ISLAMIC LEVIATHAN

RELIGION AND GLOBAL POLITICS

John L. Esposito, *Series Editor*

University Professor and Director
Center for Muslim-Christian Understanding
Georgetown University

ISLAMIC LEVIATHAN
Islam and the Making of State Power
Seyyed Vali Reza Nasr

Islamic Leviathan

Islam and the Making of State Power

SEYYED VALI REZA NASR

OXFORD
UNIVERSITY PRESS

2001

OXFORD
UNIVERSITY PRESS

Oxford   New York
Athens   Auckland   Bangkok   Bogotá   Buenos Aires   Cape Town
Chennai   Dar es Salaam   Delhi   Florence   Hong Kong   Istanbul   Karachi
Kolkata   Kuala Lumpur   Madrid   Melbourne   Mexico City   Mumbai
Nairobi   Paris   São Paul   Shanghai   Singapore   Taipei   Tokyo   Toronto   Warsaw

and associated comapnies in
Berlin   Ibadan

Copyright © 2001 by Seyyed Vali Reza Nasr

Published by Oxford University Press, Inc.,
198 Madison Avenue, New York, New York 10016

Oxford is a registered trademark of Oxford University Press

Library of Congress Cataloging-in-Publication Data
Nasr, Seyyed Vali Reza, 1960–
   Islamic leviathan : Islam and the making of state power / Seyyed Vali Reza Nasr.
      p. cm.—(Religion and global politics)
   Includes bibliographical references and index.
   ISBN 0-19-514426-0
      1. Malaysia—Politics and government. 2. Islam and politics—Malaysia.
3. Pakistan—Politics and government—1988– 4. Islam and politics—Pakistan.
I. Title.   II. Series.
DS597.2.N37 2001
322′.1′095491—dc21   00-064968

9 8 7 6 5 4 3 2 1

Printed in the United States of America
on acid-free paper

To

Lala Amjad (Syed Amjad Ali)

Gentleman, scholar, friend

and

Bhaji Kishwar (Begum Kishwar Abid Husayn)

A guiding light for truth-seekers

Preface

In 1979 General Muhammad Zia ul-Haq, the military ruler of Pakistan, declared that Pakistan would become an Islamic state. Islamic values and norms would serve as the foundation of national identity, law, economy, and social relations, and would inspire all policy making. In 1980 Mahathir Muhammad, the new prime minister of Malaysia, introduced a similar broad-based plan to anchor state policy making in Islamic values, and to bring his country's laws and economic practices in line with the teachings of Islam. Why did these rulers choose the path of "Islamization" for their countries? And how did one-time secular postcolonial states become the agents of Islamization and the harbinger of the "true" Islamic state?

Malaysia and Pakistan have since the late 1970s–early 1980s followed a unique path to development that diverges from the experiences of other Third World states. In these two countries religious identity was integrated into state ideology to inform the goal and process of development with Islamic values. This undertaking has also presented a very different picture of the relation between Islam and politics in Muslim societies. In Malaysia and Pakistan, it has been state institutions rather than Islamist activists (those who advocate a political reading of Islam; also known as revivalists or fundamentalists) that have been the guardians of Islam and the defenders of its interests. This suggests a very different dynamic in the ebbs and flow of Islamic politics—in the least pointing to the importance of the state in the vicissitudes of this phenomenon. What to make of secular states that turn Islamic? What does such a transformation mean for the state as well as for Islamic politics?

This book grapples with these questions. This is not a comprehensive account of Malaysia's or Pakistan's politics, nor does it cover all aspects of Islam's role in their societies and politics, although the analytical narrative dwells on these issues considerably. This book is rather a social scientific inquiry into the phenomenon of secular postcolonial states becoming agents of Islamization, and more broadly how culture and religion serve the needs of state power and development. The analysis here relies on theoretical discussions in the social sciences of state behavior and the role of culture and religion therein. More important, it draws inferences from the cases under examination to make broader conclusions of interest to the disciplines.

I have incurred many debts in researching and writing this book. Grants from the American Institute of Pakistan Studies and the Faculty Research Grant Fund of the University of San Diego facilitated field research in Pakistan and Malaysia between 1995 and 1997. Sabbatical leave from teaching, along with a Research and Writing Grant from the John D. and Catherine T. MacArthur Foundation, provided me with time to write. On Malaysia, the Institute Kajian Dasar (Institute of Policy Studies), Zainah Anwar, Osman Bakr, Abu Bakr Hashim, Khalid Ja'far, Muhammad Nur Manuty, Hassan Mardman, Chandra Muzaffar, Farish Noor, Fred von der Mehden, and Imtiyaz Yusuf greatly helped with the research for this project. On Pakistan, I benefited from the advice and assistance of Muhammad Afzal, Zafar Ishaq Ansar, Mushahid Husain, S. Faisal Imam, and Muhammad Suhayl Umar. I am also grateful to Mumtaz Ahmad and John L. Esposito for their support, wisdom, and many useful suggestions. I alone am responsible for all of the facts, their interpretation, and resultant conclusions that appear in the following pages.

Contents

ISLAMIC LEVIATHAN

Introduction

Defining the Problem

Over the course of the past two decades Islamism has exercised a growing in-fluence on politics in Muslim countries from Morocco to Malaysia. In some instances this trend has led to regime change as in Iran and Sudan, but more often, it has ensconced Islamic norms, symbols, and rhetoric in the public sphere, and in the process, it has had a notable impact on politics, policy making, law, and social relations. Although Islamist forces are today the principal protagonists in struggles of power with ruling elites in Muslim so-cieties,[1] they no longer hold a monopoly of speaking for Islam or acting on its behalf. Increasingly, social and political actors across the board, including state leaders and institutions—who are in many cases responsible for trans-forming Islamic politics into policy—champion Islamic causes.

It is often assumed that the greater visibility of Islamic norms, values, and symbols in the public arena, and anchoring of law and policy making in its values—what has been termed Islamization—is the work of Islamist move-ments who have forced their ideology on ruling regimes and other hapless so-cial actors. The role of Islam in society and politics is therefore the culmina-tion of Islamist activism, and in terms of what it spells for public policy, it reflects the ideological directives and political imperatives that guide the Is-lamist challenge to ruling regimes.

There is little doubt that ruling regimes and disparate social and political actors alike are pushed in the direction of Islamic politics by Islamist forces. Still, the pattern of Islamist activism and its revolutionary and utopian rhetoric only partly explain this trend. To fully understand the expanded role of Islam in politics of Muslim societies, it is important to "bring the state back in,"[2] to look at it as an Islamist actor. For the state in Muslim countries has played a key role in embedding Islam in politics. More important, as will become clear in this study, states have done so not merely in reaction to pressure from Islamist movements but to serve their own interests. State leaders have construed Islamism as a threat, but at times also as an opportunity, and in so doing have found added incentive to pursue Islamic politics. The turn to Islam is not so much a defensive strategy as a facet of the state's drive to establish hegemony over society and expand its powers and control. Islamization is a proactive rather than a reactive process, in which state interests serve as a causal factor.

Why do states Islamize? When are they likely to do so? Through what mechanisms and to what ends do they Islamize? And what is likely to be the consequence of this turn to Islam? These are the principal questions that guide the analytical narrative in this study. By providing answers to these questions, this study will look to the manner in which state interests become anchored in Islamization—first through appropriation of the Islamist discourse, and then through implementation of wide-scale Islamic policies. It is possible to think of Islamization as a critical turning point in the development process, one that alters the character of the state and, hence, the nature of state-society relations, all with the aim of renegotiating the relative powers of the two. A state's normative policies cannot be viewed as divorced from its intrinsic tendency to expand its authority and reach. These points suggest that cultural factors—Islamic norms and symbols here—are decisive in the evolution of state-society relations and can provide critical turning points on the path to development.

To identify those factors that govern state action, this study will focus on the cases of Malaysia and Pakistan since the rise of the Mahathir Mohammad and Zia ul-Haq regimes in the two countries at the juncture of 1979–80. Since that time, the state's involvement in Islamic politics in both countries has been direct and extensive, revealing a clear link between state interests and Islamization. The cases of Malaysia and Pakistan in addition suggest important causal relations between the nature and makings of state power and the proclivity to use Islam to serve state interests. The exercise of power by these states, as determined by the nature of their relations with key social forces that bolster their authority or serve as resistance to it, is consequential in anchoring social and political institutions and the national political discourse in an Islamic normative and conceptual order—Islamization, in short.

Both Malaysia and Pakistan can be characterized as weak states, wherein ruling regimes have made prolific use of Islamic symbols and policies to shore up state authority at a critical juncture—viewing Islamic politics more as an opportunity than a challenge.[3] The manner in which these states have adopted Islamic ideology and politics to chart a new trajectory of development underscores the central thesis of this book concerning the relevance of Islam to state power. State structure and the continuity and change in state-society relations are thus important in explaining the state's decision to turn to Islamization. In Malaysia the ruling party—the United Malays National Organization (UMNO)—and in Pakistan the military have also been important in shoring up state power. However, the apogee of UMNO's power in Malaysia and the military's in Pakistan coincides with Islamization, attesting to the centrality of religious politics to expansion of state power. In the cases under study here the colonial period looms large in terms of explaining the capabilities of the state.[4] Examination of relations between state and society—and by extension, state and Islam—in Malaysia and Pakistan will therefore begin with the colonial period and its institutional legacies, and trace the impact of those legacies on state formation and conduct of politics after independence.[5]

In exploring these themes, this study will draw on the theoretical contributions of New Institutionalism.[6] The emergence of Islamizing states in both Malaysia and Pakistan underscores the complexity of continuity and change in institutions in the process of sociopolitical change. By institutions I mean "the formal and informal . . . procedures, routines, norms and conventions embedded in organizational structure of the polity"[7] that shape structures and determine constraints—both formal (rules and laws) and informal (norms of behavior and conduct)[8]—that provide the context for economic and political change. The rationalist approach to New Institutionalism looks to strategic decisions made by key actors to bring about institutional change, and in time, new development outcomes.[9] The historical approach, on the other hand, focuses on the interaction between institutions in a polity as key to understanding particular development paths.[10] In this perspective the political landscape is shaped by struggles of power between institutions, and sociopolitical change is punctuated by critical junctures when the outcome of clashes between institutions revises development paths.

As such, the institutionalist approach is a useful analytical tool for understanding historical change and the sociopolitical context in which development paths materialize. However, New Institutionalism does not adequately contend with the role of cultural and religious forces in historical change. The cases of Malaysia and Pakistan show that the influence of culture and religion in transforming institutions, states, and development paths is far more significant than treating them as aspects of the institutional structure—as norms, constraints, and routines—would suggest. This study will use the evidence from the cases under study to expand the purview of the institutionalist approach just as it will use its insights to explicate Islamization in those cases.

Concerning State Power

States matter. They provide for education, defense, and health care, and account for economic development and social change. As centers of power, states regulate collection and disbursement of resources, control policy making, and deeply affect every facet of their citizens' lives.[11] Undertaking these functions, in fact, shapes states,[12] which in the process, and in turn, mold the structure of politics.[13] States are the most important determinants of sociopolitical change in modern times,[14] so much so that state leaders can and do

operate independently—and even in contravention—of underlying socioeconomic forces, interest groups, and class.[15] It is therefore not possible to satisfactorily conceive of socioeconomic changes on the scale that Islamization in
Malaysia and Pakistan has entailed without contending with the state. In Malaysia and Pakistan the Islamization period was also the era of unprecedented
expansion of state power. Therefore, the two cases serve as testament to the
rising power and importance of the state, and challenge the notion that in the
age of globalization states are necessarily on the decline.[16]

How much states can get done and how much of the lives of their citizenry
they control is a function of their strength. Therefore, what constitutes strength
and weakness in a state, and how that affects politics, economics, and social
change, is of great explanatory value.[17] Marxist and statist theories equate
state strength with capacity—the ability of a state to extract and allocate resources, as well as formulate and implement policy—and autonomy from
classes and interest groups.[18] Strong states have larger jurisdictions and are
more independent from various classes and interest groups. Their policies are
rational and effective. They can intervene in markets more directly to control
the flow of resources—to mobilize them for investment in lieu of consump-
tion without hindrance of pressures of vested interest.[19]

Organizational theories equate capacity and autonomy with the coherence
of the bureaucracy and structure of the state institutions.[20] Others place emphasis on the state's ability to use force and to penetrate its society.[21] For others
still, state capacity and autonomy is very much a function of the extent of its
domination over society.[22] States with "integrated control" over society[23] are
capable of successfully organizing interest groups without yielding to pluralism,[24] and those able to blur state-society distinction are likely to enjoy high
capacity and autonomy.[25] These theories, however, say little about the manner
in which cultural factors mediate state-society relations and can alter the balance of power between the two—directly affecting state capacity and autonomy. It is a central aim of this book to include culture in the discussion of
state power, not only as a means of bestowing states with legitimacy and
symbolic tools of control, but as the means of changing the balance of power
between state and social actors in various economic and social arenas wherein capacity and autonomy are negotiated, and the powers of the state are established. In the cases under examination here, the expansion of state capacity to manage society, and bolstering of the requisite authority to do so with
least degree of resistance, is ineluctably tied to Islamization.

States face a multitude of imperatives that vary from one state to the next.
However, every state is concerned with security, legitimacy, hegemony, revenue generation, and economic growth.[26] Of these, revenue generation has generally been viewed as most directly responsible for state formation and the
shape that state institutions take. This has been true of the early European
state, wherein financial demands of war and administration propelled state
formation,[27] as much as of the colonial state, which in many instances was
dedicated to extraction of resources from indigenous populations.[28] The crux
of the argument is that a state needs revenue, whose generation and collection

will serve as the impetus for state formation.[29] The constraints faced by state leaders in generating revenue and extracting resources from society determine their choice of structures, systems, and ultimately institutions that make up the state.[30] Conversely, state leaders shape constitutions, formal as well as unwritten rules of the game, to increase social output and maximize tax revenue.[31]

The turn to Islamization in Malaysia and Pakistan, however, does not support the attachment of so much importance to the relation between the imperative of revenue generation and state formation. For additional revenues that were generated by state collection of religious taxes, as will be discussed later, remained modest. Revenue generation was therefore not important in the turn toward Islamization in Malaysia and Pakistan from the 1970s onward. The literature on Islamism would place emphasis on the imperative of legitimacy, arguing that the turn to Islamization was a reactive policy—a type of survival strategy—to protect the state from serious challenges to its authority.[32] The cases of Malaysia and Pakistan will show that the scope and nature of Islamization extended beyond provision of legitimacy to beleaguered states. Islamization, rather, reflected the influence of two other interrelated imperatives: hegemony and economic growth. Both of these imperatives are tied to the state's need for revenue. For it is the need for revenue that led the state to dominate society, and later justified that domination, and also sustained a keen interest in investment, growth, and development in the state.[33] However, growth and hegemony pose separate challenges to state structures and help forge states in different ways.[34] As will become clear in the following chapters, Islamization was more directly tied to the imperatives of growth and hegemony than to revenue collection or legitimacy. It was a facet of expansion of state power and its project of economic growth and development.

Culture and State Power

It follows from the foregoing discussion that to explicate the advent of Islamization as a project of the state, one must take stock of the role of cultural factors in politics and state formation. There has been much written on culture and politics.[35] Earlier studies sought to explain political conduct in diverse societies in terms of their cultural beliefs. Culture explained attitudes,[36] as well as the master narrative and the very design of politics.[37] More recent treatments of the subject have moved away from cultural explanations of political behavior to view culture as an element of exercise of authority by the state[38] and a "resource," in the words of David Laitin, to be used by political entrepreneurs.[39] In this regard, cultural identity is a tool that can be used by political entrepreneurs in competitions for power and resources,[40] or by states in establishing hegemony over society.

The exercise of authority is ineluctably entwined with the trappings of culture. Culture provides politics with its repertoire of symbols that connote authority.[41] Culture is thus the means to power.[42] In the words of Clifford Geertz:

> Politics is an endless jockeying for marginal advantage under settled ("consti-
> tutional") rules of the game, and the role of the wigs and robes that everywhere
> attend it is to make the rules seem settled, to raise them above—or insert them
> beneath—the partisan struggle they are supposed to regulate. But, in all these
> views, the semiotic aspects of the state . . . . exaggerate might, conceal ex-
> ploitation, inflate authority, or moralize procedure.[43]

States can easily dominate their subjects physically; but to effectively rule over them—to establish hegemony over their lives in the Gramscian sense[44] —they must also control their subjects ideologically—that is, control the cultural underpinnings of their sociopolitical outlook.[45] The political functions of ideological and physical control are so close that, in fact, it is not always possible to distinguish between the two.[46] The importance of ideological domination lies less in its facilitation of physical control than in its making such control unnecessary. For it is "an economizing device by which individuals come to terms with their environment and are provided with a 'world view' so that the decision-making process is simplified."[47] Ideological control thus fosters uniformity, by providing states with a centripetal antidote to the centrifugal forces that could tear a state apart.[48] It also makes governance more efficient and less dependent on coercion as it facilitates greater fiscal control and makes extraction of resources easier,[49] and gives citizens a stake in the well-being of the state.[50] A state that enjoys the unfettered hegemony that results from ideological control is then free to engage in rational pursuit of economic growth.

To this end states will experiment with various ideological and institutional mechanisms to achieve an "integrative revolution," the success of which depends on their ability to resolve the tensions between primordial and legal-rational attachments.[51] The more coherent the relations between culture and exercise of authority—between spiritual excellence and political eminence, magical power and executive influence—the more complete the hegemony.[52]

It is for this reason that state power is so concerned with symbolism and theater.[53] That concern reaches its apogee in the Balinese theater state of Negara, wherein, writes Geertz, "power served pomp, not pomp power."[54] Here ceremonies and rituals of the state were ends in themselves, but also shaped the world in the image of the state. Control came from the core—the seamless continuity between the state and Balinese culture—shaping the world as an approximation of itself.

It is also for the same reason that states have laid claim to collective consciousness and the very identity of the nation.[55] The state has sought to appropriate those concepts that are foundational to people's conception of history:[56] "its traditional icons, its metaphors, its heroes, its rituals, and its narratives."[57] In short, argues Joel Migdal, "state leaders and agencies have been at the center of redrawing social boundaries to coincide with actual or desired political borders . . . . [and] states have been at the core of reinvention of society."[58]

Culture is not, however, a monolithic concept. Laitin has argued that there may be discord in a polity over the value system that underlies its working.[59] Rather than a master narrative, Laitin argues, culture provides the political system with a set of priorities or "points of concern" that may keep a political system together, or, conversely, serve as sources of real conflict.[60] Drawing on Talcott Parson's notion that changes in one subsystem require changes in other subsystems as well, Laitin argues that the relations between culture and politics is dynamic and subject to regular adjustment.[61] Hence, we can infer from Laitin to argue that greater Islamic consciousness in Malaysian and Pakistani societies necessitated commensurate changes in their respective states as well. Laitin's approach provides an explanation not just for why Islam is relevant to Malaysian and Pakistani states, but for why it was so in the 1970s and the 1980s. It also helps explain why only a relatively recent interpretation of Islam is relevant.

The thrust of the foregoing discussions has been to establish a link between culture and hegemony. The cases under study here will highlight this connection, but will also point to the importance of culture to economic growth, arguing that there exists a direct linkage—above and beyond establishing hegemony—between the cultural policies of state leaders and their designs for growth and development. Although the aim of hegemony is to free the state to pursue growth as it sees fit and, hence, culture is used to establish hegemony that then provides for growth, in Malaysia and Pakistan Islamization was directly tied to growth. This provides culture with an added role in shaping politics and forging state structures.

Religion, Hegemony, and the Postcolonial State

The imperatives of hegemony and growth are particularly challenging to postcolonial states of the Third World, as is the relevance of cultural factors to exercise of authority by the state.[62] For in postcolonial states state-society relations remain fluid, state structures are still evolving, and the goal of development looms large in society and politics. As such, it is here that the linkage between cultural factors—and more specifically, religious symbols, rhetoric, and value system—and state power comes into sharper focus.

The state in much of the Muslim world did not emerge at independence, but was inherited from colonial administrations.[63] Its machinery of government, ideologies of modernization, views on social engineering, and political control were all handed down from the colonial era, as those who ran the machinery of colonial administrations continued to wield power in the successor states and thus guaranteed a certain degree of momentum. The postcolonial state, far from a new development, has been a later growth on an old tree.

The globalization of imperialism during the colonial era, moreover, ensured the dominance of the European form of the state, which in the Third World appeared in the guise of the colonial state.[64] Therefore, even countries such as Iran and Turkey, who did not experience direct colonialism, created modern states that although modeled after the European state, more closely approximated the colonial state.[65] The postcolonial state adopted European concepts of sovereignty and self-determination along with administrative features of the state to fashion itself in the mold of the European state, but it did not replicate the relationship between the state and its citizenry that is the hallmark of the European state. Instead, the postcolonial state continued the colonial style of governance, whose limitation of popular participation in favor of decision making by an elite—albeit Westernized—is more akin to traditional rule than modern democracy.[66] Although the postcolonial state leaders have shown far greater concern with popular support and have been more attentive to demands from below, still their conception of governance has remained highly paternalistic and indeed colonial.[67] James C. Scott's depiction of colonial attitudes among the Malaysian bureaucratic elite rings true of postindependence leadership across the Third World:

> The ideal relationship between the people and their leaders, as these men [civil servants] see it, does not differ in many respects from the colonial pattern. They envision a class of people who know best and expect to rule in the interests of the people . . . independently of popular desires by virtue of its superior qualifications. [They] would encourage in the masses the traditional belief that this natural elite is best fitted to direct the nation.[68]

This tendency has been reinforced by the resurgence of traditional conceptions of authority, which have taken the form of neopatrimonialism.[69] To be sure, the legal structure in postcolonial states is modern and decision making is rational and secular, but in other aspects of governance state leaders display traditional rather than modern proclivities. Interestingly, traditional patterns of exercise of authority among modern ruling elites is itself a product of colonialism, which protected and nurtured traditional institutions of authority and furthermore bolstered its paternalistic view of governance through similar colonial conceptions.[70]

The continuity between the colonial and postcolonial states has to do with the fact that at the moment of independence an underdeveloped indigenous bourgeoisie was unable to contain the overdeveloped colonial state or to countervail the formidable alliances with key classes and social groups that bolstered colonial authority.[71] Equally significant was the fact that the ruling bureaucratic elite that had managed the colonial state remained in control after independence. They had been a product of colonialism and had internalized its values of governance.[72] They proved instrumental in shaping politics after independence, serving as conduits for colonial values in the postcolonial era.[73] These points are particularly relevant to Malaysia and Pakistan, where state structures have so closely approximated the British colonial state that they have been dubbed as "viceregal" states.

The political forces that spearheaded independence across the Third World, too, contributed to continuities between colonial and postcolonial eras. Benedict Anderson writes that nationalism developed among "bilingual intelligentsia"[74]—the products of colonialism who operated in the modern rather than traditional sectors of the colonial society.[75] The nationalist discourse did not reject foreign intellectual hegemony; rather, its struggle against colonialism remained focused on political control.[76] Thomas Hansen writes of Indian struggle for independence that "Gandhi and the entire cultural nationalist tradition in India saw the essence of the nation as residing in India's cultural communities, whereas the political realm of the colonial state remained a morally empty space, a set of lifeless procedures and culturally alien institutions. . . . This construction inaugurated [after independence] a stream of cultural 'antipolitics,' that is, a production of culture."[77] The postcolonial state sought to infuse the "lifeless" colonial state with moral authority. This was drawn from the cultural repertoire of the nation to foist an indigenous nationalism. As a result, the postcolonial state became anchored in ideologies of nationalism that were imported from Europe and contributed to cultural dualism, and ultimately the crisis of the postcolonial state. This trend has been particularly true of the Muslim world, wherein nationalism became identified as an alien idea and a project of the state, both of which limited its penetration of society and usefulness to state leaders as a tool of establishing hegemony.[78] The more states faced crises in the political and economic arena, the more the shortcomings of their ideological tools became apparent. This trend has been most visible with the decline of rent—which has been used to gain consent to rule from the population, especially in the Arab world—and the subsequent collapse of the "social contract" that sustained authoritarianism in that part of the Muslim world throughout the 1960s–1980s period.[79] The subsequent crises have made the state vulnerable to an ideological challenge from below, which took the form of Islamism—whose power rested in that it was not tainted by a connection with the West, and it had a base among the masses.[80] Some state leaders responded by turning to Islam in search of a viable state ideology. The ideological underpinnings of the postcolonial state, however, made success in such a gambit unlikely. For, in the words of Nazih Ayubi,

> [T]he fact that the contemporary state lays claim to secularism has enabled some forces of political protest to appropriate Islam as their own weapon. Because the state does not embrace Islam . . . it cannot describe its opponents as easily as the traditional State could as being simply heretic cults. Political Islam now reverses the historical process—it claims "generic" Islam for the protest movements, leaving the State the more difficult task of qualifying and justifying its own "version" of Islam.[81]

Malaysia and Pakistan, as will become evident in this study, are perhaps unique in both the degree to which they moved away from the dominant nationalist paradigm to invest in a state ideology of Islam—whose foundation lay in attitudes, arguments, and beliefs that had emerged from below and related to popular and community-based beliefs and practices—and were in fact successful in using to establish hegemony and pursue their goals of growth.

In addition, colonialism saddled the postcolonial state with attitudes and ambitions that have redoubled its desire for hegemony and yet made its attainment more elusive. The colonial ideology posited that the colonial state had to be separate from the people, based on a totally different—and superior—set of values and committed to changing society, over which it ruled in its own image.[82] This was facilitated by the fact that the colonial state generally enjoyed greater autonomy from the local society than did the European state.[83] From this emerged notions of order that would make governance efficient just as they would multiply the productive capacity of the colony.[84] These notions included new conceptions of space and personhood, as well as social organization. In particular, colonialism policy followed a policy of indirect rule—through chiefs and landlords—that had the effect of unburdening government, but reinforcing and demarcating state-society relations. The result was that as the colonial state relied on intermediaries to rule, it did not directly penetrate society.[85] The colonial state also discouraged national identity formation and in fact encouraged subnational identity consciousness by strengthening religious, ethnic, and tribal affiliations through its multilayered legal system, communalist representation, and variegated patterns of extraction and disbursement of resources.[86] The result was that postcolonial states inherited divided societies, which were not easily controlled through nationalist ideology. Over time, the colonial nature of the postcolonial state created tensions in state-society relations and proved to be a handicap for the postcolonial state that has been far more interested in hegemony over society. The more the state sought to expand its authority, the more it felt the limitations that its colonial legacy created.

This problem was compounded by the struggle for independence. The anticolonial struggle encouraged everyday forms of resistance to the colonial state and instituted legitimacy of defying the state—especially by using culture to do so.[87] The postcolonial state had difficulty in reversing this trend. Having initiated the masses to resisting authority, the nationalist elite were then saddled with the problem of establishing order over a more unruly society. Without the relations of order between the state and its subjects in place, the postcolonial state became more dependent on ideology to get consent to rule.

The postcolonial state also enlarged the colonial state's ambition of transforming the societies over which it ruled, hoping to "transform society according to its blueprint."[88] This encouraged highly interventionist attitudes in the state, which, enjoying the broad autonomy that it had inherited from the colonial state, outlined a vision of development and charged itself to pursue it in the name of common good. Statism requires restructuring society, integrating its parts into a uniform whole, and vesting that whole with broad powers in managing society and the economy. Statism also acts to limit market forces and the influence of nonstate actors. As the state seeks to rule over society and tightly manage social and economic forces, it will seek broadened hegemony. Hence, economic growth necessitates hegemony and more efficient ideologies to achieve it. This need becomes more apparent when the state's management of the economy falters, with debilitating implications for state hegemony. This has been a primary reason for the prominence of Islamist opposition in the Arab world.[89] In Malaysia and Pakistan the state concluded that an Islamic ideology would provide for more complete hegemony and hence serve the goal of economic growth.

In recent years, the limitations that restrain the postcolonial states have become increasingly apparent. As the crises facing these states have mounted, the need for more viable state ideologies that would yield effective hegemony has grown. This has encouraged some state leaders to move away from hitherto dominant state ideologies that were anchored in nationalism and secularism, and to embrace new ideologies that draw on community-based and popular cultural beliefs and practices. In India this has produced greater Hindu consciousness in politics, and in the Muslim world, greater flirtation with Islam.

Islamization, whether undertaken deliberately, or gradually and unwittingly, has been an effort on the part of the postcolonial state in the Muslim world to find legitimacy and relevance in terms of local culture and mores, and to anchor itself in its value system. In states where the mark of colonialism is most evident, such as in Malaysia or Pakistan, this function of Islamization is quite clear.[90] In these countries the turn to religion to augment state power has been most thoroughgoing, virtually reinventing state ideology with broad implications for its powers, hegemony, and ability to pursue accumulation. Creating cadence between the values of the state and those of society is necessitated by the state's desire to exert authority to a greater extent, expand its functions and capacity to control and implement public policy, and to dominate the public and private spheres more clearly. In short, state-led Islamization is in essence the indigenization of the postcolonial state—embedding it in the local value systems.[91] The dialectic of state expansion and social resistance to it has forced at least some postcolonial states to realize that it is more efficient to be Islamic than not.

Islamism and the Islamization of Postcolonial States in Malaysia and Pakistan

The ascendancy of Islamist ideology and activism over the course of the past two decades has perhaps been the most significant change in the paradigm of politics across the Muslim world.[92] Islamism both rejects and defies secular ruling regimes and the Western cultural underpinnings of their development agendas. It demands submission to the writ of Islamic law in public as well as private affairs, and promises to bring about an Islamic order that is just and is capable of attaining veritable development. It is in many regards a Third Worldist ideology that aims to complete the task that the nationalist movements of earlier decades had left incomplete: to liberate Muslim lands from the intellectual as well as the physical control of the West.[93] Ali Benhadj, the Algerian Islamist leader, perhaps most lucidly captured the heart of the matter in the following words: "My father and brothers (in religion) may have *physically* expelled the oppressor France from Algeria, but my struggle, together with my brothers, using weapons of faith, is to banish France *intellectually* and *ideologically* and to be done with her supporters who drank her poisonous milk."[94]

Islamism has appealed to those who have been disaffected by the economic and political achievements of Muslim postcolonial states, as well as those who have been alienated from the state because of the cultural chasm that separates the secular Westernized state leaders from the more Islamically conscious masses.[95] However, beyond the core group of its ardent supporters, Islamism's reach extends to a broader spectrum of the population, who have in various ways and to varying degrees turned to Islam. Islamism has thus spearheaded greater Islamic consciousness across the Muslim world and, in the process, eroded the hegemony of secular ideologies of the state. What has ensued is profound change in the nature of the public sphere in the Muslim world.[96]

That change has "deprivatized" Islam, to use José Casanova's terminology, and enshrined it as a "public religion."[97] This cultural impact of Islamism is in many ways more significant than its more direct political challenge to ruling regimes. For the Islamist challenge to the ideological underpinnings of the secular state has been far more successful than its challenge to that state's political control.[98] Consequently, even where Islamism has failed to bring about regime change it has nevertheless affected state-society relations by changing the cultural reference points of the society, and thereby forcing change in the nature of the relations between the two.

The complexity of the Islamist challenge lies in the fact that it is not an atavism—a medieval rejection of modernity.[99] Islamism is very much concerned with the modern world.[100] It fashions itself as a modern ideology in competition with other modern ideologies.[101] In fact, Islamism defies the facile religion versus secularism conception that has been prevalent in the social sciences. As a religious idea that has internalized many aspects of modernity and seeks to operate in the modern world, Islamism shows that religion is adaptable to ideological change and will do so in a continuous dialectic with society.[102] Islamism is the product of this dialectic in the postcolonial Muslim world. As such, it appeals to those Muslims who are groping for what Geertz called the "integrative revolution."[103] Geertz believed that in postcolonial states the main tension is between primordial attachments and commitment to civil sentiments and modernization and social change. Individuals are divided between the attachments that define their identity, and the goals that the modern state has set before them and which they also desire. That Muslim states have failed to articulate ideologies that would resolve those tensions has made at least the cultural—if not the more strident political—promise of Islamism relevant to a broad spectrum of Muslims. Interestingly, it is exactly this aspect of Islamism that has made it relevant to the postcolonial state's aim to reformulate its relations to society and to reestablish its hegemony.

For Malaysia and Pakistan two aspects of the Islamist ideology were particularly useful. First, that Islamism had done much to mobilize Islamic symbols and formulate new Islamic concepts of relevance to politics, and moreover, had both articulated the manner in which they should serve political ends and convinced the masses of the necessity of that process. Second, Islamism was opposed only to the secular ideology of the state, but not to state hegemony its extensive intervention in the economy and society. Islamism at its core supports statism, provided that the state is "Islamic." In Malaysia and Pakistan state leaders concluded that if the state were to be construed as Islamic, then it would be in the position to claim support from Islamism and harness its energies to support expansion of state power, provided the state would be recast in the proper cultural guise.

To begin with, throughout the 1960s and the 1970s Islamist thinkers harped on the importance of Islam to politics, reinterpreted the main tenets and myths of the faith to suggest a seamless continuity between faith and political action, and articulated new concepts such as "Islamic economics," "Islamic education," "Islamization of knowledge," and the "Islamic state."[104] All of this amounted to a repertoire of concepts that would appropriately serve the state and help it create new institutions with which to expand its capacity and social control. That Islamist ideas had permeated among the masses—and in particular the educated youth and the segments of the intellectuals—would allow the state to reinstitute its control over those social classes and segments of the society that Islamism had attracted away from secular state ideology.[105]

Generally speaking, three social groups have been the backbone of Islamism: the intellectual "counterelite," shopkeepers and small merchants tied to the petite bourgeoisie; and the unemployed urban youth and the poor—the sansculottes. Although all three oppose the secular postcolonial state and favor its replacement with an Islamic state, they do not necessarily share the same political orientation. Most notably, the petit bourgeois element is mercantilist in spirit and views society as divided along corporate rather than class lines. It is therefore not committed to revolutionary change. The political activism of the sansculottes element, however, is animated by class war and is therefore revolutionary in nature. Hence, generally speaking, this element is left of center in economic matters. In many Muslim countries separate movements or organizations represent these different elements. The most serious Islamist challenge to the state has occurred where all of these elements have been gathered in a single movement. In Pakistan and Malaysia the turn to Islam allowed the state to divide the counterelite intellectuals and the petite bourgeoisie from the sansculottes, and to co-opt the first two. The counterelite intellectuals were co-opted into various state and educational institutions and served as the means of constructing the Islamization regimes.[106] The petite bourgeoisie forged an alliance with the state and became tied to its drive to pursue its goal of accumulation. By dividing the core elements of Islamism, co-opting some and isolating the remainder, Malaysia and Pakistan were able to confound the Islamist opposition, create confusion in its ranks, appropriate their ideology, takeover some of their institutions, and ultimately diffuse its threat to the ruling regimes.[107]

In addition, state-led Islamization has thus allowed the state to organize, bolster the power of, and ultimately control institutions and social organizations that can allow it to use Islam in the service of state interests. Islamization from above allowed the state to reap the fruits of the Islamist propaganda and win the competition with the Islamist challenge from below to control the normative order, and thus construct a viable state ideology that provides for uniformity across society, as well as greater compliance with the will of the state.

Islamization makes the boundaries between state and society blurry,[108] and as such gives greater room to the state to maneuver.[109] Jamal Malik writes of increase in state patronage of religious seminaries in Pakistan in the 1980s that it was not so much an effort to placate Islamist activists or to give the state greater control through clientalism, as to use them as an outlet for conveying state ideology to the masses.[110]

Equally significant was Islamism's statist proclivity. Islamism was from inception nothing short of a rejection of both the reality and intent of the secular state's penetration of society, and as such, it was a clear attempt at undoing the impact of secular public policy in Muslim societies to date. In this regard Islamism serves as an important source of social resistance to expansion of state power and capacity, and as the focal point for the rallying of those social forces that resist state domination. Although Islamism is concerned with the state power, it is not inherently opposed to it; its opposition to that power emanates from the ability of the secular state to use it to further its secularist agenda. In effect, resisting expansion of state power and capacity is a consequence of Islamism's resistance to state-sponsored secularization, and not to statism itself. In this sense, Islamism does not purport to be some form of liberalism—as it does not engage the problematic of the dominant state—but by sticking to statist assumption promises to continue the state-centered authoritarian tendencies of the regimes it challenges. Consequently, Islamism is not a threat to the state per se, only to the secularism of the state. In fact, Islamism holds promise for a state that is open to abandoning secularism in favor of another ideology of rule. The turn to Islam, moreover, did not require of the states fundamental transformation, only a cultural orientation. "Islamic" states in Malaysia and Pakistan since the 1980s have changed little in their structure and policymaking, and display the same fundamental characteristics, goals, and relations with society that they did before the 1980s. Islamization thus did not reinvent the state—as did the Islamic revolution of 1979 in Iran—nor alter the scaffolding that sustains its edifice, but merely repackaged the postcolonial state as Islamic.

That promise was not a trivial matter. States vie to do more and to do so efficiently. For this they need legitimacy and uniform cultural domination, which Malaysia and Pakistan (as will be elucidated in this study) were lacking. States also need better levers of power and less resistance to exercising it. For Malaysia and Pakistan Islamization served both ends. By presenting Islamization as a public good to be provided by the state, the state expanded its capacity. It assumed more responsibilities and extracted more from society. In Pakistan, for instance, Islamization allowed the state to draw greater numbers of the population into the ambit of its control by creating new sources of patronage and assuming control of preexisting autonomous Islamic patronage networks and the financial and social institutions that were associated with them.[111]

It would be expected that the Islamization of the state and its appropriation of religious funds and patronage would lead to some form of religion-state conflict. This, however, did not come to pass in Malaysia and Pakistan. In these countries from the 1980s onward the state took over religious education, jurisprudence, various forms of administration, taxation, and social services with minimal resistance. These two states were able to assert far broader domination over the religious sphere with far less resistance than had been achieved in the stronger states of the Arab world and Iran before the revolution of 1979.

Islamization also diverts attention from expansion of state power and diffuses the significant challenge to state authority that comes from Islamism. Islamization must be understood in terms of both its defensive function—as a response to political and ideological challenges to ruling regimes at times of crisis—and its proactive function, to get better terms in negotiations with social forces for power and capacity. Why Islamization was so attractive for Malaysia and Pakistan was that it allowed the states to simultaneously subdue political opposition and expand state power and capacity. Contending with opposition thus also produced stronger states.

Since the Islamist ideology implies that the state has a right to be intrusive and interventionist—to expand its powers, capacity, and reach if it becomes Islamic—and calls for provision of Islamization through state power, it would be hard-pressed to mount a challenge to state-led Islamization. Malaysian and Pakistani state leaders saw in the Islamist ideology a green light to expansion of state power.[112] However, to successfully use Islam to the ends described, these states had to undergo veritable cultural transformation. It became apparent to state leaders in these countries that if the state were to be culturally in tune with Islamism and the outlook of its constituency, that ideology would support an expansion of state power and capacity. To dominate the Islamist discourse, these states had to become legitimate Islamic actors. Hence, state-led Islamization was a conscious strategic choice on the part of some states to strengthen state institutions and expand state power, capacity, and reach. In Malaysia and Pakistan this choice marked a notable turning point—a critical juncture—in the 1980s in state formation. Still, the state's turn to Islam was not an entirely new phenomenon—although it had never assumed this scope. In both Malaysia and Pakistan, since independence the state had on occasion used Islam to serve its interests. Positive returns in this regard had in fact encouraged the state in both countries to do so more frequently and had produced an institutional foundation for it. As such, the Islamization regimes of the 1980s in both countries were the culmination of the gradual turn of the state toward Islam.

As states develop, certain battles are fought and certain struggles of power are settled to determine paths of state formation. In the juncture of the 1980s Islamist opposition affected state formation, providing it with both challenges and opportunities. How the state reacted to those challenges and opportunities both determined the trajectory of state formation from that point forward and decided the faith of the Islamist discourse in politics and society. The following chapters will examine the manner in which the gradual turn to Islam set the Malaysian and Pakistani states on the path that would culminate in state-led Islamization, and why this tendency culminated in the marked cultural transformation of those states at the critical juncture of the 1980s.

Islam and State Power in Comparative Perspective

The relation between religion and state formation has not been fully explored in the social sciences. This owes to the fact that, generally, most theorists have assumed that in modern times economic changes have led, and will lead, to privatization of faith and secularization.[113] As a result, religion will not have an impact on state formation in a meaningful fashion and will most likely cease to command popular allegiance.[114] However, historical evidence shows that religion has been far more entwined with state formation than has been assumed. In Europe organized religion thrived with expansion of the modern state, using its fruits and apparatuses, including those governing fiscal regulation and violence, to augment its own powers.[115] More important for the purposes of our analysis here, states in turn used religious institutions and appropriated church lands and property to augment their powers and revenue. Thomas Ertman writes that the church was important to expansion of royal authority in the tenth and eleventh centuries in Latin Europe, and provided the Carolingian state with institutions through which to exercise authority and rule.[116] The Carolingians totally integrated the church into state apparatuses to create state administration, and took over various papal territories and ecclesiastical resources—which accounts for the Christianization of the Frankish Empire of the Carolingians after 800.[117] Similarly, Robert Wuthnow has shown that as the rise in trade in the 1500s supported both rise of the state and the Reformation in central and northern Europe, there emerged a symbiosis between the two.[118] In Sweden and Denmark the princes turned to the Reformation because it provided them with the opportunity to appropriate church lands—quadrupling Crown lands in the case of Gustav Vasa of Sweden, who dissolved monasteries in 1527 and took their land.[119]

This trend was also evident in England.[120] Here the Reformation was a revolution from above with broad implications for state power and capacity. In 1533 the king was proclaimed head of the Church of England, which placed all ecclesiastical affairs in England under state authority. In 1532 the Parliament forced the clergy to surrender ecclesiastical law to the jurisdiction of the Crown and forbade papal annates. The ties with the Vatican were further weakened in 1533 with the Act of Restraint of Appeals to Rome, which prohibited appeals by domestic courts outside the realm. In 1534 the Act of Supremacy named the king supreme head of the Church of England. In the same year the dissolution of monasteries began, which by 1539 placed all their lands in state hands; and in 1540 all property of the church was vested in the Crown.[121] This allowed the Crown to take over the ancient parish administration that had until that time been ecclesiastical. That administration was made into an instrument of poor relief and provided the Privy Council in London with a direct role in, and considerable control of, local affairs.[122] The fusion of the Reformation and nationalism thus supported the expansion of state capacity and reach.[123] In Wuthnow's words, "The English Reformation was clearly a triumph for the central regime over the decentralized, provincial power of the landowners and was recognized as such by the latter."[124]

Wuthnow furthermore emphasizes the importance of the Reformation in mediating struggles of power between towns and rising states.[125] In central and northern Europe, commercial activities were centered in cities and towns. Their greater prosperity gave the burgeoning states greater autonomy from the landed elite and revenues from the land. The conflict between the Crown and the nobility translated into the Crown's support for the Reformation, which was also championed by the mercantile classes. The Reformation here helped states consolidate their autonomy and forge a state-towns (and, hence, mercantile classes) alliance in lieu of the state's reliance on the nobility and the church. In England, the Reformation began with Henry VIII's break with Rome over the divorce of Catherine of Aragon, but soon produced the same result. As the Crown promoted trade, merchants in the Parliament came to its assistance in severing England's ties with Rome and ensconcing the Reformation in England. It is evident that the Reformation helped the rising state to establish ties with those social classes that would be most directly active in promoting accumulation and economic growth. State-led Islamization established the same ties in Malaysia and Pakistan.

Elsewhere in Europe the contribution of religion to state formation was rooted less in economic considerations, and more in ethics. Philip Gorski has underscored the importance of the "disciplinary revolution" that followed the Reformation to shape later state formation in Holland and Prussia.[126] Writing on the Dutch Republic of 1560–1650 and Hohenzollern Prussia of the 1640s to 1720, Gorski argues that it was Calvinism that provided primary support for the "social and organizational basis for establishment of a *strong system of local government.*"[127] In both Holland and Prussia the state internalized Calvinist ethics and used the strong institutions that they had formed at the base of the society to strengthen the state. This process reached its apogee under Frederick William I, who favored Calvinist recruits into state institutions. Gorski thus associates the strength of Dutch and Prussian state institutions—especially the bureaucracy—with Calvinist ethics. As will be elucidated later in this study, in Malaysia at least, state leaders looked to Islamic ethics to bring about the same "disciplinary revolution."

It is interesting to note that in all of the aforementioned cases, the successful use of religion to expand state powers led to the state's assumption of some form of religious authority—which was most evident in the English king's arrogation of the status of head of the Church of England. This confirms the observation made earlier that successful use of religion to expand, state powers requires the state to assume the requisite religious and cultural guise. It is also evident from the above cases that as states use religion to expand, they ensure certain sociopolitical roles for religion and even expand the purview of its powers. Central and northern European states used the Reformation to construct viable states, but in the process ensured the Reformation of domination over large parts of Europe. The same trend has been evident in the cases under study here.

In the Muslim world the relation between religion and state formation has been more contentious. The postcolonial state in the Muslim world looked to the modern Western state as a model. It sought to emulate its structure but also cultural and ideological orientation, which it understood to be inherently secular. The Turkish Republic established by Mustafa Kemal after World War I serves as the most lucid example here. The Kemalist state was avowedly secular and Westernized, and adopted nationalism in lieu of religion to underpin the identity of the state. The Kemalist state was dedicated to growth and development, and strove to assert broad hegemony over the population to achieve its goal. Kemalism soon became a model for state formation in much of the Muslim world, so much so that Alan Richards and John Waterbury view later state developments in the Middle East and North Africa as Kemalist at their core.[128] Pahlavi Iran (especially during the interwar years), Algeria under the FLN, Arab nationalist regimes from the 1950s onward, or Pakistan under Ayub Khan (1958–69), all to varying degrees emulated the Kemalist model, although never with the same penchant for secularism.

Secularization has led the state to look to molding the individual as a prelude to carrying out successful social change and development. This has been the avowed policy of Kemalist states from Turkey to Pahlavi Iran, and Indonesia to the revolutionary Arab states. To a lesser extent this has also been the case in Malaysia, Pakistan, Bangladesh, and Arab monarchies. The state's concern with music, dress, popular beliefs, and cultural outlook of Muslims has been prevalent.[129] It partly accounts for why for the social role of religion and the extent of state penetration of society, and more generally, cultural issues continue to be at the heart of politics in Muslim societies.

Social engineering went hand in hand with the conscious secularization of politics and the public arena. In this process the state early on secularized the judiciary and the educational system, and nationalized religious properties and endowments, thus truncating the sociopolitical role of religion just as it expanded its own powers and economic position.[130] The problematic of the secularization process in the Muslim world rested in that it did not seek to separate religion from politics so much as it sought to dominate religion, making its thinking and institutions subservient to the state.[131] This had the effect of politicizing religion as it instituted a struggle of power between the state and religious institutions in the political arena, and tied that struggle to the larger issue of state penetration of society. In Egypt, for instance, the Nasserist regime's imposition of reforms on the al-Azhar Islamic educational institution had the effect of bureaucratizing the religious scholars as a prelude to making them subservient to the state. That bureaucratization, however, imparted political attitudes on the religious establishment.[132]

In many cases, the secularization drive pushed religion out of the public sphere where it could no longer be effectively regulated or controlled by the state. As a result, religion—made more politically conscious—festered in the private arena as a potential source of support for opposition to the state and its ideology. In Pahlavi Iran the Islamic Revolution of 1979 resulted from exactly this process.[133]

As a result, Islam remained important to politics in Muslim states, and ultimately ruling regimes admitted to this as they turned to the repertoire of Islamic symbols and cultural tools to shore up their authority. The outward secular image of the state therefore was in contradiction to its own use of Islamic cultural manifestations. This contradiction became more apparent as the state faced economic and political crises, and in turn strengthened the role of Islam in politics. However, after decades of confrontation, state leaders often lacked either the legitimacy or institutional means to control Islamic forces that had been gathering strength outside of state control in the civil society and private spheres. The secular state itself, therefore, invited Islam back into the political process; and despite its continued commitment to secularism, paved the way for reentry of Islam into the public arena.

This process has been evident even in the most ideologically secular Muslim states, and those that have been viewed as strong states. Early on in socialist Arab states leaders turned to "political spirituality," namely, selective use of Islamic doctrines "to obtain consensus for secular undertakings."[134] In Egypt Nasser quoted scripture when articulating his vision of Egypt's development, whereas in Algeria FLN leaders depicted socialism as compatible with certain teachings of Islam.[135] This process only gained in momentum as Muslim states began to confront profound economic and political problems. The collapse of Arab socialism after Egypt's defeat in the 1967 war, gradual collapse of the social contract that had sustained authoritarianism, erosion of regime legitimacy, downturn in income from rent in the 1980s, and social pressures that resulted from economic restructuring in the 1980s and 1990s compelled states to use Islam more systematically. The emergence of Islamist opposition from the late-1970s onward also made turning to Islam important to contending with the legitimacy deficit that confronted ruling regimes.

As a result, from the 1970s onward, Muslim states were compelled to contend with the role of Islam in politics—and especially in the context of existing secular systems—more directly. Ad hoc uses of Islam had to give place to rethinking the relation of Islam to the state. Generally speaking, there are three types of state interaction with Islam and uses of Islamization evident in the Muslim world with differing outcomes for state, society, and the mediating role of Islam: the rejectionist secularists; the opportunist Islamizers; and the thoroughgoing Islamizers.

Algeria since the brutal military coup of 1992 and Turkey since the "soft military coup" of 1997 are examples of the first category. These states have chosen a path of retrenchment of the secular ideology of the state to the exclusion of any meaningful Islamic representation in the public arena and the political process. Algeria chose this course after Islamist activism threatened to overwhelm the secular state pursuant to the elections of 1991. Turkey has opted to exclude Islam from the political process after economic reforms of the 1980s and democratization in the 1990s opened the door for greater Islamic assertiveness in the political process. The Algerian and Turkish approaches represent a reassertion of the secular vision of the state that was prevalent in the 1950s and the 1960s; it is relying on the use of force to bolster that notion of the state despite greater prominence of Islam in society and politics.[136]

The second type of states—the opportunist Islamizers—are those that have taken guarded steps in the direction of accommodating Islam in politics—at least during critical periods—but have not committed themselves fully to a new cultural orientation. To varying degrees, the original conceptions of the state continue to define its character and relations with society. These states have shown some dexterity in using Islam to serve their objectives, but have not managed to monopolize the Islamic discourse or the flow of Islam in the political arena.

Furthermore, in these cases the state has turned to Islam primarily to address a short-term political crisis. However, the benefits that accrued from the use of Islam have at times nudged them further in the direction of utilizing Islamic symbols. In this type of state, since the state's approach to Islam has been purely utilitarian and even blatantly so, there tends to be a limited period of time during which the state has been able to control Islamic politics. Since the state does not undergo a cultural transformation, it cannot speak for Islam, and has to rely on Islamist forces and their ideology to provide it with support.

The inherent secularism of the state, and limited mandate of its Islam policy, means that ultimately any alliance between the state and Islamist forces will end. In the process, however, Islamist forces get a foothold in the political arena, and the state does develop certain degree of Islamic consciousness and legitimacy.[137] As a result, whether intended or not, the state develops certain cultural indigenization. It does not manage to gain control of Islamist institutions and ideology, or completely resolve the dilemmas of the postcolonial state, but becomes more stable than the first category of Muslim states. Still, these states remain arenas in which fierce battles between the state and its Islamist opposition rage.

Egypt since 1971, Turkey between the 1980 coup and the 1997 "soft coup," Jordan since the 1950s, and to some extent Indonesia in the 1990s exemplify this type of state. All of these states have been secular postcolonial states. Of the four only Jordan, as a monarchy, has been anchored in traditional cultural institutions and has had a claim to representing indigenous cultural values. Turkey has been a secular pro-Western republic, and Egypt and Indonesia after periods of socialist secularism have now become pro-Western capitalist republics.

The four states have all grown close to Islamic forces at critical periods, and have been instrumental in entrenching the Islamist discourse and its spokesmen in their political arenas. In all these cases the state has held on to the view that it needs Islam only for the narrow purpose of accomplishing a particular political objective. It has not viewed Islam as essential to the expansion of state authority. It has therefore accepted some degree of Islamization while it strives for its objectives, but once the goals have been attained, it has sought to end Islamization, and usually this has been when its conflict with Islamists has arisen. In Jordan and Egypt since the 1980s this development compelled the state to stay the course with its Islam policy.[138] Here, the state has concluded that its connections with traditional Islamic institutions and moderate Islamist forces were useful in constricting the radical Islamist organizations that had now gained a foothold in the political process.[139] By controlling the flow of Islam in the public arena, these states have sought to deny it to their Islamist oppositions. The state's Islam policy has been a policy of policing and controlling the public sphere.

In Jordan in the 1950s, in Egypt in the 1970s, in Indonesia in some regards, and in Turkey in the 1980s secular states turned to both traditional Islamic thinkers and Islamist activists to constrict the Left and dismantle their organizational networks. In Indonesia in the 1960s and the 1970s the state followed a similar policy, but since the 1980s the desire to combat the Left has ceased to animate its Islam policy.[140] Beginning with King Abdullah I the Jordanian monarchy gave Islamist forces a great deal of room to maneuver. The monarchy's aim was to constrict Nasserists, Ba'thists, Palestinian nationalists, communists, and other left-of-center critics of the monarchy. This utility of the Muslim Brotherhood became more important after the Black September of 1970, and in dividing the ranks of the Palestinians.[141]

In Egypt, beginning in 1971, Anwar Sadat bolstered the Muslim Brotherhood to destroy the Nasserist base of power and outmaneuver his rival, Ali Sabri.[142] The Brotherhood weakened the Nasserists' presence on campuses, in unions, and in political institutions.[143] In Turkey, after the military coup of 1980, General Evren used Islamist groups, which later became the nucleus for the Islamic Salvation Party and Refah and Virtue parties to weaken leftist labor unions and student groups, and to minimize leftist resistance to the coup and to the restructuring of the economy.[144] In fact, the rise of Islamism in Turkey is directly linked to the process of economic reform since the coup.[145] In a more sinister case, the Turkish military encouraged the growth of a militant Islamist group, Hizbullah (Party of God), in the 1980s to constrict the Marxist separatist Kurdish movement, PKK.[146] In 2000 Hizbullah was accused of the torture and murder of more than 1,000 people, clearly the most violent expression of Islamism in Turkey.

In each of these cases, the political leadership felt threatened by the Left. In each case, furthermore, the Islamist forces viewed the Left as a grave danger as well. This provided for a tactical alliance between the secular state and the Islamist forces. In each case the political leadership adopted a sympathetic posture toward a role for Islam in politics and society to broker an alliance between the state and the Islamist groups.[147] In these cases states encouraged religious education and facilitated a role for it in society in order to make it immune to leftist activism.[148] In the end, however, each of these leaders would prove to be more tied to the interests of the state than to those of Islam and would ultimately prove unable to maintain his unique position.

In Jordan, Egypt, and Turkey, the eventual demise of the Left removed the state's need for Islam. The growing power of Islamist groups under state patronage and in battle against the Left would turn them into a formidable force. Eventually the battle ceased to be between the state and the Left, and became one between the state and its former partners among the Islamist groups. The state made it obvious that with the demise of the Left it intended to end its alliance with Islamist groups, who, having tasted power, let it be known that they would like to lay claim to the state.

The principal political leaders in these states had to choose which camp they belonged to. In these cases, the limited interests of the state in Islamic politics, its refusal to accommodate Islam at a fundamental level, and the transitory nature of the alliance with Islamist forces produced an untenable situation: it led to the rise of a powerful social movement that the state, owing to its essentially secular nature, could never fully control.

In response to this challenge Turkey has opted to move back in the direction of uncompromising secularism,[149] whereas Egypt and Jordan have sought to retain control of the flow of Islam in politics. To do so they have constructed more solid alliances with traditional Islamic institutions and incorporated Islamic symbols and values to a greater extent into state ideology and its working.[150] In this regard, they have moved in the direction of the thoroughgoing Islamizers—Malaysia and Pakistan—to which my discussion will now turn.

Malaysia and Pakistan: Riding the Tiger and Expanding State Power

Malaysia and Pakistan are the most interesting cases. Here state leaders went beyond using Islam and Islamist forces in a limited fashion to contend with a political crisis and rather viewed Islam and the need to anchor the state in indigenous cultural values as central to the state's efficient functioning and expansion of its power and capacity. In Malaysia under Prime Minister Mahathir Mohammad (1980–present) and Pakistan between the military coups of 1977 and 1999, Islamization of society has occurred under the aegis of the state, and in far more thoroughgoing fashion than in Egypt or Jordan. In Malaysia and Pakistan the state became the agent of Islamization and undertook this effort in close collaboration with Islamist forces.

In each case the state's turn to Islam has been explained as a reactive strategy. Both Malaysia and Pakistan turned to Islam at a time of profound crisis before the ruling regimes. Pakistan faced a rising tide of Islamist activism in the form of the Order of the Prophet (Nizam-i Mustafa) movement of 1977, which threatened not only to topple the Pakistan Peoples Party Governmant of Zulfiqar Ali Bhutto but to wash away the postcolonial state, part and parcel, as had happened in Iran in 1979.[151] The Islamic challenge was complemented with rising ethnic tensions in the country, which the state believed could be contained through greater reliance on Islam. Throughout the Zia period (1977–88) the growing importance of ethnic politics in Sind, NWFP, Baluchistan, and Southern Punjab deviated from, and perhaps accounted for, the state's preoccupation with Islam.[152]

In Malaysia, too, the ruling UMNO party was faced with a serious challenge for its control of Malay politics by the resurgent Partei Islam Se-Malaysia (Malaysian Islamic Party [PAS]—Pan-Malayan Islamic Party [PMIP], before 1951) that made solid gains prior to the May 13, 1969, riots, as well as the newly educated middle- and lower-middle-class youth, under the leadership of Anga-tan Belia Islam Malaysia (Malaysian Islamic Youth Movement [ABIM]) in the 1970s.[153]

In each of the two cases the state made a strategic choice: to champion the cause of Islam in order to shore up its authority and legitimacy, outmaneuver its opposition, and gain stability. In this, Malaysia and Pakistan, it is usually suggested, have acted as Egypt, Turkey, Indonesia, or Jordan did, except that here Islamization became more broad based and the state committed itself to it beyond the scope of resolving a single crisis. Also in Pakistan and Malay-sia the state chose to manage Islamization itself rather than rely on Islamic or Islamist intermediaries to spearhead it. More important, the Malaysian and Pakistani states proved willing to give up on their secular ideology to do so. By Islamizing the public sphere, they brought Islam into the public arena and established a measure of control over its flow in society and politics. In this process, the state was interested in regulating Islamist politics, extending its control over Islamic institutions and Islamist movements. Islamists in turn wanted access to state resources and influence in public policy making. Is-lamization was designed to create circumstances in which Islamists would perceive their interests to be compatible with those of the state.

Pakistan and Malaysia may have opted for this different course because of the vulnerabilities that were particular to their state structures. Both Malaysia and Pakistan are new states with weak notions of nationality—states that were literally conceived of at the moment of birth and lack continuity in time. They are, moreover, multiethnic states that include important population groups that were not included in the new states willingly. Both Malaysia and Pakistan lack a strong notion of nationalism born of a sustained struggle for independence against colonialism. In both countries the ruling elites closely collaborated with the British to the very end—to stave off Hindu hegemony in Pakistan's case and the communist Chinese threat in Malaysia's. In both cases the populations that inherited the state were beneficiaries of colonial largesse. The areas in Northwest India that were included in Pakistan were deemed as strategic and hence received much patronage from Delhi during the colonial era. Similarly, the British interest in Malaya was until the mid-1800s limited to their concerns with supporting the China trade from India. Thenceforth, British economic interests in resources on the Malayan penin-sula were tied to the Chinese and Indian businesses and labor, whereas the Malayan oligarchy and peasantry were enticed to facilitate the burgeoning colonial economy. As a result, throughout the colonial period, the British maintained strong patronage links with the Malays. The close connection to colonialism in both cases made for states that were not forged through the crucible of the struggle of independence, but were rather handed down—cre-ated—at independence. These states emerged after intricate negotiations over power between future state leaders, colonial powers, and various ethnic and social groups. For instance, in the case of Malaysia, the British forced the concept of a multiethnic state on a reluctant UMNO, and then secured guar-antees for the Chinese and Indians in the future Malaysian state. The Malaysian and Pakistani states were therefore greatly constricted as the scope of their powers was decided by those negotiations and was from the outset controlled by checks and balances that obviated the possibility of formulating effective economic and social policy.

Both Malaysia and Pakistan were weak states, not only for the reasons just mentioned but also because they lacked effective machinery of government. In Malaya the Chinese and the Indians were the backbone of the British order, which at any rate operated as much through Singapore as Kuala Lumpur. In Pakistan's case the impressive government of the British Raj was left behind in Delhi. The new Pakistani government had to govern out of a hotel in Karachi without the rudiments of a national government over provinces that had no natural grid among them, and some of which were reluctant participants in the Pakistan movement.

In addition, in both Malaya and northwest India, the British ruled through intermediary power brokers. In Malaya it was the sultans and in northwest India, princes and landlords who maintained control over local populations. As a result the Malaysian and Pakistani states were born with strong social institutions that immediately restricted the power and capacity of the new states.

As a result, both Malaysia and Pakistan were born as weak states, confronting a formidable task of state building in fractured societies with strong social institutions and power brokers, and while lacking even the ideological tools that were available to other Muslim states in the form of nationalism. That secular nationalism was so weak in Malaysia and Pakistan made these states both more vulnerable to the Islamist challenge and yet more interested in using Islam as a basis for state ideology. In Malaysia the expansion of UMNO has been a source of power for the state. In Pakistan the military has performed the same function. However, in both cases these institutions have bolstered state authority since the 1980s by advocating state-led Islamization, attesting to the linkage between expansion of state power—whether facilitated by UMNO or the Pakistan military—and state use of Islam.

Given the limitations to state power and capacity in Malaysia and Pakistan, state leaders reacted differently to the challenge of Islamism. They were more hard-pressed to reject encroachment of Islam into the public sphere in the manner witnessed elsewhere in the Muslim world, but by the same token were more likely to identify its promise.

In Malaysia and Pakistan Islamization helped reinvent the postcolonial state and its relations to society. Under Islamization state power in Pakistan was restored, and in Malaysia it was expanded and its domination became more pronounced. It was during the Islamization era that corruption and predatory behavior reached its apogee, attesting to greater state role in the economy and society. It was also owing to changes in state power and capacity that Malaysia and Pakistan showed notable progress in at least one of the main indicators of development during the Islamization era. It was then that Malaysia took giant strides in the direction of capitalist development, and Pakistan in the direction of democratization. Whatever the shortcomings of these processes in Malaysia and Pakistan, the two countries have exceeded secular Muslim states elsewhere in progress on these fronts. This indicates that Islamization has allowed these countries to remove some of the obstacles to development in society and politics. How the Islamist threat was turned into an asset is captured in the manner in which Mahathir and the UMNO leadership deftly depicted Islamization as the equivalent of capitalist development. In the words of Deputy Prime Minister Musa Hitam in 1984:

> Through a complex process of accommodation . . . cooptation . . . and confrontation . . . we *Sunni* Muslims of Malaysia will remain on top of the situation. . . . We see absolutely no contradiction between Islam and modernisation. Indeed Islam of the 21st century must be a core element of our modernisation programme.[154]

So the state replaced large swaths of colonial ideology of the state with Islamic ideology. Such an act of accommodation was not merely reactive, but proactive. In fact, such a fundamental voluntary reorientation of a state can be explained only as a rational choice to further the interests of the state. The state would internalize Islamic values, not only to combat Islamist challengers to its authority but also to become stronger and to expand its powers.

By actively endorsing the cultural language of the opposition and the prevailing norms of the larger society, the state not only receives greater legitimacy but also manages to reduce resistance to its continued expansion, which is at the heart of the postcolonial state. For instance, despite much pressure brought to bear on Pakistan since 1993 to increase taxation of the agricultural sector, the ruling regime has failed to do so. The only agricultural tax to have been levied and collected over the last twenty years is the Islamic land tax (*kharaj*) that was imposed in the 1980s. Hence, Islam alters the balance between state and society in struggles that involve extraction of resources from society, pointing to the importance of culture to discussions of state formation.

While much attention has been focused on how education, economy, state institutions, and the like become Islamic—posing the issues as the passing of secularism in favor of Islam, less attention is paid to what Islamization of these arenas of public life means for state power. Islamization is not just about Islam but also about the state.

In the long run, however, Pakistan and Malaysia produced different results. In Malaysia ultimately state interest completely dissolved ABIM interests and for much of Malaysian history marginalized PAS. In Pakistan, eventually Islamists asserted their interests within the state to a greater extent. This had to do with the fact that in Malaysia UMNO was a strong party, which co-opted ABIM and was able to contend with PAS. In fact, in Malaysia UMNO became the means for co-opting Islamism, and as a result became an instrument of Islamization. In Pakistan Zia's military regime had no party and was therefore less successful in fully co-opting the Islamist forces and establishing control over their constituency. As a result, in Pakistan the state conceded more to Islamists and had greater difficulty in managing them.[155] More important, the alliance between the state and the Islamists in both Malaysia and Pakistan proved untenable. Islamists ultimately concluded that the interests of the state—despite its significant Islamization—were incompatible with the Islamist worldview and that the state in Malaysia and Pakistan had changed culturally, but little had changed in its structure and working. These tensions came to the fore in the late 1990s as the Asian financial crisis in Malaysia and IMF-imposed reforms on Pakistan forced a breach between the state and its Islamist constituents. Still, the twenty years of Islamization is an important *phase* in the development of Malaysia and Pakistan, one that has profoundly changed the shape of the state in the two countries. Islamization has left an indelible mark on society and politics, the state and its institutions, with far-reaching implications for sociopolitical changes and economic developments from this point forward.

Plan of the Book

This book is divided into three parts. Part I deals with the origins of the state in Malaysia and Pakistan and early state formation in the two countries. Chapter 1 will elaborate the manner in which the colonial experience formed the essential characteristics of the state in the two countries in general, and the relation with Islam and society in particular. Chapter 2 will examine the manner in which relations between early state formation shaped politics, setting the stage for the encounter of Islam and the state in the 1980s.

Part II discusses the critical juncture of the late 1970s through the early 1980s. Chapter 3 examines the crisis that confronted the secular state in Malaysia and Pakistan between 1969 (May 1969 riots in Malaysia and fall of Ayub Khan regime in Pakistan) and the 1977–80 period (escalation of Islamist challenge to the ruling order in Malaysia and fall of the Bhutto regime in Pakistan). Chapter 4 presents a broad account of the nature and scope of the Islamist challenge to the ruling regimes in the two countries.

Part III analyzes the responses of the Malaysian and Pakistani states to the challenges before them. Chapter 5 elaborates on the Islamization initiative in the two countries—the policies that they entailed and the ends that they served. Chapter 6 discusses the consequences of Islamization for Malaysia and Pakistan. What was the impact of this strategy on state-society relations, the attainment of state objectives, and the long run prospects for development, stability, growth, and democracy?

I

THE MAKING OF
THE NEW STATES

The Colonial Legacy

Malaysia and Pakistan did not exist, even as an ideal, before colonialism. Their final shape and borders were in fact determined only on the eve of independence. Their societies reflect the deep impact of colonialism, just as their machinery of government displays uncanny similarity to that of the colonial era. The colonial era is therefore the beginning of the modern state in Malaysia and Pakistan. It was then that both the capabilities and vulnerabilities of the state were decided, as were the particular institutional characteristics of the state that account for why and how culture and religion would become so central to later stages of state formation, and its projects of hegemony and economic growth. The story thus begins with the colonial era.

One Malay State or Many? Britain and the Creation of Malaysia

With the Anglo-Dutch Treaty of 1824 Malaya became a sphere of British influence. Until well into the mid-1800s colonial rule in Malaya was not concerned with extraction of resources from peninsular Malaya so much as it was aimed at maintaining control over the strategically located Straits of Malacca and its environs. As a result, initially at least, Malay territories were peripheral to British interests in Southeast Asia, and later when the British found ample reason to penetrate those territories, Malays were supplanted with imported labor and were thus removed from the thick of the colonial economy. This marginality would prove consequential for state and society in Malaysia.

The British presence was first established in the three Straits Settlements of Penang, Malacca, and Singapore, all of which were directly ruled by the British and had a mixed population of Malays, Chinese, and Indians. The security of these city-states was dependent on some form of control of the Malay interior. That, however, was more easily achieved through local structures of authority than through direct British rule.[1] The British policy therefore became one of preserving those structures of authority that were controlled by a Malay ruling class in various sultanates (*kerajaan*) under the rule of the *raja* or *sultan* (king).[2] This ruling class controlled the Malay peasantry—which at the time constituted the vast majority of the Malay population—through time-honored patron-client relations.[3] The British found indirect rule through the various sultans who ruled over patches of territory on peninsular Malaya to be both effective and cost-efficient. Colonial state formation from this point forward would not be concerned with land or extraction of resources, but control of the local population.

The Malay Peninsula at the time consisted of several sultanates with distinct boundaries and ruled by separate dynasties. Only the Malay lingua franca and Islam tied these disparate political entities together. The British did not at first have a conception of the Malay Peninsula as a single unit, but as a region that consisted of many political entities.[4] That conception changed in the 1871–74 period as political chaos, first in the sultanates of Selangor and Perak, and then further east, threatened British commercial interests and stability in the Straits Settlements.[5] The chaos compelled the British to take a more active interest in Malay politics and to develop a coherent policy toward control of the interior.[6] This produced the Forward Movement in 1871, which began the consolidation of British authority over Malays.[7] That process would gain momentum with the Treaty of Pangkor in 1874 and culminate in the Federated Malay States in 1895, which by 1910 covered all of peninsular Malaysia and was governed by a high commissioner.[8]

The Treaty of Pangkor brought nine Malay sultanates or states (as they came to be known) mainly on the western and southern parts of the peninsula—known as Negri Sembilan—under British protection. The treaty would later serve as the basis for extending that protection to the eastern and northern parts of the peninsula as well. Under the Federation Agreement the British protection covered all of today's peninsular Malaysia, but remained weakest in states under Siamese suzerainty—which have traditionally been the most Islamic in their culture—Kedah, Perlis, Kelantan, and Trengganu. This was significant for future Malaysian politics, for UMNO, too, is weakest in these states, which happen to serve as the base for Islamist challenges to state authority.[9]

The period of the 1870s–1890s witnessed growing Chinese and British interest in the economic potential of the Malay interior.[10] Capital accumulation in the Straits Settlements had led to new places for investment, and attention turned to the Malayan interior.[11] The Chinese already held investments in the interior, but were soon overshadowed by Europeans, who dominated foreign investment in the interior, especially in rubber. By 1913 Europeans controlled some 60% of land planted with rubber in Malaya.[12] This interest necessitated more direct control of the Malay Peninsula in order to protect the lucrative investments in tin and rubber that soon constituted the lion's share of the colonial government's revenue.[13] Stability in the Malay states was now a greater imperative, which justified the formalization of the British protectorates into a coherent system. In addition, the growing local European population demanded a greater say in colonial policy making and favored it to be managed centrally outside of the hold of individual sultanates. British commercial interests thus favored centralization of administrative functions in Kuala Lumpur.

The result of all this was the Federation Agreement that formalized the British protectorate system in Malayan states. However, although the British had moved in the direction of looking at their Malayan territories as one entity—which was reflected in the fact that they adopted the same policies and used the same treaties in dealing with all Malayan sultanates—they continued to uphold the sovereignty of individual sultans and their states—which was evident in the Federation Agreement. The British consolidation of power therefore both entrenched individual state identities and promoted the conception of the Malayan Peninsula as one cultural and political unit.

The aim of the protection was merely to bring order to the Malay states through the steady hand of British supervision. The British did not wish to rule directly over the Malays, but to merely minimize political instability caused by internal struggles of power. The British would thus provide advice to the sultans and help them in administration, but would refrain from direct intervention in the government of the states.

The British advice was conveyed through a "resident" who served as the link between the sultanate and the British center in the Straits Settlements. The resident would oversee the economic and political affairs of the state and would dispense advice to the sultan with the aim of minimizing political turmoil. Direct British intervention in the affairs of the state would occur only if the sultan failed to heed British advice or interfered with British commercial interests.[14] The intervention would, however, be limited to either forcing the sultan to mend his ways or replacing him on the throne with a more pliable relative.[15] Those rulers—and the upper ranks of the aristocracy—who followed the British lead were in turn protected from challenges to their authority by rival states, or claimants to power and status from within their own states, and were moreover richly rewarded by substantial regular incomes in keeping with their status.[16]

The limited nature of the British intervention, therefore, meant that colonialism would not infringe upon the sultans' prerogatives, or disturb the nature of the sultans' authority and relations to the Malay peasantry. The British presence did not affect the power and status of the Malay aristocracy or the social standing of the Malay peasantry. In fact, by relying on the Malay oligarchy to control the Malay masses, the British bolstered the powers of that social class just as it co-opted it into the British system through education in modern subjects and recruitment into the British administrative system.[17]

One result was to retard the growth of a Malay middle class. The British compensated for that by nurturing Chinese and Indian middle classes that performed the function of the bourgeosie.[18]

Hence, on the Malayan Peninsula British rule perpetuated the myth of Malay sovereignty, vested in individual Malay states, and strengthened their traditional cultural and political institutions. In fact, under the British the sultans became symbols of Malay political sovereignty although they had little power to make real decisions.[19] The British system also strengthened the ties that bound Malay states to Islam. The British took over the functions of lower-ranking chiefs, who had traditionally served as magistrates and tax collectors.[20] Greater administrative efficiency under the British improved collection of religious taxes and management of religious endowments, Islamic courts, and pilgrimages to Mecca, and encouraged formation of a religious advisory council (Majlis Ugama Islam) to assist sultans in management of religious affairs.[21]

The council became the basis for a religious bureaucracy in all Malay states, and as such both entrenched the role of religion in Malay politics and gave the religious establishment a vision of a larger Malay polity that extended beyond individual states. Therefore, during the heyday of colonialism the rise of religious bureaucracies in Malayan states bolstered the authority of the sultans and placed control on the flow of Islam in society and politics. This control would, however, be short-lived. For the ulama that were inducted into state religious administrations tended to be rural religious functionaries that were tied to the syncretic Islam of rural Malaya. In cooperation with the sultans they acted to limit the powers and influence of orthodox reformists (the Kaum Muda—young group), who grew in prominence in the late nineteenth century as a result of greater contact with the Arab heartland of Islam.[22] The reformists were thus excluded from the power structure that the British and sultans set up, and would in time serve as leaders in the emerging Malay nationalist movement that evolved outside of the British system of control and in defiance of it.[23] These Islamic leaders provided for use of religion in mass politics in competition with the hierarchical control of rural Islam by the sultans.

Legal reforms proved equally important for the powers of the sultans. The British preserved the traditional Islamic courts, although they were made subservient to the new civil code that was modeled after the Indian Penal Code.[24] Still, those areas of the law that most directly affected the Malay masses—family law, inheritance, and minor offences—were dealt with in Islamic courts under the sultans' control. Moreover, although British reforms reduced the powers of Islamic courts by codifying legal relation in a feudal and hierarchical society, they augmented the powers of the sultan as the titular overseer of the system.[25] The consequence was that during British rule, in civil and legal matters a clear distinction between religion and the state—the domain of the British civil authority and the sultans' cultural and religious prerogatives—was established.[26] However, the political role of the sultans precluded a complete separation of religion and politics.

The growing economic penetration of the Malay interior encouraged legal and administrative changes, including changes in private property rights, contractual obligations, and land ownership.[27] These changes produced new administrative systems in various states under the supervision of the residential system. The need for financing such an undertaking led to a rationalization of fiscal systems and centralization of tax collection.[28] Hence, the Federation Agreement produced far more administrative centralization than it did political centralization. British Malaya continued to consist of three Straits Settlement colonies and nine separate Malay states. Each of these states had joined the Federation through a separate treaty with Great Britain, which was negotiated independently and at different points in time. As a result, the very process of creation of the Federation underscored rather than downplayed the sovereignty and individual identity of the Malay states.[29]

Yet, the federal administrative system became increasingly centralized with the resident-general at its apex. It standardized administrative practice across the Malayan Peninsula and even the Straits Settlements.[30] This development encouraged a peninsular conception of authority in Malaya that extended beyond individual states. It had a uniformalizing function, encouraging the conceptualization of the peninsula as a single unit, managed from a center, which by the 1900s had moved from the Straits Settlements to Kuala Lumpur.[31] The apparent anomaly between political decentralization and administrative centralization would affect state power in Malaysia after independence as the administrative center would serve as the foundation of the future Malaysian state, and political decentralization would ensure certain devolution of power to the individual Malay states and their sultans.

By the turn of the century Malays, too, became participants in this growing bureaucracy.[32] Education had equipped many Malays of aristocratic background with skills to join the civil service, and many had been recruited by the British to serve in state bureaucracies—but not in the colonial bureaucracy. The growing Malay civil service eventually became a strong source of support for a united Malay civil service.[33] This produced the Malaya States Civil Service, which was manned by recruits from the Malay oligarchy and elite bureaucrats in various states.[34] The Malay bureaucrats now constituted a "rentier cum aristocratic class"—which after independence would form the core of the bureaucratic elite and leadership of UMNO.[35] For instance, Onn Ja`far, who was a key figure in the formation of UMNO, was a member of the royal family of Johor, and Tunku Abdul Rahman, Malaysia's first prime minister, was the brother of the sultan of Kedah. Both men were officers in the British administration of Malaya. This class, the "administocracy" in Jomo K. S.'s words, would continue to manage the state and the economy, limit the Malay bourgeoisie, collect rent, and dispense patronage.[36] The rise of this class, however, promoted a conception of the Malay polity—and ultimately the state—that superseded individual Malay states and that coincided with the boundaries of control of the civil service.[37] This class would both articulate new ideas such as "progress," "territorial state," and "Malayness," thus laying the foundations for a nationalist discourse,[38] and would become the conduit for the transmission of the colonial conception of the state into postindependence Malaysia.[39] The Malay elite who were integrated into the British administration would also contribute to the rise of Malay nationalist parties, most notably, UMNO.[40] The Malay elite, who had all along felt disadvantaged in the British administration, were able to translate their feelings of frustration into a nationalist discourse that addressed the demands of the Malay middle classes as well.[41] The Malay elite therefore performed the peculiar function of both representing and articulating Malay nationalism, and yet ensuring the continuity of the British order in Malaysia.

Under the Federation the economic value of peninsular Malaya grew.[42] Tin mining and rubber plantations proliferated, bringing other forms of trade and investment.[43] Malaya became a large source of revenue for Great Britain—a bright jewel in the British Empire. Between 1900 and 1913 British government revenue went up from $15.6 million to $44.3 million.[44] One estimate places British revenues in Malaya in 1927 at twenty million sterling.[45] However, the British did not make money in Malaya through direct revenue generation. In fact, British revenues and expenditures were often very close, and the colonial administration would on occasion experience deficits.[46] The British, rather, made money in trade as well as managing currency and credit flows. In fact, the Malayan economy was largely trade dependent. In 1926 overseas imports of British Malaya were 117 million sterling, and exports 147 million. These figures exceeded "the whole of the rest of the Colonial dependencies put together."[47] The foreign exchange contribution to Great Britain, especially during the difficult post–World War I years, would prove significant.[48]

The economic value of Malaya to the British prompted greater concern for stability and control. British rule was not benefiting from, and hence was not being shaped by, direct extraction of revenue, but by trade. This made exercise of territorial control over land, crops, and labor unnecessary, especially since labor was provided by imported Chinese and Indian migrants. Trade required stability, which could be secured through indirect means of control. The British continued to look to Malay states for that stability and control. Economic boom in the twentieth century therefore further entrenched the sovereignty of Malay states and sociopolitical standing of the sultans and the Malay oligarchy just as it strengthened the skeleton of the British administrative system.

The growing colonial economy benefited the Malay rulers and oligarchy. Investment in Malay states increased, as did both the incomes and rent that they received. The economic boom, however, did not affect the mass of Malay peasants, whose livelihoods continued to depend on rice farming and who experienced greater poverty during the colonial era.[49] The British relationship with Malayan rulers supported the feudal relationship in rural Malaya and kept the Malayan peasantry on the land where they could be controlled by their traditional institutions of authority. The British, furthermore, had no interest in Malays as laborers.[50] They were viewed as lazy and therefore better kept on the land, in the *kampongs* (villages) and under the control of the sultans.[51] The British instead imported Chinese and Indian labor to serve the colonial economy. As a result, the expansion of the colonial economy in Malaya changed the ethnic composition of Malaya—with profound implications for later state formation—but had minimal impact on the social characteristics of the local population. Since the British did not directly exploit Malay labor, British rule did not produce a mobilization of Malay peasantry into an anticolonial movement.

It was all along the avowed policy of the British to improve the lot of the Malay masses, but their policies, in effect, contributed to their misery and poverty.[52] The expansion of the colonial economy, especially the spread of rubber plantations, increased competition for land and produced a money economy in rural areas, which contributed to growth of poverty.[53] In effect, the British policy toward Malays was one of benign neglect. They were not included in the colonial economy and were left to their own devices in their own increasingly marginalized *kampong* economy. They were shepherded by the Malay oligarchy, whose own economic interests rested not with the economy of their Malay subjects, but with the colonial economy in which their subjects had no place.

The colonial era, however, did affect Malays in other ways. The rise in the number of Chinese and Indian laborers reinforced Islamic identity among Malays,[54] as did greater access to education, communication, and roads. As more Malays read or made pilgrimages to Mecca, their interest in their Islamic identity grew, and their view of Islam changed—extending beyond the local traditions that were tied to the sultans.[55] These changes loosened the control of the sultans over segments of the Malay population and opened the door for Islam to become an aspect of Malay nationalism, if not a surrogate for it.[56] The British system, which had emphasized oligarchic control of the masses, had left the door open to mass politics. The new interpretations of Islam that were tied to the rising Malay educated and middle-class elements, and were not controlled by the sultans, became a claimant to that mass politics. Islam therefore emerged on the political scene in Malaya in the early years of the twentieth century as a competitor for secular nationalism and the traditional relations of politics in the sultanates.[57] The rise of the Partei Islam Se-Malaysia (Islamic Party of Malaysia [PAS]) as a challenger to both UMNO and the authority of sultans is reflective of this development.[58]

The pattern of consolidation of colonial rule and later its retrenchment were also significant in determining both the shape and capabilities of the future Malaysian state. From 1895 onward British rule over Malaya became increasingly centralized. Colonial rule, however, did not formally unify the Peninsula and the Straits Settlements. The former continued to be divided into separate states under the umbrella of a federation, whereas the British governed the latter directly. The Federation of Malay States, meanwhile, provided for a uniform legislation and administration, and encouraged Malays in secular as well as religious administrations to focus on the federation rather than its constituent parts. Still, the federal arrangement moved in the direction of a single Malay polity only very slowly. To begin with, the Federation Agreement recognized and reinforced the status of sultans, who, at any rate, were not keen on the administrative centralization that followed the agreement.[59] Along the way the British made many concessions to the sultans regarding the powers of the federal legislative body and the extent of central administration's infringement on their powers. The nature of relations between the colonial economy and the Malay masses encouraged such concessions further, as did the fact that each Malay state had joined the federation after negotiating separately and directly with the British.

As the colonial economy expanded, so did the scope of tensions between the states and the central British administration. The colonial economy demanded development spending, which translated into increase in central administrative powers. The sultans and their British residents resented this centralization. They believed that administrative centralization would undermine the authority of the sultans before their subjects and would ultimately destabilize Britain's indirect rule over Malays. In the 1920s the British high commissioner, Sir Laurence Guillemard, acquiesced to these demands by decentralizing administrative powers and functions from Kuala Lumpur to various state capitals.[60] This move was not tantamount to devolution of power to states—as British administration continued to manage development spending—but recognized state sovereignties and lowered the status of the burgeoning Malay center in Kuala Lumpur.[61] Guillemard's concession was in turn unpopular with European investors, who favored contending with one administrative authority that would be beyond the influence of sultans and residents.[62] The Europeans favored a colonial administration that would be solely responsive to European interests and would not include Malay influence in its decision making.

The debate was greatly influenced by developments in the Middle East.[63] In the 1920s the British were devising a protectorate system in the Arab lands of the Ottoman Empire.[64] In the Middle East, under the provisions of the mandate system of the League of Nations, the British formed a regional order that consisted of politically separate although culturally and religiously uniform Arab polities and states. The similarity made the Middle Eastern developments directly relevant to British Malaya. The wisdom that emerged from the Middle East was that given the international climate of the post–World War I era and the resources available to Great Britain, indirect rule would serve its interests most directly. In Malaya this wisdom would mean moving in the direction of strengthening Malay states rather than the British center in Kuala Lumpur.

The decentralization effort was directed at transforming the Federation of Malay States into what was then termed the Union of Malay States.[65] The Federation of Malay States was based on the idea of a singular Malay political and administrative arena that would supersede the sovereignty of individual states and would in time dissolve them. The Union of Malay States would give up on the existence of a united Malay political and administrative space, favoring the presence of many sovereign Malay states loosely held together. The Union would be more akin to the British Arab mandates after World War I, whereas the Federation would have been closer to the British Raj.

In effect, World War I forced Great Britain to reevaluate where it was heading with its rule over Malaya. The federation idea made for better administration—and was favored by local European capitalists. However, the federation formula suggested a united pan-Malayan political and administrative space that could potentially make rule over Malaya more difficult, for it would allow more broadly based nationalist political resistance to surface— what the British were encountering in India in the form of the Indian National Congress. Just as the conception of India produced Indian nationalism, the concept of Malaya would produce Malayan nationalism. The British policy in the Middle East suggested that after World War I Britain favored unburdening colonialism by getting maximum economic advantage with minimal political commitment. Decentralization in Malaya would serve that purpose. It would shore up the identity of separate Malayan states and encourage popular loyalty to them. It would also weaken the broader conception of Malayness and possibilities of broad-based peninsular opposition to British rule. Decentralization would provide for more possibilities of divide and rule, and compartmentalizing the Malay identity and politics.

The upshot of the struggle over decentralization was that political formation in Malaya was kept suspended between development of individual Malay states and the merging of state sovereignties into a larger Malay entity. The implication of this for later state development was that the Malaysian state's powers were limited and it was saddled with strong institutions of authority that were not vested in the political center of authority in Kuala Lumpur. The tensions inherent in this would determine the dynamics of state formation after independence.

The advent of World War II proved decisive for the debate over decentralization. During the war the Japanese drove the British from Malaya and were able to get support from indigenous Malays. The occupation also pitted the Chinese and Malays against one another, with the former opposing the occupation and the latter either supporting or remaining insouciant before its policies. The end of the occupation witnessed Chinese-Malay clashes.[66] In the absence of a national and peninsular-wide leadership, Malays turned to the ulama and religious leaders—especially the orthodox and reformist of the *Kaum Muda* type—for guidance.[67] These religious leaders were interested in defending Malay rights and interests in tandem with demanding liberation from colonialism,[68] infusing communal interests, enmeshed with Islamic consciousness, into the nationalist discourse. The Japanese, therefore, changed Malay politics. Japanese occupation removed the British system of control in one swoop, precipitated tensions with the Chinese that underscored the importance of peninsular-wide political organization to the Malays, and brought Islam into their politics. The Japanese interregnum therefore raised Malay political awareness.[69] This awareness laid the foundations of peninsular-wide Malay nationalism. That nationalism, moreover, included Islamic arguments and symbols, not only because the Malays had turned to orthodox and reformist ulama for leadership during the Japanese occupation—the time when their nationalist perspective was taking shape—but also because a peninsular-wide conception of Malay nationalism needed the uniformalizing influence of Islam. Across the Malay Peninsula significant variations in custom (*adat*), popular religious practices, and dialect existed, distinguishing between regions and states.[70] In the absence of a widely shared sense of nation in lieu of allegiance to states and sultans, Islam became an indispensable component of peninsular-wide Malay identity and nationalism.

The emerging nationalism opposed the Union of Malay States in urban areas. British-educated Malay aristocratic and bureaucratic elite, along with Malay middle classes, articulated a "pan-Malay" nationalist discourse and demanded a unified Malay polity. This movement took the form of UMNO (formed on May 12, 1946). UMNO's first leaders, especially Onn Ja'far, advocated a nonracial British style of governance, thus allaying British fears regarding rights and privileges of the Chinese and Indian minority.

Weakened by war, the British were unable to immediately resume formal control over Malayan politics, especially since the surging Malay nationalist movement was a new development outside of their traditional sphere of control. In addition, the British now faced a Chinese-Malayan communist movement. Hoping to contain the communists, placate the nationalists, and also protect British economic interests and the status of the Chinese and Indian minorities, in 1946 the British proposed a single Malay Union including Penang and Malacca Straits Settlements. The move toward decentralization was thus abandoned, not because of local European pressure, but because of Malay demands.[71]

The British offer, however, faced resistance from the sultans who continued to wield power over large areas of the Malay Peninsula and lord over the majority of Malays. British interest in tin and rubber made the British susceptible to their pressure as well. The Malaysian state was therefore carefully crafted to satisfy both sides. A unitary Malay polity would coexist with the individual Malay states.

The establishment of Malaysia was ultimately a victory for the unitary polity. This owed to the fact that the Malay states had no relations with the economically powerful Straits Settlements and could not serve the interests of the economic actors who were critical to both the British and the future prosperity of Malays.[72] UMNO, on the contrary, proposed to replicate British rule and thus provided for a viable relationship between the Straits Settlements and the Malay interior that would be acceptable to the Straits Settlements and to the Chinese, the Indians, and the British interests therein. As a result, UMNO was able to secure Malaysia by committing itself to the colonial model of state, internalizing its values and following its methods of administration. The Malaysian state was thus made possible by Malay nationalism's formal commitment to preserving the continuity between colonial and postcolonial eras.

The Malaysian state, however, had to also accommodate the Malay state system, although as subordinate to the unitary Malay polity. This meant that UMNO's victory came at the cost of limiting its power and reach in favor of state rights and powers, and prerogatives of the sultans. The future Malaysian state was born with limited powers and has since sought to eliminate the vestiges of British indirect rule, not only to finalize the triumph of the unitary Malay center but also to expand its powers.

From Muslim Separatism to the Muslim Vice-Regal State: Britain and the Making of Pakistan

British rule over North-West India—areas that would later constitute Pakistan—shows great similarity with rule in British Malaya. Here, too, colonialism produced the fundamental characteristics of the state and determined the nature of its relations with society. British rule endowed the future state with machinery of government, along with relations of patronage and powerful social organizations that were vestiges of its policy of indirect rule.[73] In India, too, British rule was shaped by trade rather than revenue extraction—especially during its latter part—and relied on intermediaries to establish control.[74] Pakistan, too, inherited a powerful oligarchy—in the form of a feudal and tribal elite—that confounded state formation from the outset. All this was particularly true of North-West India. In this area, too, as was the case in Malaya, the nationalist movement did not take shape in a struggle against British rule, but in a competition with the Congress party and its notion of a secular India, which Muslims believed was a euphemism for Hindu domination. The implications for Britain's "soft colonialism" in North-West India was to produce a weak and fractured state in Pakistan. However, in Pakistan the impact of colonialism on the social structure—producing not only a dominant oligarchy, but entrenching tribal, racial, ethnic, and religious divisions—and the struggle for securing a state in the form of Pakistan played a more important role in determining not only the powers of the future state but also the relevance of Islam to it. The impact of each will be considered here.

The British earned very little in taxation in India. In fact, the low taxation accounts for the success of the British Raj in governing India.[75] The British earnings in India came for the most part from managing credit and currency flows that were used by Indian and British entrepreneurs. It also benefited from trade, and from taxing British manufacturers and merchants that made money through trade with India.[76] In fact, the government revenue and expenditure in India during the 1914–45 period was very close, and many years the government experienced deficits.[77] But direct revenue was not what made India the "Jewel in the Crown" of the British Empire. As was also the case in Malaya, absence of taxation made direct control of labor, crops, and the vast territory of India unnecessary. What mattered was stability, which could be achieved through indirect rule.

In North-West India, however, the emphasis on control and stability went beyond the needs of trade. British attitudes toward this region were greatly influenced by perpetual fears of a Russian threat. British investments and patronage, and, more generally, benevolent colonialism, unburdened British rule and gained a measure of acceptance for it. As a result, in North-West

India different state-society relations emerged. Here, unlike in the rest of India, patronage played a prominent role in securing consent to rule, and trade and revenue was less important to the colonial administration than stability.

The British ruled over the vast territory of India through an elaborate hierarchy of indirect rule.[78] At the apex were the Indian princes—the closest to Malayan sultans—who ruled over their peasants under the watchful eyes of British residents. More ubiquitous were tribal leaders, landlords, and rural intermediaries (*taluqdars* and *zamindars*) who collected revenue from the peasantry on their lands and repaid official recognition of their titles with loyalty. The British hoped for a "stable stratum of landowners who, in the British fashion, would combine support for the government with economic development of their estates" and, as "counter-parts of the English squire and Scottish laird," would serve as a "benevolent, improving landlord[s] with a stake in the country."[79] More important, they would provide stability and control in rural areas that facilitated trade, which enriched urban India and the British.[80]

British rule also relied on managing social divisions: horizontally between the masses and the elite, and vertically between tribes, races, and ethnic groups. The system of indirect rule rested on bifurcation of society into masses and elites—who served as the pillars of British rule. Although this vision of the society served the imperatives of indirect rule, it also drew on Britain's ideologies of colonial rule. Britain's thinking on India, especially between 1858 and 1919, was premised on the notion of India's difference from Britain, and the "White Man's Burden" to govern and change India in the image of Britain.[81] This view was central to the colonial state's conception of its own role being one of imposing discipline on an otherwise unruly and inferior society. This paternalistic attitude toward society—which interestingly was particularly evident in the British administration in Punjab[82]—would remain a hallmark of the postcolonial state in Pakistan, wherein state leaders have retained both the colonial conception of the state's role and its view of society.

The colonial attitude was particularly evident with regard to Islam. Muslims were seen as fierce invaders, prone to waging holy wars, intractable, resistant to change and modernity, fanatical, despotic, and devoted to backward views and practices. They were hard to rule over and were always a threat. Even after Britain subdued Muslims and co-opted many Muslim leaders, these attitudes persisted.[83] In North-West India, the British enjoyed close relations with Muslim landlords and tribal leaders, yet remained preoccupied with the Muslim threat, manifested in the challenge of the Afghan tribes in the "Great Game" on the frontier.[84] That the Raj was particularly disparaging of Islam, and viewed Muslims as ruled by their religious sentiments, has been important in the attitudes of later generations of Pakistan leaders—whose views on administration and government was shaped in the British military and bureaucracy—toward religion and its role in society.[85]

The British also divided Indian society vertically along the lines of tribe, race, language, religion, and ethnic identity, and privileged cultural values in lieu of religious ones, for instance emphasizing the notion of honor in serving society (*izzat*) in recruiting into the British military. All this made social control easier, but it also strengthened community and identity in politics, and entrenched a social structure that would confound later state formation. The primary instrument of the British in this regard was the law.[86] The British legal system made everyone equal before the law as property owners, but still reinforced group identity by reinforcing personal law,[87] which was premised on traditional, tribal, and feudal norms.[88] Hence, the British promoted modern norms and classes in public and commercial matters, but not in personal law. This bifurcation politicized and reified communal, tribal, feudal, and traditional identities, and made them relevant to questions of proper rule and authority. In later years in the postcolonial state the reified identities would make claims to the state.[89]

During the colonial period Anglo-Muhammadan Law developed to establish a clear relationship between the British order and its Muslim subjects.[90] It entailed new legal interpretations and institutions, and gave Islamic law authority in a modern legal setting by fixing fluid practices and legal concepts that were followed by Muslims in categories that could serve as the basis of political and legal procedures and institutions. It thus confirmed a place for Islamic law in the colonial order, but clearly as subservient to British norms and laws. In this it closely resembled the relations between British and Islamic laws and courts in Malaya. The Anglo-Muhammad law, much like its counterpart in Malaya, had the function of establishing the idea that a "secular" colonial state can oversee the implementation and management of Islamic law and make it subservient to secular law. This precedent would prove important to both Pakistan and Malaysia in later years.

In North-West India, the British looked more narrowly to feudalism and tribal affiliation to rule. Colonialism therefore supported customary law— rather than Islamic law—as the basis of personal law.[91] The British saw tribal law as the more fundamental essence of indigenous life in North-West India, more so than Islamic law.[92] After all, the one thing the British were not was Islamic. Hence, they preferred non-Islamic conceptions of law and political order, especially given their fears of Islam.[93]

As a result, politics in North-West India, and especially in Punjab, became anchored in tribal affiliations. The idiom of authority in Punjab became tribal and was co-opted by the colonial administration. Both tribal rule and feudalism emphasized kinship. In Punjab tribal and feudal norms were distinct from religion. The British helped articulate the role and powers of tribal leaders (and later landlords), whose authority depended on British rule and who benefited from customary law and the political structure associated with it.[94] The British system encouraged tribal loyalty and the vertical and corporate division of society and precluded broader-based political affiliation.

Support for tribal affiliation was later extended to feudalism as landed magnates became more prominent in western Punjab and development of agriculture made landlords more important to social control.[95] Reforms in the structure of colonial administration from the turn of the century onward further entrenched the sociopolitical role of British intermediaries. The Morley-

Minto reforms of 1909 provided for provincial councils, elections, and new arenas for conduct of politics. Still, the reforms were designed to rest power not in those who wanted change, but in those on whose cooperation the British had long relied. Hence, the opening of colonial rule to mass participation was done in such a manner as to strengthen British intermediaries, and hence British rule.[96]

The feudal and tribal authorities were also tied to rural Islam as well. Islam in rural Punjab and Sind is closely tied to shrines and their hereditary keepers (*pirs* and *sajjadahnishins*).[97] Indian ulama, however, were not part of this arrangement. Their socioreligious role as interpreters of the faith under Muslim rulers could not have a place in British rule; nor could their *shariah*-based conception of the sociopolitical order fit British customary law, nor its patronage of rural shrines. British rule thus spurred Islamic reform movements that were anti-British. These movements were supported by the ulama, and sought to preserve the role of Islam in society by reviving faith and its claim to societal and political life.[98] From Shah Waliullah of Delhi to the Deoband, Ahl-i Hadith, and Jama`at-i Islami (Islamic Party), Islamic actors and movements had sought to either create *shariah*-based realms and spaces or to roll back the British order.[99] They were thus inimical to tribal and customary law and rural Islam, and articulated Islam as a force for unity, rooted in a broad-based conception of society in contravention to the tribal idiom of colonial rule. Their vision would facilitate a greater role for Islam as a force in politics at the end of the colonial era.[100]

In Malaysia there was no tribe, and the sultans were closely associated with the *shariah*. Hence, there, British rule supported traditional Islamic institutions in tandem with traditional political institutions. The British therefore enjoyed some relations with *shariah*-based law, ulama, courts, and institutions. In India, the British support for traditional political institutions precluded a relationship with the ulama. For instance, in Malaya the British helped the sultans in management of religious endowments, whereas in India an effort to manage these endowments in the public domain in 1894 was rebuffed, and religious endowments were returned to private control in 1913.[101] As a result, in India British rule failed to connect with Islamic institutions. They gained strength and a role in politics because they were mobilized against British rule rather than co-opted by it. The ulama and, more broadly, Islamic institutions thus found a role in politics outside of the control of the intermediaries of power that were instead tied to rural Islam. In Malaya the sultans retained control over ulama and Islamic institutions; in India the princes, tribal leaders, and landlords enjoyed no such control. As a result, in India Islam became more readily mobilized as a political force and entered the fray at an earlier stage—during the struggle for independence.

The reification of tribal and feudal affiliations, however, was challenged by the spread of anticolonial politics during the interwar years. The anticolonial forces rejected customary law as a vestige of British order,[102] and instead foisted Islamic law as the counterweight to customary law, Islamic universalism in place of patrilineal loyalties. The *shariah*-based Islam of the ulama and

Islamist activists thus became a tool for broad-based political mobilization in the service of the nationalist struggle. This trend began with the Khilafat (Caliphate) movement after World War I and quickly became central to Muslim politics in India. The rise in the fortunes of Islamic universalism was supported by the Pakistan movement and the Muslim League as well, although the ulama and Islamists did not support the demand for Pakistan, nor did the League advocate Islamic rule. The League rather understood that in order to promote Muslim nationalism as a credible force in Indian politics it had to cut across parochial political loyalties to build a broad-based movement. The demand for Pakistan was, after all, a nationalist struggle, one that saw tribal affiliation as a stumbling block to the creation of a uniform society to support state formation in North-West India. After the Morley-Minto reforms opened provincial and national-level politics to nationalism, Islam became an important force in galvanizing localized Muslim communities into a larger unit capable of competing in the broader political arena.[103] Meanwhile, the ingrained vertical division of society allowed the advocates of Islamic politics to appeal to Muslims in communal terms just as they sought to integrate them into a larger whole. This process culminated in the Pakistan movement and eventually occluded tribal affiliation as a dominant marker in Muslim politics. The creation of Pakistan, in fact, finally ensured Islam's triumph over tribal and customary law in defining the foundations of the state[104]—a process that would be pushed further along with Islamization in the 1980s.[105]

In sum, British rule brought to the fore conflicting impulses. It strengthened rural Islam through patronage, and also provoked the mobilization and strengthening of the ulama and *shariah*-based Islam. In politics British rule bolstered the authority of the tribal and landed elite and a corporatist division of society. By so doing, it encouraged the ulama and the leadership of the Pakistan movement in the Muslim League to promote an Islamic, integrative, and broad-based political movement. Since the Pakistan state both inherited colonial rule and embodied the Pakistan movement, it included all of these impulses. As successor to the British order, the Pakistan state continued to operate through the tribal and landed elites, and to maintain ties to rural Islam. In fact, it was by appealing to these powerful political institutions that Muhammad Ali Jinnah was able to win Pakistan.[106] Pakistan was from the outset ruled by a bureaucratic and military elite who had been in the service of the British Raj, in alliance with the intermediaries that had also supported British rule. Jinnah became governor-general at independence; Pakistan's military was under the command of a British general until 1951; the country was ruled by the same bureaucratic, military, and oligarchic elite—the "salariat" in Hamza Alavi's words[107]—who had also managed the British apparatuses of power; and the law of the land was the India Act of 1935. Consequently, Pakistan was aptly dubbed the "vice-regal" state—a continuation of the administrative and political structures and practices of the Raj. This would ensure continuity between colonial and postcolonial states.

Still, the idea of Pakistan drew on a more universalist notion that came from ulama and Islamist conceptions of Muslim society. Pakistan's politics was from the outset caught between British structures of authority and the Is-lamic tide that had risen in opposition to it. These contradictory forces made the task of state formation difficult, and account for the weakness of the state and its conception of authority.[108]

Pakistan was the culmination of Muslim separatism that emerged as a corollary of decolonization of India. The demand for Pakistan gained in strength during the interwar period, but its roots ran deeper. British rule in India had all along encouraged communal affiliations in lieu of a shared sense of "Indianness." Even reform measures designed to expand the social base of support of colonialism, such as the Morley-Minto reforms, reinforced these tendencies through its system of separate electorates. The Muslim League was established in 1906 to safeguard Muslim interests in the commu-nally conscious colonial polity of India. Muslim communalism, however, be-came a notable political force only after secular nationalism failed to bridge the communal chasms that colonialism had entrenched in India. As Gandhi nudged the Congress party in the direction of Hinduism, secular Indian na-tionalism found its hold on Muslim elites and middle classes slipping.

The Muslim League gained in stature and prominence under Jinnah's lead-ership to further the interests of Muslims after independence.[109] The interwar period was a time of great uncertainty for Indian Muslims. They had already lost their position of dominance during British rule and were now anxious about their fate in independent India. The Muslims had never been reconciled to British rule over India and were, therefore, the natural constituency for the Congress party and its struggle for independence. For many Muslims, how-ever, the prospect of living under Hindu rule was also quite daunting. Their dislike of the British was tempered by their apprehensions about what they were to expect of a "Hindu Raj." Jinnah and the Muslim League did not view the struggle against the British to be the paramount concern of the Muslims and remained apprehensive about living as a minority in a predominantly Hindu India. Jinnah, therefore, demanded special constitutional rights and privileges to protect Muslim interests in independent India. The Congress Party would not countenance the demands he put before the future Indian democracy to give Muslims a true say in shaping the Indian republic. The re-sult was the partition of the Indian Subcontinent and the birth of Pakistan.

As Indian nationalism emphasized the uniqueness of the Hindu commu-nity, especially after Gandhi appeared on the scene, that link to pluralism and democracy in the eyes of Muslims like Jinnah and his followers became weaker. They were propelled into action by their distrust of the Congress party and by the belief that Indian democracy, far from safeguarding their in-terests, would in fact marginalize them. Jinnah's camp eventually articulated Muslim nationalism in rejection of Indian nationalism. The demand for Paki-stan was not about religion, but about safeguarding Muslim rights and privi-leges in Hindu India. Still, it was closely associated with Islam as identity and would in time serve to mobilize it.

As the Muslim League sought to establish itself as a viable force before the Congress Party, it was compelled to create bridges between disparate

Muslim communities. As a result, the league began to put forth an Islamic posture that would transcend local cultural differences and the boundaries of control of individual tribal leaders and landlords to confirm the existence of a single Muslim polity, political platform, and demand for power—on which the league's claims rested. The secular defender of Muslim rights thus found itself advocating Islamic universalism.

In the elections of 1937 the Muslim League did poorly, especially in those areas that were to constitute Pakistan. This defeat compelled Jinnah to appeal more directly to Islamic sentiments in order to garner support for Pakistan. A famous battle cry of the league at the time was: *"Pakistan ka matlab kiya hey? La ilaha ila'llah"* ("What is Pakistan about? There is no god but God"). Jinnah was also compelled to make deals with the intermediaries of British rule in North-West India, who controlled the local population, and could deliver them during elections and plebiscites. Pakistan was thus born despite the obstacles that the colonial social structure placed before it. A successful Muslim nationalist movement was possible only in defiance of the British hierarchy of intermediary rule and emphasis upon tribal, racial, linguistic, and other local affiliations. Jinnah was able to achieve this feat by, first, appealing to Islamic universalism, the language and rhetoric of which had been made available to the league by ulama and Islamists' discourses in response to the structure of colonial rule. In a sense, the colonial rule set up mobilization of Islam and its subsequent use to construct a Muslim nationalist movement. It also set a precedent for the Pakistan state to continue to use Islam to compensate for the limitations that have been placed before its authority by the system of colonial control. Second, Jinnah used the pillars of the colonial system, and by so doing guaranteed their continued prominence in Pakistan. As a result, the scramble for Pakistan vested the future state with both colonial-era social structure and intermediaries of power, and Islamic universalism. The first would ensure the use of the latter, just as had been the case on the eve of the partition. The colonial era thus not only determined the fundamental characteristics of the state, the nature of its authority and relations with society, but also the role of Islam in it. The relations between Islam and politics after 1947, including during the period examined in this book, are closely tied to the manner in which colonialism shaped both state-society relations in Pakistan and the relevance of Islam to managing them.

In both Malaysia and Pakistan, therefore, the fundamental characteristics of the state and the role that Islam would play in state and society are a legacy of the colonial era. Colonialism gave these states their machinery of government, ideologies of rule, and social structure. Indirect rule saddled the future states with obstacles before their exercise of power and provided them with little with which to manage mass politics. The absence of a struggle for independence denied the states strong ideological moorings. Mass politics remained outside the state and close to Islamic forces that were not part of the colonial system of control. Benevolent colonialism thus produced "vice-regal" states that have been particularly weak and also prone to using religion to compensate for those limitations that were inherited at birth.

2

From Independence to 1969

Malaysia and Pakistan arrived at independence without a prolonged struggle for independence. Muslim Indian and Malay nationalists demanded independence for Pakistan and Malaysia, but their attentions were primarily focused on ethnic squabbles, with the Chinese and Indians in Malaya and Hindus in India. The British, more often than not, were tacit allies rather than adversaries in these competitions for power. Malay domination of the state in Malaysia and the birth of Pakistan were in good measure facilitated by the process of decolonization that was managed by Britain. As a result, Malaysia and Pakistan were born as nation-states in new territorial spaces, but with little in the form of nationalist ideology to support state formation. What existed at independence in the form of nationalism was tied less to the territorial boundaries of the state and more to the ethnic interests of the dominant community. Even then, nationalism had to compete with strong allegiances to competing identities: ethnic identities in Pakistan and fidelity to sultans and Malay states in Malaysia.

The state in Malaysia and Pakistan did not replace the colonial state so much as it took over its operation. In Pakistan, for instance, Muhammad Ali Jinnah became governor general at independence in 1947, and the India Act of 1935 served as the operative constitution until 1956. In Malaysia, the country's first prime minister, the anglicized and aristocratic Tunku Abdul Rahman, fashioned the country's leadership as "designated heirs of colonial rulers."[1] In many regards, therefore, independence did not change the nature of the state, but merely supplanted those who controlled the levers of power. The state retained its colonial setup, functioned as it did under colonialism, and even retained the ideologies of colonial rule along with its systems of control. This indigenization of the colonial state was made possible by the absence of a prolonged and serious nationalist struggle for independence, but did not mean that such a struggle had altogether been averted. In fact, in good measure, decolonization would continue in Malaysia and Pakistan after independence as the relations between state and society would undergo change. The postcolonial state in Malaysia and Pakistan was not the culmination of the nationalist struggle for independence, but insofar as the state inherited the mantle of colonial rule, it would be compelled to contend with growing mass politics as an adversary. This greatly limited the powers of state and also compelled it to indigenize itself, both to shed its colonial coloring and also to augment its powers. In fact, in large measure, state formation in Malaysia and Pakistan has been conditioned by the state's attempts to contend with the circumstances of its birth—to compensate for its lack of a nationalist legacy and to shed the colonial one.

The problem here has been that the political institutions and social structure that were left behind by colonialism constricted state power and reach.[2] In both Malaysia and Pakistan, the bureaucracy, judiciary, military, and police were assets to the state, but also ensured colonial inertia in postindependence states.[3] The state leaders who assumed power in Malaysia and Pakistan were from among not the nationalist counterelite, but the administrative and military elite of the colonial establishment. In both Malaysia and Pakistan the instruments of indirect British rule—sultans, princes, tribal leaders, and landlords—continued to wield great power in the new states. In Malaysia the British accepted a peninsular conception of Malaya very late in the game. Consequently, Malaysia arrived at independence with Malay states and sultans whose long entrenched authority rivaled—if it did not supersede—that of the new state. Malaysia had to coexist with Malay states; and Malaysian state leaders had to cede significant powers to Malay sultans. In Pakistan the same trend held true. In fact, the prospects of formation of Pakistan strengthened tribal leaders and landlords as Jinnah and the Muslim League were compelled to turn to these intermediary powers to win independence. The state in Malaysia and Pakistan therefore inherited not only the machinery of government but its intermediaries. That would have implied that state leaders would continue to rule in the manner of the British. State leaders in Malaysia and Pakistan, however, were not keen on indirect rule. They became increasingly interested in more centralized control, especially as they sought to transform their economies from a component of Britain's global trade network into self-contained and growing markets. National interest, inherent in the nation-state, nudged state leaders in Malaysia and Pakistan to look for a different relationship between the state and the economy, and hence the state and society. The indigenized colonial state thus parted with the colonial state as it sought to strengthen the center at the cost of the intermediaries of power. The dialectic of this process would not always prove successful—keeping Malaysia and Pakistan relatively weak—and would consequently involve Islam in politics.

Equally important were the fractious societies that Malaysia and Pakistan inherited from the British era. Chinese and Indian labor migration had

changed the ethnic composition of Malaya, creating an axis of conflict between migrants and "sons of soil" (*bumiputra*). The Malays were locked in
the agricultural sector and predominated in rural areas, whereas the Chinese
and Indians dominated in urban areas, especially the commercially important
Straits Settlements. They were also more prominent in British administration
and in trade and financial activities. The migrants served as the bourgeoisie
of Malaya although they had no links to the emerging Malay nationalism. In
fact, following the Japanese occupation, tensions between the Chinese and
Malays turned into racial violence.[4] Since Malaysia lacked a Malay bourgeoisie, it had to coexist with the Chinese bourgeoisie. The legacy of the
racial violence, however, made this difficult. This became apparent early on,
when on the eve of independence, the nationalist leader, Onn Ja`far, tried to
fashion Malay rule in the image of British rule—as nonracial—by opening
UMNO to non-Malays, but failed.[5] The anomaly of a state that is dominated
by Malays but relies on a Chinese bourgeoisie, amidst the racial and economic divide that separates the two communities, has greatly constricted the
Malaysian state.

The Pakistan state was similarly constricted by its social structure.[6] Muslim separatism had been popular in those Indian provinces where Muslims
had been a minority, fearing Hindu domination most: Bihar, Hyderabad, and
the United Provinces, to name the most important. Pakistan, however, was
created in the Muslim majority provinces of North-West India—Punjab,
North-West Frontier Province, Sind, Baluchistan, Western Kashmir—and
East Bengal. While all of these provinces were predominantly Muslim, ethnic, linguistic, and cultural distinctions set them apart from one another and
from the Muslim populations of the Muslim minority provinces. The language of the Muslim minority provinces was Urdu, which had very little following in Sind, Baluchistan, or even Punjab.[7] Hence, language immediately
distinguished Muslims from Bihar, Hyderabad, or the United Provinces from
those in Sind, Baluchistan, or Bengal. Nor did Sindhis, Punjabis, Bengalis, or
Biharis and Hyderabadis follow the same customs and mores; they were different people, who except for their religious faith, shared more with their
Hindu neighbors than with Muslims of other provinces.

Yet, as Islam dominated the struggle for independence in India, Muslims
from disparate ethnic backgrounds, following different cultures, and conver-
sant in different languages were thrown together. Millions migrated from the
Muslim minority provinces to the two wings of Pakistan, settling among
people who were their coreligionists, but who were not as enthusiastic about
Pakistan as were the newcomers. Furthermore, the residents did not share the
language and culture of the newcomers, or of people living in the other provinces of the new state, for that matter. The problem was evident at the highest
levels. Most of the leaders of the ruling party, the Muslim League, were born
and raised in provinces that had remained in India, and hence they had had no
political base in their new country. The influx of the newcomers and their
domination of politics, seen in such measures as declaring Urdu the national
language, raised the ire of the "sons of soil" and precipitated ethnic tensions.

These tensions, as was the case in Malaysia, too, reduced the maneuverability of the nascent state and complicated state formation. In time, as will become evident, it would encourage state leaders to turn to Islam in order to override the differences between "sons of soil" and migrants (*muhajirs*), and between the provinces and the center. Islam thus became the main legitimating force in Pakistan's politics, underlying the viability of the federal unit.

The state in Malaysia and Pakistan was born weak. It lacked a strong nationalist ideology and popular support, and it confronted powerful political institutions and unbridgeable social divides. It was largely a continuation of the colonial regime in spirit as well as practice. State formation early on meant overcoming the handicaps of the circumstances of independence. State leaders sought to shore up state authority, expand its penetration of society and control over the economy, and more generally, to produce stronger apparatuses of governance that would be capable of transforming society and supporting economic development. These goals could not have been satisfactorily pursued by a weak state and would therefore serve as impetus for change in state-society relations. State formation up to c. 1971 was a game of political brinkmanship as state leaders had to negotiate with power brokers and social and economic forces, to augment central control in the face of social resistance, and to provide the society and polity with ideological vision. The vicissitudes of this process shaped the states and their relations with society, it also determined the role of Islam in politics. The successes and failures of state leaders early on and the manner in which they engaged religion and culture to achieve their goal of change set the stage for the more concerted use of Islam to serve state power from the 1980s on.

Malaysia, 1957–c. 1969

Malay nationalists in UMNO and the bureaucracy inherited the colonial state in 1957. To do so they compromised with the British on two important issues—both of which had direct bearing on the powers of the state and would remain a preoccupation of state leaders in the years to come. First, UMNO accepted a limited sovereignty for Malay states along with a political role—albeit largely ceremonial—for their sultans. The states would have their own governments, certain control over their budgets, and the ability to legislate and implement laws. Just as the Constitution of 1957 was largely secular in character and reinstated the British order, during the same time period Malay states passed legislation of their own in Islamic matters—suggesting that the federal center and individual states were moving in different directions with regard to the place of Islam in society and politics. These legislations, such as the Selangor Muslim Law Enactment of 1952, provided for religious councils, departments of religious affairs, Islamic courts, collection of religious taxes, and regulation of preaching.[8] Religious courts (courts of *khadis* and *khadi besars*) remained under the jurisdiction of the sultans, who appointed judges and prosecutors. The courts dealt with personal and criminal matters of Malays only, but remained subservient to civil courts—a continuation of the colonial practice.[9] As a result, after 1957 Islamic issues were largely left to the states and their sultans.[10] That individual Malay state identity persisted in Malaysia somewhat limited the scope of the national identity that was to underpin Malaysia.

Second, although UMNO rejected Onn Ja'far's conception of nonracial governance, it agreed to an intricate power-sharing arrangement with other ethnic groups. Malays would rule over Malaysia politically, but would not infringe on the dominant position of the Chinese and Indians in the economy.[11] Harold Crouch has argued that until 1969 state authority was based on "an alliance between Malay aristocrats-bureaucrats and Chinese business in the context of an economy dominated by foreign capital."[12] The Malay political establishment would refrain from interference in economic matters and would leave the economy open and market-oriented. This meant that the Malaysian state early on was thwarted from the kind of interventionist policies that other Third World states were following. This did not, however, mean that the government would remain completely aloof from economic matters, but that its efforts to improve infrastructure[13]—especially in rural areas—and spur growth would not affect Chinese and Indian economic interests, nor those of British firms that were ubiquitous at the time of independence.[14] In fact, cabinet posts overseeing the economy were early on reserved for the Chinese.[15] Stability in the economic arena was important to UMNO's political ambitions, for its control of Malay politics and competition with the sultans for allegiance of Malays hinged on its ability to funnel money into that community.[16] That money came from the British and ethnic-minority-dominated economic sector. Hence, weak linkages between the Malay rulers establishment and the Malay masses made those state leaders dependent on foreign and minority economic interests.

As a result, the state leadership enjoyed only a limited role in Malaysia's economy and governed the country in cooperation with ethnic minorities, on the one hand, and state-level leaders and sultans, on the other. The Malaysian state was greatly constricted and enjoyed only a limited role. The story of state formation from this point forward is one of overcoming this handicap, and expanding the state's role in the economy and power over the federal structure. UMNO would achieve these goals in part by expanding its base of support so that it would include economic actors and also gain control of various state assemblies and governments. UMNO's success as a party in resolving the limitations before state power in Malaysia was, however, facilitated by its dexterous use of Islam.

UMNO was initially charged with the task of managing Malay politics with the aim of fostering stability needed for economic prosperity. This required UMNO to expand its base of support into rural areas where the majority of Malays lived, a task that required lavish expenditure on rural areas. Whereas during the colonial era authority and tradition had provided for control, the greater degree of political participation after independence forced the ruling order to be more responsive to the demands of the general population, and

Malays in particular. Moreover, since UMNO was in competition with the sultans for the control of Malay politics, it had no interest in reinforcing the traditional ties of authority and sought to wean greater numbers of Malays away from clientalist ties to the sultans by integrating them into national politics through participation.

Between 1957 and 1960, one-eighth of the GNP was allocated to the rural economy.[17] Consequently, early on the industrial sector grew slowly.[18] Since the government's rural expenditures greatly depended on its income from other economic activities, it was compelled to take a more active role in the economy, which was then largely dominated by British and Chinese interests.[19] This necessitated a greater say for Malays in the economy, to assert a symbolic presence in that arena as well as to ensure generation of wealth and the allocation of a greater share of it to UMNO's expanding Malay national constituency.

The state and UMNO's elite thus argued that effective control of Malays—which had been in the interests of the foreign and minority economic actors since the colonial days—required greater allocation of resources to Malays, which in turn required more rapid generation of wealth. These tasks justified expansion of a custodial role for the state in the economy[20]—not to supplant the private control of business, but to manage its growth and distribution of the wealth it generates. The change in government strategy was welcomed by foreign and minority economic actors, for it would redirect investment from rural areas to the commodity and industrial sector to the benefit of British, Chinese, and Indian interests. Even if Malays would ultimately benefit from this, so would the foreign and minority interests.

The government thus initiated import-substituting industrial ventures and sought to reduce the blatant British and minority ethnic control of the economy through mixing private enterprise with state intervention—which stood for Malay participation in the economy.

The government's greater assertiveness in economic matters was justified in terms of the imperative of maintaining control over Malays and rural areas to the benefit of the economy as a whole. That it would be the state rather than a Malay bourgeoisie that would make its presence felt in the economic arena made these changes more acceptable to the foreign and minority economic interests. As a result, from the outset, while UMNO supported the Chinese bourgeoisie, it stifled the growth of the Malay one.[21]

At a more fundamental level, however, the greater role of the state in the economy was reflective of the colonial ethos of the governing Malay elite. The prominence of the Malay colonial bureaucrats in UMNO leadership meant that from the outset UMNO would develop the same paternalistic view of the economy and society that was characteristic of the British period. It was Prime Minister Tun Abdul-Razzaq, a product of the British-era civil service, who fashioned this policy as development through trusteeship of the state on behalf of Malays in the 1970s.

The influence of the bureaucracy in itself meant that the state would not remain uninvolved in the economy for long.[22] The bureaucratic element was at the time co-opted by British interests. It functioned as an elite corps, serving in that capacity as an intermediary between foreign and minority capital and the Malay peasantry and petite bourgeoisie that UMNO was targeting and that the state sought to control.[23]

The bureaucratic element put forth the idea of "bureaucratic capitalism"—namely, generation of wealth by using the state, over which UMNO had a domination. State activism, moreover, would serve rather than hinder entrepreneurial activity. The colonial state's claim that it was fair and benevolent, and that it would provide for the long-run interests of all, especially the Malays, underpinned that activism. This was a compromise to satiate the Malaysian state's appetite for expanding its reach and support its claim to be serving the society—and especially for the Malays. This activism gradually opened the door to greater use of business to serve UMNO's ends, and in time the greater use of UMNO by business to serve its ends.[24]

The expanding role of UMNO and the state ultimately involved the question of the role of Islam in society and politics. During Malaysia's early years language functioned as the most important force in Malay nationalism.[25] The Constitution of 1957 was secular and ascribed to Islam a largely ceremonial role relegated to the domain of the sultans, whose decisions, if in contravention with UMNO and the ruling elite's, could be overruled by the federal center.[26] Prime Minister Tunku Abdul Rahman elaborated on the role of Islam in Malaysia in the following manner: "I would like to make it clear that this country is not an Islamic state as it is generally understood. We merely provide that Islam shall be official religion of the state."[27] The UMNO leadership resisted using Islamic rhetoric and symbols, preferring to fashion itself as secular-nationalist.[28] This was not only in keeping with the ethos of the dominant elite but was viewed as necessary for maintaining comity between the various ethnic groups.

Still, the state leadership and UMNO elite could not remain insouciant toward Islam for long. To begin with, in Islam they saw a useful instrument for promoting social cohesion, discipline, solidarity, and national unity.[29] Secondly, it soon became evident that it was imprudent to deny the fact that Malay identity is ineluctably intertwined with Islam. To successfully articulate and dominate a nationalist discourse—especially in the absence of a strong nationalist ideology developed during decolonization—state leaders and UMNO's elite must address the issue of Islam.[30] The Malaysian state had been set up based on the assumption that Malay nationalism was secular in nature. This perception was fostered by the anglicized elite of UMNO and found support among Malay teachers, who constituted the bulk of UMNO's rank and file at the time and who were principally concerned with language and ethnicity rather than religion.[31] However, after the Japanese occupation, that nationalism included Islam and orthodox ulama and reformist Islamic leaders. The exclusion of that dimension of nationalism in postindependence conceptions of Malay rule and UMNO's politics led to the creation of Islamist Malay nationalist parties, most notably the Pan-Malayan Islamic Party (PMIP, which later became PAS) in 1951.[32] The rise of PMIP/PAS underscored the folly of UMNO's secular posture, and threatened to limit its reach into Malay society and the control of its politics. For Islam was not merely an aspect of rural Malay politics and the sultans' authority but a growing aspect of urban Malay political life and the constituency in which UMNO operated. In addition, UMNO's ties to the commercial and industrial interests created tensions in its relations with the rural sector, leaving the lower ranks of the peasantry open to PMIP/PAS.[33]

Consequently, from 1960 onward UMNO became more open to Islam.[34] UMNO's 1960 constitution "vowed to promote the advancement of Islam as 'modus vivendi' for all Muslims in Malaya." In the same year the government established PERKIM (Pertubuhan Kebajikan Islam Se-Malaysia, the All-Malaysia Muslim Welfare Organization).[35] The following year the government built the National Mosque (Masjid Negara) and instituted the National Qur'an Recitation Contest.[36] Hence, the ebbs and flows of ethnic tensions pushed the government to make symbolic gestures toward Islam. Attempts to pacify the ethnic minorities had created problems for UMNO among the Malay population. The turn to Islam was an attempt to placate that constituency and to preclude the possibility of an Islamic bid for Malay leadership to take advantage of UMNO's predicament.

The 1960s proved to be a period of turmoil for Malaysia. Communist activity, largely associated with the Chinese, escalated—although its threat to the state remained limited. Singapore, with its majority Chinese population, first joined then left Malaysia, with notable impact on Chinese-Malay relations. Indonesia put forward irredentist claims to Malaysia, and the Philippines did the same to the province of Sabah in Borneo.[37] The communist challenge and the Singapore saga encouraged state leaders to turn to Islam. Both of these events were seen as Chinese bids for power that necessitated the underscoring of Malay identity and interests—especially against the ideological lure of communism to poor rural Malays. The irredentist claims to Malaysian territory had the opposite effect. Since Indonesian ulama were important to Islamic debates in Malaysia at the time, there had existed an argument for Islamic solidarity—if not unity—between the two countries.[38] Malaysia found it prudent to deemphasize its Islamic character in order to argue that Malaysia and Indonesia had little in common. Similarly, since Sabah is not Malay, and was then not Muslim either, an ethnically plural and secular Malaysia would have a stronger claim to it (although in time, as people of Sabah and Sarawak were counted as *bumiputras* [sons of soil] to raise the number of Malays, who are *bumiputras,* vis-à-vis the Chinese and Indians, Islam became important. The people of Sabah and Sarawak are not Malays, but have been converting to Islam. The *bumiputra* identity, if not the Malay one, had to be Islamic). The more apparent impact of these crises was that, collectively, they created a stage of siege among Malays, who found their control of Malaysia under attack by Chinese communists and the inclusion of Singapore in the federation, and the very existence of their country challenged in one form or another by other regional powers. The result was that the contentious debate over Malay interests, the setup of the state, and the place of Islam in society and politics as downplayed, and UMNO proved more open to alternate views in the hope of generating Malay solidarity. These issues, however, returned to center stage in the late 1960s once the sense of siege was lifted.

By 1969 the ruling regime's token and largely Islamic policy was no longer enough to contain the opposition. Since 1957, despite state intervention in the economy, foreign and minority domination of the economy had continued unabated. Government attempts to generate wealth had disproportionately benefited the foreign and minority interests. Malays in both urban and rural areas had not enjoyed the benefits of economic growth, although the state had spent generously in rural areas. In 1969–70 almost half of the population of peninsular Malaysia lived in poverty—in rural areas the share of the poor was 59%. Overall 74% of the poor in the country were Malay.[39] Malay ownership in various sectors of the economy stood at only 1.9% of the total (0.9% in agriculture, 0.7% in mining, 2.5% in manufacturing, 2.2%in construction, 13.3% in transportation and communications, 0.8% in commerce, and 3.3% in banking and insurance).[40] The combined number of Malay students in the two existing universities in Malaysia and Singapore in 1963 was only 11% of the total, although Malays were half of the population.[41] At the University of Malaya, Malays were 20.6% of the student body, and only 6 percent of those who studied sciences and 0.4% of those who studied engineering.[42] The marginality of Malays to the economy produced dissent, which, combined with income discrepancy between non-Malays and Malays, translated into political tensions.

State and UMNO leaders were not able to claim impartiality between ethnic communities, as did the British, for these leaders were representatives of Malay power and its control of the state. Malays therefore blamed state leaders for the plight of their community in a country in which they predominated and over which they ruled. The tensions erupted in the form of violent racial riots in May 1969.[43] The riots, which involved significant loss of life and property, shook the Malaysian state.[44] First, the disturbances were an eruption of ethnic enmity in a state that was premised on cooperation between its ethnic communities. Second, it revealed the extent of Malay discontent with distribution of wealth in society and the perceived privileged position of the Chinese and Indian communities. Third, it exposed the fact that the Malay state leadership and UMNO's policies of neutrality between ethnic communities—which mimicked the style of British rule—had lost all legitimacy among Malays. The Malay population expected UMNO and the state leadership to advocate its cause rather than keep its political energies and ambitions at bay. The state's attempt to remain above the ethnic fray had undermined its nationalist credentials—which at any rate were weak, owing to the absence of a struggle for independence—as had its secular posture, which created distance between the state and important segments of the Malay community. The riots underscored the imperative of expanding state power and reach in Malaysia to two interrelated although distinct ends: first, to increase its control of Malay politics; and, second, to allow it to more tightly govern the economy to facilitate that control. After 1969 state power became a more central preoccupation of Malaysian rulers. The state moved away from its erstwhile role of mere custodial oversight of the society and the economy to more active management of change. The transformation of the state would ultimately involve its relations to Islam.

After the 1969 riots the era of cooperative management of the affairs of the state was replaced by tighter control of social, economic, and ethnic relations. The state became more openly the advocate of Malay interests, abandoning the colonial style of governing in cooperation with all ethnic communities while remaining above ethnic divisions. The anglicized and accommodationist Tunku Abdul Rahman was replaced at the helm of UMNO and the state by the more pro-Malay Tunku Abdul Razzaq. UMNO now decided to more actively intervene in the society and economy to even the playing field for Malays.[45] A new strategy was put forth in the form of the New Economic Policy (NEP) and its corollary, the New Education Policy. These broad-based economic and social initiatives (which will be discussed in the next chapter) provided respite for the state just as they justified and facilitated expansion of its power and capacity, but they did not altogether resolve the crises it faced. The solution to those crises required concentration of power in the state.

Pakistan, 1947–1969

At independence, the state in Pakistan shared many similarities with its Malaysian counterpart, although in many regards it was a weaker state. In Pakistan, too, an anglicized and bureaucratic elite inherited the colonial state and ruled over a fractured society through the same intermediaries of power as the British.[46] However, in Pakistan the Muslim League never developed the same power and control as UMNO did in Malaysia. Instead, in Pakistan the military and the bureaucracy dominated. Unlike in Malaya, where the indigenous population had little presence in the British military, in India Punjabis and Pathans were prominent in the Indian military, the result of which was that half of that military's officers and soldiers ended up in Pakistan, ensuring a say for the military in the new state's politics.[47] The military and the bureaucracy were, moreover, colonial institutions, and their attitudes toward politics, social control, and proper government were those of the colonial era. The British order in India had privileged law and order over participation. This attitude conditioned the thinking of the military and the bureaucracy. Their prominence in Pakistan's politics therefore infused the new state with ideologies of British rule. In Pakistan the "vice-regal" state was a military-bureaucracy condominium in which the political class—especially after Jinnah's death in 1948—was the junior partner.[48] This alliance first asserted itself in 1954 when the governor-general, Ghulam Muhammad, a member of the bureaucracy, dismissed the Constituent Assembly in order to prevent its devolution of power to East Pakistan.[49] Ghulam Muhammad's assertion of the paternalistic prerogatives of the administrative elite in lieu of democratic practices thus established the primacy of the bureaucratic and military elite over and above the politicians in Pakistan's politics.

In addition, in Pakistan the tribal leaders and landlords constituted a powerful social organization, with far more impact on state formation than the sultans and the Malay oligarchy. To begin with, populism or socialism did not influence the Pakistan movement as was the case with Indian nationalism, and therefore was not inherently opposed to the landed elite. In fact, the Pakistan movement had early on become the refuge of Muslims of privileged classes who distrusted the economic policies of the Congress party and the socialist rhetoric of some of its leaders like Jawaherlal Nehru. In addition, once Pakistan was created, the state needed the landed elite in much the same fashion as had the British, namely, to establish order in rural areas.

The Muslim League had little following in the provinces that later formed the new state. The support of the landed elite, especially in elections in the decade preceding independence, had been crucial to the Muslim League.[50] The landed elite in Punjab, Bengal, and Sind supported the Pakistan movement, and in so doing guaranteed their influence on the future state. The circumstances of Pakistan's birth therefore militated a different balance of power between the new state and the colonial institutions of control.

The Pakistan state was from inception a weak one. Its roots in the provinces it had inherited were tenuous. These provinces had little in common save for the fact that the majority of their populations were Muslim. Their economies were not linked and were instead tied to the central grid of Indian economy from which they were now cut. The new state had only rudimentary machinery of government, confronted a massive refugee problem, was in a state of war with India, and faced economic ruin and severe food shortages. These problems led to concentration of power in the hands of the bureaucratic and military elite,[51] whose domination ensured continuity between colonial and postcolonial states.

Still, the concentration of power in the bureaucracy and the military did not resolve the problems confronting the state. To exert social control, and to establish its authority, the state very quickly turned to tribal leaders and the landed elite,[52] on the one hand, and Islam, on the other. Indirect rule through the oligarchy, moreover, encouraged rather than discouraged reliance on Islam. For the alliance between the state and the oligarchy impeded the state's efforts to either effectively pursue development or satisfactorily contend with inequities in distribution of resources through state institutions, forcing the state to instead look for alternate channels for alleviating poverty and to even contemplate a different structure of authority through which to expand its capacity to rule.[53] The result has been that the state turned to Islam and its social institutions to achieve both ends. The turn to Islam in Pakistan is therefore a product of the attempts by a state that is held captive by the oligarchy to augment its power and autonomy of action.

In addition, in return for helping establish state authority, the oligarchy secured their social and economic position. The tribal leaders and the landed elite thus became intermediaries in establishing political order in rural areas.[54] The state gave them great discretion in local affairs, with the effect of confirming and strengthening their authority. As the local role of the landed elite became integrated into the organizational design of the new state, the seeds of future weakness of the state were sown. The state had, for the immediate future at least, closed itself out of the rural areas, helped bolster the authority of a powerful sociopolitical force, and created a relationship of dependence between the state and the oligarchy. Throughout the 1947–58 period the state would prove unable to extract agricultural surplus for economic growth—either in the form of taxation or controlling the price of agricultural goods[55]—or to even guarantee the supply of food to the population. The oligarchy, meanwhile, was able to use its local power to also influence politics at the provincial and national levels. By the middle of the 1950s it had effectively taken over the ruling party, the Muslim League, and was broadly represented in the national and provincial cabinets, as well as in the Constituent Assembly. The position of power of the oligarchy at the helm ensured it of access to state resources and patronage, which was used to further strengthen its power at the local level. The Muslim League thus proved unable to defend its turf against encroachments by the oligarchy to the extent that had UMNO.

The alliance between the military, the bureaucracy, and the oligarchy helped establish the state, but ensured limitations before its authority and capacity. While state leaders favored a strong central government, the oligarchy through whom they ruled favored a weak center.[56] State leaders ruled through the vice-regal state, but were unable to invest it with the authority that it had enjoyed under the British. This reality deeply influenced the transformative agenda of the state and complicated its task of governance. It also mired national politics in petty squabbles and jockeying for power that undermined the legitimacy of the political system in the eyes of the general population.[57] The state's turn to Islam from the 1940s onward must be understood in the context of the problems that are inherent to the setup of the state, and the distribution of power between state institutions and its instruments of indirect rule.

The deep-seated ethnic divisions in Pakistan were also important. The aforementioned problems confronting the state made it particularly difficult for the ruling establishment to effectively contend with tensions between the Punjabi and Muhajir elite and Bengali and Sindhi nationalists in the provinces. The problem that confronted the political center immediately after the partition was how to keep East Pakistan at bay—avoid its domination of Pakistan politically and culturally—and how to produce an ideology capable of keeping the country together under the control of the West Pakistani elite—Punjabis and Muhajirs for the most part. That East Pakistan was separated from West Pakistan by the breadth of India, and was more populous than West Pakistan (at the time of the first census in Pakistan in 1951 there were 41.9 million East Pakistanis and 33.7 West Pakistanis)[58]—which itself was divided into ethnically distinct provinces—made the state particularly susceptible to secessionist demands. Immediately after the partition, the political center faced a strong demand for distribution of power and resources in the state. East Pakistan insisted on a greater share of economic investments and military expenditures, and greater representation for East Pakistani Bengalis in government service.[59] The political center rejected redistribution of resources and devolution of power to East Pakistan. As a result, the Bengali population in the east, gradually but surely, was alienated from the state.

The dilemma that East Pakistan placed before the state manifested itself soon after independence in the constitution-making process, which lasted some nine years.[60] The debates over distribution of powers between West and East Pakistan, the question of national language, and the role of Islam preoccupied the political elite.[61] Meanwhile, the state used a host of ad hoc measures to manage the situation. The polity became increasingly Islamized, both as a consequence of the constitutional impasse and as a means of diverting attention from the standoff between the two wings of Pakistan. The Muslim League began to lose all support in East Pakistan. In response, state leaders began to emphasize Islam as a force of unity to a greater extent.[62]

As a consequence of the problems facing the state, in Pakistan Islam became important to national politics far earlier and affected state formation far more directly. As a result, state leaders in Pakistan were compelled to contend with Islamic demands and negotiate with Islamist actors far more frequently and as a part of their strategies of development.[63]

State leaders at first resisted giving Islam a central role in national politics. However, a state built in the name of Islam and as a Muslim homeland, confronted with insurmountable ethnic, linguistic, and class conflicts, quickly succumbed to the temptation of mobilizing Islamic symbolisms in the service of state formation. This tendency was only reinforced over the years as the state has failed to address fundamental socioeconomic issues, carry out meaningful land reform, and consolidate power in the center. This has opened the door for Islamic parties to enter the fray.[64] Islamist activism thus influenced the national political discourse, the manner in which key questions were framed, and ensconced Islamism in the political process.[65] The incremental sacralization of the national political discourse has clearly favored a political role for those who claimed to speak for Islam and advocate Islamization. Their activism, in turn, strengthened the impetus for Islamization.[66] The secular state resisted this trend only briefly. By 1949 the elite had accepted a political role for Islamic forces, compromising their original conception of Pakistan as a thoroughly secular state. In that year the government adopted the Objectives Resolution, which was demanded by the Islamic forces as a statement of intent with regard to the future constitution.[67] The resolution formally introduced Islamic concerns to constitutional debates and committed Pakistan to greater Islamization. Subsequent state policy, culminating in the Constitution of 1956, only reinforced this tendency.[68] As a result, by the end of the first decade of Pakistan's existence Islamic forces were fully included in its political process and had moved to appropriate the national political discourse from the state.

In both Malaysia and Pakistan the bureaucracy (and military) and intermediaries of British rule had been tied to the colonial order. The nationalist parties (UMNO and the Muslim League), too, were tied to the British, but also included Islamic elements (ulama and Islamist activists). In Malaysia the secular and colonial element was able to dominate and marginalize the Islamic one more effectively and for a longer time. In Pakistan the state succumbed more quickly and adopted the Janus face of inheriting the British order but seeking to represent Islamic universalism. This meant that although the state accepted a place for Islamic forces in national politics, it was not willing to abandon secularism, nor to permit any Islamization of society and politics outside the purview of its direct control. The state therefore resorted to regulating the flow of Islam in the political process, hoping to gradually negotiate arrangements with Islamic parties to that effect. Although the state never formalized a workable arrangement and was not able to avert frictions and confrontations, still it succeeded in retaining control over the flow of Islam in politics and limiting the scope of Islamization. The state oversaw the inclusion of Islamic forces into the political process by using regulatory arrangements. The manner in which these arrangements took form also accounts for the particular role that Islamic parties have adopted in Pakistan's politics, the limits they have faced in their drive for power, and the structure of their discourse on politics and society.

The state did not, however, adopt a clear policy regarding Islam until 1958 when the military under the command of General Muhammad Ayub Khan took over and proceeded to resolve many of the anomalies that had confounded state formation.[69] Ayub Khan attempted to strengthen state institutions, and to expand their control over the society, economy, and politics. Once freed of its shackles, the state would be able to do away with the encumbrances of ethnic conflict and Islamist activism, and to embark on development.[70] The Ayub Khan regime was avowedly secularist and justified the coup in part as an effort to save the state from an Islamist takeover.[71] The military regime revamped the political system, replacing politicians with the most anglicized, and hence secular, Pakistani leadership from among the civil service and the military.[72] By suspending the democratic process, the coup immunized the power structure against Islamic activism of any sort. Ayub Khan did not believe that Islam could provide a notion of Pakistani nationhood that would serve the national goal of development.[73] The military regime therefore set about changing the focus of the constitutional debates from "why Pakistan was created" to "where Pakistan was heading," that is, from ideological, and hence Islamic, to developmental concerns. This approach left its imprint on society and politics during the 1958–1969 period. Modernization and industrialization, combined with the secularization of society, in large measure divided Pakistani society into a secular and Westernized ruling class and the mass of people living according to time-honored Indo-Islamic traditions. Each adhered to its own cultural, social, and political outlook, which resulted in alienation between the rulers and the masses.

Still, Ayub Khan was unable to extricate either ethnic conflict or Islam from Pakistan's politics. He chose to crush the first and to manage the second. The state during the Ayub Khan period sought to incorporate Islam into the state's discourse on sociopolitical change and at the same time limit the role of Islamic parties—the self-styled advocates of Islamization—in the political process.[74] Here the state sought to appeal to the emotive power of Islam at the same time as it sought to depoliticize it by limiting the political uses of faith by nonstate actors.

During the Ayub Khan period the state acknowledged a role for Islam in politics, albeit begrudgingly.[75] Ayub Khan came to power at the helm of a military coup that sought not only to consolidate power in the central government but also to modernize Pakistani society. Islam had no place in the generals' vision of the future and could only serve as an obstacle to it. Hence, Ayub Khan initially tried to extricate Islam from politics. Soon after he assumed power, he tried to formulate a new agenda for state construction, one that would be both secularizing and yet a unifying force—thus replacing Islam as the glue that kept Pakistan together. However, the general found it impossible to undo the impact of a decade of gradual Islamization of national politics, especially as his autocratic style met with popular opposition and his plan of action raised the ire of various Pakistani ethnic groups, notably in East Pakistan.[76] Ayub Khan was compelled to appeal to the emotive power of Islam to boost the legitimacy of the state. The Ayub Khan era witnessed the emergence of linkage between Islam and state power—and more particularly, the state's efforts to manage development. It was also during the Ayub Khan era that the state first tried to control Islam's flow in society and politics with the aim of harnessing its energies in the service of the state. The manner in which this occurred and its ramifications for society and politics would be important for the more concerted Islamization policies from the 1980s on.

Soon after it took over power, the Ayub Khan government chose to gain control of and manage Islamic politics rather than to expel Islam from politics. Although Ayub Khan and his coterie of advisors were secular in orientation, they understood that the Pakistan state lacked the kind of centralized control that made the more strident secularism of Nasser's Egypt or Pahlavi Iran possible.[77] Moreover, ethnic tensions in Pakistan compelled the state to harp on Islamic solidarity, which precluded the kind of secularism that was in vogue in Iran and the Arab world at the time.

Between 1958 and 1962 Ayub Khan tried to use Islam for socioeconomic and development purposes. He tried to portray Islam as a progressive force and to use it to justify development.[78] Central to this effort was the appropriation of the right to interpret Islam from the ulama and the Islamist parties, and to wrest control of Islamic institutions from Sufi shrines to mosques and religious endowments.[79] The West Pakistan Waqf (Endowment) Properties Ordinance of 1959 initiated state takeover of religious endowments and domination over rural religious leaders.[80] In rural areas these endowments were closely tied to rural religious leaders who had once served as intermediaries of British rule. The state thus expanded the purview of the colonial state's control in rural areas. The endowments also allowed the state to assume control of welfare services that were associated with these endowments and that affected the lives of many among the rural population.[81] By taking over the management of the shrines, state leaders were able to use them to propagate a new interpretation of Sufism and rural Islam as compatible with development.[82] Sufi doctrines were depicted as enjoining a positive work ethic, and rural religious festivals were used as venues for agricultural and industrial fairs. By becoming the keeper of shrines, the state was able to find a presence in rural areas, which was otherwise closed to it by the landed elite.

Ayub Khan was able to take over religious endowments and their lands and property in rural areas largely because he was able to claim that he was doing the bidding of the ulama and Islamists, who were strongly opposed to rural religious leaders and their institutions.[83] Ayub Khan thus used the religious cover of ulama and Islamists to expand the powers of the state in rural areas. The lesson would not be lost on state leaders from this point on. In fact, Ayub Khan soon indicated his desire to extend similar control over ulama and preachers to also use their institutions and mass following to serve development.[84] In May 1959, soon after he consolidated power, Ayub Khan addressed a gathering of the ulama from both East and West Pakistan. In his speech the general encouraged the religious leaders to interpret Islam in ways that would help the country's developmental agenda.[85]

All this would make the state the chief spokesman for Islam and permit it to set the pace for the flow of Islam in politics. The state, in principle, conceded to a political role for Islam but only if it would control its interpretation, institutions, and politics. As a result, the state used an Islamic rhetoric when necessary and paid lip service to Islamic ideals.[86] Soon after, government-sponsored institutions such as the Advisory Council for Islamic Ideology, the Institute of Islamic Research, and the Institute of Islamic Culture were charged with the task of formulating a modernist view of Islam.[87] The government then proceeded to implement measures that clearly reoriented the state's policy on Islam to date and redefined the role of Islam in politics. The Family Law Ordinance of 1961, for instance, effectively secularized family law, precipitating a confrontation with the ulama and Islamic parties.[88] The Constitution of 1962, in the same manner, removed "Islamic" from the official name of the state, which now became the "Republic of Pakistan."[89] By 1967 the government had introduced a host of bills to reform Islamic law and practice with the aim of accommodating the state's modernizing agenda.

The success of the state's policy depended on both a successful articulation of its interpretation of Islam and its ability to effectively marginalize Islamist movements that could challenge its hold on Islam. The state's efforts to regulate and control Islam eventually failed. The failure owed to, first, the shortcomings of the state's vision of Islam. The Islamic pretense of the secular state was at no point convincing to the masses. Its interpretation of Islam did not grow roots and was easily challenged by the ulama and Islamist activists.[90] It was obvious that the state was not serious about Islam and had no authority to interpret it.[91] In the end, the state initiated control of Islam to serve state interests,[92] but was not able to sustain that control. It did, however, provide an example for instrumentalist uses of Islam to augment the powers of the state.

Second, the collapse of state authority in the late 1960s made effective control of Islam difficult for state leaders. The Ayub Khan regime was committed to development in Pakistan. In this it followed in the path of other late developers and Third World states in promoting industrialization through state intervention in the economy.[93] It sought to reduce the scope of political participation and to vest greater powers in state institutions in order to increase investments in the industrial sector. The Ayub Khan regime also followed the Kemalist model of secularizing the state and society with the aim of facilitating development. These efforts greatly changed Pakistan's economy. It gained an industrial infrastructure, experienced sustained growth rates, and took giant strides toward development. This development was accomplished at great social and political cost, however.[94] The development process went hand in hand with greater authoritarianism and weakening of institutions of civil society. It followed economic policies that in different ways mobilized important segments of the population against the government. Ayub Khan's strategy for spurring industrial development led to corruption and flagrant income inequalities between social classes, economic groups, and, most ominously, the various provinces of Pakistan. It led to mobilization of industrial labor and the urban poor, led by the intelligentsia and ethnic parties.[95] Between 1963 and 1967, the percentage of the poor—those whose incomes were below Rs. 300 per month—had somewhat declined in both the rural and the urban areas, from 60.5% to 59.7% and from 54.8% to 25%, respectively,[96] but the disparity in the distribution of wealth between the provinces and between the propertied classes and the masses had increased.[97] According to Mahbub ul-Haq, "By 1968 22 families controlled 2/3 of Pakistan's industrial assets; 80% of banking; 70% of insurance."[98] Economic growth had favored the industrial sector at the cost of the traditional economy, the cities at the cost of the hinterland, and Punjab and West Pakistan at the cost of East Pakistan. The business elite had amassed great fortunes, as had senior civil servants and high-ranking members of the armed forces, while the middle class and the poor had lost ground. Corruption, which by 1967 had infested the country, had only further discredited the government's promise of economic progress in the eyes of those who had not shared in its fruits. Agricultural policy had caused large-scale migration to the cities, while industrialization had generated grievances among the labor force, whose numbers had risen threefold in the 1960s. The costs of development in the end delegitimated the Ayub Khan regime, with the effect that it was unable to contain rising ethnic and Islamic activism at the end of the 1960s.

Pakistan's defeat in the 1965 war, combined with disaffection with authoritarianism, secularism, and economic inequities, eroded government legitimacy and produced wide-scale antiregime political activism. The Left and Islamists articulated antistate ideological positions, prodemocracy movements demanded end to authoritarian rule, and ethnic forces, especially in East Pakistan, demanded autonomy and secession. Weakened and under attack, the ruling regime buckled, and the concentration of power at the center collapsed. Ayub Khan resigned in 1969. The military ruled another two years, only to lose East Pakistan after a bloody civil war and defeat in a war with India.

In the end, the Ayub Khan era proved to be an anomaly in Pakistan. A strong and secular state, committed to development and able to formulate and implement policy with relative freedom from social resistance, proved to be a transient phenomenon. The collapse of the Ayub Khan regime thus ended the attempt to construct a strong secular state that would control Islam, and would initiate development and social change from above using the power concentrated at the center.

In both Malaysia and Pakistan the period between independence and 1969 was a time of adjustment for the new states. In both cases weak states born of colonialism sought to establish social control and extend their power and reach, but only tentatively. Saddled by the institutions and legacy of colonialism, both Malaysia and Pakistan were weak states from inception. The state in Pakistan was saddled with more problems than its Malaysian counterpart. During the period under discussion Pakistan produced two constitutions— the first, nine years after independence. However, Pakistan was also able for a time during the 1958–69 period to concentrate greater powers at the center, approximating those at the disposal of many Third World states at the time.

The bureaucracy, military, judiciary, and the political elite—nationalist leaders as well as the oligarchy—of the British period continued to wield power in the new states as well. In Malaysia the nationalist political elite were able to dominate at the center and to keep the oligarchy at bay. In Pakistan, the nationalist political elite were unable to contain the oligarchy and were eventually altogether sidelined by the bureaucracy and the military in 1958. Both states sought to manage the social structure that they inherited from the colonial era in the manner that had the British. Malaysians sought to balance the interests of Malays, Chinese, and Indians, whereas Pakistanis followed British divide-and-rule policies. In both cases the state failed to manage ethnic tensions. Malaysia erupted in race riots in 1969, and Pakistan became embroiled in an ethnic civil war in 1971 that led to secession of East Pakistan and the creation of Bangladesh.

The limitations of state power eroded secularism in Pakistan more quickly and also led to instrumentalist uses of religion to serve state power. Islam does not feature in Malaysia's politics as a notable force during this period, and has little role in or impact on state formation. Pakistan's first constitution, unlike Malaysia's, was avowedly Islamic, and concentration of power at the center during the Ayub Khan era used Islam to vest power in state institutions even as the state claimed secularism.

Finally, state formation in the period under discussion, in both Malaysia and Pakistan, came under a great deal of pressure from distribution of wealth between ethnic groups and sectors of the economy, as well as from the challenges that were inherent in economic change and industrialization. The year 1969 marked an abrupt interruption in state formation as social uprisings led to regime change in Pakistan and overhaul of national politics in Malaysia. These changes would provide respite for the postcolonial state in the 1970s, but did not remove the underlying causes of crisis in the secular postcolonial state.

II

THE 1970S

Political Turmoil and Cultural Change

3

Secular States in Crisis

The crises that confronted the Malaysian and Pakistani states in 1969 resulted in major changes in the setup of the states and the ways in which they interacted with society. In Malaysia the post-1969 era witnessed a profound change in the character of the state and how it perceived its role in society and politics. In Pakistan the post-1969 era was one of tumult during which the country went through civil war, war with India, secession of East Pakistan, democratization, and recalibration of state-society relations through a new constitution and large-scale restructuring of the economy. In both cases, these changes alleviated some of the problems that had besieged the state before 1969. However, the changes did not remove those problems altogether, and in seeking to do so created new crises. As a result, by the end of the 1970s the secular state began to decline, reaching the limits of its power, capacity, and social control. The decline of the secular state resulted in greater Islamic consciousness in the political arena. This occurred at a time of Islamist resurgence across the Muslim world, which made Islam more directly relevant to the crisis that confronted the state in the 1970s. Islamic resurgence would contribute to that decline, would benefit from it, and would in the end also provide solutions for reversing it. The manner in which Islam would become entangled with the state, however, began with the decline in state authority and power.

Malaysia, 1969–1979: The NEP Era

Between 1969 and 1979, Malaysia, under the leadership of Tunku Abdul-Razzaq (1969–75) and Husain Onn (1975–80), sought to defuse sociopolitical tensions that had led to the 1969 riots through aggressive intervention in the economy and society. In so doing, the state would not only expand its powers and capacity but change its relations with the majority and minority communities.[1] The expansion of state power and capacity faced little resistance and acted to limit the scope of pluralism in Malaysia, producing a mix of authoritarianism and democracy, which would become more apparent in the 1980s during the Islamization era.[2]

Authoritarianism grew with relative ease in the 1970s, for the minority Chinese and Indian communities were persuaded that expansion of state power was in their interests. Such expansion, they believed, would allow state institutions and UMNO to better placate the disgruntled Malay community. Malays favored expansion of state power and capacity because it would be directed at furthering their interests.[3] After 1969 the Malaysian state moved away from its original colonial conception of being above all ethnic communities and serving all of their interests equally. It would no longer be autonomous and equidistant from all ethnic communities. After 1969 the state became more openly an advocate of Malays—their representative and instrument. This change was necessary if the state and UMNO were to control Malay politics to the benefit of all. Still, the change signaled an important turning point in state formation. The closer affiliation with Malay interests after 1969 would subject state formation to influences to which it had hitherto been immune. The political, social, and cultural forces that were internal to the Malay community now more openly affected the working of the state.

That the Malaysian economy was largely foreign and minority owned, combined with the weakness of the state, prevented the state from wide-scale nationalization of industries (which would occur in Pakistan in the 1970s, as well as in parts of Africa with foreign and minority interests).[4] The state instead turned to acquiring, rather than appropriating, property to achieve redistribution of resources. As a result, state intervention in the economy remained somewhat limited, leaving the economy relatively free and under foreign and minority control, but increasing the share of Malays in the wealth that it would generate. This was not a strategy of giving Malays control of the economy, but of gradually increasing their say in it—and then through the agency of the state—while generating wealth for all concerned by encouraging industrialization and trade. It did not change the structure of socioeconomic relations, but fine-tuned them by imposing certain compromises. The strategy benefited Malays as Malaysia experienced growth rates exceeding other middle-income countries.[5] Between 1971 and 1980 the Malaysian economy grew at the annual rate of 7.8%.[6] Still, it did not produce the kind of political capital for the state that more aggressive intervention in other Third World countries had done. Between 1970 and 1986 the share of Malays in the private sector rose from 14.2% to 30.5%.[7] This translated into some redistribution of wealth, but kept the Malays at the lowest rung of the economic ladder. It also left foreign and minority interests dominant in the economic sector, with obvious political implications. Hence, the failure to nationalize foreign and minority economic interests, although economically beneficial, was politically a problem. For it denied the state the kind of legitimacy and social control that other Third World states were enjoying. This had partly to do with the fact that although NEP had some of the trappings of Third World-ist and nationalistic state-led industrialization, its principal "enemy" was not foreign interest, but the domestic Chinese and Indian one. This placed certain limits on nationalist zeal in dealing with the "enemy" in the economic sector.[8] The upshot of all this was that the state would eventually have to look to Islam to get what other Third World states got from anti-imperialism.

The principal tool for bringing about socioeconomic change was the NEP, which was implemented in 1971. Its main objectives were to eliminate poverty, especially among Malay peasants; to enhance Malay social and economic standing through a system of quotas for Malays in education, employment, and government contracts; and to change in the ownership of corporate equity holdings through state funding of *bumiputra* (sons of soil) "trust agencies" that would purchase and hold equities for the Malay community.[9] Large government and quasi-government agencies would acquire corporate equity in favor of Malays, especially in trade, finance, and industry. For instance, Bank Bumiputra (Sons of Soil Bank) was established to provide credit to these ventures.[10] This approach produced a strategy of development by "trustee-ship"[11] managed by a state bourgeoisie rather an a Malay entrepreneurial class. In fact, NEP led to a "subsidy mentality" among Malays that retarded their entrepreneurial zeal.[12]

NEP provided for interethnic parity in ownership of corporate wealth through state intervention in public enterprises. This intervention led to an increase in the role of the state agencies and actors in the corporate scene. Large financial allocations were made available to public enterprises to help economically weak Malays.[13] However, as the state became the agent of Malay activity in the private sector, it spawned a new relationship of patronage among the UMNO, the state, and Malays, which served the state's interests in controlling Malay politics. That the Malays' stake in the economy still depended on the performance of foreign and minority interests made both the state and Malays dependent on those interests.

NEP temporarily neutralized formal Malay opposition. Throughout the 1970s the government increased the flow of funds to the rural economy. More important, by creating educational and employment opportunities, a Malay presence in the private sector, and—symbolically, at least—asserting the Malay supremacy in Malaysia, NEP placated Malays. As part of NEP the government increased the quota of Malay students in universities and created new ones to specifically serve them, such as the National University of Malaysia (Universiti Kebansangan Malaysia). Many more students received government scholarships to study in Australia, Europe, and the United States. These students were then recruited into government service, universities, and the private sector. Consequently, NEP began to change the face of Malay society.[14] It increased the size of the Malay urban middle classes, and extended the control of UMNO and the state over them. That control, as discussed later, would be less than total.

In the short run NEP accelerated the growth of Malay urban and middle classes, and helped UMNO to gain a following among them. This bolstered UMNO's—and, hence, state leaders'—claim to represent the Malay community in lieu of sultans and other contenders such as PAS.[15] The balancing role that UMNO played between Malays and minority economic interests gave state leaders increasing powers and room to manuever. Management of the delicate economic and political relations was eventually formalized in the Barisan Nasional (National Alliance),[16] which also ensured UMNO domination of national politics. The alliance between UMNO and Chinese and Indian parties in the alliance produced a stable ruling coalition that re-created in the political arena the pact that existed in the economic one. Even PAS was part of Barisan Nasional between 1973 and 1977.

NEP's social and economic successes in the end were short-lived, undermining its promise of political stability. It expanded government power and capacity, created new relations of patronage and clientalism between the state and the Malay community, and reduced social and ethnic tensions. By the mid-1970s, however, NEP faced new challenges. First, NEP's record fell short of expectations. Second, social changes that NEP brought about produced new demands on UMNO and the state, which NEP alone was not able to contend with.

Between 1970 and 1975 the Malay share of manufacturing jobs rose from 25% to 32% and the Malay share of managers in the private sector rose from 11% to 17%.[17] In 1975 Malays owned no more than 8% of all capital. In fact, by all counts NEP had failed to realize its goals by 1975.[18] The pace of change was viewed as too slow and soon produced disenchantment with the powers-that-be. This disenchantment was even evident in UMNO and led to severe criticism of the party's leadership by a number of younger leaders, among them Mahathir Mohammad.[19]

In addition, the industrialization initiative encountered the same problems with backward and forward linkages that are evident in import-substituting industrialization everywhere. These problems compelled the government to intervene in the market to a greater extent but with diminishing returns. In addition, the wide-scale presence of state actors and UMNO leaders in the private sector, especially in various corporations and industrial projects, soon made UMNO an avenue for generation of wealth. This not only provided UMNO and state leaders with means to use patronage for political control but tied UMNO to private sector interests, and, furthermore, opened the door to corruption.[20] Also, as state and UMNO leaders, for personal as well as political reasons, developed a vested interested in the growth of companies in which government enterprises held equity, they increasingly supported business interests, leaving Malay rural areas and urban middle and lower middle classes by the wayside.[21] By the end of the 1980s businessmen had replaced teachers—the original founders of UMNO—in the party's leadership positions.[22] NEP was benefiting large businessmen, who served as instruments of state intervention in the market or acted as middlemen between the government and foreign and minority interests. The large business interest used its access in UMNO to protect its position and reduced NEP to a source of rent for a few powerful Malays. This meant that in practice the state was not so much a "trustee" of all Malay interests as a "facilitator" for enrichment of the Malay elite.[23] This trend would become more pronounced after 1980, but it was already undeniably shaped by the late 1970s.[24]

By 1975 it was also clear that most antipoverty subsidy programs had failed.[25] There was more urban and rural poverty,[26] as well as income in-equality—between Malays and minority communities, and between rich and poor Malays. NEP was designed to reduce ethnic tensions. Therefore, it did not concern itself with social tensions within the Malay community. These tensions were, however, notable, with roots in the colonial era.[27] As NEP calmed ethnic tensions, it brought into the open grievances within the Malay community.[28] The unevenness of NEP's social and economic impact had ag-gravated class conflict among Malays. The wealthy Malay beneficiaries of NEP flaunted their wealth—which owed less to entrepreneurship and more to connections—displaying ostentatious lifestyles that created resentment among rural and middle-class Malays toward NEP.[29] Soon the fact that NEP trusteeship was, in effect, a support system for wealthy Malays caused politi-cal tension. Those left behind by NEP turned to social activism, which often took the form of Islamic voluntarism.[30] The movements that resulted from this development, which will be examined in the next chapter, created a po-litical arena from which NEP, UMNO, and state control were excluded. The growth of these movements signaled that expansion of state power and reach under NEP had reached its limits, and might actually experience a reversal.

These tensions produced anti-UMNO and antistate Malay forces. These forces were prominent among students and in rural areas. They opposed UMNO and the state's economic strategies, rejected conspicuous consump-tion of the wealthy few, and criticized NEP for its narrow focus on wealthy Malays, on the one hand, and its failure to alter the balance of wealth in the country in favor of Malays. The challenge to NEP, UMNO, and state leaders was serious. Malay students had been an important force in the riots of 1969 and in Tunku Abdul-Rahman's fall from power.[31] They were also an impor-tant constituency of NEP, whose quota policies had been designed to benefit students in education and employment. NEP had increased the number of Malay students from 11% of the total in 1963[32] to 57.2% by 1975 and 66.4% by 1978.[33] It had increased their numbers but had not established control over them. Unrest among the students was a significant blow to NEP. It also was a source of concern since students were integrated with urban middle classes and their numbers were far higher than in 1969.

Equally important was unhappiness with NEP in rural areas. That unhap-piness had limited UMNO's penetration of rural Malay politics, which ap-peared as a potential threat to UMNO and state leaders' position of power after PAS left Barisan Nasional in 1977 to exploit the rising anti-NEP and anti-UMNO mood.[34] PAS's departure, along with the students' Islamist lean-ings (which will be discussed in the next chapter), underscored UMNO and state leaders' "Islamic deficit" at a time of pending crisis. The state in Malay-sia had remained largely secular. It had sought to control Malays through NEP, and beyond that by championing language and Malay nationalism. It had assumed a secular Malay identity. The turn to Islam among Malay rural and middle classes—and their rejection of NEP as a gateway for Western consumerism and domination[35]—caught UMNO and state leaders off-guard.[36]

The NEP era also produced greater authoritarian tendencies in the Malaysian state. Although Malaysia remained a democratic polity, state encroachment into the economy and society through NEP, the extension of its control over Malay politics, and the rise of controlled democracy through Barisan Nasional reduced the scope of democracy. This development presented the Malaysian state with problems that Alfred Stepan has argued are typical of statist responses to socioeconomic crises. He writes:

> Statism seeks to structure society, integrating its many parts into a solidaristic whole. It vests power in that whole, but still assumes self-management of the parts (as reflected in continued presence of market forces and social groups). This attempt to strike a balance between the liberal and Marxist conceptions of the state is untenable. It creates tensions. Statism ultimately acts to limit market forces, and also empowerment of non-state actors (since both could threaten the state's role and social harmony and common interest.) Hence, Organic-statist systems seek to manage social groups (with varying degrees of success). These states often emerge after crises of pluralist systems, and vie to limit the freedom of action of social forces under the pluralist regime in favor of controlled and tight state management. Achieving this end may be difficult.[37]

Stepan believes that statism can contend with these problems through corporatism. In the Malaysian case, however, the solution would rather come from Islamization.

The socioeconomic problems created by NEP found added significance as Malaysia witnessed a marked increase in Islamist activism. This phenomenon was in part a response to the failures of NEP, but also dovetailed with the global resurgence of Islam in the late-1970s—which made it a greater threat to the balance of power in Malaysia. The rise in Islamism was, therefore, the other part of the political equation in the late 1970s. To understand why the Malaysian state reinvented itself in the early 1980s the problems inherent in NEP must be examined in conjunction with the dynamics of Islamist politics during the decade of the 1970s. This relationship will be discussed in the next chapter.

Pakistan 1969–77: The End Game of the Secular State

The Ayub Khan regime fell from power in 1969 amidst growing sociopolitical tensions across Pakistan. The decade of authoritarianism and rapid industrialization had generated class conflict and aggravated ethnic tensions. Pakistanis of all political hues demanded an end to military rule and return of democracy. The Ayub Khan regime, the strongest to date in Pakistan, was unable to contain the rising tide of the opposition, especially the combination of Islamist demand for an end to secularism, leftist agitations for social justice, and Bengali and Sindhi demands for autonomy and secession. The depth and breadth of these demands were such that they rolled back the gains made by the state under Ayub Khan. After a decade of consolidation of state power, Pakistan witnessed successful social resistance to state power. In East Pakistan a total collapse of state authority led to civil war and secession of that province. In the western portion of Pakistan, the collapse of state authority led to regime change and a reformulation of state-society relations. This effort would fail to satisfactorily restore power to the state, leading state leaders to turn to Islam in the 1980s to create stability in state-society relations and to vest in the state the powers that it lost in 1969.

Ayub Khan's regime was replaced by a martial law administration under General Yahya Khan. The military's second direct intervention in politics would last until 1971. Yahya Khan's administration sought to see Pakistan through two crises: first, transition to democracy, which was to take place through general elections in December 1970; and, second, resolution of ethnic tensions between East Pakistan and the center. The latter crisis was particularly important to the state leadership, for it involved the territorial integrity of Pakistan and the delicate balance of power with India.

Faced with a strong leftist challenge to state authority in both wings of Pakistan and a resurgent Bengali nationalism, the Yahya Khan regime turned to Islam. The generals believed that Islam was the only ideology that could confront the Left and provide a basis for keeping Pakistan together.[38] The state's instrumentalist use of Islam more openly related questions of state power to religion. Islam, however, did not prove to be the panacea that the martial law administration had hoped for. In particular, Islamic solidarity failed to subdue Bengali nationalism.

The East Pakistan debacle followed immediately after Pakistan's first general elections, which were held soon after Yahya Khan took over. When Pakistan went to the polls in December of 1970, Bengali grievances against the central government were already threatening the unity of the country. Sheikh Mujibur Rahman and the Awami League had mobilized support in East Pakistan around their for demand for what was, in effect, a confederation between the two wings of the country, in which the eastern wing would receive parity and broad autonomy.[39] In East Pakistan, Zulfiqar Ali Bhutto's Pakistan People's Party (PPP) and its left-of-center populist platform had resonated with the masses. The elections produced the curious results in which the Awami League won 160 of 162 National Assembly seats allocated to East Pakistan (of the total of 300), but won no seats in West Pakistan, whereas Bhutto's PPP won 81 of 138 seats allocated to West Pakistan, and won no seats in East Pakistan. After the elections Bhutto and the military refused to allow the Awami League to form the government and devolve power to East Pakistan, pushing that province to secessionism.[40] The Pakistan military then resorted to brute force to prevent that outcome, with disastrous results—loss of East Pakistan after military defeat to India.

After the military debacle of East Pakistan Yahya Khan handed over power to Bhutto's PPP. Throughout his campaign for power Bhutto had promised to bring fundamental changes to the country. He systematically attacked the dominant military and bureaucratic elite, and their instruments of power among the oligarchy and the industrial elite, who had emerged during the Ayub Khan era. Bhutto had promised to disenfranchise the structures of power that Pakistan had inherited from the colonial era, and to distribute power and wealth from the dominant ethnic groups and provinces to the smaller ones, and from the wealthy and powerful to the plebian masses. His campaign slogan was *kapra, roti, makan* (cloth, bread, shelter—the three bare necessities for the poor).[41] Bhutto combined socialist rhetoric with Islam, talking of Islamic socialism and *musawat-i Muhammadi* (Muhammad's justice).[42] Bhutto intended to use strong popular support to push through social change, and in the process to empower the state and expand its capacity.[43] Whereas Ayub Khan had sought to concentrate power at the top in order to bring about social transformation, Bhutto would do so from below.

The PPP government, however, did not live up to expectations. It never managed to institutionalize Bhutto's charismatic appeal, and in time the regime fell back into the mold of Pakistan's politics. The PPP rose to power at a time of greater popular participation in politics. To its detriment, it proved unable to either harness or suppress that participation. Bhutto failed to exploit the military's moment of weakness to institutionalize the PPP's popular support. In fact, the PPP was never made to resemble a popular party, but at all times remained an extension of its leader. As the PPP failed to provide Bhutto with a satisfactory base of support, he resorted to authoritarian measures, and ultimately relied on the oligarchy and the military to rule.

The party's populist agenda affected the industrial elite, but not the rural areas, wherein many more of the poor lived. Bhutto failed to carry out effective land reform, leaving intact the rural power structure and failing to alter its impact on poverty and national politics. The failure to contend with the military, the bureaucracy, and the oligarchy made the task of restructuring the state unattainable, especially as Bhutto was compelled to rely on these institutions in place of a strong party to rule. The populist regime thus began to resemble the one that it had replaced. Far from reinventing the state, it continued with the apparatuses of power of the colonial state. The failure of the PPP, however, further eroded state authority, with debilitating consequences for stability and economic growth.

Throughout the 1970s the PPP relinquished its populist agenda for a balancing act between various interest groups. Bhutto was compelled to eviscerate his agenda of its substantive content, purge his party of its left-of-center workers, and push it in the direction of patrimonial politics. By the mid-1970s the PPP—populist by claim and leaning to the right in practice—was paralyzed. As a result, it was not able to fully benefit from, nor control, the new policies that it implemented in the economy.

The nationalization of industries and the use of the public sector to foster greater economic equity, which followed PPP's rise to power, had benefited the bureaucracy and the state bourgeoisie, whose powers had been increased to allow them to oversee the new state-run industries, more than it had the labor force.[44] With the influx of its erstwhile enemies—landed gentry and business leaders—into the ranks of the PPP following its ascension to power, Bhutto's populist agenda was turned on its head. The party was transformed into a patronage machine to benefit those with political clout rather than the poor—as was also the case with UMNO in Malaysia. Bhutto's appeal to Islamic symbols and to the support of the traditional elite and interest groups and his strong-arm tactics in dealing with the Left disheartened loyal party workers and eroded the PPP's base of support among the modern social sector, whose expectations had remained unfulfilled.

The opposition also found ample ammunition in PPP nationalization and land-reform measures. The propertied elite and the Islamic parties—the first motivated by its economic and business interests and the second, by its belief in the sanctity of property—joined forces to denounce the government's economic policies. Their opposition manifested itself in a host of anti-PPP issues. The government's halfhearted efforts at land reform in 1972 and the nationalization of agribusinesses—cotton-ginning and rice-husking mills—in 1976 (shortly before national elections) allied the landed gentry, small landowners, rural politicians, shopkeepers, and merchants, who saw their economic interests threatened.

The scope of the disgruntlement eventually spread to constituencies that had initially supported Bhutto. The PPP had generated much expectation that the economy could not meet. In fact, the impact of populism on the economy was to slow its pace of growth. Between the Ayub Khan and Bhutto periods, annual average real growth rates in agriculture fell from 3.4% to 2.1%, and in large-scale manufacturing from 10.9% to 3%. Total exports fell from 9.5% to 7.4%. With a shrinking economy Bhutto's hold on power became more tenuous.[45]

The opposition to Bhutto, however, did not focus its attention on economic issues alone. Islamic and political arguments were thought to provide a more effective basis for a social movement and had the added advantage of taking the debates beyond individual policies to challenge the legitimacy of the government as a whole. The alliance between the state and the bourgeoisie, which was the PPP's avowed aim, produced a more significant alliance between the rural masses and the landed elite. Bhutto responded with efforts to find his own base of support in the rural areas, but in line with the PPP's dilemma of meeting the demands of diverse interest groups, the move was interpreted by city dwellers as having an "anti-urban bias" and further pushed the middle and lower-middle classes into the fold of the anti-PPP alliance.

The opposition to the PPP quickly adopted Islamic form. In the 1970s the ideological hegemony of the Left—that had brought down Ayub Khan—ran out of steam and was supplanted by Islamist ideology (the nature and scope of which will be discussed in the next chapter). This shift made the state even more sensitive to Islam. Furthermore, as Bhutto confronted more concerted opposition to his rule, he, too, sought to use Islam to serve the needs of his regime and those of the state.

The 1970s witnessed the apogee of antistate Islamist activism in Pakistan. Much as the race riots of 1969 brought Islam into Malaysian politics, the loss

of East Pakistan more definitively anchored Pakistan's politics in Islam.[46] Islamist parties had all through the East Pakistan debacle blamed the crisis on
the state leaders' secular ways and lackluster adherence to Islam. At one rally
an Islamist student responded to the question "What broke up the country?"
with the answer "Wine."[47] After the secession of east Pakistan this sentiment
became prevalent in all sectors of society and even among some in the military. The calamity that had befallen Pakistan was thus seen as a consequence
of secularism, a view that led many to turn to Islam for solace at a time of national crisis. This kind of change in the political climate clearly did not favor
the Bhutto government.

In addition, the loss of East Pakistan underscored the vulnerability of the
country to further disintegration along ethnic lines. This experience redoubled adherence to the ideological underpinnings of the country, which were
rooted in Islamic identity. Throughout the 1970s Pakistan became palpably
more Islamically conscious. This mood was evident even in one of the principal bastions of secularism, the military. As mentioned earlier, some among
the officers blamed the loss of East Pakistan on secularism and the military
and state leaders' secular ways. Their dissatisfaction with their superiors
translated into greater Islamic consciousness. More generally, the military
had recruited greater numbers from the lower middle classes in the 1960s and
had not successfully transformed their worldviews. As the new recruits
moved up the ladder in the military, they made that institution more open to
Islam.[48] The influence of this trend became more pronounced in the 1970s as
the military, having suffered a humiliating defeat in East Pakistan and been
blamed for a decade of authoritarian rule under Ayub Khan, was eager to regain respect and restore public confidence in itself, and to this end became
more open to Islam. Finally, during the 1970s the military was under the command of General Muhammad Zia ul-Haq, who not only vaunted his own reli-
giosity but was insistent on promoting Islam in the military.

The loss of East Pakistan, in effect, created a crisis of identity for Pakistan
that Bhutto and the PPP's leftist populism failed to resolve. As a result, the
population turned to Islam for answers. This opened the door for Islamists and
traditional religious institutions to become more directly involved in politics.[49]
The fate of the state from this point forward would involve them as well.

The new-found importance of Islam would make it central to all struggles
of power in the 1970s. The salience of Islamic arguments in politics became
immediately evident in the debates surrounding the Constitution of 1973.[50]
The debates produced a constitution that was more amenable to Islam than
Ayub Khan's 1962 constitution, and, more important, debates over division of
power between state and social institutions and actors were enmeshed with
concerns for Islamic norms and practices. The constitution, which included
all Islamic features of the earlier constitutions, made Islam directly relevant
to the state—and also its powers and authority.[51]

This constitution would further weaken the Bhutto regime, which, given
its secular image, was at a disadvantage in the face of the growing prominence of Islam. This disadvantage became clear soon after the promulgation

of the Constitution of 1973 as the government confronted a series of challenges to its authority that were couched in Islamic language or involved Islamic issues. These varied from opposition to Pakistan's recognition of Bangladesh to pressuring the government to declare the Ahmediya minority non-Muslim. Bhutto was taken unawares by how quickly Islam replaced ethnic and leftist ideologies at the political center stage. He did not openly resist the rise of Islam, nor assert the prerogatives of the secular state. Rather, he sought to ride the tide of Islamic consciousness in order to use it to stymie his opposition by forcing political debates to move beyond Islam to political and social issues. Resisting Islam would only focus all politics on the role of Islam in society and politics—which in the 1970s was a losing proposition for the secular state. By easily conceding on Islam, Bhutto hoped to make Islam a nonissue and refocus attention on the issues that had brought him to power.[52] Stymieing Islamist opposition to the secular state by making such an opposition moot was a strategy of survival that would only be perfected by General Zia in the 1980s.

Having opened the gateways of politics to Islam, Bhutto had no intention of giving up all claims to it. To the contrary, opening politics to Islam made him all the more interested in harnessing the energies of Islamism and Islamist forces, and using them to the advantage of the state, its institutions, and its leaders. This course of action would also limit the Islamists' and ulamas' ability to dominate the political arena.

Bhutto's strategy rested on manipulation of both popular Islam and the high Islam of Islamists and ulama.[53] Bhutto's campaign for power had since inception been close to the popular Sufi Islam of rural Punjab and Sind.[54] Bhutto was himself attached to rural Islam and the cult of saints in Sind.[55] More important, however, Bhutto understood that rural Islam resonated with the poor, and it provided him and the state with a powerful tool with which to control those masses, and then to transform society and politics. Bhutto aimed to mobilize the urban and rural poor in support of his drive to restructure state and society.[56] To this end, he sought to create a strong nexus with their religious worldview. Bhutto's campaign of change ran aground early on, but his interest in rural Islam continued. In the 1970s he hoped to gain legitimacy from his devotion to the shrines and saints of Sind, and even to use the power of rural Islam and Sufism to combat the Islamists and the ulama. In this, however, he failed. Popular Islam did not empower his regime, and, more important, did not save him from Islamist and ulama opposition.

As a result, Bhutto was compelled to compete more directly with Islamists and ulama for control of the burgeoning Islamic politics. In this regard, he sought to fashion the state as a legitimate agency for managing the role of Islam in society and politics—a function that would become associated with the state in the 1980s. Unlike Ayub Khan, Bhutto did not seek to reinterpret Islam to serve the needs of development. His notion of Islamic socialism and appeal to popular Islam had been designed to serve populism. However, as Islamists and ulama dominated the Islamic discourse in the political arena, Bhutto abandoned all efforts to interpret or reform Islam, and resorted to symbolic measures that were designed to placate Islamists and ulama and to give the state legitimacy in terms of their vision of Islam. In 1974 Pakistan hosted the first Islamic Summit, which forged strong bonds between Pakistan and the Persian Gulf Arab states. Bhutto hoped that these ties would give his regime Islamic legitimacy just as they would buoy Pakistan's sagging economy through investments and labor remittances. The Persian Gulf states were eager for Bhutto to abandon socialism and were keen on strengthening their ties with Pakistan based on Islamic solidarity. The government's turn to Islam thus also had an economic and foreign policy component.

After the summit the state's symbolic appeal to Islam became more blatant. It sponsored the International Seerah (Life of the Prophet) Conference in 1976,[57] commissioned the printing of an "error-free" Qur'an, relaxed regulations governing pilgrimage to Hajj, made Arabic a component of the educational curricula and increased the Islamic theology and history component of it, changed the national holiday from Sunday to Friday (the Muslim sabbath), changed the name of Pakistan Red Cross to Red Crescent, empowered the Council of Islamic Ideology that had become dormant, and established the Ministry of Religious Affairs to formalize and regulate relations between the state and the ulama and Islamists.[58] Bhutto even dubbed Pakistan's nuclear weapon the "Islamic bomb."

These measures set the state on the path to Islamization—adopting Islamic coloring in order to serve the interests of the state and its leaders. However, at this stage the turn to Islam did not serve Bhutto's project of power. The Bhutto period continued to witness collapse of state authority as the scope of opposition to his regime broadened to include ever-increasing segments of the population. That opposition maintained a tight control over Islamic politics so that while the state became increasingly open to Islam—thus legitimating its flow in politics—it was unable to benefit from that openness. It became clear that the secular state and secular state leaders would not be able to effectively manage Islamic politics. Bhutto was compelled to dabble in Islamic politics but only to ensconce Islam in the political arena and seal the fate of his own regime.

The scope of this problem became clear in 1977 when Pakistan went to the polls. The opposition to Bhutto formed a nine-party electoral alliance—the Pakistan National Alliance—which included Islamist and ulama parties as well. The alliance mounted an effective bid for power, which served as a testament to both the erosion of Bhutto's power and secular authority in Pakistan. The election results, however, did not reflect the popularity of the opposition, which led to widespread belief that the election results had been tampered with. The opposition turned to street agitation, which between March and July 1977 spread across Pakistan. The direct challenge to Bhutto was the Nizam-i Mustafa (Order of the Prophet) movement.[59] The confrontation with the ruling order was thus cast in an Islam-versus-secularism mold.

In a last-ditch effort to maintain control of the flow of Islam in politics Bhutto adopted the demands of the Islamist opposition.[60] He banned the serving of alcohol, ordered the closure of casinos and nightclubs, and banned gambling and all other social activities proscribed by Islamic law.[61] He hoped that by surrendering the right to interpret Islam to the Islamic groups he could mollify them. But Islamists and ulama were in no mood to be placated. Freed of the restrictions of state control, they were determined to use Islam to take over power. They continued their anti-Bhutto campaign, which came to an end only when the military staged a coup in July 1977.

By the end of the 1970s the state in both Malaysia and Pakistan faced a crisis. In Malaysia NEP's usefulness to support the postcolonial state had reached its limits and had in fact placed new challenges before state leaders that could not be dealt with in its existing setup. In Pakistan the collapse of state authority during the 1969–71 period initially pointed to radical changes in state-society relations—an end to the colonial moorings of the state and redistribution of power and resources in society. This, however, did not come to pass. Rather, the state resumed its erstwhile mode of operation—relying on the military, bureaucracy, and the oligarchy to rule—albeit behind the façade of Bhutto's populist regime. Tensions that were inherent in this arrangement, combined with economic downturns and a growing chorus of Islamic opposition to the state, eventually undermined state authority, which reached crisis proportions in 1977 when the tidal wave of social resistance threatened to sweep over the state. The end of the Bhutto era thus witnessed a near collapse of state authority in Pakistan—a crisis of the secular state that far exceeded the challenge that faced the state in Malaysia. At the juncture of the late 1970s both the Malaysian and Pakistani states faced an impasse. The secular state had reached the limits of its power and was in fact experiencing a reversal in its power and capacity. The crisis of the state was occurring in an environment of greater Islamic consciousness in society and politics, which included the state as well. With no ideological tools available to the state through which to protect its position, state leaders began to look to Islam itself as a panacea. The choice made by the state can best be understood in the context of the nature and scope of Islamic politics in Malaysia and Pakistan during the 1970s, and the promise and challenges that inhered in it.

4

The Islamist Challenge in Malaysia and Pakistan

The decade of the 1970s was a period of ideological tumult in Malaysia and Pakistan. At the time when secular states were experiencing crises of governance, the society was in the throes of reexamining its foundational identity. That process led to greater Islamic resurgence across society and in politics that was evident in greater adherence to Islamic norms in private and public lives. Change in dress and patterns of social interaction, as well as increase in membership in Islamic societies, Islamic activism, attendance at mosques, and pilgrimage to Hajj, indicated a turn to Islam in Malay and Pakistani societies.[1] This phenomenon empowered and emboldened Islamist and ulama activists and parties who articulated an Islamist discourse of power through that decade, and formed or expanded existing sociopolitical organizations to serve the directives of that discourse. These activists and organizations both promoted the resurgence of Islam and were supported by it. In time they defined the place of Islamic ideas and activism in the political arena—thus changing the nature of demands on the state and casting anew the nexus between state and society. Islamist activism in the 1970s, and its ideological vision, both defined the challenge to the secular state and determined the direction in which the state would develop along at the end of that decade.

Islamist Activism in Malaysia in the 1970s: PAS, ABIM, and *Dakwah* Movements

The 1970s witnessed an intense ideological battle over Malay identity between Islam—as conceived of in the new wave of Islamist activism—nationalism, and traditional conceptions of Malay community tied to sultans[2] and rooted in language and custom (*adat*).[3] Islamic resurgence during that decade was rooted in the race riots of 1969, which ignited interest in Islam as an important distinguishing dimension of Malay identity in Malaysia's polyglot society.[4] That interest, however, became more pronounced in the 1970s as an unintended consequence of NEP.[5] The relationship of patronage between the state and the Malay community reinforced Malay identity just as it distinguished between Malays and non-Malays.

Social tensions born of NEP were also important in this regard. The decade of the 1970s witnessed rapid economic and social change.[6] The growth in Malay urban middle classes, migration and the rise of urban poverty, and income inequality between communities, classes, and urban and rural areas all fueled Islamic resurgence.[7] NEP had been designed to address ethnic imbalances, not class, sectoral, or regional ones. Islamism focused on exactly those chasms that NEP had created but was not equipped to bridge. Islamism in the 1970s created a student-peasant-worker alliance, thus clearly demarcating the boundaries of NEP's influence and opposition to it.[8] NEP not only laid the foundations for an antistate political platform around demands for social justice but also threatened to divide Malays along the line of support or opposition to UMNO and NEP. This would have sharply reduced the purview of UMNO and state leaders' power and opened important space in Malay politics for other contenders to speak for that community and represent its interests. Moreover, once divided, Malay's control of Malaysian politics may have come under question as well.

Islamism emerged in the 1970s as both a challenge to UMNO and a response to social ills that had followed NEP. Islamism was therefore both a political force and a social force. It was largely associated with urban youth, many of whom also had ties with rural areas. Although PAS continued to serve as a political platform for Islamism[9] and was important in underscoring the relevance of Islam to Malay identity in the 1970s,[10] it did not act as the principal vehicle for Islamic resurgence during that decade. For, despite its antistate rhetoric, it remained more a rival to UMNO than a threat to the state.[11] In fact, for a time in the 1970s PAS joined the ruling Barisan Nasional to support the Malay state.[12]

Islamic resurgence was, instead, most prominent among students and *dakwah* (propagation) movements that were directly or indirectly associated with them.[13] *Dakwahs* had two aims: to make Muslims more vigilant in observance of their faith and to do social work. All *dakwah* activity in Malaysia emphasized these two goals, but to varying degrees. *Dakwah* activity had emerged soon after independence to emphasize the role of Islam in Malay life.[14] UMNO and the government had encouraged it as a means of spreading Islam in Borneo—especially through PERKIM—whose population were counted as *bumiputras* to bolster the number of Malays vis-à-vis the Chinese and Indians.[15] The number and scope of *dakwah* activity, however, expanded significantly in the 1970s, and more important, involved students.

The two most important *dakwah* movements in the 1970s were the Islamic Youth Movement of Malaysia (Angkatan Belia Islam Malaysia [ABIM]) and al-Arqam. Both were rooted in student Islamic activism, worked to propagate Islamic observance in private and public life, and were opposed to UMNO and NEP. ABIM was more concerned with urban middle classes and the poor, whereas al-Arqam was devoted to addressing issues associated with rural poverty and rural development. Between them, ABIM and al-Arqam included the most significant anti-NEP social groups in Malaysia, and sought to establish a broad-based antistate and anti-NEP sociopolitical alliance.

Al-Arqam developed as a self-contained community that closely followed the teachings of its leader, Shaykh al-Ashaari.[16] It combined al-Ashaari's teachings with community-based rural development projects and businesses. Its impact on the rural scene where it was active was notable, but its overall impact on rural economy and society was limited. This owed to the cultlike structure and teachings of the movement along with limitations that exist in organization across the rural areas of peninsular Malaysia. Al-Arqam therefore did not pose the kind of challenge to the government that ABIM did. In fact, the government did not contend with al-Arqam until 1994, when it was banned and its leader was arrested. The organization's particular reading of Islam and its sartorial regulations had by then set it apart from mainstream Islam in Malaysia and made it easier for the government to crack down on its activities.

The challenge of ABIM was both more direct and far-reaching. ABIM was the culmination of student political activism that had begun in 1969. Students at the University of Malaya had been instrumental in the race riots and in bringing down the government of Tunku Abdul-Rahman.[17] As a political force, their power only grew in the 1970s. The National Education Policy component of NEP provided for new universities, increase in the number of Malay students, and scholarships for education abroad.[18] The number of Malay students in universities rose by 65% between 1970 and 1975, by which time some 6,000 Malay students were studying abroad on government scholarships.[19] By 1979 66.4% of university students would be Malay—90% at the National University of Malaysia.[20] The government investment in education did not translate into control over their politics and activism. In fact, as early as 1971 the government felt compelled to limit their activism through the University Colleges Act of 1971.[21] This only further encouraged the students' turn to Islamist activism since by organizing as *dakwahs* rather than student bodies students could avoid the government clampdown.[22]

More significant than the increase in the number of students and their penchant for activism was this turn to Islam, which signified a tuning out of nationalist politics in one of the most significant segments of the Malay community—wherefrom its future leaders and the core of its middle classes would emerge. For instance, Anwar Ibrahim, who began his political career by establishing ABIM, had parents who were both active members of UMNO.[23] The impact of this trend was already evident in the 1970s. It was then a source of embarrassment to UMNO that in elections PAS candidates tended to be better educated than UMNO ones, and the general perception was that the educated youth were not to be found in UMNO but in ABIM and PAS. In short, given the education gap between UMNO and its Islamist opponents, it appeared that the future belonged to the latter. UMNO became particularly worried about this trend after PAS's strong showing in the 1960 elections, when it took nearly half of the Malay vote.[24]

The turn to Islam owed to a number of factors. First and foremost was disenchantment with UMNO and its secular nationalist ideology.[25] The students had become more conscious of Islam in the post-1969 period, and saw little reflection of that consciousness in UMNO and NEP. ABIM would characterize UMNO's brand of nationalism as an un-Islamic attachment to race—as *asabiyyah*—that contravened the universal conception of community that is enjoined by Islam.[26]

International influences were also important. The turn to Islamism in Malaysia came during a decade when Islamism rose in prominence across the Muslim world. This surge ended the Bhutto regime in Pakistan in 1977, mounted a strong challenge to the Sadat regime from 1977 onward, and brought down the Pahlavi monarchy in Iran in 1979. Malaysian students were exposed to these trends and imbibed the ideology of Islamism in contacts with Islamist movements abroad as well as through Islamist literature in Malaysia.[27]

In Malaysia contacts between ulama and centers of Islamic learning in the Arab world had always been strong. Many among the Malaysian ulama—and PAS leaders—for instance, have been educated at the al-Azhar in Egypt or at various institutions in Saudi Arabia.[28] International Islamic organizations, as well as movements dedicated to propagation of Islamic orthodoxy—such as the South Asia–based Tablighi Jama'at (Propagation Society)— served as conduit for ideas between the Middle East and South Asia, and Malaysia.[29] These contacts had exposed Malaysians to developments in relations between Islam and politics in the Arab world and South Asia. PAS, for instance, has followed the example of Islamists in the Middle East and South Asia in demanding implementation of Islamic law and restrictions on women's participation in public affairs and economic activities.[30]

In the 1970s, however, the influence of the Arab world extended beyond religious channels of communication. The Arab-Israeli war of 1973—which animated ABIM's activism—and ascendancy of OPEC supported feelings of Islamic solidarity and empowerment, which extended to Malaysia as well.[31] With the flow of wealth to the Middle East came greater economic contacts between Malaysia and the Persian Gulf states, and investments by states, companies, and entrepreneurs from that region.[32] As was the case with Pakistan, fecund economic ties between Arabs and Malaysians strengthened Islamic unity and identity. Greater ties with the Middle East also opened the door to infusion of funds into religious schools and projects across Malaysia.[33] Eager to assert its claim to leadership in the Muslim world, Saudi Arabia favored patronage of Islamic projects across the Muslim world, which also strengthened direct ties between Malaysians and Saudi religious leaders.

All this had the effect of bolstering the role of Islam in Malaysian identity.

During a decade when the Middle East experienced wealth and empowerment, Malaysians were drawn to Islamic unity, wishing to belong to the Islamic world. That wish contributed to Islamic consciousness that quickly exceeded UMNO's position on Islam.

The Iranian Revolution of 1979 had the effect of transforming the rising Islamic identity that had resulted from economic and political ties with the
Middle East into a political consciousness that more closely paralleled Middle
Eastern Islamism.[34] The revolution in Iran suggested to some activists and intellectuals that advocating a confrontational, aggressive, and antiestablishment
form of Islamism would make them more important and relevant.[35] This belief
then spread to some politicians as well—for instance, precipitating internal
schisms in PAS that led the party to explore the promise of greater activism
by leaving Barisan Nasional.[36] Iran thus served as an example in suggesting
new avenues for discourse and mobilization with greater returns to activism.
In addition, the revolution—along with other expressions of Islamism—
was then deemed to be progressive whereas Malaysian society was viewed as
decadent and stagnant. Islamism for many Malays held the promise of true
development and progress that NEP and its notion of trusteeship had failed to
deliver. It was therefore a foil to NEP just as it was a suitable ideology of opposition. For instance, in September 1979 the United Association of Malaysian Students in Britain rejected NEP as capitalist and materialist, benefiting
only a corrupt elite, and irrelevant to the poor.[37] The attack on NEP then set
the stage for advocating an Islamic solution to the problems facing Malays
and Malaysia. ABIM hoisted Islamism not only as an alternative to UMNO's
brand of Malay nationalism but to show that UMNO and state leaders were
not serving Malay interests.[38]

The state leadership also viewed the Islamist wave as a concern for Malaysia's regional policy. Muslim separatism in the Acheh region of Sumatra,
Pattani region of Southern Thailand, and the Mindanao region of the Philippines was on the rise in the 1970s. Muslim populations of these regions are
either Malay or have had historical ties to Malays. Islamism in Malaysia
therefore had the potential to influence political stability in the region and to
affect Malaysia's delicate relations with its ASEAN partners.[39]

Malaysian students abroad were also changing through interactions with
Islamist trends from South Asia and the Middle East.[40] In Britain, Australia,
and the United States many formed Islamic student societies (Persuatan
Islam) and joined Islamic student associations, emerging as important actors
in the Muslim Student Association in the United States or the Federation of
the Organization of Islamic Societies in Britain.[41] They formed the Malaysian Islamic Studies Group, Suara Islam (Voice of Islam), and the Islamic
Representative Council.[42] It was in these forums that they studied the works
of radical Islamists from the Arab world and Mawlana Mawdudi of Pakistan,
and integrated Islamist arguments about social justice and the Islamic state
into their political worldview.[43]

These ideas came back to Malaysia with the returning students to gel with
ideas that were being promoted in Malaysian universities by ABIM, in rural

areas by al-Arqam, and in mosques by al-Azhar and Saudi-trained ulama, who had already initiated Islamist political activism.[44] The popularity of Islamism among returning students also indicated that religious activism was increasingly flowing up to the more privileged segments of Malay society and its future leadership. For instance, Prime Minister Husain Onn's daughter returned from her studies abroad observing the Islamic code of dress for women.[45]

By the middle of the 1970s Malaysia was clearly in the throes of a widespread Islamic resurgence that extended from greater personal observance to political activism. The students had emerged as the most important actors in the Islamist movement. They were present in various *dakwah* movements and in PAS. However, their most important vehicle was ABIM, which in the 1970s became not only the most powerful *dakwah* and activist organization, but a direct challenge to UMNO's hold on Malay politics and its conception of the Malaysian state.[46]

ABIM was formally created in 1972 with 153 members. It was the culmination of student activism of the 1969–71 period,[47] bringing together the message of *dakwah* that was ubiquitous outside of campuses and the political demands of students for sociopolitical change on campuses.[48] ABIM was from the outset closely associated with its charismatic leader, Anwar Ibrahim, who served as ABIM's president between 1974 and his resignation in 1982. Anwar had been at the University of Malaya during the race riots of 1969 and had been instrumental in relating Malay identity after 1969 to Islam. In ABIM he proved very effective in relating the question of "survival of Malays"—that had become central to Malay politics after 1969—to Islamic identity.[49] ABIM emphasized morality in tandem with demands for social justice and Malay rights, and popularized the notion that Islam is the panacea for all social ills and economic problems.[50] ABIM, however, never openly called for an Islamic state, and instead advocated change in the sociopolitical system from below based on Islamic values. It, moreover, advocated interpreting those values so as to accommodate Malaysia's pluralist society.[51] ABIM advocated an Islamic state, to be based on Islamic laws and values. ABIM recognized the problems that confronted the campaign for an Islamic state, given the ethnic composition of Malaysia. As a result Anwar and ABIM admitted that Middle Eastern and South Asian Islamism could not be readily imported into Malaysia, and that while Islamic ideology born in the Middle East and South Asia could provide a model for Malaysians to follow, it had to be tempered to fit the needs of a multiethnic society.[52] In a speech before ABIM's annual congress in 1979 Anwar declared: "Islam is the solution for the problems of a plural society."[53]

Under Anwar's leadership ABIM became dominant in both Islamist and student politics in the 1970s, and fused the energies of the two to create a potent political force.[54] ABIM's membership in the middle of the 1970s stood at around 40,000 and 100 branches.[55] It received recognition outside of Malaysia and accolades from Saudi Arabia, Pakistan, and Ayatollah Khomeini in Iran.[56] ABIM's Islamism was modern and reformist, and as such was different from the more traditional Islamism of PAS and rural *dakwah* movements. For this reason, it had broad appeal in urban areas and among the rising middle classes. ABIM advocated sociopolitical change by instilling Islamic values in society. It emphasized education, and to this end it established Islamic secondary schools (Yayasan Anda) that were to spearhead its aim of overhauling social values and carried its message beyond campuses and deepened its social base. ABIM was not a political party, although in many regards it posed as such, especially during the time when PAS was a part of Barisan Nasional—when ABIM was the principal Islamist opposition force. Rather, it operated as a *dakwah* movement dedicated to propagation of Islam.

ABIM's criticisms of UMNO, corruption of state leaders and the political elite, nepotism, failures of NEP, and secularism and "Westernized" culture of the elite, was more direct and uncompromising.[57] Siddiq Fazil, an ABIM leader characterized the organization's position in the following terms:

> The leaders were condemning corruption, but they were enriching themselves. They talked about Malay nationalism, but they were alienated from Malay masses. They were obsessed by the West. They were too accommodating to non-Malay sentiments. They were extremely slow in implementing national policies in education and langauge. We were impatient and angry about the plight of the Malays, their education, rural development, rural health . . . . We were very angry, disgusted and critical of the government. There seemed to be no moral foundation and no spiritual guidance. We turned to Islam to fill this vacuum and to look for guidance.[58]

ABIM also criticized the government's use of the Internal Security Act—a vestige of the British period, which gives broad powers to the government to suspend civil liberties—demanding greater personal freedoms and limits on state exercise of power. These kinds of views were expressed in the organization's organ, *Risalah* (Message), and accounted for its popularity beyond its student base of support.

ABIM also created a broad-based organizational structure that extended across Malaysia. Through study cells, lectures, and seminars the organization propagated its ideas far and wide and continued to recruit among the youth and urban professionals. By the middle of the 1970s the sheer size of ABIM's organization became a source of concern to UMNO, which understood the potential of a rival that claimed the membership and following of as many Malays as did ABIM.

Some in UMNO looked to sultans and ulama to contain *dakwah* activity. For instance, Tunku Abdul-Rahman at one point chastised the sultans for not controlling extremist *dakwahs*.[59] However, since *dakwah* activity of the 1970s rejected *adat* and custom as un-Islamic, it rejected the authority of the sultans, which was based on *adat*.[60] UMNO leaders therefore had to equip the state with the means to contain ABIM and other *dakwah* movements. UMNO and state leaders initially responded to the Islamist challenge by bolstering the government's Islamic legitimacy, mostly through symbolic acts and proclamations. In 1972 the government declared that NEP had been rooted in the

Qur'an and Islamic legal sources. Fines were levied on Malays for consuming alcohol.[61] By the late 1970s use of Islamic language in public discourse and pronouncements of state leaders had become routine.[62] Television broadcast call to prayers and government sponsorship of mosque building increased, as did the frequency with which UMNO and state leaders appeared in religious functions. Foreign policy became more pro-Arab, and in 1973 trade with Israel was ended.[63] Finally, the inclusion of PAS into Barisan Nasional was also designed to provide the ruling regime with Islamic legitimacy.

These measures did not, however, stem the tide of Islamism, especially the growing influence of ABIM. This became apparent during the Baling uprising of 1974—a peasant protest movement in which ABIM took part. The uprising was of great concern to state leaders. For until then communists led by Chinese activists had led this kind of opposition, which the government had easily dealt with by relying on Malay identity. The Baling uprising was the first instance of a Malay-based and Islamically inspired peasant uprising—a confrontation between Malays and the Malay leadership. State leaders responded to what they saw as the Islamist threat to their position and ABIM's rise through strong-arm tactics. In 1974 Anwar, along with 1,169 ABIM members, was arrested.[64] In the same year UMNO put forth plans for an expansion of federal religious bureaucracy, including Pusat Penyelidekan Islam Malaysia (Islamic Research Center of Malaysia [Pusat Islam]); and established the Pusat Dakwah Islamiyah (Islamic Missionary Center) in the prime minister's secretariat;[65] set up the National Fatwa (Religious Decrees) Council, and charged the Religious Council for the Federal District (Majlis Ugama Islam) with the task of regulating *dakwahs*.[66] The government also created its own *dakwah* organization through PERKIM in 1975. The former secular prime minister, Tunku Abdul-Rahman, mobilized support for PERKIM within Malaysia as well as across the Arab world, fashioning it as an international Islamic movement dedicated to conversion of non-Muslims of Malaysia to Islam, especially in Borneo. PERKIM received funds and support from Saudi Arabia, Kuwait, and Libya, and provided the government with some Islamic legitimacy. For instance, in 1983 Tunku Abdul-Rahman received both the Faisal Award from Saudi Arabia and the National Hijrah Award from Pakistan for service to Islam.[67]

Through these measures UMNO not only sought to assume an Islamic image—in particular by becoming a part of the *dakwah* movement—but to regulate *dakwah* activity in general. In particular by the late 1970s UMNO had become worried about labor and peasant disturbances that had connections to *dakwahs*,[68] as well as the rise of anti-Hindu extremist *dakwahs* that led to attack on Indian temples and property during the Kerling incident in 1981.[69] Worried about escalation of violence and militancy, UMNO made a distinction between "proper" *dakwah* and "false" *dakwah* (*dakwah song-sang*), justifying use of force against the latter. UMNO's strategy was to divide and rule *dakwah* movements by isolating radicals and extremists, along with small groups with small bases of followers, in tandem with co-opting larger mainstream *dakwahs* through PERKIM.[70] However, the distinction made by the government was somewhat arbitrary. According to one survey, in 1981 there were 40 extremist *dakwahs* with 30,000 members.[71]

These measures, however, failed to slow the spread of Islamism, which with PAS's departure from Barisan Nasional constituted added threat to UMNO. The apparent change in the balance of power between secular regimes and Islamist oppositions in the Middle East and South Asia convinced PAS that it had much to gain by leaving Barisan Nasional. PAS believed that once it left the ruling coalition it would be in a position to capitalize on the political mood in the country and to harness the energies of urban and rural Islamist movements to mount an effective challenge to UMNO. From 1977 onward PAS, too, became a notable Islamist threat to UMNO and state leaders.

Since its creation in 1951, PAS had kept Islam relevant to Malay identity and nationalism, but had not been able to challenge UMNO either ideologically or politically. PAS's influence had remained limited to the more purely Malay and Islamically conscious northern provinces of Malaysia, notably, Kedah, Kelantan, and Terengganu.[72] Since its creation PAS had advocated Islamic rule for Malaysia. Its vision of Islam was more strident and also more ethnically chauvinistic than that of ABIM. Although PAS accepted democracy, it favored a direct role for the ulama in governance, which hinted at theocracy. PAS also equated Islamization with disenfranchisement of the "yellow culture"—Chinese influence over Malaysia.[73] PAS had, in the first place, left UMNO after independence in part because of the party's accommodation of the Chinese and Indian communities, which it equated with ambivalence toward Islam.[74]

PAS's view of Islam was in concert with the religious sensibilities of small-town and rural voters that supported the party. It also reflected the thinking of those ulama and religious leaders who had been educated in the Middle East, at al-Azhar or in Mecca and Medina, as well as in South Asia at conservative institutions such as the Deoband. For this reason, PAS had never been able to make an effective bid for urban and middle-class Malay vote.

In ABIM PAS saw an opportunity. Anwar and ABIM had opened urban areas, middle classes, and professionals to Islam and Islamism, in essence creating a unique opportunity for PAS. PAS left Barisan Nasional to explore the possibilities that *dakwah* activity in the 1970s, and ABIM in particular, had brought to the fore.[75] PAS's own membership had undergone change in the 1970s to make the party more open to those possibilities. In the 1970s the old guard was gradually replaced by younger Islamist activists and ulama, many of whom had been ABIM leaders or had been involved in student activism in Britain. These younger voices sought to revamp PAS to turn it into the vanguard force for the creation of an Islamic republic in Malaysia. They initiated recruitment, training, and organization drives, and changed PAS's platform to increase its appeal to ABIM's constituency. Since ABIM was not a party, it could retain control over its members only for a finite period of time. Furthermore, it could not use student mobilization directly in the political arena. PAS, however, was a political party and was the most natural destination for ABIM's "graduates." The new leadership in PAS, especially the ideologically strident Hajji Abdul Hadi Awang (chief minister of Terengganu since 1999), made the creation of an ideological and organizational nexus between PAS and ABIM the bedrock of an effective Islamist bid for power.[76]

After leaving Barisan Nasional, PAS had quickly adopted ABIM's rhetoric. It made the demand for an "Islamic state" central to its program, and depicted UMNO and Malay nationalism as too narrowly communal. PAS also criticized NEP and industrial development in Malaysia along with its Westernizing cultural influence.[77] With this prelude Awang and PAS approached Anwar after he was released from jail in 1975 to formalize an alliance between PAS and ABIM.

However, PAS remained more radical than ABIM, for it had recruited from among the more radical ABIM and Malay students in Britain. The party more closely followed the teachings of Egypt's Sayyid Qutb and Pakistan's Mawdudi, and after 1979 Iran's Khomeini. Its vision of an Islamic state was closer to the Middle Eastern and South Asian models than that of ABIM. It in fact saw in Islamic universalism the means to reduce Malay attachment to nationalism and hence to end UMNO's domination. In many ways ABIM was from the outset uncomfortable with this dimension of PAS's activism. ABIM, too, was impressed with Islamist forces outside of Malaysia, but did not seek to emulate their radicalism. These differences made the alliance between the two Islamist forces problematic. In particular, Anwar remained cautious. He was wary of PAS's strident rhetoric and uncompromising Islamism, and believed that PAS's approach was not likely to work in multiethnic Malaysia, and might alienate Malay middle classes as well. Anwar and ABIM's vacillations prevented a united Islamist challenge against the state at the critical juncture of the late 1970s. It also opened the door for UMNO to make a bid for ABIM's support.

Between 1977 and 1982 UMNO and PAS competed over ABIM's support. In 1982 UMNO came out victorious. In that year Prime Minister Mahathir Mohammad persuaded Anwar to join UMNO. Anwar resigned from ABIM and, along with many of its leaders, joined the ruling party and various state institutions. ABIM continued to function as a semiofficial youth movement, but lost its independence, and in due course, power and influence. Anwar would rapidly rise in the ranks of UMNO to become deputy party leader, as well as deputy prime minister and acting prime minister in 1997, before his dismissal and arrest in 1998 (which will be discussed in later chapters).

Anwar's decision to choose UMNO over PAS was a pragmatic one.[78] Anwar saw PAS as dominated by ulama and posed to grow more radical in response to events in the Middle East and South Asia. He believed that ABIM's urban and middle class base of support would not be comfortable with PAS's radicalism, nor with following the lead of its ulama. ABIM had all along favored a "Malaysian Islamism" that would borrow from outside ideas, but would adapt them to the needs of Malaysia. Anwar's own background had convinced him of the necessity of such an approach and made it difficult for him to follow PAS's lead. He came from a Hindu ancestry and was raised in Penang—

one of the original British settlement colonies with a large Chinese entrepreneurial community. PAS's approach was more in tune with the cultural am-
biance of the more predominantly Malay northern states of Malaysia. Anwar
understood early on the limits to Islamist radicalism—and in this he was far
ahead of Islamist thinkers everywhere—whereas PAS would remain enam-
ored with radicalism for far longer, expecting it to produce for PAS what the
revolution had done in Iran. As a result, ABIM and PAS disagreed over the
utility of radical action, and the scope of Islamization in society and politics.
Whereas PAS's position emulated the Iranian and Arab models, Anwar was
moving in the direction of an accommodationist Islamism.

Moreover, PAS had traditionally been strong only in Kedah, Kelantan, and
Terengganu. UMNO, on the other hand, was a national organization. ABIM
was more likely to influence the state and the broader spectrum of Malay
community through UMNO. Many Malays, although critical of UMNO, were
still attached to it and would not have followed ABIM into PAS. UMNO thus
provided for a more tenable marriage between Islamism and the modern state
that ABIM's followers desired than PAS's platform.

Soon after Anwar was freed from jail, Mahathir Mohammad, who was a
rising star in UMNO at the time and knew Anwar through family connections, invited the ABIM leader to join UMNO and to bring ABIM's message
into the party. Anwar's rapport with Mahathir was critical in ABIM's decision
in favor of UMNO. ABIM had until that point rejected overtures from UMNO.
Anwar, however, trusted Mahathir—whose position on Malay rights had received support from ABIM—and chose the nationalist party as the appropriate vehicle for projecting ABIM's influence onto the state and the broader
Malay society. The pact between ABIM and UMNO also committed the latter
to greater openness to Islam, which, in turn, ensured Mahathir's rise to the
helm in the party.

PAS's failure to forge a pact of unity with ABIM, and its decision to vest
its fortunes in a Middle Eastern and South Asian style of antistate and puri-
tanical Islamism, compromised Islamism's potential to win the state. UMNO,
having lost its Islamic legitimacy after PAS left Barisan Nasional, was quick
to exploit the differences between PAS and ABIM. Thus UMNO and state
leaders stymied the progress of Islamism toward power, but they had to do
more to completely contain its threat. That would not come to pass until the
1980s when Mahathir Muhammad would commit the state to Islamization.

Islamism in the 1970s also held some promise for UMNO, which some
like Mahathir were quick to understand and, in time, exploit. Islamism was
generally supportive of state power. It promoted the idea of a powerful state
that faced no hindrance in its efforts to change society. Only such a state
could guarantee social harmony and genuine development by instituting Islamic values and laws. Whereas PAS envisioned such a state to be narrowly
rooted in Islamic law and approximating a theocracy, ABIM had put forth
a more flexible view. Anwar and ABIM had argued for adherence to Islam
by state leaders, and not necessarily rebuilding the state de novo based on a
preconceived Islamic blueprint. The mark of Islamicity of the state was not

simply in its adherence to narrow interpretations of Islamic law nor in leadership by the ulama, but in good governance and acceptance of Islamic values. Anwar argued, "[W]e have seen the hypocrisy of the so-called modern political elite . . . . [W]e felt rampant corruption and moral decadence. So we moved to see the relevance of Islam in a societal context."[79] Islam provided an ideology for better government. The Islamic state was a desired end not only because it was Islamic but because it was good. This line of reasoning was therefore open to coexistence with minorities in an open economy so long as the state abided by Islamic norms and guaranteed socioeconomic equity. In fact, Anwar argued that Malaysia's multiethnic reality made the uncompromising Islamism of the Middle East and South Asia—that PAS sought to emulate—unfitting to Malaysia.[80] Anwar thus placed greater emphasis on values than law, on morality than hard-and-fast strictures, in defining his desired Islamic order. Anwar had in many regards stepped out of the rigid confines of Islamist ideology to formulate a broader interpretation of what was the Islamic state was, what sort of state would qualify as Islamic, and why it should be established. This interpretation gave state leaders greater latitude in contending with the Islamist demands placed before them.

The Islamic state in ABIM's formulation was in essence an argument for concentration of power in the state and expansion of its capacity. To be Islamic, the state had to do more, control more, regulate more, and do all of that more efficiently and within the moral bounds of Islam. In addition, ABIM argued for hard work, discipline, and unity, all values that the state would also promote in the 1980s as a basis for its pursuit of economic growth. In the 1980s the state would respond to the threat that was posed to its authority by Islamism, but would also seek to capitalize on the possibilities that inhered in it.

The Islamist Challenge in Pakistan in the 1970s: The Jama`at-i Islami and the Nizam-i Mustafa

The principal Islamist actors in Pakistan in the 1970s were the Jama`at-i Islami (Islamic Party) and its student wing, Islami Jam`iat-i Tulabah (Islamic Student Movement [IJT]). Also important were the ulama parties, most notably, Jam`iat-i Ulama-i Pakistan (Society of Pakistan's Ulama [JUP]) and Jam`iat-i Ulama-i Islam (Society of Ulama of Islam [JUI])[81]—both of which had become more interested in politics and adopted some of the rhetoric, organizational features, and policies of political Islam owing to the influence of the Jama`at and IJT.

The Jama`at was formed in 1941 in what was still united India.[82] It was the brainchild of Mawlana Sayyid Abu'l-A`la Mawdudi (d.1979), who also served as the party's chief ideologue and titular head until 1972.[83] Since its formation, the Jama`at articulated a distinctly political interpretation of Islam and demanded the restructuring of society and politics and the establishment of a state that would embody the spirit of Islamic law—replacing the secular state with an Islamic one. The Jama'at is perhaps the first movement of its kind to develop systematically an Islamic ideology, a modern revolutionary reading of Islam, and an agenda for social action to materialize its vision.

Pakistan's particularly arduous experiences with nation building and consolidation of the state, the deep-seated cleavages in its polity, uneasy coexistence between democracy and military rule, and civil war and secession of the majority of its population made the emotive power of Islam increasingly more appealing, and its promise of unity ever more poignant.

Following the creation of Pakistan, Mawdudi and the Jama'at quickly closed ranks with the ulama and other self-styled religious movements in pressing the newly formed state for an "Islamic" constitution. The Jama'at's ideas and policy positions featured prominently in the ongoing debates between the government and the religious alliance from 1947 to 1956, most notably in the Objectives Resolution of 1949. In this climate the Jama'at successfully anchored constitutional debates in the concern for the Islamicity of the state.[84] Jama'at's activism in these years eventually culminated in an open confrontation with the government over the role of religion in politics.

In 1953, the ulama and religious activists led agitations to demand the relegation of the Ahmediya sect to the status of a non-Muslim minority.[85] They argued that this measure would serve as a litmus test for the government's commitment to Islam. The Jama'at's role in this affair proved critical. As a result, once the government clamped down on the agitations, Mawdudi was charged with sedition and was subsequently sentenced to death. That sentence was later commuted and was eventually reversed by the country's Supreme Court.

By pitting the Jama'at against the state over a popular cause, the anti-Ahmediya issue enhanced the party's political standing and following. Moreover, the agitations placed Islam more squarely at the center of the constitutional debates regarding the nature of the Pakistani state, all to the Jama'at's advantage. As a result, the Jama'at became more directly involved in politics. It used its growing power to exert renewed pressure on the government, this time around the issue of the Constitution of 1956.

During the Ayub Khan years, the political establishment became dominated by an authoritarian and bureaucratic elite, who actively promoted religious modernism as a way of retarding the drive for the Islamization of the country. Advocates of Islamic revival and an Islamic state were increasingly pressed into retreat. The Jama'at's offices were closed down, its leaders were excoriated in government-sponsored publications, and its activities, networks, and operations were restricted. Mawdudi himself was imprisoned twice during Ayub Khan's rule. The government had launched an offensive against Islamist activism with the hope of freeing Pakistan and General Ayub's modernization schemes of the menace of the clamor for Islamicity.

The result of this transformation was clear in the Jama'at's policies in the post-Ayub period. In 1970 it participated in national elections with the aim of capturing power. Those hopes were dashed when the party won only four seats to the National Assembly and four seats to the various provincial assemblies. In 1971, the Jama'at responded to the advent of civil war in East Pakistan by mobilizing its resources in support of the central government and by joining the conflict to prevent East Pakistan from becoming Bangladesh.

The secession of East Pakistan, and the rise of Bhutto to power in 1971, intensified the Jama'at's political activism. The socialist content of the PPP's political program was particularly instrumental in prompting the Jama'at into action. Viewing Bhutto's populism as a direct challenge to the Islamic basis of Pakistan, and to its place in the country's political order, the party directly confronted the government on numerous political issues. The Jama'at, however, did so increasingly through the agency of its student organization, IJT.

IJT was formed in 1947 with twenty-five students. Much like ABIM, it was initially conceived of as a *da'wah* (Arabic and Urdu equivalent of *dakwah*) — a voluntary expression of Islamic feelings among students.[86] Its aim then was to influence the education of the future leadership of Pakistan through recruitment and spread of propaganda on campuses. It was not long, however, before it turned its attention to politics, first on campuses, and eventually on the national scene.

Throughout the 1950s, concern with the Left increased. The ideological dichotomy between Islam and Marxism soon culminated in actual clashes between IJT and leftist students. These clashes politicized IJT. The new orientation became important as in the 1960s IJT became locked in battle with the Ayub Khan regime. IJT created unrest on Pakistani campuses, initially to oppose the government's educational initiatives, but eventually to register its dissent on such national issues as the Tashkant Agreement of 1966, which ended the war between Pakistan and India. The agitations elicited government reaction, leading to clashes and, subsequently, to the arrest and incarceration of numerous IJT activists. The impact on IJT was profound. It institutionalized agitations, increasingly in lieu of religious work, as the predominant mode of organizational behavior, but also attested to the power and potential of student activism.

It was therefore not surprising that IJT was pushed further into the political limelight between 1969 and 1971 when the Ayub Khan regime collapsed and the civil war in East Pakistan led to the dismemberment of Pakistan. IJT, also with the implicit encouragement of the government, became the main force behind Jama'at's national campaign against the PPP in West Pakistan and Bengali secessionists in East Pakistan. The campaign confirmed IJT's place in national politics, especially so in 1971, when IJT began to interact directly with the military government of East Pakistan in an effort to extirpate Bengali nationalism. As a result of these contacts, IJT joined Pakistan military's counterinsurgency campaign in May 1971.

Clashes with the Left in West Pakistan and the civil war in the East left an indelible mark on IJT. The organization's penchant for radical action now clearly eclipsed its erstwhile commitment to an agenda of religious work. It saw the political situation at the end of Ayub Khan's rule and, later, during the Bhutto period, in apocalyptic terms, wherein the end thoroughly justified the means.

The ideology of the Jama'at was firmly imprinted on the ethos and identity of IJT, enough so as to shape the student organization's worldview. IJT thus extended the ideological reach of the Jama'at into a broader spectrum of the population through campuses. IJT's ability to mobilize large numbers of students in addition provided the Jama'at with valuable manpower needed to wage demonstrations, stage agitprop, and conduct electoral campaigns. IJT's activism proved particularly important to Islamist resistance to Bhutto in the 1970s because the principal Islamist party at the time, the Jama'at, had been routed at the polls in 1970, while IJT, fresh from a "patriotic struggle" in East Pakistan, defeated the PPP's student federation in a number of campus elections in Punjab and Karachi. IJT's victories breathed new life and hope into Islamism and the dejected Jama'at. IJT had taken on the PPP successfully, parrying Bhutto's political momentum. The victory had, moreover, been interpreted to mean that Islamism could stop the Left—which led anti-Bhutto social forces to rally behind the Jama'at.

Following its victory, IJT became a more suitable vehicle for launching anti-PPP campaigns. The student organization soon became a de facto opposition party and began to define the parameters of its political activism accordingly. It performed its oppositional role so effectively that it gained the recognition of the powers-that-be. IJT leaders were among the first to be invited to negotiate with Bhutto later in 1972, once the PPP decided to mollify its opposition.

IJT's rambunctious style was a source of concern for the newly formed PPP government. The student organization had not only served as the vehicle for implementing Jama'at's political agenda, but was poised to take matters into its own hands and launch even more radical social action. While the Jama'at advocated Islamic constitutionalism, IJT had been harping on the demand for Islamic revolution. The tales of patriotic resistance and heroism in East Pakistan imbued IJT with an air of revolutionary romanticism. IJT thus became the mainstay of such anti-PPP agitational campaigns as the Non-Recognition of Bangladesh movement of 1972–74, the anti-Ahmediya controversy of 1974, and the Nizam-i Mustafa (Order of the Prophet) of 1977. As a result, IJT found national recognition as a political party and a new measure of autonomy from JI. The organization also developed a psychology of dissent, which, given the fact that it was as an extraparliamentary force, could only find expression in street demonstrations and clashes with government forces.

The Jama'at-IJT combination became the vanguard force in anti-Bhutto Islamist activism throughout the 1970s. Their aim and program of action was more akin to that of PAS. The Jama'at and IJT were revolutionary and anti-establishment forces that sought to establish an Islamic order that was narrowly based on their austere reading of Islamic law. Their vision of the future and mode of activism was uncompromising and left little room for the broader inclusive interpretations that were evident in ABIM's program.

The success of the Jama'at and IJT made Islamism the pivot of the anti-Bhutto activism in the 1970s. The social forces and economic interests that rejected Bhutto's populism and style of rule began to lend support to Islamist forces and to adopt its rhetoric in expressing their dissent. This was even true in the military, where officers that were unhappy with the PPP gravitated toward the Islamist stance. This success made the Islamist position more strident and less open to compromise. From 1972 onward, Islamist activism would increasingly weaken the Bhutto regime and limit the possibility of restoration of power to the state after the tumult of the 1969–71 period. The prospect of overwhelming the state would underscore the utility of radical action in lieu of accommodation and compromise. Thus, the 1970s would witness a more powerful and radical Islamist onslaught against the state, one that posed a more serious threat to the state and its leadership than Islamism did in Malaysia.

No sooner had Bhutto assumed power than the anti-PPP opposition reared its head. This opposition soon assumed an Islamic front and became dependent on the Jama'at to mount a successful campaign of political agitation. Bhutto initially tried to control the activities of the Islamic parties, but, given the gradual rise in the popularity of Islam, the weakening of the state following the civil war, and the mistakes made by the ruling party, it failed. This led to further decline in the state's authority. By the end of the Bhutto era, Islamist forces, led by the Jama'at, were in a position to make a direct bid for controlling the state.

The inability of Islam to keep the two halves of the country united had not diminished the appeal of religion either to politicians or to the people. Oddly enough, it even increased it. The precariousness of Pakistan's unity led Pakistanis to reaffirm their Islamic roots. The PPP government, much as Ayub Khan's regime, sought to both manipulate Islam and marginalize its principal spokesmen, but did not succeed. Although not the main force behind the return of Islam, the Jama'at proved to be its main beneficiary. For, given the prevailing climate, its views on an array of national issues were for once in tune with those of a larger number of Pakistanis. Its growing influence in the army, the most secular and anglicized of state institutions, was indicative of this trend.

This trend was reinforced in the subsequent years, thanks in part to Bhutto's choosing General Muhammad Zia ul-Haq as the army's chief of staff. Zia had long been sympathetic to the Jama'at. He had been greatly impressed with Mawdudi's works, and following his investiture as chief of staff, used the powers vested in his office to distribute the party's literature among his soldiers and officers. Bhutto was greatly dismayed at this development and had summoned the general before the cabinet to explain his actions. Later during his trial before the Supreme Court, Bhutto was to remark, "I appointed a Chief of Staff belonging to the Jamaat-i-Islami and the result is before all of us."[87] His statement underscores the Jama'at's increasing influence in the armed forces and the party's role in bringing down his regime.

The PPP's credo from its inception had been "Islamic Socialism"; Bhutto had said "Islam is our faith, democracy is our polity, socialism is our economy," but under the pressures of Islamization, as he lost his grip over the hearts and minds of the people and with growing ties with the Persian Gulf states, he had to forego the second two in favor of the first.[88] The Constitution of 1973 reinstated "Islamic" as part of the official name of the state. But because Bhutto had been one of the most secular of Ayub Khan's lieutenants, and his ties to Islam had been through popular religion, his gestures toward Islam were not thought to be genuine by the Islamists and ulama.[89] Bhutto was all along viewed as a rabid secularist. The ulama and the Islamists made much of his open disregard for religious values and mores, and accused him of receiving financial and organizational backing from the Ahmediya community.[90] By 1974 the Ahmediya connection had become sufficiently damaging to the government to compel Bhutto to declare that community to be a non-Muslim minority, but despite this concession, the government never managed to develop a following among the Islamically inclined Pakistanis. It was caught in a situation of Islamizing the national political discourse, while it was unable effectively to appeal to Islam. In fact, given Bhutto's policies and style the Islamization of national politics would not favor him or his party. The secularism of the PPP never ceased to be a political issue.

This became all the more the case when PPP found itself at loggerheads with the ulama party, JUI, in provincial politics. JUI had formed the government in Baluchistan and NWFP in coalition with the Pathan nationalist National Awami Party. Although JUI's rise to power in these provinces was not the result of an Islamic campaign, after assuming power JUI pushed for the first "Islamization" measures to be instituted by a governmental body in Pakistan, including strict observance of the fast during Ramadan. In this the JUI/NAP governments were the first instances of Islamic government in Pakistan and added to the momentum for Islamization in the 1980s.

Eager to consolidate power, in 1973 Bhutto used strong-arm tactics to dismiss the only two non-PPP provincial governments in Baluchistan and NWFP. The Baluch resisted, and a brutal guerilla war broke out, which by December 1974 pitched the Baluch tribes against the Pakistani army. The conflict harkened back to the East Pakistan debacle and intensified opposition to Bhutto just as it brought the military into politics. In fact, the Jama'at used the occasion to put Bhutto's record in East Pakistan on trial. Meanwhile, since JUI had been a partner in the dismissed governments, Bhutto's actions were interpreted as an assault on ulama and Islamist parties.

The Baluchistan and NWFP imbroglio made the resolution of other crises more difficult. For instance, it took the convening of the Islamic summit of heads of Muslim states in Pakistan in 1974 to overcome the opposition to the recognition of Bangladesh. The anti-Ahmediya agitation ended only after the government buckled and declared them a non-Muslim minority. The agitation strengthened IJT and underscored the weakness of the ruling order. Bhutto had not only failed to create a strong state, but presided over further erosion of state power as politics became mired in agitational politics in a climate of growing Islamic consciousness.

The weakening of Bhutto led to the emergence of more broad-based opposition to his regime that gained strength on the back of Islamist agitation in the streets. In 1975 opposition leaders decided formed a multiparty anti-PPP coalition, the United Democratic Front. In a move indicative of the increasingly central role that Islam was playing, the group chose Mufti Mahmud, a member of the ulama and leader of JUI, as its leader. The Front was able to translate the agitation staged on the streets by the Jama'at and IJT into a political movement that could challenge the PPP through formal channels. It soon became a force to contend with and was able to challenge the government on a host of issues in the parliament.

When the government announced national elections for March 1977, the Front changed its name to the Pakistan National Alliance (PNA). It was composed of nine parties, including the Jama'at, JUI, and JUP. The alliance adopted an Islamic platform, popularly known as Nizam-i Mustafa, which favored the ulama Islamist parties. PNA gave a large number of its election tickets to the three ulama and Islamist parties, who, in turn, provided PNA with workers and activists—mostly from IJT—to push its agenda on the streets and in the election campaign. The Jama'at was by far the most active and prominent of the Islamic parties in the PNA, owing to both its long history of political activism and the central role that IJT had been playing in anti-Bhutto politics since 1971.

In the 1977 elections, of the 168 seats PNA contested, the Jama'at's share was thirty-two seats. The PNA won thirty-six seats, of which the Jama'at's share was nine. The Jama'at did surprisingly well in these elections, tallying 25% of PNA's seats. (Along with JUI and JUP, the share of the religious seats was even higher).[91] If the results of the rigged elections were any indication, the Jama'at had been headed for domination of PNA and the political order that elections were to produce.

The PNA's results fell far short of expectations and were not in keeping with its apparent popularity. As a result, PNA accused Bhutto of rigging the elections. The PNA then began a national campaign to demand new elections. As politics moved from elections and the democratic process into the streets, PNA became more reliant on the Jama'at and IJT to produce mobs and activists, and to keep the pressure on the government through demonstrations and agitation. By July 1977, as a result of PNA's postelection agitational campaign, Jama'at's popularity had risen still further, enough to suggest that it would have done even better if new elections were held.

Bhutto remained defiant in the face of mounting opposition. He dispatched the police to combat demonstrators and ordered the arrest of PNA leaders. Bhutto had all along regarded the Jama'at, and its leader, Mawdudi, as a major force behind the PNA. He decided that the agitation was in essence a demand for Islamization and moved to resolve the crisis by dealing directly with the Jama'at on Islamic issues. In April Bhutto met with Mawdudi in the hope of defusing the crisis. After that meeting he openly championed Islamization in the hope of co-opting a part of the opposition. He announced that in recognition of the demands of the Nizam-i Mustafa casinos and nightclubs would be closed down, sale of alcoholic drinks and gambling would be banned, and generally activities proscribed by Islam would be against the law. In addition, he would reconvene the Council of Islamic Ideology under the supervision of Mufti Mahmud, the leader of JUI and PNA, so it could oversee the implementation of government-sponsored Islamization. The Islamic parties rejected this idea and again demanded new elections.

With no way out of the impasse, Bhutto turned to Saudi Arabia, hoping that using its moral and financial leverage, the kingdom could help end the stalemate. Saudi Arabia proposed negotiations between the government and PNA, which began again on June 3. The PNA was represented by a three-man team, two of whom—its chair, Mufti Mahmud of JUI, and a representative from the Jama'at—hailed from ulama and Islamist parties. The PNA contingent was careful to keep negotiations on the elections of 1977, the legitimacy of the government, and new elections. Islam and the Nizam-i Mustafa, on which Bhutto was willing to make substantial concessions, did not figure prominently. Bhutto now tried to divert attention from the negotiations by rallying Pakistanis around a nationalist and anti-imperialist platform, charging that the PNA and the Jama'at were being led by the United States, who had been opposed to the PPP's socialist and Third World leanings, and to Pakistan's nuclear program. For instance, in a speech before the parliament on April 28 Bhutto had stated, "The person inflaming the country in the name of Nizam-e-Mustafa, Maulana Maudoodi."[92]

Negotiations went on for a month. During this period, Bhutto's resolve gradually waned, and he became increasingly amenable to new elections. It is not certain whether the government and PNA actually reached an agreement or not. All sides, however, concur that the delay in reaching a final agreement during the last hours before the coup owed much to General Zia's counsel to Bhutto.[93] The general had warned him against entering into an agreement with PNA based on preliminary understandings reached in the negotiations because the army would not accept its requirement of leaving Baluchistan in two months and releasing from custody National Awami Party leaders who had fought the army in that province. Bhutto's indecision augured ill for the stability of the country. On July 5, 1977, the Pakistan army, led by Zia, staged a military coup, removed the government, arrested political leaders from both sides of the conflict, and imposed martial law.

The Bhutto years saw the apogee of Islamist activism. The government failed to reverse the erosion of state authority that had followed the fall of Ayub Khan and the loss of East Pakistan. Rather, the PPP's social, economic, and political policies produced an intractable opposition, whose activism continued to corrode state authority. That opposition took heart from Islamist activism led by the Jama'at and IJT, and, in turn, helped propel those forces to new heights of antiestablishment politics. In Pakistan there were no fissures among Islamist and ulama forces, nor did their ideological perspectives distinguish them, as was the case in Malaysia. In Pakistan the ABIM stance did not emerge, and, as a result, Islamism remained resolutely strident in its ideology and politics. Pakistan in the 1970s witnessed a full-fledged power struggle between Islamism and the state, the scope of which far exceeded that of Islamist politics in Malaysia. By 1977 Islamism in Pakistan was posed to overwhelm the state, only to be thwarted by a military coup.

Islamist activism also ensconced new assumptions, beliefs, and modes of behavior in Pakistan's politics that provided state leaders with new possibilities in managing state interests. Islamist ideology in Pakistan, too, advocated the creation of an omnipotent Islamic state that could resolve the problems facing the country. Islamists provided detailed signposts showing how the Islamic state was to be created, and more important, the extent of its powers, the scope of its control of society and economy, and the duties of the citizenry before it. Beyond its assurance of an Islamic order, the Islamic state promised a strong state with little or no resistance to its powers. As Islamists hacked at the roots of the postcolonial state, they instilled in Pakistanis the virtues of a strong state—albeit an Islamic one.[94]

At the critical juncture of 1977–80 in both Malaysia and Pakistan the postcolonial state faced a serious crisis. Its strategies of survival and efforts to shore up state authority and pursue economic development—NEP in Malaysia and the PPP's populism in Pakistan—had faced resistance. That resistance had parlayed into Islamist activism that threatened state authority and, in the case of Pakistan, came close to debunking the state altogether. State leaders were thus compelled to look for new ways in which to bolster state authority and augment its powers. The task of empowering the state would inevitably become anchored in the ideas and political tools of Islamism, for the decade of Islamist activism greatly affected social norms and values, and the relation of society to the state. Creating cadence between state and society compelled state leaders to take stock of the place of Islam in society and politics, and to repackage the state in accordance with the Islamist conception of the state.

III

HEART OF THE MATTER

5

Malaysia, 1981–1997

Islamization and Capitalist Development

In 1981 Mahathir Mohammad became the head of UMNO and prime minister of Malaysia. With Mahathir came profound changes in the nature and workings of the Malaysian state. It grew in power—as did UMNO—to oversee a prolonged period of economic growth and development in the country. All this occurred in tandem with state-sponsored Islamization, which instituted Islamic values and norms in society and politics with far-reaching impact on various aspects of Malaysian public life, societal relations, and economic transactions.

During the Islamization period (1981–1997) Malaysia experienced a period of great political stability. Factionalism within UMNO declined, and the party was able to exercise effective power through the absolute majority of a broad-based ruling coalition. This stability allowed the state to expand its powers as well. Islamization extended the reach of the state into the private lives of Malays, as well as into social and economic activities from which the state had until then been excluded. Islamization thus provided the state with more social control. The stronger state then oversaw economic development. By the close of the 1990s Malaysia's per capita GDP was close to $9,500 (having risen by 5.7% per annum on average during 1985–95 period), the annual GDP growth rate stood at 8.1% on average, life expectancy had risen to 71 and the literacy rate to 78.5%.[1] In the meantime absolute poverty had gone down to 12% from 49.3% in 1970.[2] At the time of the Asian financial crisis of 1997 Malaysia stood at the threshold of qualitative social and economic transformation, and held on to a lofty vision for its future—the much vaunted Vision 2020 that was introduced in 1991. Islamization was thus the handmaiden of empowerment of the state and economic growth. The contribution of Islamization to state power was not, however, in the new revenue extraction possibilities that it brought to the fore but in growth and supporting development.

Mahathir rose to the helm in Malaysia at a time of crisis for both UMNO and the state. The crisis before NEP was straining relations between the Malaysian political elite and Malay masses, and resurgent Islamism posed a serious challenge to the secular state. Mahathir saw the solution to the crisis in rapid growth and development, which would increase the size of the economic pie, thus relieving tensions between ethnic communities as well as within the Malay community. This was a task that required greater state control of the economy—although to put in place a different economic strategy than had NEP. The Mahathir era was not just one of state intervention in the economy on behalf of Malay interests, but of greater state intervention in the economy, *period*.[3] It was Mahathir's specified aim to erect a strong Malay-dominated capitalist state in Malaysia.[4]

This, in turn, required the state to overcome the resistance that confronted it and to create greater harmony in state-society relations. Since the main source of challenge to the ruling establishment in the late 1970s came from Islamism, which was also defining popular political attitudes and identity, the state had to contend with that force. Mahathir understood the challenge of Islamism, but also saw that ideology as a potential tool for empowerment of the state. As a result, he sought to co-opt rather than crush the Islamist opposition; to harness its energies and appropriate its popular political and ideological tools, rather than assert the primacy of the secular state by force. Mahathir understood that Islamism had already created a powerful social base, enjoyed wide popular support, and had convinced many Malays of the importance of the state—albeit an Islamic state—to veritable development. If the Malaysian state was willing to compromise on secularism, it stood to benefit from the fruits of a decade of Islamist activism just as it would subdue it as an oppositional force. For Mahathir, therefore, Islamization was a means to pursue capitalist development.

In addition, whereas UMNO's leadership had since 1957 viewed secularism of the party and the state to be essential for ethnic peace, Mahathir argued that it was a moderate Islamic UMNO and state that could provide ethnic peace. He argued for responding to Islamism with more Islam. Mahathir was not interested in Islamic revival, a fact that distinguishes him from General Zia ul-Haq in Pakistan. In fact, in many regards Mahathir has more in common with secular modernizers such as the shah in Iran than with Islamically oriented political leaders in the Middle East and South Asia. Nationalism expressed through pursuit of progress to carry the nation to great heights—Vision 2020 in Malaysia and the Great Civilization in the shah's Iran—the drive to empower and enrich the country through development and close alliance with the West, and the belief in the necessity of a top-down social and cultural revolution as a prelude to development were hallmarks of the shah of

Iran's leadership as well. Mahathir, however, was more sensitive to the importance of Islam to society and politics, and was more willing to compromise on
secularism to achieve a viable balance between religion and modernization.

As a veteran of politics in Kedah, where PAS is a force to contend with and
where local politics bore the influence of Islamic values, Mahathir was both
more sensitive to the importance of Islam to politics and less openly secular.
He favored grafting an Islamic national identity to the secular state in order
to strengthen it. Mahathir believed that UMNO faced a potential crisis. Students were coming back from abroad bearing the imprint of the Iranian revolution and ascendant Islamism. They were entering various walks of life and
were likely to choose PAS if the choice was between Islam and secularism.
The consequences of the exodus of the educated to PAS could be far- reaching.
In the early 1980s in many elections PAS candidates were better educated than
UMNO ones. This meant that as PAS would absorb the better educated and
Islamically oriented students it would become the party of the future, the party
of the elite (intellectually speaking) of Malays. UMNO could not afford to let
this to happen. Mahathir argued that unless UMNO was able to appropriate
the Islamic discourse PAS would dominate Islamic politics—recruit ABIM
workers and even absorb the student organization.[5]

If PAS were to become a force in national politics, there would be an up-
surge in radical Islamism that would be far more dangerous to ethnic peace
than would UMNO's moderate Islamic image. In 1982 elections PAS won
16% of the vote and five seats in the parliament.[6] Mahathir believed that these
modest numbers masked PAS's potential threat to UMNO's domination in
Malay politics. PAS continued to show strength in the four northern states of
Kelantan, Perlis, Kedah, and Terenganu, which are next to one another—and
hence, made PAS into a regional power—and which have an overwhelming
Malay majority. Control of Malay politics there could put PAS in the position
to influence Malay nationalism as well.

Through a moderate Islamic image UMNO would actually contain and
control Islam, and marginalize PAS in the process so as to preserve ethnic
peace.[7] The ethnic peace would provide for economic growth and development that would benefit minority economic interests as well as those of
Malays. Non-Malays accepted moderate Islamism as a necessary step to contain more radical Islamism.[8]

The same argument held for foreign investment, which was to be at the
crux of Mahathir's growth strategy. As early as 1978, Mahathir, who was then
minister of commerce and industry, argued that resistance of Islamist forces
to foreign investment was making things complicated. He suggested that
such investments had to be in accordance with Islam.[9] An "Islamic" state was
thus put forth as a prerequisite for growth and prosperity. UMNO and the
state would have to include both Islam and the private sector, and Islam had
to be interpreted in a manner to make such a feat possible.

Between 1975 and 1977 UMNO and PAS had cooperated in the Barisan Nasional. That alliance had, however, fallen apart. That experience had proved
to many in UMNO that there was little to be gained by ad hoc alliances with

Islamist parties and that UMNO and the state it controlled would do better by being in the position to directly control Islamism rather than rely on a third party to do so. Mahathir was perhaps the first UMNO leader to fully conceptualize the meaning and potential of reinventing the secular postcolonial state as an "Islamic" state.

Mahathir had been minister of education in the 1970s and had seen up close the scope of ABIM and Islamist student activism. He understood the extent of the influence of Islamist ideology on the Malay youth and saw that Islamism was not likely to dissipate easily, and that UMNO and the state would not quickly contain it. In addition, he was not personally as secular as his predecessors, and as an ardent Malay nationalist he had received support from ABIM in the past. In fact, Mahathir's "Look East" and "Buy British Last" policy[10] and criticism of Western values and imperialism had given him certain support in the constituencies that also supported ABIM or PAS.[11] In the 1990s his opposition to Western imperialism gave place to defense of Asian values.[12] This, too, was popular with the Islamic constituency as it defended cultural values that are closely tied to Islam in Malaysia. He was therefore not as adamant on secularism as were his predecessors, or his Middle Eastern counterparts. He was open to coexisting with Islam, co-opting Islamism, and conceptualizing the ideology of the state altogether differently. His aim was to create a stable political center under UMNO's leadership, through which the state could assert its prerogatives and manage the economy. The ideological underpinnings of that center would be moderate Islamism cum nationalism. Whereas in 1979–81 UMNO leadership was pushing for a crackdown on Islamism and such measures as banning the use of the term "Islamic" in party names, Mahathir did not favor a confrontational approach.

The crux of Mahathir's program was to revamp NEP and push forward with industrial deepening and economic growth.[13] State control of Islam was to facilitate this process. The Malaysian economy had traditionally been a mix of public and private sector. Malays had been generally active in the public sector—especially through NEP—whereas the private sector had been largely dominated by Chinese business interests. Mahathir wanted to open the private sector to Malays as well. He was supportive of NEP's use of public enterprises to acquire assets for Malays, but believed that this was not enough.[14] NEP limited the Malay economic role to the public sector, and then as shareholders rather than entrepreneurs. NEP, moreover, made Malays dependent on Chinese entrepreneurship.[15] He argued that Malays ought to be the vanguard force in industrial development as entrepreneurs rather than as overseer bureaucrats.[16] Under Mahathir NEP's emphasis on eradication of poverty as the means to uplift Malays gave place to creating a Malay entrepreneurial and capitalist class.

Hence, despite its claim to representing all Malays, after 1980 UMNO and the state became increasing tied to the Malay business elite—to some extent in lieu of the party and the state's traditional ties to the Malay middle classes. UMNO and the state relied to an increasing extent on Malay capitalists to spearhead growth and uplift of Malays, and to this end encouraged foreign investment and provided corporate welfare. Middle-class Malays supported this development to some extent, but rural Malays—PAS's base of support in the north—were opposed to it.[17] The size of the middle class had grown to 32.6% of the population from 20% in 1970, and that of the peasantry had declined from 56.4% to 28.3% during the same time period. Still, the peasantry constituted close to 30% of the population, and 21.3% of the 32.6% middle class were the less privileged and more Islamically conscious lower middle classes.[18]

Since UMNO's support for Malay capitalists is depicted as a nationalist project, then it has to be tied to debates over Malay nationalism, to which Islam is relevant. Therefore, embarking on the project of creating a Malay capitalist class required UMNO to gain control of Islamic politics, and to define Islamic values for Malays so as to prevent an alliance between the middle and lower classes around an Islamic demand for social justice.

Mahathir turned to the East Asian model of development, emphasizing export-led growth. The strategy proved successful. In the 1980s the growth rate stood at 7–9% a year on average and per capita income rose above $2,000; manufacturing was 26% of GDP, and 50% of manufacturing was export oriented.[19] State-run enterprises continued to play a central role in the economy, but the private sector became more important to growth. A privatization initiative opened the economy to foreign investment and more aggressive entrepreneurial activity.[20] The growing private sector was dominated by foreign and Chinese interests, but soon included Malay businesses as well. Mahathir was particularly keen on this development. He argued that a viable Malay entrepreneurial community must be nurtured to serve the economic interests of Malays. He was aware that NEP fostered dependency on the state and was not compatible with nurturing entrepreneurial skills. If there was to be a strong Malay presence in the private sector, then the state need not represent Malay interests through NEP's policy of acquisition of industrial assets. In fact, all such assets could be turned over to Malay businesses. Mahathir therefore was willing to reduce the role of the state in the market, provided that it would be replaced by Malay rather than Chinese business interests. The problem was that in the early 1980s there did not exist a viable Malay entrepreneurial community. It had to be created. According to Mahathir, "the best way to keep shares between Bumiputra hands is to hand them over to the Bumiputra most capable of retaining them, which means the well-to-do."[21]

Mahathir was committed to promoting Malay capitalism. He openly advocated emergence of Malay millionaires.[22] From 1980 onward the government encouraged the rise of Malay-owned conglomerates. The result was the emergence of very wealthy Malay entrepreneurs with close ties to party leaders such as Daim Zainuddin.[23] The rise of the private sector, however, also increased the state's control of the economy. Through support for new business ventures as well as UMNO-business alliances the scope of state intervention in the economy expanded—although the intervention was not direct.

Mahathir also believed that the development of Malay capitalism required changes in attitudes toward work and the economy. For him development was

first and foremost built on correct values that could then support technological leaps and industrial deepening.[24] His Look East policy had meant looking
to Japan and South Korea as "values" models.[25] In those cases he saw qualities
of hard work, discipline, loyalty, group cohesion, order, and cleanliness. These
were characteristics that were key to development, and that Mahathir saw
lacking in Malaysia, especially among Malays.[26] He blamed poverty on the
unwillingness of Malays to work, show initiative, and take advantages of economic opportunities. He reiterated colonial-era characterizations of Malays
as lazy and uninterested in work. In 1982 he asserted, "We are not worka-
holics. We think we should be."[27] NEP is not just division of assets and patronage, he asserted, but it also meant that Malays had to work.[28] Mahathir
did not, however, believe that Malay culture and religion was inherently anti-
capitalist. Rather, it was the misunderstanding of Islamic teachings in the cultural life of Malays as well as in their politics that was responsible for dilemmas
that Malays faced. NEP had, moreover, further entrenched these tendencies.
Correct interpretation and application of Malay and Islamic beliefs and
mores could support capitalism. In 1982 he compared Malaysia and Japan,
concluding that the Japanese "are not very religious, but their cultural values
are akin to the kind of morals and ethics that we have in this country or would
like to acquire in this country. They may not be praying all the time but . . .
[for them] profit is not everything."[29]

In Islamist activism of the 1970s Mahathir saw the means to change local
values to support economic growth. For that activism had shown altogether
different character traits than those Mahathir had associated with Malays.
ABIM and its allies had been disciplined and hardworking, and they had promoted positive work ethics and values for governance and social relations.
Mahathir thus turned to Islam to articulate the values and ethics that were
necessary for the development of Malay capitalism, setting in motion the as-
similation of Islamic values (*penyerapan nilai-nilai Islam*) into state policy
making. The government promoted the values of justice, honesty, efficiency,
dedication, diligence, and self-discipline as Islamic values for government
administration as well as entrepreneurial activity.[30] In numerous speeches
Mahathir characterized the ideal civil servant as *berish, cekap, dan amanah*
(clean, efficient, trustworthy).[31] In the early 1980s seminars for government
administrators advocated hard work in the context of Islamic belief and practice.[32] The government also argued that economic development could not be
devoid of spirituality—that development needed spiritual regeneration and a
morally upright society.[33] The Fourth Development Plan (1981–86) specified
commitment to Islam.

Mahathir used Islam to revamp state administration, and in essence defined the state as an "Islamic developmental state." Malaysia's entire strategy
of growth from the 1980s on, changes in the bureaucracy, and the rise of a
Malay private sector were all tied to the burgeoning Islamization strategy.[34]

Since Malay entrepreneurs were to assume control of enterprises that had
hitherto been under the control of the bureaucracy, the latter could not oversee the formation of the former as had been the case in East Asia. As a result,

the task of creating and nurturing a Malay private sector was directly over-seen by UMNO, and the circle of advisors close to Mahathir, notably Daim Zainuddin. This opened the door to close business-party relations,[35] creating corruption, mismanagement, and income inequality.[36] It also changed the image and distribution of power in UMNO. As UMNO became dominated by businessmen and pursued private-sector development, it encountered some problems with its traditional base of support. This time, the problems of equality and social justice were not ethnic and intercommunal, but internal to the Malay community. The drive for Chinese-Malay parity thus created social tensions in the Malay community.[37] These tensions, in turn, made it neces-sary that the state maintain control of Islamic politics, both to provide legiti-macy for its development strategy and to reduce the possibility of Islamism spearheading an effective social resistance. Thus, the game of ethnic parity went hand in hand with concentration of power in the state.[38]

Export-led growth required keeping the price of labor down while the gov-ernment supported the enrichment of the Malay capitalists who managed the business ventures. This made the ruling order susceptible to the kind of rhet-oric that ABIM had used against UMNO in the 1970s. Export-led growth also required including women in the labor force to a greater extent, which had been criticized by PAS.[39] The problem was all the more serious since in the early 1980s Malaysia experienced an economic downturn owing to declining oil and tin prices and a recession in its export markets.[40] It is therefore not co-incidental that the Islamization initiative was launched during the 1982–86 time period when the economy was in the throes of a recession, and when UMNO was becoming more entangled with capitalist interests and corruption.

The government was also concerned with the implications of Islamist ac-tivism for foreign investment and also for Malaysia's international image. Export-led development was reliant on foreign investment and required fa-vorable reception of Malaysian goods in foreign markets. In the early 1980s the government was wary of Islamist reaction to foreign investment.[41] It therefore sought to cloak itself in Islam in order to minimize resistance.[42] For instance in 1981 the finance minister declared that the government intended to create a new economic system that would be compatible with Islam.[43] Simi-larly, the government was concerned about Islamic extremism, emphasis on imposition of strict Islamic legal codes, and a theocratic and intolerant image for Malaysia. Not only would this disturb the ethnic peace that underpinned economic growth,[44] but it would also damage Malaysia's international image, with implications for its trade earnings. This was especially a concern be-cause in the 1980s Malaysia became the world's largest exporter of compo-nents assembled and tested—mainly in electronics and then mainly for American firms.[45] Malaysia was thus highly dependent on the global econ-omy and the United States in particular. Given tensions between Iran and the United States in the 1980s and generally the negative image that Islam had in the United States, Islamist activism was viewed with concern by the powers-that-be. Mahathir was eager to keep Islamism moderate and away from radi-cal influences from the Middle East. Throughout the 1980s and the 1990s, just as Malaysia promoted Islamization it kept its distance from Iran.[46] Throughout the Mahathir period, despite symbolic concessions to Islam, Malaysia's foreign policy has been guided by the needs of export-led growth and the imperative of globalization.[47] It has been oriented primarily toward ASEAN rather than the Muslim world.[48] In fact, commitment to ASEAN required a more moderate approach to the question of Islam in politics in order to avoid complicating Malaysia's relations with Indonesia as well as with Burma, Cambodia, the Philippines, Thailand, and Singapore, which have significant Muslim minorities—with separatist tendencies in the Philippines and Thailand.

Since 1980 the government has shown great sensitivity to those expressions of Islam that could adversely affect Malaysia's image. In 1993 when PAS announced that it passed a bill in the Kelantan state assembly to implement punitive strictures of Islamic law (*hudood*) it faced stiff resistance from Mahathir.[49] He has in addition criticized regulating interaction of the sexes, and in 1996 when demands for strict observation of modest dress by women (*hijab*) created a furor, he remarked, "Everyone looks to our Islam, some here look to Islam elsewhere." Not only did he defend moderation, but also by casting it as Malaysian Islam versus "outsider's" Islam, he placed advocates of harsher Islamism on the defensive. He also hoisted moderate Islam as a Malaysian export product, one that could affect Islam elsewhere, arguing that "[h]ow Malaysia handles Islam will directly affect world perceptions of Islam in general."[50] This approach also related to Malaysian pride and ambition, and hence gave moderate Islam a nationalist dimension. Mahathir thus early on set the tone for the state's strategy of defining the "Islamist middle," occupying it, and asserting its hegemony. In 1982 he declared that "Islam is a pragmatic and flexible religion which takes into account the condition of the day."[51] This was not only to keep Islamism moderate but also ensure state control of Islam, and full utilization of whatever means to power Islamism could provide the state.

The government decided that to tackle these issues it would have to assume control of the Islamic discourse. In a manner that was reminiscent of Ayub Khan's attempt to reinterpret Islam in the service of development in Pakistan in the 1960s, Mahathir set out to wrest control of interpretation of Islam and to promote a version of Islamism that would be compatible with Malaysia's economic growth strategy. To do this successfully, however, the government would have to co-opt or marginalize other contenders for interpreting Islamism—ABIM and PAS in particular. Moreover, the state had to be viewed as a genuine Islamic actor. It would have to be in a position to claim that it is more Islamic than any other force in the political arena.[52] It was in this spirit that in 1984 Mahathir responded to PAS's accusations that UMNO is "un-Islamic" (*kafir*, lit. infidel or unbeliever) by challenging PAS to a television debate to see who is more Islamic.[53] In the 1990s Mahathir would announce with confidence that even the Prophet of Islam could not have done more for Islam than he had. In later years as he received the accolades of the Muslim world—including the prestigious Faisal Award from Saudi Arabia for services rendered to Islam—he became bolder in responding to Islamist critiques of his policies.

The attempt to gain control of the flow of Islam in politics first led to an intricate policy of managing Islamist groups, and then to the Islamization initiative. The government devised a multipronged approach to containing and managing Islamism and curbing its extremism. It sought to co-opt moderate Islamist forces, marginalize and silence the extremists, and generally regulate all Islamic activity—which would be tantamount to extension of state reach into the private sphere.[54] The first was necessary in order to provide the government with legitimacy to undertake the other two. It was with this in mind that Mahathir began to "Islamize" UMNO's image and made a bid for co-opting ABIM.

Soon after he became prime minister Mahathir began to change UMNO's image. In 1981 UMNO declared that it was "the largest Islamic party in Malaysia" and that undermining it would damage Muslim and Malay interests.[55] Shortly thereafter UMNO leadership declared UMNO to be "the largest Islamic party in the world,"[56] and asserted that to "oppose the policies of UMNO was to also oppose Islam as UMNO was set up to champion the cause of Islam."[57] Mahathir then went further, charging the party to assume the role of the principal advocate of Islamization in Malaysia. He told UMNO:

> UMNO defeated the Malayan Union. UMNO won independence. UMNO redeemed the dignity of the colonized Malays. UMNO has preserved and upheld Islam in Malaysia. UMNO has ruled justly and brought about development, and many other things. These are the results of UMNO's struggle. But I repeat, UMNO's struggle has not ended. Today we face the biggest struggle—the struggle to change the attitude of the Malays in line with the requirements of Islam in this modern age. . . . UMNO's task now is to enhance Islamic practices and ensure that the Malay community truly adheres to Islamic teachings. . . . Naturally this cause is far bigger than the previous struggles of UMNO. Of course it is not easy to succeed. But UMNO must pursue it, whatever the obstacles, for this is our real cause.[58]

UMNO even sent teachers to villages and *kampongs* (traditional Malay villages) to teach the peasants to equate UMNO with Islam.[59] UMNO's turn to Islam began Islamizing the state to the extent that UMNO and state were not separable.[60]

This set the stage for UMNO's bid for ABIM. Mahathir had known Anwar since the 1970s, and the two were distantly related and held one another in high esteem.[61] Mahathir was a new breed of UMNO leader. He, much like Anwar, was an outsider to the ruling circle. He did not come from an aristocratic background, and, much like Anwar, came from a humble background—which in both their cases included Indian migrants. Mahathir too, had been antiestablishment and had at one point been expelled from UMNO. Mahathir was aware that with the existing UMNO leadership the party could not oppose PAS and might lose control of Malay politics. UMNO had strong nationalist credentials, but if Malay politics was to be dominated by Islam UMNO could not afford to be out of touch with it and leave Islam to PAS. ABIM could supply Islamic legitimacy to UMNO, and provide it with intellectual and organizational tools to control Islam.

Mahathir had viewed much of the *dakwah* activity of the 1970s as retro-gressive and too radical in tone.[62] In his book *The Challenge* (1976) he criti-cized *dakwahs* for removing Malays from modern society and diverting their attention from pursuit of economic development. However, Mahathir saw ABIM differently. ABIM had a modern profile; it called for Islamic revival, but its principal aim was to change Malaysia, espousing values and goals that were not all that different from those Mahathir advocated.

Mahathir met with Anwar, and argued that ABIM was more likely to have an impact on state and society in Malaysia if it were to join with UMNO than with PAS. UMNO was the best vehicle for Islamization. He furthermore ar-gued that it was not time to push for full-fledged Islamization, but Malaysia could move in that direction.[63] Mahathir in effect argued that he favored a grad-ual Islamizaiton approach, postponing full Islamization to some future point in time, but showing concrete progress in that direction. PAS was arguing for either full Islamization, or, at least, greater commitment to progress in that di-rection.[64] Not only was PAS's ideology too strident to be mainstream, but PAS was not an actor at the center. Mahathir also promised Anwar that UMNO would serve as an appropriate vehicle for the realization of ABIM's goals.

ABIM then faced a choice, joining PAS in a grand Islamic alliance against UMNO or joining UMNO after it indicated it was turning away from secu-larism toward Islam in 1981–82. Anwar favored joining UMNO, for it pro-vided for greater consensus in the Malay community, whereas an ABIM-PAS alliance would have opened a wide chasm at the center of Malay politics and society. In addition, Anwar agreed with Mahathir that PAS's ideology was a threat to ethnic peace, and was likely to undermine economic growth and po-litical stability. At the time young firebrand ulama, who had been educated at al-Azhar in Egypt or at Medina University or Darul Ulum of Mecca in Saudi Arabia had taken over PAS and pushed it to radicalism. The lay-educated ABIM would have been uncomfortable in an ulama-dominated party. Anwar believed that if ABIM merged into PAS a clash between ulama and their ways and the lay Islamists would have been inevitable. In the end, Anwar was not confortable with an organization that was dominated by the ulama, particu-larly ones with radical leanings.

PAS was also strong in northern Malaysia, where the scope of influence of Islamic orthodoxy had been different from in southern Malaysia where local cultures and customs held sway. Although PAS offered Anwar the presidency of the party, Anwar saw in UMNO a more influential vehicle for change.

ABIM also had to consider that it would face far more pressure from the government if it were to remain in the opposition. In 1981 the government passed the Societies (Amendment) Act of 1981 to control extremists.[65] Al-though the act, which strengthened the Societies Act of 1966, was meant to curb the activities of extremist and deviant *dakwahs,* its ultimate target would have been ABIM. Direct confrontation would have radicalized ABIM in a manner that Anwar was not willing to accept. Anwar understood that UMNO and the state's control was too strong for ABIM to become anything but a marginal force as PAS had been. PAS, in the meantime, hoped to use ABIM to break UMNO's clientalist hold on Malay politics. It was better, concluded Anwar, to join the system rather than fight it.

The rank and file of ABIM were not supportive of Anwar, nor were all members of UMNO keen on "Islamizing" the party. Whereas Anwar had some following among UMNO youth, the old guard was opposed to dealing with ABIM. For instance, Tunku Abdul-Rahman openly opposed Anwar's admission into UMNO, arguing that UMNO was a secular nationalist party.

In 1982 Anwar resigned from ABIM and joined UMNO. Without Anwar ABIM lost much of its power and influence. It continues to operate as a semi-official youth movement—however, without the same energy and influence that characterized its activism in the 1970s. Many ABIM leaders and sympathizers followed Anwar into UMNO, or joined the bureaucracy and the private sector. In subsequent years Anwar was able to use these ABIM alumni to strengthen his own position in UMNO. Anwar would rise quickly in the ranks in UMNO, first as youth leader, but subsequently in the national cabinet as minister of culture, minister of finance, deputy prime minister, and acting prime minister in 1997. He was dismissed from his official positions and tried for corruption and sexual misconduct in 1998, an event that marked a turning point for the Islamization regime and that will be discussed in the Conclusion.

Anwar's entry into UMNO gave the party's new "Islamic" orientation legitimacy and credibility—not only because of ABIM's Islamic credentials, but also because at the time Anwar symbolized global resurgence of Islam in Malaysia.[66] Anwar's decision proved to be a turning point for UMNO and the ideological underpinnings of Malay politics. It could be read as either Islamization of Malay nationalism or pragmatic Malay nationalism co-opting elements of Islamism to stave off the tidal wave of global Islamic resurgence.[67] UMNO and the state forced changes on Islamism through Anwar, but were themselves conquered by the moderate Islamism that they promoted as the foil to PAS and the more radical Islamism that was emerging across the Muslim world at the time. In time Anwar became an UMNO politician and built an impressive political base of support within the party.[68] By the time of his dismissal in 1998, his career was directed at securing the premiership rather than ensuring Islamic revival.

Anwar's most important contribution to UMNO and the state was to legitimate the conceptual foundations of Mahathir's intended Islamization initiative. Mahathir wanted to define Islamism as a moderate ideology that would accommodate pluralism, capitalism, globalization, and Malaysia's foreign policy. It would provide Malays with positive work ethics and social values, but would not insist on rejecting modernity and sequestering Malays from the pursuit of wealth. For him there was no point in having Islamic revival (for revival's sake) unless it led to material advancement and progress of Muslims. Serving Malays was serving Islam, but not vice versa. Revival had to accommodate Muslim economic, social, and technological needs. Islamization was not so much about law and politics as it was about values and progress.[69] This was a daring posture that Mahathir could advocate without more credible Islamic credentials. Anwar and ABIM had those credentials. In time, Anwar would also prove to be an articulate spokesman of that approach, in many ways appropriating that discourse from Mahathir.[70] In the end, Mahathir and Anwar reduced Islamic views on economic issues to concerns for human dignity—a broad concept that allowed capitalist development. Accumulation of wealth and capitalism would be acceptable so long as they would not degrade human dignity.[71] The concern for human dignity conveniently became a justification for favoring Malays, and favoring Malays was equated with Islamization.[72] By the time of the Seventh Development Plan (1996–2000) Islamic rhetoric was openly used to justify government support for Malay businesses.[73]

In addition, Islamization was used to strengthen ties of patronage between Malays and UMNO and the state. The flow of resources to various social groups in the name of Islam benefited Malays only. In fact, Islamization in many regards became the means of providing resources to Malays. For instance, when in 1983 the government established the International Islamic University, it rejected the proposal for the Chinese Merdeka (Independence) University. The International Islamic University was for all practical purposes a Malay venture; however, since it was not defined as an ethnic undertaking but a religious one, the government did not feel compelled to provide to the Chinese community in kind.

Anwar put forth a moderate and inclusive vision of Islamism that embraced globalization and capitalism along with cultural pluralism within Malaysia as well as the region, and deemphasized Islamic revival as understood in the Islamist ideological literature. He carefully distinguished between the "Southeast Asian" view of Islam that is tolerant of minorities and is open to capitalist development and the West and the Middle Eastern and South Asian views on Islam that are more exclusionist.[74] He argued that Buddhism has imparted a psychological condition on Islam in Southeast Asia, namely, that salvation is generally a personal matter, and hence notions about the needs of an Islamic social order do not have cadence with Malay culture. Anwar's ideas soon found regional support, especially in the views of Indonesia's Abdurrahman Wahid, who also advocates an inclusive and pluralist view of Islam.[75] Anwar later further embellished these ideas to produce a more comprehensive vision for Malaysia's role in the region and the Islamic world in a book entitled *The Asian Renaissance* (1997).

Anwar argued that Islamic values and lessons of its history must be first rediscovered, and only then recovered—that is, made into the basis of society and politics. This meant a gradualist approach to Islamization that would conveniently postpone full Islamization to a distant future. Anwar's line of reasoning also meant that Islamic ideals, symbols, and thinkers would be appropriated and defined by the state to serve its own ends. In 1996–97 Institut Kajian Dasar (Institute of Policy Studies), Anwar's main policy-making think tank, held a series of conferences on key Islamic revivalist thinkers, such as Jamal al-Din Al-Afghani and Muhammad Iqbal, in conjunction with non-Muslim Asian thinkers, such as José Rizal and Rabindranath Tagore, in the context of Anwar's Asian renaissance approach. The aim of the conference was to redefine these figures in such a fashion that their life's work would support Malaysia's conception of Islamization.

Tolerance of pluralism in effect argued against imposition of Islamic law, which has been the bedrock of Islamism across the Muslim world. UMNO argued that it was not possible to treat the Chinese and Indians as *dhimmis* (non-Muslims that are accorded special rights by Islamic law and are subject to a poll tax) and to make them subservient to Islamic law without shattering the ethnic peace and undermining economic growth on which the Malays depended. This line of reasoning was convincing to most Malays outside of PAS. This meant that the Chinese and Malays had a right to engage in activities that were proscribed by Islamic law, such as gambling, consumption of alcohol, or patronizing bars, Western-style restaurants, and clubs. These activities would be available in Malaysia, but technically for the minorities only. The government would ban Malays from such activities to the extent possible—such as forbidding Muslims from entering casinos in Malaysia—but generally it was up to Muslims to adopt a "moral filter" and avoid harmful activities. Thus it was not up to the state to act as the moral police, but individual Muslims should accept responsibility for their own morality. This also meant that an Islamic society for Malays does not need Islamization of the state or the Malaysian society as a whole.

This live-and-let-live approach—and especially absolving the state of the responsibility of ensuring Islamicity—is clearly at odds with the directives of Islamist ideology and was opposed by PAS as unacceptable. It was, however, popular with urban Malays, who understood the importance of cultural pluralism to economic stability and prosperity. In sum, this was a happy compromise between Islamization and open society. The state would push for Islamizing Malays but keep Malaysia pluralist and open, a distinction that was not convincing to all, and a segment of Malays continued to support PAS—which recovered in 1990 by winning elections in Kelantan to UMNO's embarrassment—and other small *dakwah* movements. Nor was the pursuit of capitalist development readily compatible with Islamization—even the government version.[76] PAS's electoral victory in Kelantan, forming the government in that state, proved that the center's domination over Islamic discourse was far from complete. Still, by and large the UMNO-ABIM combine managed to dominate the Islamist scene in Malaysia and to ensconce its vision of moderate, inclusionary, and prodevelopment Islam in society and politics.

Ideological hegemony, in turn, gave legitimacy and support for official regulation of Islamic life and thought. The state set out to draw clear boundaries for Islamic activism and social institutions. It accepted *dakwahs* if they would avoid revolutionary activism, would not insist on implementation of Islamic law (especially *hudood* laws), would not divide Malays into "real" and "nominal" Muslims, would accede to the state's view of Islam as tolerant and inclusionary, would support education and economic development, and would not demand of their followers beliefs and modes of behavior that would be inimical to modernization. *Dakwahs* that did not fit this image were defined as "false" (*dakwah songsang*).[77] The government would use the Societies Act to suppress the activities of these *dakwahs*. In 1983 the government cited forty-five groups with 40,000 members as targets for suppression.[78] A number of the more radical Islamic peasant movements were crushed by the state, most notably after the revolt of Ibrahim Mahmud, a renegade activist with ties to PAS, which involved the use of the military and left thirteen dead and 159 wounded.[79] In 1994 the government shut down the largest rural *dakwah* movement, al-Arqam—whose cultlike organizational setup and sartorial distinction flew in the face of the dominant view of Islam.[80] The government also looked to end student radicalism abroad. In 1983 it introduced a program of socializing students before going abroad as well as after their return, and sent ulama overseers to supervise Malay students.[81]

While the attempt to prune the *dakwahs* was initially directed at moderating Islamism, it soon extended into a policy of extending state's reach by assuring it of uncontested domination in the Islamic arena. The elimination of the al-Arqam was justified in terms of the movement's deviation from accepted *dakwah* beliefs and behavior. However, the government was also motivated by the fact that in the 1990s al-Arqam expanded its social and economic activities. The al-Arqam developed strong business networks, marketing, and production of goods, especially in rural areas, and increased its investments abroad, all without use of government loans, subsidies, or other support. Not only did this accomplishment threaten the logic of the "trusteeship" relationship that ties Malays to UMNO and the state, but it purported to create social and economic arenas outside of state control. The threat to UMNO and the state's primacy and domination over Malay society and economy was thus eliminated through the state's Islamic policy.

Generally, Mahathir favored uniformalizing Malay Islam as a necessary prerequisite for development. This meant that the phenomenon of *dakwahs,* with their particular readings of Islam and their tendency to create separate communities within the larger Malay community, were at odds with the the state's agenda. Hence, the government also cracked down on Sufism and missionary movements such as the Ahmediyah after 1982. The government strongly discouraged conversion to Shi'ism that had gained currency after the Iranian revolution. UMNO even justified its objection to PAS in similar terms. However, UMNO stopped short of denouncing *dakwah* as an institution, and in place of the *dakwahs* it closed down established its own *dakwah*. In 1981–82 the government even appointed its own "*dakwah* attaches" to its embassies abroad.[82]

The tendency to use Islam to expand state power and reach was also evident in UMNO and the state's dealings with the sultans and ulama. Whereas ABIM, PAS, and *dakwahs* were a threat to the state, sultans and ulama were traditional institutions that merely impeded consolidation of power under UMNO in the federal center. Mahathir believed in the necessity of a united Malay society and polity under a single political leadership dominated by UMNO. He therefore was opposed to those political structures that divided the Malay community into smaller political units (the sultans) or claimed leadership over them (sultans and ulama).[83] In 1983 Mahathir moved to reduce the powers of the sultans by introducing a bill to the parliament that would reduce the scope of the sultans' veto power over government legislation.[84] The sultans were tied to the ulama, their office had religious symbolism, and most religious laws were in the domain of states in which they were the nominal sovereigns. The issue therefore had religious significance. Mahathir's move against the sultans was popular with middle-class Malays.[85] It was, however, feasible because the state benefited from its claim to Islamism. Islamist ideology in Malaysia was disdainful toward the sultans and *adat* (custom, tradition)—although after Mahathir's challenge they grew closer to PAS—and favored a centralized republican state. Mahathir took full advantage of Islamism's opposition to monarchy—fully expounded upon by the principal ideologues of Islamism such as Khomeini or Mawdudi—and extended the federal center's claim to the powers of the sultans, and those federal religious bureaucracies to state level ones, all under the pretext of fulfilling an Islamist demand: replacing monarchy with Islam.[86] In fact, Anwar's entry into UMNO went hand in hand with relocating adminstration of Islamic affairs away from Malay states to the federal government, which Anwar initiated in his first official post in the prime minister's office dealing with Islamic affairs.[87]

In the 1990s Mahathir and Anwar would continue to nibble at the sultans' powers using Islam as a cover. In 1992–93 federal-level *shariah* courts ruled against immunity of sultans from prosecution.[88] The government argued that variations between interpretation and application of Islamic laws in various states were harmful to Malay society, and at any rate since the Malaysian state at the center was more Islamic—and "genuinely" Islamic—than the sultans' administrations, it was the appropriate seat for interpretation and application of a single Islamic legal code. Since 1987 the government has sought to uniformalize the working of Islamic law (*shariah*) courts in various states and to move some of their function to the federal level, and has even upgraded the status of *shariah* judges in order to facilitate these measures.[89] Since 1996 there has been an attempt to integrate *shariah* courts (that oversee family law) with other courts that are based on English common law.

Mahathir and Anwar were no doubt keen to reduce the power of state courts after Kelantan state's decision to implement *hudood* laws in 1993. Wresting control of Islam from the various states would eliminate such a possibility. Throughout the 1990s Mahathir supported the work of the feminist Islamic group, Sisters in Islam, who favored centralization of application of Islamic law in order to close loopholes in enforcement of divorce and polygamy laws that result from differences in various states' laws. In addition, Sisters in Islam believed that women would fare better before a lay Islamic bureaucracy in Kuala Lumpur than before ulama in provincial settings.

UMNO and the state's triumph in its showdown with the sultans in 1983–84 led to greater authoritarianism. With no real resistance before its authority, and having successfully adopted an Islamic image and already expanded its powers, the state began to assert itself prerogatives more clearly. In 1988 Mahathir moved to weaken the judiciary by cutting the powers of the judges and removing their autonomy from the executive branch.[90] The assertive state thus began to use its power to consolidate its position and to cut down those legal and civil society institutions that impeded its exercise of authority.

The ulama presented a more complex challenge. The religious divines exercise a great deal of influence on Malay religious and social life, but do not form a single organization with clear-cut boundaries. Moreover, the nature of its interaction with the state has been varied. Whereas many ulama, especially in northern Malaysia, have traditionally followed PAS, the Grand Mufti and the government-sponsored ulama congregation, Majlis Ugama, and the National Fatwa (Religious Decrees) Council have supported the central government, most notably in contending with extremist *dakwahs* after 1974.[91] Religious decrees (*fatwas*) by ulama in the National Fatwa Council and Pusat Islam (Islamic center) were used against the al-Arqam, after which their properties were seized and offices closed.[92] The government's desire to reduce the ulama's powers stemmed from the belief that, first, the ulama were a retrogressive force whose influence on society would subvert modernization and, second, the ulama were also a powerful social institution whose influence could serve state interests. The state could penetrate society under the aegis of the ulama if it were to co-opt them. The Islamic image of the state provided such a possibility.

The government has protected ulama power, but sought to limit it to "those [who are] truly versed in Islam and have given proof of their adherence to and reverence for the teachings of Islam,"[93] that is, those who are moderate, apolitical, and accommodating toward state policy.

Mahathir greatly used Anwar and ABIM as the means of wresting power from the ulama by claiming support from a class of "lay" keepers of religion whose popular ideology was not kind to the ulama. Anwar and ABIM have served to legitimate both the state's claim to speak for Islam in lieu of the ulama, and a lay bureaucratic management of Islam through state institutions.

The government has been generally supportive of anti-ulama modernist interpretations. Sisters in Islam's feminist critique of the ulama receives government backing, as do modernist works such as the controversial book by Kassem Ahmad that was published in 1986 and that rejected aspects of Islamic belief. Ahmad was close with UMNO, and the book was withdrawn only after vociferous opposition by PAS and the ulama.[94] It has, however, been clear that the ulama cannot be easily challenged through such means. The government has therefore sought to establish tight control over them by defining, controlling, and even bureaucratizing the ulama—standardizing their education, licensing their practice, and organizing them hierarchically, all to control them and to limit their political potential. The aim is to use the ulama's position to sanction policy and to use their social-religious role to enhance state capacity. Already in 1982 the federal government had over 100 ulama employed in the prime minister's office and 715 in the ministry of education.[95] Ulama associations and councils such as the Persatuan Ulama Malaysia (Malaysian Ulama Association [PUM]), Pusat Islam (Islamic Center), and the religious affairs division of the prime minister's office featured in policy making. Still, the state's control over the ulama remained tenuous, and increase in it involved conflict.

A principal arena of conflict is mosques and preaching. Over the course of the past two decades the government has invested massively in mosque building across Malaysia. Beyond its symbolic value, this undertaking has been a means of establishing the state's presence in every village and hamlet. The government provides preachers and ulama for these mosques, which ensures that local Islam remains politically subservient. The extension of state power into regulation of mosques was made possible by its Islamic image. That image did not, however, remove all resistance. Many ulama and PAS members have refused to accept government preachers and continue to congregate around their own preachers. Others have created their own small places of worship (*surau,* equivalent of Arabic *musalla*) to compete with state-controlled mosques.[96] The government has, in turn, sought to establish a licensing system on preachers, forbidding unlicensed preachers from government mosques, which in many areas are the only mosques. For instance, in March 1982 the Islamic Council of Kuala Lumpur declared that "no one without official permits from the council is allowed to preach Islam in mosques [in the city]." In November a bill was introduced to the parliament to make it illegal to challenge religious authority of the Council, or build a mosque without permit."[97] As a result, mosques and preaching has become an arena for struggle between PAS and UMNO, the state and the ulama. The state's success here would end the autonomy of the ulama and transform them into a state institution—expanding the scope of the state's social control significantly.

The government has also sought to gain control of the training of ulama. Most ulama are trained in religious seminaries in Malaysia and across Southeast Asia. Increasingly, they have received their education in Egypt, Saudi Arabia, Pakistan, and India. Neek Abdul-Aziz, the PAS chief minister (Mentari Besar) of Kelantan, was, for instance, educated at the seminary of Deoband in India. The government views the Middle Eastern and South Asian influence on the ulama to be retrogressive and politically radical. It prefers educating them in Malaysia. Foreign education also makes it impossible for the government to control the education of the ulama. The government has proposed establishing the University College of Islamic Studies of Malaysia outside of Kuala Lumpur to train ulama. If this scheme were to prove successful, it would further increase the state's control over the thinking and social function of the ulama, and through them social and political attitudes of Malays.

The Islamization Policies

In order to control the flow of Islam in politics UMNO and the state had to operate as a legitimate Islamic actor. This required formulating and implementing policies that would fulfill the popular demands for a greater role for Islam in society and politics. This led the state to put forward a broad-based Islamization program in 1983 that included law, the economy, social relations, and politics. It involved much use of Islamic symbols, but also changed many aspects of Malay as well as Malaysian society and politics. Initially, state-led Islamization was based on three initiatives: the establishment of an Islamic financial sector, an Islamic higher education system, and an Islamic bureaucracy. The creation of an Islamic bank, and the International Islamic University—along with the introduction of courses on Islamic civilization for university students—and expansion of the religious bureaucracy at the center were the pillars of Islamization.

Islamist ideology has included demands for an "Islamic economy" as a part of its promised utopian order. An Islamic economy is to operate free of interest rates and would provide social justice, equity, and harmony.[98] Credible Islamization, therefore, had to include financial and economic transactions as well. Muslim states have found it easier to accommodate Islamism on economic issues than on political ones. Moreover, they have seen Islamic economics to be a useful means of gaining some Islamic legitimacy. As a result, Muslim states from North Africa to Southeast Asia have created Islamic financial institutions. These, however, operate on the margins of the regular economy and cater to a minority of economic actors, while providing the state with Islamic legitimacy. In Pakistan in the 1980s interest-free banking dominated the financial sector, but accounted for only a fraction of banking services, over 90% of was which were carried out by foreign banks.

Malaysia was no exception to this trend. Islamic banking was introduced by the government in 1983 as an option in the banking sector for those who wished to engage in interest-free banking. Islamic banking did not apply to the banking sector in its entirety. Bank Islam Malaysia was established with government support, which accounted for 30% of its paid-up capital—the remainder coming from PERKIM, religious departments of various states, and other government Islamic ventures.[99] By 1995 Bank Islam had sixty-three branches across Malaysia.[100] In 1993 another state-controlled bank, Bank Rakyat (Peasants Bank) too began to offer interest-free banking. The role of interest-free banking in the banking sector has been marginal and, moreover, has not contributed to government revenue. Instead, it has provided UMNO and the state with Islamic legitimacy, and extended their reach into society by bringing social groups that had largely shunned state-run financial institutions—and in the case of peasants and the pious, all banking operations—under the control of state-run financial institutions. Interest-free banking, for instance, has increased the scope of the state's economic ties to the peasantry, who have by and large operated outside of the mainstream financial system and have been more closely tied to PAS or al-Arqam.

The experience with banking was replicated in insurance with the establishment of the Islamic Economic Development Fund in 1984, and Syarikat Takaful Malaysia (Malaysia's Insurance Cooperative) in 1985.[101] The Islamic insurance scheme, too, avoids interest and operates as a trustee profit-sharing operation. In the 1990s Islamic pawnshops were introduced—mainly in rural areas—along with an Islamic brokerage scheme in 1994.[102]

The Islamic economic initiative also included collection of Islamic taxes and disbursement of the resultant revenues. The most important tax in this regard is the *zakat* (alms tax), which is a 2.5% compulsory flat tax. According to traditional law, Muslims must calculate the tax themselves and can give the funds to educational or religious causes, or to the poor directly or through the ulama and religious institutions. Only a genuinely "Islamic" political authority can legitimately assume the collection of the tax and the disbursement of the revenues. As a result, the collection of *zakat* by the state was necessary to legitimate its claim to being "Islamic," and popular compliance with the state's collection of that tax was a litmus test of the public's acceptance of its Islamicity.

In Malaysia, *zakat* had been traditionally collected by government agencies. In rural areas state administrations collected *zakat,* and in the cities an equivalent tax was levied by the state.[103] The numbers had traditionally been modest. For instance, in 1968 only $3.5 million was collected in *zakat* in rural areas. In the Kelantan, wherein PAS has been very strong and Islam plays an important part in society and politics, only 6% of the crop went to *zakat*.[104] These *zakat* funds went to Majlis Amanah Rakyat (Council of the Peasants Trust). The trust invested them in commercial, educational, and infrastructure projects for Malays.[105] Hence, *zakat* funds did not go to the poor directly, but followed the logic of alleviating poverty through trusteeship that was also the basis of NEP. Some *zakat* funds went to building mosques, training ulama, and organizing pilgrimages to Mecca (the Hajj).

In the 1980s the state streamlined the collection and disbursement of *zakat* funds. Although the funds were still collected and disbursed locally, much more emphasis was placed on the collection of the tax as a mark of the Islamicity of the state. Still, compliance rates remained modest, 8% in 1988, over 90% of which came from rural areas.[106] The contribution of *zakat* funds to state revenue was (and continues to be) negligible. It has, however, bolstered the state's claim to legitimacy, and extended its control over education, mosque building, religious activities, and infrastructure projects in rural areas—where UMNO and the state had been traditionally weakest. Here, it is not tax collection that has been shaping the state, but the state's political needs that have necessitated control over taxation.

This imperative has also been evident in the evolution of the Lembaga Urusan dan Tabung Haji ([Hajj] Pilgrims' Management Fund Board, [LUTH]). LUTH was originally formed in 1957 as a government service for those who wished to perform the Hajj. It was designed to encourage gradual savings for a pilgrimage in lieu of sale of agricultural lands to that end. It became more centralized after 1969. LUTH collects regular deposits into individualized savings accounts toward the cost of pilgrimage to Mecca. In addition, it organizes the pilgrimage itself. Over time LUTH became very popular with Malays. In 1965, 5,229 Malays performed Hajj through LUTH, whereas by 1980 the number stood at 14,846.[107] By the mid-1980s only a small percentage of pilgrimages in Malaysia were organized outside of LUTH by PAS or al-Arqam; 5% in 1984, and a total of 9,302 in 1975–88.[108]

Over time LUTH has become an important financial institution with large financial holdings and assets invested in various state and private sector enterprises. The size of its fund grew from RM0.4 million in 1974 to RM132.8 million in 1974.[109] In 1981 LUTH had total resources of RM300 million. Its deposits stood at RM108 million from 51,000 accounts. By 1991 LUTH had RM1.2 billion in funds in 1,753,678 accounts and 86 branches.[110] It had invested RM200 million in acquisition of stocks in various industrial projects.[111] It had 40 branches, three fully owned subsidiaries, and equity participation in 25 private and 50 public companies. It had a profit rate of 9% for depositors (based on profit-sharing rather than interest).[112] LUTH has been viewed as a success case of interest-free operations in a capitalist environment. LUTH thus provided impetus for other ventures, notably, Bank Islam, 10% of whose paid, up capital came from LUTH.[113] LUTH's success has also helped other interest-free projects such as the Islamic insurance, whose assets reached RM287 million by 1991, and whose growth, along with that of LUTH and the Bank Islam, showed that interest-free financial activities were popular with Malays.[114]

The interest-free institutions, and LUTH in particular, have been a means of mobilizing savings—particularly from amongst those who may not use the regular financial institutions—to support various economic projects. After NEP, LUTH invested in acquiring stocks in various industrial projects and is today one of the largest holding companies in Malaysia; as such, it provides the state with significant control over various aspects of the economy.[115] More important, however, was the fact that LUTH's domination of Hajj tied increasing numbers of religiously conscious Malays to a state-controlled financial institution—making them dependant on the state to perform a central article of their faith. LUTH also gives the state the means to control the extent of Malays' contact with Islamist trends in the Middle East and South Asia, which was especially important in the 1980s when Iran used the Hajj as the forum for spreading its revolutionary ideology.

LUTH's example led the government to extend the purview of its control to religious endowments (*waqf* property) as well. In the Seventh Development Plan (1996–2000) the government openly laid claim to religious endowments.[116] Anwar Ibrahim advocated developing *waqf* property to help realize Vision 2020, and encouraged the Mufti of Penang to join Shahdah (Testimony), a development company that was formed with that aim in mind.[117] By the late 1990s UMNO was more openly using its Islamic rhetoric and interest-free institutions to mobilize previously untapped domestic savings to support its agenda of growth, just as it minimized resistance to its overall growth strategy.

The government undertook equally important steps to Islamize education. Primary and secondary educational curricula, along with those of university education, were changed to include classes on Islamic civilization.[118] An Islamic Teachers Training College was established in 1982 to train teachers for these tasks. The most important institutional development was the International Islamic University (IIU), which was established on the outskirts of Kuala Lumpur in 1983.[119] IIU was closely associated with Anwar, who took particular credit for conceptualizing its Department of Revealed Knowledge.[120] Anwar served as the nominal chancellor of the university and appointed its principal directors. The university was based on Islamist notions of "Islamization of knowledge" which had been put forward by the Palestinian-American Islamic scholar Islam`il al-Faruqi, who had influenced Anwar in the 1970s when he taught in Malaysia.[121] Islamization of knowledge was an effort on the part of Islamist intellectuals to make various modern academic disciplines compatible with Islam, and thus lay the foundations for an educational system and an intellectual tradition that would "Islamize modernity."[122] In many ways, IIU was incompatible with Mahathir's vision of Islam. Anwar, however, saw in IIU a means to retain his relations with Islamism of old and, in particular, to continue to be viewed as an Islamist leader internationally— to maintain Islamist legitimacy. He also used IIU to co-opt and silence critics of Malaysia in international Islamist circles. As scores of South Asian and Arab Islamist intellectuals were employed by IIU or received scholarships to study there, Malaysia was able to establish some control over the manner in which its experiment with Islamization was presented in Islamist circles. Early on, IIU also served as a think tank for the Mahathir administration on Islamic issues and was important to countering leftist criticisms of its economic policies.[123] In time, IIU also came to be viewed as a Malay university, one that trained Islamically conscious civil servants for the state. It acquired engineering and medical faculties, and expanded in size and influence.

The government also established other Islamic institutions of higher learning and expanded the scope of Islamic education in Malaysia's existing universities. The Islamization of education spawned numerous think tanks and research institutes that recruited from among university faculty and graduates, and provided policy-making guidelines to UMNO and state institutions.

Islamization from 1980 onward required establishment of new institutions and revamping of old ones. It also involved new policy initiatives that found embodiment in the institutional changes. Pusat Islam was reorganized and expanded in 1983–84. The religious affairs department of the prime minister's office was expanded under Anwar's supervision. By 1987 it had a staff of 608, up from eight in 1968.[124] Two nationwide committees were formed to guide Islamic policymaking: Badan Perundingan Islam (Islamic Consultation Board), to recommend Islamic policies; and Lembaga Bersama Penyelarasan Kegiatan Islam, Malaysia (Joint Committee on Management and Implementation of Islamic Activities, Malaysia), to monitor the implementation of all decisions and programs that the government had agreed to establish according to Islamic tenets. New national-level committees were formed to contend with various aspects of Islamization: Majlis Kebangsaan Bagi Hal Ehwal Agama Islam, Malaysia (National Council for Islamic Affairs); Jawatankuasa Kemanjuan Hal Ehwal Agama Islam, Malaysia (Board for the Promotion of Muslim Welfare, Malaysia); Majlis Syura (Consultative Council); Jawatankuasa Peringkat Kebangsaan Menyelaras Perlakasanaan Undang-Undang Sivil dan Syarie diMalaysia (National Board for the Implementation of Civil and *Shariah* Laws, Malaysia); and Lembaga Penasihat Penyelarasan Pelajaran dan Pendidikan Agama Islam (Advisory Board for Islamic Education and Curricula).[125]

The institutional developments went hand in hand with increase in the Islamic content of radio and television broadcasting; introduction of requirement of religious knowledge into civil service examinations (1991); creation of an Islamic Medical center (1983); plans for Islamic villages in urban centers (1988); regulation of sale of alcohol and relation between the sexes; increase in censorship of films and publications (1991); imposition of taxes on cigarettes and alcohol to be used to implement an Islamic value system (1992); and an acceleration in mosque building—including grand state mosques—and use of Islamic architectural concepts in showcase projects.[126] There was also a great deal more Islamic activity in the foreign-policy arena. Malaysia took a more active role in the Organization of Islamic Conference after 1981. It also adopted a more pro-Arab foreign policy that sat well with the Islamic constituency. It held the Palestine Solidarity Day in 1992 and an "International Conference on Palestine" in 1983, when Anwar participated in the PLO Summit in Algiers; and in 1984 Yasser Arafat visited Malaysia.[127] In the 1990s Malaysia took an active role in political change in Albania as well as in the Bosnian crisis. In addition to giving the countries financial and political support, Malaysia admitted hundreds of students from these areas to IIU and the University of Malaya on government scholarships.

At the state level, too, new institutions were created. The Jawatankuasa Hal Ehwal Agama Islam Negeri (State Committee for Muslim Affairs at the State Level) was set up to streamline Islamic activities at the state level. It was to be chaired by Mentari Besar (chief minister). This institution's work was to complement that of the Majlis Agama Islam, which itself was reorganized. However, whereas Majlis Agama was directly answerable to the sultan, Jawatankuasa Hal Ehwal Agama Islam Negeri was to advise the state government and the chief minister.[128]

Since Islamic courts and law was the domain of state governments, institutional changes in these regards occurred at the state level. *Shariah* courts were freed from oversight by the sultan or the chief minister, and the status of the judges was raised to be on par with that of their counterparts in the civil judiciary. Hence, *shariah* courts became more powerful. In 1984 the scope of jurisdiction of *shariah* courts was extended beyond RM5000, and in 1988 they were recognized as the equal of civil courts and were given broad powers to protect the sanctity of Islamic law.[129] The rise in power of *shariah* courts was not in keeping with Mahathir's aim of limiting Islamization to matters of ethics and values. In fact, controlling the *shariah* courts as they became more powerful became a challenge to UMNO and the state. Still, the *shariah* courts provided the state with the means to wrest power away from Malay states, to gain more control over Islamic issues—especially to deny states control over Islamic politics—and to use Islamic law to assert social control.

Encouraged by Islamization after 1983 various states introduced their own Islamic codes in various criminal and civil matters. In 1990 Article 121 of the constitution was amended to stipulate that the High Court and subordinate courts have no say in matters that fall under *shariah* court jurisdiction.[130]

The government also created mechanisms to make sure that Malaysian laws do not contravene Islamic laws. It hoped that this would reduce demands for implementation of Islamic law and limit the discussion of the topic to one of bringing Malaysian law into accordance with Islam rather than introducing a new legal code. In 1993 after PAS introduced its Hudood Bill in Kelantan the government's position came under pressure, for PAS's proposal for implementation of Islamic law went far beyond the government's limited approach, rendering it as inadequate. The proposal underscored PAS's assertion that UMNO's Islamization was largely cosmetic, "long on symbolism, short on substance."[131]

Finally, whereas the government had been able to limit discussion of implementation of Islamic law to one of ensuring that Malaysian laws did not contravene Islamic law, it could not, however, stave off the various codes that were added in Malay states—including the PAS bill in Kelantan. Islamization therefore created an unexpected struggle for power between Malay states and the federal center.

The increase in the number and diversity of new Islamic codes across Malaysia was also a source of concern insofar as it bolstered individual states' autonomy vis-à-vis the center. In addition, various businesses and civil society groups decried the difficulties that were inherent in contending with the many codes. The feminist Islamic group, Sisters in Islam, for instance, has pointed to the fact that variations in marriage, divorce, alimony, or inheritance laws across states means that what may be a violation of law in one state is lawful in another. By the end of the 1990s the government capitalized on the unhappiness to argue for a uniform Islamic code managed by the center. Mahathir stated that "if the end result of the implementation of Islamic laws is chaos . . . it is not any good."[132]

However, it was Anwar who took the lead in this regard to argue that the federal center was a bona fide Islamic state, rightfully entitled to manage Islamic law and its application. Islamic law was therefore used at first by states to assert their autonomy and identity, but in the end became a tool in the hands of UMNO and the federal center to wrest control of Islamic affairs, which had until the 1990s rested in states, and situate it in the center—to increase the power and control of the center at the expense of Malay states. *Shariah* courts at the center are now directly responsible to political leaders and are used by UMNO and the state to legitimate policy making or actions against opponents, such as the crackdown against the al-Arqam in 1994.

The most interesting institution to emerge in the 1980s, insofar as Mahathir's aim of relating Islamization to globalization and capitalist development is concerned, was the Institut Kefahaman Islam Malaysia (Institute of Islamic Understanding of Malaysia [IKIM]).[133] IKIM was formed in 1992. It was initially a think tank for the government on Islamic issues. Mahathir no longer viewed IIU as a suitable think tank for policy making, and no other institution was properly organized to provide the government with the kind of policy formulation it needed. IKIM also served as the means of establishing control over Islamic thinkers and intellectuals through patronage that was dispensed in the form of retainers, research positions, and project funding.[134]

In fact, the scope of IKIM's research projects was so broad, and included so many intellectuals and writers, that the institute exercised great influence on the direction that research work on Islam in Malaysia would take.

In time IKIM was given a more specific charge, to justify capitalist development, globalization, and Vision 2020 in Islamic terms, and to articulate a moderate vision of Islam that would support Mahathir's agenda. IKIM's objectives were spelled out in the following manner:

> To correct the image of Islam which has been wrongly portrayed as promoting terrorism, conservatism, fanaticism, backwardness, poverty and degrading stereotypes to present Islam as a religion that promotes the concept of truthfulness and that thrives on tolerance and dynamism and full of extraordinarily pure and valuable universal precepts to nurture a harmonious society whereby Muslims and non-Muslims can live and prosper side by side to provide a platform for Muslim and non-Muslim scholars to discuss or analyse issues of mutual importance to create an in depth awareness and understanding of international issues having direct impact on Muslims.[135]

IKIM was to portray capitalist development as compatible with Islamic values, and in so doing provide an ideological response to PAS's attacks on government development policy as un-Islamic. IKIM seeks to justify the pursuit of wealth, the administrative values and practices that are needed for managing it, and to rationalize globalization, consumerism, foreign investment, limited labor rights, income inequality, and the like in terms of Islam.[136] It seeks to develop Islamic values of capitalism and articulate the notion of an "Islamic developmental state." It openly equates Vision 2020 with Islam, and hence globalization and corporate culture with Islamization.[137] IKIM also places emphasis on those Islamic values that would support growth, equating Islamic values with Asian work ethics, discipline, and entrepreneurship.[138] A quote on IKIM's web site in 1999 read: "Islamic nations need not invent systems of Government because systems can never be perfect and can never guarantee good government. What creates good Government is the quality of the people who are entrusted with ruling the country." Islamization is not about the Islamic state, but about producing Malaysians needed by the development process.

IKIM has argued that Malaysia should adopt institution formation on the model of the West. It has been publishing prolifically on the relation of Western corporate culture to Islam. The issues are purely economic and modern, and the aim is to find some kind of Islamic angle for promoting American or Japanese corporate cultures.[139] IKIM's discussions of corporate culture give an Islamic basis to Vision 2020.[140] However, the role of Islam in corporate culture here is purely ethical—limited to the role Confucianism plays in Asian corporate culture.[141] The aim is to promote the right kind of corporate culture and industrial strategy.[142]

IKIM has argued that revival of Islam should be seen in empowerment and enrichment of Muslims. It places emphasis on the broader concern of re-creating glories of Islam and capturing the spirit of the faith and its history in

lieu of the more narrow interpretation of the revival of Islam as mere implementation of the *shariah*. It promotes a moderate and circumspect definition
of Islamic revival.[143] This definition is also used to convince foreign interests—as well as the minority Chinese—that Malaysian Islamism would not
be a threat to their investments.

In 1985 Anwar gathered a number of ABIM activists to form his own think
tank, Institut Kajian Dasar (Institute of Policy Research [IKD]). In the 1990s
IKD became more active, and provided Anwar with policy-making advice independent of government channels. It also did much to articulate and propagate Anwar's own views on moderate Islam and its relation to Malaysia's development. IKD, however, did not have the same impact as IKIM. IKIM has
perhaps been the most ambitious attempt on the part of the Mahathir administration to moderate Islamism and harness its energies in the service of growth.
More than any other institutional manifestation of Islamization, IKIM captures
the essence of Mahathir's aganda, to ride the tiger of Islamism, but also to
use Islamic values to expand state power and push for rapid growth through
globalization.

By 1997 when the Asian financial crisis set back Malaysia's economic development and tarnished its industrial policy, the Malaysian state looked
nothing like the weak postcolonial state of the 1957–80 period. The state control of society and the economy had increased markedly. The state had pene-
trated many more social arenas, and exerted much control over cultural and
religious discourses. It controlled more aspects of Malay life and politics—
especially those of middle-class and urban Malays. That domination, moreover, appeared to be absolute. In the process civil society had weakened—despite growth of the private sector. The UMNO-business alliance stifled rather
than promoted pluralism in politics. Democracy had become largely controlled, the judiciary had been weakened, the sultans had lost power, and PAS
was caged in Kelantan. Authoritarian tendencies were on the rise under the
guise of Asian values.[144] There was a direct correlation between Islamization
and expansion of state power. Religious politics had been successfully used
by the state to lessen resistance to its projects of power and growth. Islamization was the handmaiden of the rise of a strong late-developer state in Malaysia in lieu of the weak state that was the legacy of the colonial era. Islamization had provided the Mahathir administration with means to compensate for
weaknesses of the state and to revise its institutional structure in such a fashion as to shore up its authority.

Still, as much as Islamization helped expand state power in the 1980s and
1990s it did not produce political stability, nor a firm basis for state-society
relations. The Asian crisis produced fissures in the Malaysian body politic
that will be discussed in the next chapter. Those fissures may well have
marked the Islamization period—at least in the form that it took between
1980 and 1997. However, regardless of the fate of Islamization the strong state
will remain in place. Malaysian politics from this point forward will have to
contend with the fruits of the Islamization era.

6

Pakistan, 1977–1997

Islamization and Restoration of State Power

In July 1977 the Pakistan military, under the command of General Muhammad Zia ul-Haq, staged a coup. Months of agitations against the government of Zulfiqar Ali Bhutto had eroded authority at the center in Pakistan and mobilized antiregime forces—and especially Islamists—to an unprecedented degree. It was therefore not altogether unexpected that regime change in 1977 led to inclusion of Islamic values and laws into policy making. The state initiated a broad-based Islamization scheme that had a profound impact on Pakistan's society and politics. Here, too, Islamization was very much a project of the state. It was designed to stave off the Islamist challenge to state authority, but also to strengthen state institutions and expand their reach into society.

There were, however, important differences between Malaysia and Pakistan that account for variations in the two countries' experiences with Islamization. To begin with, Pakistan faced a far graver crisis at the time of the 1977 coup than did Malaysia when Mahathir came to power. Pakistan did not have strong political parties and hence relied on the military. Finally, in Malaysia UMNO and state leaders were concerned with state authority, but in tandem with economic growth and development. In Pakistan restoration of state authority was the paramount concern.

At another level, in Pakistan Islamism had all along been both more powerful and more radical, and became even more so through the crucible of the 1977 agitation. In Pakistan in 1977 there was no moderate Islamist force like ABIM. Whereas in Malaysia at the time the most significant Islamist force

130

was also the most moderate one, in Pakistan it was the Jama'at-i Islami or JUI that dominated the scene. As a consequence, whereas the UMNO-ABIM combine would produce moderate Islamization in Malaysia, the alliance between the military and the Islamists in Pakistan would produce far more thoroughgoing and ideologically strident Islamization. In Malaysia UMNO managed to dominate the Islamist discourse and to harness the energies of Islamism to serve UMNO and the state's interests. In Pakistan Islamism at all times dominated the Islamist discourse. State-led Islamization in Malaysia was thus far more moderate in tone than it was in Pakistan. Still, the aims of the state in both cases were the same: to expand state power and reach, and to do so by posing as the principal agents of Islamization in society and politics and the chief implementers of Islamic laws. For both states, Islamism presented challenges, but also new possibilities, to allow the state to overcome the handicaps of its colonial legacy. Islamism could endow the state with the requisite legitimacy and provide it with ideological moorings and institutional capabilities that it had lacked before the Islamization period.

The military coup in Pakistan came at a time when Pakistan's politics was at an impasse. Months of agitation had precipitated a serious crisis. Negotiations between the government and the PNA had proceeded slowly, and there is dispute as to whether in the end they produced an agreement, and if so whether it would have been viable. Many in the PPP and PNA argue that such an agreement had been reached,[1] but the military was opposed to some of the compromises Bhutto had made, notably, those regarding release of Baluch separatists from prison. General Zia argued that Bhutto had intended to use the agreement as only a respite after which to order a military crackdown on the opposition.[2] That would have further undermined state institutions, political stability, and law and order. In addition, Zia argued that politicians had proven themselves incapable of ruling the country effectively, and more so, of resolving the crisis that they had created.[3] The military thus concluded that the collapse of the state was imminent, and that neither Bhutto nor the PNA would be able to reverse that trend. In fact, Bhutto had become the obstacle to restoration of order. In addition, many in the military sympathized with the PNA, and hence the military was not willing to act under Bhutto's command, which would have put the military at odds with the popular opposition movement.[4] The military intervened in the political process independent of Bhutto in order to avert a bloodbath or a civil war in which the military would have to take sides.[5]

The military coup's first aim was therefore to restore order, a task that took place through gradual regime change between 1977 and 1979.[6] However, although by 1979 it appeared that Pakistan had put the worst of the crisis behind it, the military proved reluctant to return to barracks. First, the military believed that restoration of order depended on removing Bhutto from the political scene. The scope of PNA agitation and the speed and ease with which the PPP fell from power had initially convinced the military that Bhutto and the PPP were finished.[7] After Bhutto was received by a large crowd in Lahore in August 1977 when he was released from custody, the military understood that it was not going to be that easy. The generals concluded that they had to stay in power until the PPP was rooted out and Bhutto was finished off. Zia also concluded that democracy was likely to be disruptive, and, hence, an obstacle to restoration of state power. If Pakistan was to have a strong state, it would have to create it in lieu of democracy.[8] The military would postpone elections and suggest revision of electoral laws—especially adoption of proportional representation, which was believed to favor Islamists and right-of-center parties—to make a PPP comeback through elections difficult.[9] The military regime redoubled its efforts to destroy the PPP's organizational capabilities and to see to Bhutto's execution.[10] Zia understood very well that to deal with the PPP politically the character of Pakistani politics had to be Islamized and the electorate had to be reoriented toward right-of-center and Islamic politics.

Second, the military viewed the rising tide of Islamism to be a threat to political stability and ultimately state interests in Pakistan.[11] As was the case in Malaysia, here, too, the military decided to "ride the tiger" rather than try to suppress Islamism.[12] To begin with, the military needed the PNA's support in its attempt to restore stability, and especially to suppress the PPP. For instance, the Jama`at-i Islami's support was crucial to the execution of Bhutto.[13] In addition, the military was not keen on confronting Islamism at the height of its power, and at the same time that it was cracking down on the PPP, although it wanted to keep Islamism at bay and away from the levers of power.[14] It therefore decided to follow a conciliatory policy toward the PNA, adopt the Islamist agenda, and use its influence to legitimate military rule.[15]

After Bhutto's execution in 1979 Pakistan's politics stabilized, but this only strained relations between the military and the PNA. The former dragged its feet in holding elections whereas the latter became impatient with military rule. Zia was not eager to return power to the politicians, lest political order collapse again and state authority once again erode. That in 1979 the monarchy in Iran fell to an Islamic revolution that affected Pakistan directly, India became embroiled in conflict with Sikhs in Punjab, and, most important, the Soviet Union invaded Afghanistan made the military eager to hold on to the levers of power. In fact, Zia believed that since the primary vehicle for national integration was the state, the military should remain in power until that consolidation was complete.[16]

In addition, Zia believed that the job of restoring state authority was not complete in 1979. In fact, Bhutto's execution and the marginalization of the PPP were not the end of the process, but rather the beginning. In particular, Zia was keen to undertake political and economic reforms, in order to undo the effect of Bhutto's populism. Zia's initiatives in this regard did not go very far. This compelled him to increasingly rely on Islamization to legitimate military rule.

In fact, between 1979 and 1988 the Zia regime became increasingly concerned with staying in power in order to ensure expansion of state power in the face of challenges that regional politics and conflict placed before Pakistan, and in order to immunize Pakistani society against the PPP and its brand of populism. Zia did not look to political institutions to achieve this end, but rather to Islamization.[17] In fact, the Zia period is remarkable for its paucity of new political institutions, given that the ruling regime's aim was restoration of the state.

Zia, however, showed more interest in stabilizing the economy. Wide-scale nationalization of industry in the 1970s had overwhelmed the bureaucracy and led to economic inefficiencies, slow growth, and inflation.[18] Soon after the military took over, it put forward a five-year plan (1978–83) to spur growth. Hence, early on, growth and development were very much on the mind of Pakistan's new rulers. Given the fact that the military blamed economic stagnation on Bhutto's socialism, it looked to capitalist development to generate growth. Hence, much as was the case in Malaysia, in Pakistan, too, the private sector featured prominently in the new regime's plans for the economy. The sixth five-year plan (1983–88), for instance, looked to shift the economy away from state-led socialism to state-led capitalism. It therefore envisioned a greater role for the private sector, and favored deregulation and some privatization. It laid the basis for a private sector-state alliance.

Economic growth, and the role of the private sector and capitalist development in that process, however, did not dominate politics at the top to the extent that it did in Malaysia. To begin with, domestic and regional political crises were a greater concern for the Zia regime. Second, the flow of rent to Pakistan's economy increased noticeably in the 1980s, dampening the urge to pursue growth. Labor remittances from Pakistani workers in the Persian Gulf rose from $365 million in 1975–76 to the average of $2.4 billion a year in the 1982–88 period, and a total of $25 billion between 1977/78 and 1986/87,[19] constituting some 40% of foreign exchange earnings and 8% of the GNP.[20] In 1981–84 labor remittances stood above 80% of merchandise exports.[21] An additional $10 billion is estimated to have come from the drug trade.[22]

Similarly, Pakistan's income from foreign aid rose sharply after the Soviet invasion of Afghanistan. In the 1976–79 period foreign aid had stood at around $900 million a year.[23] In the 1981–85 period it stood at around $1.3 billion a year.[24] In 1981–87 Pakistan received $3.2 billion in grants from the United States, and was promised another $4.1 billion for the 1987–93 period.[25] In addition, Pakistan benefited directly from aid to the Afghan fighters and refugees that in 1986–89 reached $1.2 billion a year from American and Saudi sources alone.[26] This form of aid also found its way into the Pakistan economy through both siphoning off of the funds and expenditures by the recipients. The average per year increase in Pakistan's income from aid in comparison with the 1976–79 period therefore was close to $1 billion in the 1981–90 period—Pakistan was receiving close to $2 billion a year in foreign aid in the 1980s. The revenue generated by Islamization measures—through taxes and the like—was only a fraction of the revenue generated by rent. As was the case with Malaysia, the turn to Islamization, as a phase in state formation, was therefore not motivated by the imperative of revenue collection, but by state interests and economic growth.

The flow of rent produced rapid economic growth in the 1980s—between 1977/78 and 1986/87 the GNP increased cumulatively by 76% and per capita income by 34%[27]—without much structural change in the economy,[28] or the degree of investment in the private sector and capitalist development that was evident in Malaysia. During the Zia period the government did not privatize large nationalized industries nor adopt a new labor policy, but concentrated on improving the performance of state-run industries.[29] In fact, during the Zia period public sector development continued to grow.[30] In 1978–88 it rose by 4.9% compared to 1970–78.[31] The sixth plan (1983–88) promised to continue state management of nationalized industries and even to expand the state's role in the agricultural sector.[32] The continued domination of the public sector caused unhappiness among the industrial elite and the entrepreneurial class that had expected wide-scale privatization of nationalized industries. Still, since the Zia regime protected middle-class values and interests, and the economy grew to produce a good climate for business—which became the cornerstone of Zia's economic strategy in lieu of private-sector-led growth—that unhappiness did not translate into meaningful opposition. In fact, to the contrary, an alliance was soon forged between the military and the private sector.[33]

Whereas in Malaysia the burgeoning state–private sector alliance was rooted in Mahathir's growth strategy, in Pakistan that alliance was first and foremost motivated by political considerations. Bhutto's populism had affected the industrial elite in particular. The Bhutto regime had nationalized industries and championed the cause of labor. In fact, it was only in the industrial sector that the PPP's program had come close to realizing its aims. As a result, from early on the industrial elite and the entrepreneurial classes were a critical source of opposition to Bhutto. In opposing him, they joined forces with lower-middle-class merchants, and more important, with Islamist forces. Throughout the 1970s businessmen and entrepreneurs provided financial and logistical support to the Islamist opposition to Bhutto. Increasingly the ambient culture of this class became Islamic in tone. By 1977 the private sector, although weakened by Bhutto's populism, exercised much influence on the PNA and the Nizam-i Mustafa movement.

Zia saw the private sector as an important base of support for his regime. It was a powerful economic class that was opposed to Bhutto and his policies, was closely tied with Islamist forces and the Islamist parties that spearheaded the fall of Bhutto, and could serve as a counterbalance to feudalism, which in Sind and parts of Punjab was resisting military rule. The private sector was also key to Zia's attempt to create a middle- and lower-middle-class base for his regime as a counterweight to the PPP's lower class base of support. The private sector became an integral part of the ruling military regime and tacitly supported its policies. By the mid-1980s the private sector became more directly involved in politics. In alliance with Islamists it formed a right-of-center political bloc that supported Zia, and served as a counterweight to feudalism and a resurgent PPP under Benazir Bhutto's leadership after 1981. As mentioned earlier, the private sector did not see eye to eye with the Zia regime over the pace and scope of privatization of nationalized industries, or the dominant role of the public sector in the economy. The private sector, however, continued to support Zia in his attempt to restore order and keep the resurgent PPP at bay. Since in Pakistan the state depended on the political support of the private sector, the private sector developed far more autonomously of the state than was the case in Malaysia. That autonomy parlayed into more open political activism by the private sector, which made it a pillar of right-of-center politics during the post-Zia period.

Changes in the private sector's political role were apparent by the middle of the 1980s. It was then that with Zia's prodding, Mian Nawaz Sharif, an industrial magnate in Punjab became active in the Muslim League, and ultimately became the chief minister of Punjab. Sharif's ascent signaled a more direct political role for the private sector, first in competition to the landed elite in the Muslim League, and ultimately as claimants to power when Sharif became prime minister in the 1990s.

Islam and the Entrenchment of Military Rule in the 1980s

After 1979 Zia's main concern became civilization of military rule.[34] There was not going to be a return to democracy, and the military would continue to rule Pakistan until state authority had been fully restored and domestic and regional crises had been left behind. Legitimation of military rule, however, required constitutional and political maneuverings, which turned Zia's attention to Islam.

In 1981 Zia promulgated the Provisional Constitutional Order as the means of reconciling military rule with the constitution.[35] It limited the powers of the judiciary and gave Zia broad powers to implement new laws. The main problem facing the state was the growing demand for restoration of democracy, which by 1979 also included the PNA and Islamist parties.[36] Zia's response was similar to that of Bhutto in the face of PNA demands for fresh elections: to give in on Islamic demands but not on demands for elections. In addition, Zia and the military had viewed Islam to have been more important to the success of the PNA than the alliance's purely political demands, and, hence, believed that by adopting an Islamic veneer they would be able to subdue and outmaneuver the PNA. The power of the Nizam-i Mustafa movement had meanwhile convinced the military of the ideological and political potential of Islam in the service of the state.

In addition, ethnic challenges to the state reinforced the tendency to rely on Islam to organize national politics. The Bhutto years had clearly aggravated ethnic tensions in Pakistan. The ascendance of ethnic politics, in turn, had mobilized the Muhajirs and the Punjabis, who were wary of rising ethnic tensions, and who were eager to steer national politics away from ethnic concerns. The Nizam-i Mustafa movement that resulted from the mobilization of the two communities focused on democracy and Islam—denouncing Bhutto's secularism and autocracy—thereby removing ethnic concerns, at least for the time being, from the political center stage. The Zia regime, which was clearly worried about ethnic tensions, especially in Baluchistan and Sind,[37] appealed to Islam in the hope of obfuscating soaring ethnic tensions, and hoped to bring stability to Pakistan, once again in the name of Islamic solidarity. It also aimed to downplay the Punjabi domination of the state under the aegis of the military by harping on Islamic themes. In sum, Islam would allow the military to limit resistance to its continued rule over Pakistan and to its goal of restoring authority in the state.

When the generals took over power, they had no clear plan of action. Operation Fair Play—as the coup was dubbed—had been a military contingency plan rather than a political operation.[38] Once the military decided to remain in power, it had to come up with a political program. The military regime had few ideological tools with which to legitimate military rule, and fewer still to shore up state authority. It therefore turned to Islam and the political platform put forward by the Nizam-i Mustafa movement to achieve its ends.

Much like Mahathir in Malaysia, Zia in Pakistan was critical in bringing about the ideological changes with which state formation would be associated from that point forward. Zia was instrumental in convincing the military that the turn to Islam was the best course of action for that institution in serving the interests of the state.[39]

To begin with, Zia was himself pious. In the military he was affectionately called "maulvi" (religious scholar).[40] He had read Islamist works since his youth, and was particularly under the influence of the works of Mawlana Mawdudi of the Jama'at-i Islami, who placed great emphasis of the incumbency of the Islamic state as a religious necessity as well as a panacea for sociopolitical problems. Zia had been promoted out of turn to lead the military. Bhutto had viewed him as dilettante who could not threaten his civilian government. Still, as the army chief Zia opened that institution to Islam.[41] He encouraged soldiers to pray and fast. Following his investiture as chief of staff, he used the powers vested in his office to distribute Islamist literature among the soldiers and officers. Zia also proposed including Mawdudi's works in the examination "for promotion of Captains and Majors," which led to his reprimand by Bhutto before the cabinet.[42] At his trial before the supreme court, Bhutto remarked, "I appointed a Chief of Staff belonging to the Jamaat-i-Islami and the result is before all of us."[43] In many regards the Islamization process began first in the military in the 1970s before it spilled over onto Pakistani society as a whole in the 1980s.[44]

In addition, Zia's thinking was shaped by how he understood the successes and failures of the military regimes of Ayub Khan and Yahya Khan to properly construct a more viable military regime. He concluded that Ayub Khan's policies were good, but his regime failed owing to its secularism. Yahya Khan sought to remedy that shortcoming, but his turn to Islam fell short because he was not a credible champion of Islamization.[45] Zia also believed that the demand for an Islamic system was the main animus behind the anti-Bhutto agitation, and hence, by delivering on that demand the military would be able to establish political control.[46] He therefore came to a similar conclusion as had Mahathir; namely, a state that is construed as a legitimate Islamic actor can both ride the tiger of Islamism and harness its energies in the service of the state. General Arif, who was a member of the military command that ruled Pakistan in the 1980s, recollects that Zia emphasized that in Pakistan sovereignty belongs to Allah. Hence, an Islamic state (i.e., the state as a legitimate Islamic actor) would be an instrument of God with uncontested sovereignty.[47] An Islamic state was therefore the most powerful form of state, one whose powers far exceeded those of the secular postcolonial state. The notion of the Islamic state also suggested that the most important duty of the state was to Islamize society, and to that end it had free reign to expand its powers and reach. To Zia this meant that military rule would continue without much resistance—and would be able to achieve its goals—so long as state-led Islamization continued. What Zia and the military in the end aimed for was to parade the postcolonial state as an Islamic state, and thereby to enjoy the powers that an Islamic state would have without bringing about fundamental changes in state institutions.

Zia's personal faith in Islamism parlayed into close collaboration between the new state leaders and Islamist parties, first and foremost the Jama'at, but ultimately a wider array of ulama and lay Islamist activists, movements, and thinkers. The general had been an admirer of Mawdudi and the Jama'at for a long time. He had looked to the Jama'at as an intellectual force that could serve the same function in his regime as the Left had done in the PPP in the 1969–73 period. Jama'at's ideology tended to support authoritarianism, and contained a powerful critique of both the Left and Western democracy to the military advantage.[48] The fact that the Jama'at had been the main ideological adversary of the Left since the 1960s and had always claimed to have a blueprint for the Islamization of the state further led Zia to draw parallels between the Jama'at and Pakistan's leftist intelligentsia. Hence, not only were Jama'at leaders placed in charge of sensitive cabinet portfolios and invited to serve on such prominent state-sponsored organs as the Council of Islamic Ideology, but a number of pro-Jama'at thinkers, writers, and journalists were inducted into the inner circle of Zia's advisers with a view to laying the foundations for a viable machinery for the Islamic state. In addition, after the Jama'at performed well in municipal elections in 1979, the party took control of important cities, most notably, Karachi—thus serving as a governing partner with the military at the municipal level.[49]

The military's close collaboration with the Jama'at was similar to UMNO's co-optation of ABIM. However, in Pakistan, since the military was not a party, it was not able to fully integrate the Jama'at, and in fact, soon strains developed in their relations. After Bhutto's execution, Zia reneged on his promise of elections and return to democratic rule. The Jama'at believed that the years 1977–79 were the pinnacle of its popularity and was eager to capitalize on that popular sentiment at the polls. It therefore began to view the Zia regime as an obstacle to the realization of its political ambitions. Zia, in turn, sought to placate the party by accommodating its Islamic demands but not its political ones. In fact, between 1977 and 1979 Zia successfully manipulated the demand for Islamization and the fate of Bhutto to keep Islamist parties away from the polls until their moment of enthusiasm had passed.

The Zia regime decided that it would be the state that would undertake Islamization and would do so without reliance on any one Islamist party. In this manner it would be the state that would be the principal agent of Islamization. Islamization would thus legitimate military rule and help restore state dominance without empowering any one Islamist party so that it could pose a threat to the state. The military regime furthermore created the institutional means to organize Islamist interest groups within the state, and encouraged them to participate in politics through these institutions. Islamization thus created a framework for co-optation of Islamism. The institutions associated with Islamization served to inform state leaders of the demands of Islamist groups and to distribute resources among them. Islamization thus worked in a manner reminiscent of what Alfred Stepan has termed "inclusionary corporatism."[50] The military regime sought to preserve the structure of the post-colonial state just as it modified its outward appearance to be accommodating of Islam. Despite its commitment to Islamization, state leaders during the Zia period were first and foremost committed to the interests of the state. Islamization was therefore a part of the state's project of power.

To serve state interests Zia sought to increase normative compliance with the state[51] and to harmonize relations between the state and civil society.[52] This was achieved through a combination of ideological and punitive measures that were encapsulated in Islamization. Islamic norms and ideals were to provide the state with normative tools for exercising social control. They were also intended to bring state-society relations and interests into alignment by providing a discourse of power that straddled the boundaries of the two, while Islamic penal law, along with martial law, was to delegitimate dissent. In particular, Islamic values and laws were used to bring order to the productive sectors of society by guaranteeing sanctity of private property and restoring confidence among private investors, all of which had been undermined by Bhutto's populism.[53] For instance, the Federal Shariat Court at one point challenged Bhutto's land reform, asserting that it was in contravention to Islam's respect for right to private property.[54] Islamization was thus used to both establish the authority of the state and to facilitate its greater reach into society.

In addition to Islamists, the Zia regime also appealed to rural religious leaders (*pirs* and *mashayakh*) and ulama.[55] This move expanded the state's base of support and provided it with entry into rural areas. This was important in that Bhutto's most important link with Islam had been through the folk Islam of rural areas centered in shrines. Whereas Islamists and urban ulama parties were influential in PNA and urban areas, rural religious leaders were important to gaining control where the PPP had been strong. That meant appropriating the interpretation of rural Islam and control of its institutions as well. The Zia regime used its Islamic image to gain control of religious endowments, and through them, of the shrines, as well as appointment of prayer leaders in mosques.[56] Those rural religious leaders who resisted the state's intrusion were subdued by use of coercion that was justified in the name of establishing proper Islamic practices in lieu of heterodox ones.[57]

Zia also resuscitated state Islamic institutions that had been created earlier but had fallen into disuse. Most notably he revived the Ministry of Religious Affairs and Awqaf (Endowments)[58]—that he used for the state's push into rural areas—and increased state control over mosques.[59] Finally, he placed much importance on the Council of Islamic Ideology that he charged with advising state leaders and institutions on Islamic matters.[60] The council included members from sundry ulama and Islamist parties, and as a result, was a legitimate representative of the Islamist movement in Pakistan. The council also served as a means of co-opting Islamism into the state. It put forth proposals on a host of social, economic, and legal issues that formed the basis of the Islamization regime. It was the Council of Islamic Ideology that recommended the creation of an Islamic state in Pakistan, thus providing Zia with the legitimate excuse to expand the state's reach into society and to perpetuate military rule.[61] In addition, many new Islamic agencies and organizations associated with Islamization measures emerged to equip the state with additional institutional tools with which to exert greater control over society.[62]

The Islamization of State, Society, and Economy

Between 1979 and 1983 the military regime put in place an elaborate Islamization regime. For reasons of expediency the Islamization process in Pakistan, unlike in Malaysia, started with imposition of Islamic penal laws[63] and, more generally, was narrowly focused on enforcement of the *shariah*—Islamization in Pakistan was in essence "Sharitization," to borrow Mumtaz Ahmad's term.[64] Its main elements were the implementation of *hudood* laws (Islamic penal laws), Islamic judiciary, Islamization of public sphere, Islamic education, an Islamic economic system, and an Islamic taxation system (based on collection of *zakat* and other Islamic taxes). With the exception of *hudood* laws, the other elements of the Islamization regime were also present in Malaysia, although they differ in the scope and manner of implementation in the two countries.

In February 1979 the military regime promulgated the Hudood Ordinances that were designed to replace the British criminal code with an Islamic one.[65] Although its impact on the criminal system was marginal, it was used to control dissent and the extent of social resistance to state policy making. These laws, which in particular dealt with theft and robbery, were to put a check on the lower-class expectations that were raised by Bhutto and to reinstitute respect for the sanctity of private property.[66] They were exclusively implemented against the poor.[67] It was the tool for a state that sought to reinforce property laws.

In 1978–79 Shariat Appelate benches were made operational in high courts.[68] These benches were given jurisdiction over appeals made against the implementation of *hudood* laws and to hear original "*shariah* petitions."[69] In 1980 the Federal Shariat Court was instituted—although its operation would be modified 28 times between 1980 and 1985 through twelve presidential ordinances.[70] The Federal Shariat Court was granted appellate jurisdiction over convictions and acquittals from district courts involving newly implemented Islamization schemes; exclusive jurisdiction to hear "*shariat* petitions" challenging laws or portions of them for being repugnant to the *shariah,* the Qur'an, and the prophetic traditions (*hadith*). The Islamization of the judiciary under the aegis of the court, it was hoped, would produce a legal system that was embedded in local beliefs and mores, and would provide speedier justice than the cumbersome Anglo-Saxon law.[71]

The mandate of the Federal Shariat Court could potentially have given it broad powers, especially since its oversight of all laws and legislation could have led to large-scale legal changes. In fact, Zia once claimed that between 1980 and 1987 some 500 laws were either amended or changed by the court.[72] The controversial Law of Evidence is perhaps the best known. It also provides a glimpse of what the scope of those changes could have been. Pursuant to the Council of Islamic Ideology's review of all laws dating back to 1834 to eliminate those repugnant to Islam, the Federal Shariat Court supplanted an 1872 British law on testimony of women.[73] The new law counts a woman's testimony as worth half that of a man.

Changes on the grand scale did not come to pass, however, because the exercise of such powers was limited by two restrictions. First, the court's power in criminal cases and its power to declare a law un-Islamic was made subject to appeal to the Shariat Appellate Bench of the Supreme Court. Second, the Federal Shariat Court's jurisdiction was limited by the fact that the constitution, Muslim personal law, and laws governing procedure in tribunals and courts were excluded from the Federal Shariat Court's jurisdiction. In addition, at the outset there were few judges and lawyers that had been properly trained for work in the Federal Shariat Court. This meant that the court would have to rely on civil court personnel. Of the twenty-one judges who served on the court between 1980 and 1989 sixteen had served on civil high courts and eighteen had received secular legal education.[74] This, too, limited the scope of the court's influence.

In practice, the court was used by the state to push through laws that would extend state powers and social control such as the state's claim to control of religious endowments and nationalization of industries.[75] The court shows the Janus face of Islamization, preserving the foundational structures and institutions of the postcolonial state while accommodating Islamist demands. The Federal Shariat Court was in the end used less as a means of creating an ideological system of justice and more as a powerful tool of social control in the hands of state leaders.[76] Zia directly appointed the court's judges, and the court's mandate closely followed the military's agenda.

Islamization of the judiciary was a cover for curbing its powers. During the first years of military coup the judiciary, rather than political parties and actors, served as the main source of resistance to military rule. The courts were in a position to render judgment on the legitimacy of the coup and to determine the fate of the PPP and Bhutto. Zia first curbed the powers of the judiciary by using the siege mentality facing Pakistan at the time to implement the Provisional Constitutional Order in 1981.[77] The order made the military leaders and their decisions exempt from judicial oversight. Islamization of the judiciary was a continuation of the process of limiting its powers. By arguing that he wished to "decolonize" and "Islamize" the judicial system, Zia diverted attention from the executive's encroachment on the powers of the judiciary. Moreover, he created a dualism in the judicial system, which although limited in its importance, still portended to divide that system from within. The weakening of the judiciary in turn weakened civil society institutions before the state and made extension of the state's reach into society easier.

Concomitant with imposition of Islamic penal laws and Islamization of the judiciary was an increase in religious observance mandated by conscious increase in the Islamicity of the public sphere. Implementation of Islamic penal laws—often carried out in the form of public floggings—did much to relate Islamization to individual conduct and societal relations. New restrictions were imposed on interactions between the sexes, and the state took it upon itself to enforce the sanctity of *chador* and *chardivari* (modest dress and household). Beyond this, state leaders instituted the use of Islamic symbolism in public discourse. It became common to begin all public meetings with recitation of the Qur'an, and more important, the state took it upon itself to enforce prayer and fasting—obligatory religious practices that had hitherto remained matters of private concern.[78] The Council of Islamic Ideology supported the state's arrogation of the right to police compliance with prayers.[79] In 1984 Zia appointed a Nazim-i Salat (Organizer of Prayer) to encourage prayer and also to submit reports to the government on popular behavior.[80] The government accelerated building of mosques, including the grand state mosque (Faisal Mosque) in Islamabad. The government also ordered all public offices to provide a place for prayer—which was tantamount to enforcing prayer on all employees—and used the media to encourage compliance among the population. Government support for Hajj pilgrimage also increased, as did its sponsorship of various other Islamic programs. The military also made much of symbolic measures such as a grand celebration of the birthday of the Prophet (*milad al-nabi*) as a national holiday and occasion for affirming the Islamicity of the state.

The state thus intruded into the private sphere to regulate social transactions and individual lives to an unprecedented extent, and to mold the citizenry and their worldview in a manner to facilitate greater state domination over them. An Islamically conscious citizenry would readily submit to an Islamic state. Having committed the state to Islamization, Zia sought greater normative compliance with the state by Islamizing the citizenry. The state's aim here was not only to increase religious observance but to instill in the population that vision of Islam that would support the domination of an Islamic state and that would foster harmony across society, as well as in state-society relations.

Beginning in 1979 the military regime initiated a process of educational change with a view to bringing it into alignment with the Islamization process.[81] Education was important to that process in that it would inculcate in the population the values that Islamization policy wished to promote and would create normative compliance with the state's central role in Islamization. If Islamization was meant to strengthen the state and the success of that endeavor hinged on popular acceptance of the notion of an Islamizing state, then education would properly orient the population to facilitate realization of those ends. Moreover, the military regime hoped that by instilling Islamic values in Pakistanis through the educational system they would become immune to leftist politics. This was an important issue for Pakistan after the Soviet Union arrived on its borders with Afghanistan in 1980, and for Zia, who hoped to extinguish all enthusiasm for Bhutto and the PPP in the populace.

Educational changes emphasized use of Urdu in place of English—posing the issue as one of decolonization rather than Islamization. In addition, educational curricula included greater emphasis on Islamic history, faith, and practice. Higher education received particular attention. Zia hoped that the new educational system in the universities would train the needed manpower for the Islamization regime. Universities across Pakistan were endowed with *shariah* departments, dedicated to providing Islamic education to all students, as well as training specialists in religious matters for employment in public and private sectors.

Zia, much like Anwar, believed in "Islamization of knowledge"—that modern and Islamic education systems can coexist and that modernity can be infused with Islamic values. To this end, Zia helped establish the International Islamic University of Islamabad. Like its sister institution in Kuala Lumpur, the International Islamic University of Islamabad sought to provide the state with modern and yet pious manpower that would be capable of operating in modern sectors of the economy and would help administer society in compliance with dictates of the Islamic faith.

Also important was the Zia regime's policy toward religious seminaries (*madrasahs*). The seminaries, which train the ulama and which had been outside of the formal educational system and the control of the government, had grown in number throughout the 1970s as Islamic consciousness had grown, and generous funding from Saudi Arabia and labor remittances from the Persian Gulf had supported seminary education.[82] The Afghan war would further raise the number of seminaries and, moreover, make them important to Pakistan's politics. The war made seminaries instrumental to recruitment and training of guerilla fighters in Afghanistan.

As a part of the Islamization initiative, the Zia regime provided financial and other support to seminaries, and enabled Islamic parties, social groups, and ulama to do the same.[83] Most notably, from 1980 onward seminaries became notable recipients of *zakat* funds that the government collected. In 1984, for instance, 9.4% of *zakat* funds went to support of seminaries, benefiting 2,273 seminaries and 111,050 students.[84]

The Zia regime also encouraged the proliferation of seminaries by increasing opportunities for employment of their graduates in government agencies and state institutions. Recruitment into government service, however, went hand in hand with changing the social and intellectual functions of traditional Islamic education. In 1979 the National Committee on Dini Madaris (Religious Schools) produced a report that encouraged seminaries to reform their curricula in order to be more relevant to the needs of the changing society and economy.[85] The conclusions of the report raised the ire of the traditional ulama, who rejected the state's attempt to judge the quality of their curricula or to modernize it.[86]

In 1982 the government announced that it would view seminary certificates as the equivalent of formal school certificates if seminaries were willing to undertake certain reforms in their curricula.[87] The announcement opened the door for seminaries to recruit from a broader spectrum of students, and through them, to play a more central role in society as whole, as well as in national educational and political institutions.

With the government willing to provide financial support and accommodate their graduates, many seminaries looked beyond training ulama to provide the Islamizing state with its new "Islamic bureaucracy." Various ulama organizations and parties, as well as self-styled Islamist parties, also looked to new seminaries to help them expand their base of support. Greater role for seminaries in national education would produce a citizenry that would more likely vote for Islamic parties and consider Islamic ideology an appropriate anchor for the conduct of politics. Zia may have seen in seminaries the possibility of changing the character of the Pakistani electorate and strengthening Islamic parties—which were closer to his regime—to the detriment of the secular national parties, the PPP in particular, that were likely to oppose his regime.

As a result, the number of seminary graduates jumped from 1,968 in the 1978–80 period to 3,601 in 1984–85.[88] Whereas 5,611 ulama had been trained in Pakistan in the 1960–80 period, 6,230 were trained in the 1981–85 period alone.[89] Umbrella organizations were set up under the supervision of the Ministry of Religious Affairs to shepherd the seminaries.[90]

State support for seminary education also meant greater state control of seminaries. The ulama had hoped to benefit from state patronage and jobs, but retain control of their seminaries. The ulama's resistance to extension of the state's reach into their educational domain led to tensions in relations between the two. As early as 1982 various ulama began to complain that reliance on *zakat* funds, disbursed by the government, had reduced voluntary contributions to seminaries, which at times exceeded government contributions, and could at any rate jeopardize seminaries' relations with society. Mufti Mahmud, the influential leader of JUI, who was personally close to Zia and his Islamization regime, at one point asked seminaries associated with JUI to refuse *zakat* funds, lest his party and the tradition with which it is associated lose control of their seminaries to the state.[91] A number of ulama in Sind declared government funding to be a form of political bribe and hence objectionable. Still others, who sought to altogether shut down the flow of government funds to seminaries, declared that the funds should not be accepted on religious grounds.

As the state's control over seminaries grew, Islamic groups and parties began to show their unhappiness by opposing government policy making. Since they were hard-pressed to challenge the government's Islamization policies, they began to criticize the government on a host of other issues. The result was that the scope of Islamic opposition to the state expanded, as did the purview of Islamist groups' political activism. The expansion of state control over Islamic institutions therefore broadened the scope of the state's competition with Islamist parties over policy making, the right to interpret Islam, and control of Islamic institutions.[92]

The Zia regime, compared to the Mahathir administration in Malaysia, paid less attention to the potential of Islamization for managing economic growth. Still, Islamization in Pakistan included new approaches to the economy. The Report of the Islamization Committee of 1980 emphasized addressing income inequality, wealth tax, economic growth, universal education, social security, and antipoverty measures.[93] The report, which was the most serious statement of government intentions at the time, made the argument that economic growth must occur with greater income equality. In this regard it recommended land reform and a more progressive inheritance tax. It also encouraged greater government management of the economy through five-year plans and encouraged a moderate rate of growth.[94] The report made no real impact on planning, which continues to be driven by non-Islamic goals and concerns.[95]

The military regime, however, changed the banking system to make it interest-free. Although most of Pakistan's banking happened through a small number of foreign banks, the Islamization of the banking system provided the powers-that-be with symbolic legitimacy, as well as greater control over the financial system.[96] Interest-free banking was particularly important to the relations between the Zia regime and its base of support among the lower middle classes, small shopkeepers, and merchants.

More important were the imposition of religious taxes, *zakat* and *ushr* (a 5% land tax on value of harvests of irrigated lands or 10% on rain-fed land), and, more generally a tax collection and distribution bureaucracy that purported to be an Islamic welfare system (see table 6.1).[97] Zia entrusted the state to collect and distribute *zakat* and *ushr* funds, and made them compulsory. By taking over the collection and distribution of religious taxes, he also bolstered the claim of his regime to be truly Islamic.[98] The general saw the taxes as the cornerstone of an Islamic welfare system.[99] Moreover, in the case of *ushr* the state had finally introduced an agricultural tax, but after disguising it as an Islamic tax. Islamization therefore provided the state with some leverage, if not a convenient cover, in carrying out some of the measures that had been effectively resisted before.

The state's takeover of the collection and distribution of religious taxes was aimed at improving social welfare, but also decreasing the government's budget deficits.[100] In fact, since 1988 *zakat* and *ushr* funds have been officially integrated into the government revenue accounts.[101] The contribution of these taxes to state revenue is modest, but they represent an increase in tax revenues, filling in for taxes that ought to be collected directly and are not. Although direct tax rates are quite high—60% for individuals in the highest

Table 6.1. *Zakat* Revenue as Proportion of Government Receipts and Expenditures *(Rs. Million)*

	1980–81	1981–82	1982–83	1983–84	1984–85
Total government revenue	46,349	51,166	59,080	72,309	77,777
Indirect taxes	29,325	31,883	37,267	41,808	43,062
Direct taxes	7,184	8,486	8,943	8,836	9,619
Expenditures	39,216	43,103	56,183	68,949	84,114
Social spending	1,350	1,496	1,804	2,300	2,506
Zakat and *Ushr*	0.844	0.799	1,031	1,263	1,417
Ushr	—	—	0.176	0.252	0.186
Land tax	0.241	0.230	0.189	0.169	0.219
Zakat distribution	0.750	0.500	0.750	0.750	1000

Source: Jamal Malik, Colonization of Islam: Dissolution of Traditional Institutions in Pakistan (Delhi: Manohar, 1996), p. 97.

bracket and 65% for companies—tax revenue recovery remains quite modest. Evasions of income and corporate tax are common, and the agricultural sector has been exempt from income tax. In recent years direct taxes have made up only 13–18% of the tax revenues.[102]

A Central Zakat Administration was formed under the Ministry of Finance to collect religious taxes. It had cells in every level down to villages, thus providing the state with an elaborate revenue collection organization. By 1983 there were some 37,000 *zakat* committees across Pakistan, employing some 260,000 people.[103] The system co-opted some 126,000 mosque preachers and placed them under government supervision.[104] This represented a significant revenue extraction administration with considerable reach into society. In 1983 the Ushr Assessment and Collection Rules were introduced.[105]

Zakat and *ushr* did not generate much revenue, but they were important in a country wherein tax evasion is pervasive and some segments of the population such as the landed elite pay little or no taxes.[106] The *ushr* tax, for instance, is a notable agricultural tax levied on an economic sector that pays very little in tax. This shows that relations between state and society over revenue extraction vary depending on the nature of ideological and cultural forces that set the context for that encounter.

Between 1980 and 1990 the government collected a total of Rs.15.1 billion (about $1.18 billion) in *zakat* and *ushr* funds.[107] This was only a fraction of government income from remittances or aid. In fact, religious taxes constituted some 2% of government revenue.

Religious taxes were distributed among the poor, but were also used to support Hajj and religious seminaries. In 1980–88 only 58% of religious tax revenues were disbursed among the poor.[108] Between 1980 and 1990 Rs.9.3 billion ($688 million) in religious tax revenue was disbursed to the poor.[109] This sum is not very large. Still in a country where in 1994 government disbursement to the poor constituted merely 0.5% of GDP the religious tax revenues constituted a significant increase in welfare disbursement.[110] The religious tax revenues, moreover, complemented revenues that the state took over from religious endowments, shrines, and charities, in the name of Islam. Centralizing tendencies of Islamization thus nudged the state to produce a welfare system, in which revenues generated by religious taxes have formed the basis of the state's redistributive efforts. Limits before state power in effectively redistributing resources to the poorer segments of the population—owing in large measure to continued prominence of feudalism—have compelled the state to look to Islamic symbols and institutions to achieve distribution of resources. This trend reached its apogee under Zia. Zia saw redistributive institutions to be important to expansion of state power.[111] He used Islamization to gain control of existing redistributive mechanisms tied with religious endowments, shrines, seminaries, and mosques, and to create a new Islamic welfare system under the control of the state.[112] Religious taxes therefore were more directly relevant to the state's project of power than to its revenue base.

The Islamization measures amounted to an elaborate state-led initiative to establish state hegemony over the public and private spheres, and to bring relations between state and society into harmony. The success of Islamization in achieving these ends, however, greatly depended on the vicissitudes of Pakistan's politics in the 1980s.

Islamization and Pakistan's Politics in the 1980s

Pakistan's Islamization initiative was both more thoroughgoing in terms of areas of society, law, and economy that it covered, and was closer to the ideological demands than the Malaysian approach. However, in Pakistan the state was not able to establish the same degree of hegemony over the political process, or exercise the same degree of social control that was evident in Malaysia. That Malaysia's Islamization was "soft" in comparison to Pakistan's may account for its greater success. Also, although troubled by political turmoil in the late 1970s, Malaysia enjoyed far more stability and political continuity on the eve of the Islamization initiative than did Pakistan. UMNO's steadying hand in the political process, meanwhile, ensured a more seamless fusion of state policy and Islamism than the military could produce in Pakistan. Another important factor was that Pakistan's society is more fractured along ethnic and sectarian lines, thus making state hegemony less tenable. Whereas in Malaysia the primary divisions are between Muslims and non-Muslims (Chinese and Indians)—and the Muslim Malay community is fairly homogeneous—in Pakistan the important identity fault lines are internal to the majority Muslim community.

The military regime thus faced increasing resistance to Islamization and was unable to fully establish hegemony on politics. Therefore, after 1983—when opposition to the military regime gained momentum—Islamization became increasingly an ad hoc process, whose vicissitudes were decided in the political process and as part of the struggles of power between state and social actors.

The military regime faced resistance from three separate although increasingly interconnected political constituencies: ethnic forces, Shi'is, and prodemocracy forces. The Zia regime took over power at a time when Baluchistan was in throes of a rebellion against the center and Sind was reeling from ethnic tensions between Muhajirs (in urban areas) and Sindhis (in rural areas).[113] That the military was active in suppressing the Baluch, had removed a Sindhi prime minister, and was itself primarily a Punjabi force heightened ethnic tensions. The advent of the Afghan war further aggravated tensions in Sind as the flow of funds from the war empowered Pathans and Afghans in Karachi.[114]

Initially the Zia regime used the rhetoric of Islamic solidarity, and more generally Islamization, in the hope of obfuscating soaring ethnic tensions. It also aimed to downplay the Punjabi domination of the state under the aegis of the military by harping on Islamic themes. JUI and the Jama'at used their influence among the Baluch and Pathans, and the Muhajirs, respectively, to promote ethnic peace under the aegis of the Islamic state. As useful as this approach may have been in the short run, it was unlikely that it would prove viable in the long run. Zia had been aware of the fact that as appealing as Islamization may have been to Muhajirs, Punjabis, and a host of other Pakistani ethnic groups, it was unlikely that it would have assuaged Sindhis, who had lost out with the fall of Bhutto.[115] Therefore, in practice the Zia regime was compelled to acknowledge the ethnic reality of Pakistan's politics. Islamization at the official level was thus complemented with ethnic politics at the practical level. As a result, during the Zia period Pakistan's politics experienced greater ethnic tensions just as it became anchored in Islamic solidarity. This entwined Islamization with ethnic politics, predicating the fomer on the imperatives of the latter.

The Islamization initiative also had an impact on Shi'i-Sunni relations in Pakistan, which were already undergoing change owing to Shi'i mobilization that had followed the Iranian revolution of 1979.[116] Zia's Islamization was largely a Sunni affair, and hence viewed Shi'i activism as a threat. This became apparent when Shi'is refused to submit to Zia's *zakat* law. Faced with the strong Shi'i protest—manifested in a large-scale and violent demonstration by some 25,000 Shi'i demonstrators from across Pakistan on July 5, 1980, that shut down the capital, Islamabad—and significant pressure brought to bear on Pakistan by Iran, the Zia regime capitulated. It recognized Shi'i communal rights and exempted Shi'is from all those aspects of the Islamization package that contravened Shi'i law.

The Shi'i victory was deemed ominous by many in the ruling regime. In addition, the state's capitulation to Shi'i demands in 1980 was seen by Zia's Sunni Islamist allies as nothing short of constricting their envisioned Islamic state and diluting the impact of Islamization. The Zia regime began its efforts to contain Shi'i assertiveness by investing in Sunni institutions in general, and Sunni seminaries in particular.[117] This, it hoped, would entrench Sunni identity in the public arena and in various state institutions and government agencies. The state thus promoted Sunni Islamism only to confront the polit-

ical and geostrategic threat of Shi'i Islamism. The Islamization period therefore also witnessed the rise of a sectarian division in Pakistan's society that in
the 1990s would pulverize civic order.[118]

The greatest challenge to the Islamization regime, however, came from resistance to military rule and the demand for restoration of democracy.[119] The
Zia regime proved unable to remove this issue from the political arena and to
anchor politics in its entirety in concern with democratization. By the middle
of the 1980s the combination of ethnic, Shi'i, and democratic forces greatly
constricted the hegemony of Islamization.

In June 1981 Zia charged the Council of Islamic Ideology to prepare a
draft for an Islamic system of government. More specifically, he directed the
council to study what system of government would be compatible with
Islam—thus laying groundwork for changing the political system in the
name of Islamization. The council formed a commission led by Mawlana
Zafar Ahmad Ansari.[120] The Ansari Commission relied heavily on Islamist
writings on the concept of the Islamic state, and hence recommended a presidential system for Pakistan with concentration of power in state institutions
and leaders.[121] The commission, however, allowed for elections, provided
they did not include political parties. The Ansari Commission therefore laid
the groundwork for reducing the scope of democratic rights and practices,
and concentrating greater powers in state institutions in lieu of civil society
ones, in the name of Islamization.[122]

In 1983 pro-democracy joined in alliance with ethnic and Shi'i parties
under the leadership of Bhutto's daughter, Benazir, to form the Movement for
Restoration of Democracy (MRD). The rise of MRD proved a serious chal-
lenge to the Zia regime, especially since Pakistan was then involved in the
Afghan war, and the 1983–84 period was one of heightened tensions with
India.[123] MRD's activism threatened the process of expansion of state power
in the name of Islamization. First, it included the most important political
constituencies that were outside of Islamization's purview of control: Shi'is,
Sindhis, Baluchis, some Pathan ethnic parties, and the remnants of the PPP.
Second, the movement was led by Bhutto's daughter, resurrecting the PPP
and the ideological and political forces that the military had sought to eliminate. Finally, MRD rejected limiting the scope of democratic rights and practices in the name of Islamization.

Zia's response to MRD was to open the political system somewhat—re-
lent on the demand for democracy—but to reemphasize the imperative of Islamization to retain the ideological upper hand in confronting opposition to
his regime. In 1983 a new constitutional framework was set to work to revise
the 1973 constitution in line with the Ansari Commission's report.[124] In 1984
Zia asked Pakistanis to vote on his regime in a national referendum. The
question put before the voters, however, was whether they favored Islamization. In this way Zia clearly blurred the line between type of regime in power
and the goal of Islamization, equating the latter with military rule and concentration of power in the state.

In 1985 Pakistan went to the polls to elect a parliament. The elections were open but did not allow party affiliations. This led the PPP to boycott the elections. As a result, the partyless elections produced a government favorable to Zia that was led by the Muslim League leaders—although without openly claiming to represent that party—with a Sindhi landlord, Muhammad Khan Junejo, as prime minister. The elections and the subsequent government were designed to take the wind out of MRD's sails by restoring the parliament and a civilian government. By replacing Islamists with the Muslim League, Zia sought to curb the ideological image of his regime, while the greater presence of the landed elite, and the choice of a Sindhi landlord for prime minister were designed to broaden the base of his regime.[125] Zia's appeal to the landed elite was particularly important since this class had been at odds with Zia owing to the military regime's efforts to tax the agricultural sector and to concentrate powers in state institutions. The inclusion of the landed elite in the ruling coalition was not, however, free of tensions. The private sector that had supported Zia all along was not altogether reconciled to the greater prominence of the landed elite at the center. These tensions would eventually translate into open rivalry between Nawaz Sharif and Junejo over the leadership of the Muslim League.

The elections of 1985 were a concession to popular demands for democracy but did not derail Islamization. Rather, the elections provided Zia with a new venue to pursue the project of state power through Islamization. The elections had followed the recommendations of the Ansari Commission's report, most notably in banning party affiliations. After the elections the resultant parliament had no clear internal structure of discipline based on party affiliation, and thus was very much subservient to the president. Zia used the parliament to "legitimately" transfer greater powers to the presidency, thus fulfilling the central demand of the Ansari Commission. The most notable step in this regard was the Eighth Amendment to the constitution that gave broad powers to the president to dismiss the prime minister and the parliament as he saw fit, thus placing democracy at the mercy of the president.[126]

Zia also found the new parliament a more effective means for pushing through his Islamization initiative. The greater presence of Islamist legislators was also important in this regard. Therefore, after 1985 the parliament became the focus of Islamization of the judiciary.[127] Limits before Federal Shariat Courts were now removed through legislation that sought to broaden the mandates of those courts and remove constraints that faced their operation.[128] The preoccupation with Islamization of the judiciary thus turned attention away from socioeconomic and political issues to Islamization. It obfuscated the chasm between democracy and Islamization that MRD had pointed to by focusing the attention of the parliament on Islamization and turning it into an instrument for its implementation.

This, however, presented Zia with new challenges. The effort to relieve Federal Shariat Courts of their constraints implied that Islamization to date had been inadequate. The parliament in fact devised a Shariat Bill to address the issue,[129] and in 1986 the Senate passed the Ninth Amendment to the constitution to give Federal Shariat Courts the power to declare any law repugnant to Islam. The demand for that bill soon became the focus of parliamentary activity, and when the bill faced an impasse in 1988 Zia used the excuse to dismiss the parliament. There were many reasons that Zia lost patience with the parliament. However, as far as Islamization was concerned, the parliament had conveniently made the Shariat Bill a highly visible issue, and the failure to pass it was viewed by Zia as a credible excuse to do away with the parliament. In addition, Zia did not wish the parliament to replace him as the chief "Islamizer" in Pakistan, and thus devolve powers from state institutions and leaders to the parliament. After the parliament was dismissed, Zia issued the Shariat Ordinance to achieve what the Shariat Bill had promised.

Shortly afterwards, Zia was killed in an airplane crash. His death quickly opened the political process. The military allowed for open elections based on party affiliation, thus ending the reign of the Ansari Commission's report. The elections brought to power Benazir Bhutto and the PPP in a weak ruling coalition that was greatly constrained by the military and remnants of the Zia regime.

Islam and Politics During the Democratic Period, 1988–99

Zia died before the Islamization initiative had been completed and attained its objectives. In 1988 Islamization in Pakistan still did not enjoy the degree of hegemony that it did in Malaysia, nor had its institutional and political goals been fully put in place. More important, Islamization in Pakistan had subdued other contestants for power, but had not completely vanquished them, nor had the state completely appropriated the right to interpret Islam and speak for it from Islamist forces. Islamization had restored state power in Pakistan, but in 1988 it had to produce the kind of stability and control that UMNO enjoyed in Malaysia.

With Zia's death the opponents of Islamization—who had earlier gathered in MRD—mounted an effective bid for redefining the ideology, function, and goals of the state. The political alliance that had sustained Islamization was, however, still strong. As a result, Pakistan's politics became polarized between the pro-Zia forces (notably, the military, Islamists, and the private sector) and the PPP and its allies among the landed elite, ethnic parties, and the Shi'i.[130] The Muslim League under Nawaz Sharif formed the core of the pro-Zia faction—forming the Islamic Democratic Alliance (IDA)—and the PPP under Benazir Bhutto that of the anti-Zia one. The elections of 1988 gave the control of the central government to the PPP, but that of Punjab to IDA. More important, neither PPP nor IDA enjoyed solid majorities and were at the mercy of precarious coalitions. Consequently, financial deals and strong-arm tactics replaced real issues in determining political allegiances and the coalitional constellations of parliamentary representatives. This exploded financial corruption and led to political decay.

The petty squabbles and corruption complicated democratic consolidation, economic reform, and stability.[131] During the decade of democracy that followed Zia's death Pakistan's economy weakened, its growth rate declined, and levels of external debt forced the government to succumb to IMF dictates in the late 1990s. Ethnic tensions in Sind escalated to a civil war in Karachi, adversely affecting commerce in the country's largest city and financial center. Elsewhere in Pakistan collapse of law and order, sectarian violence, and political tensions signaled declining state authority. Democracy thus produced a crisis of governability and reversal of gains that state power had made under Zia. The president and the military used the powers that Zia had vested in the presidency on three occasions to dismiss elected governments (Benazir Bhutto in 1991 and 1996 and Nawaz Sharif in 1993) and parliaments and to call for fresh elections (1990, 1993, and 1997). In 1999 the military intervened to suspend what it called the "sham democracy" altogether. Between 1988 and 1999 Pakistan went through four general elections and had seven governments led by five prime ministers. During the decade of democracy (1988–99) no government completed its electoral mandate.

There is little doubt that the crisis that faced Pakistan's democracy eroded state power and weakened its institutions. The sudden death of Zia left the consolidation of power at the center incomplete. In fact, a reversal in that process began as a consequence of the collapse of democratic rule into the rivalry between Benazir Bhutto and Nawaz Sharif, which led to the polarization of national politics, corruption, and political decay. The repeated interventions of the military and the presidency in the democratic process were in part an effort to reverse this trend.[132] In 1999 the military concluded that democracy in its existing form could not help restore authority and power to the state, and that this end could be achieved only by ending democratic rule.

Political developments during the democratic era redefined the relation of Islam to the state. Islam continued to be important in the political arena. Islamist parties remained active in politics, generally supporting Nawaz Sharif and the Muslim League against Benazir Bhutto and the PPP. Islamist political institutions and organizations continued to proliferate, and a new penchant for violence and sectarianism became apparent, especially after the rise of the Taliban in Afghanistan.

At the official level, however, Islamization suffered a setback. First, the rise of Benazir Bhutto and the PPP undermined Islamization's claim to universal support and put some of the policies that were associated with it in question. In fact, early on, the rivalry between the PPP and IDA was very much defined by the struggle to dismantle or preserve the Islamization regime. Benazir Bhutto's failure to win a clear mandate in the 1988 elections limited her ability to challenge the Islamization regime. Islamization, and the laws, policies, and institutions associated with it remained intact, but lost the prominence that they enjoyed under Zia. Nawaz Sharif, on the other hand, continued to support Islamization, proposing new legislations to its reach. Still, even during Nawaz Sharif's tenure of office Islamization did not regain the stature it enjoyed during the Zia period. Nawaz Sharif promulgated a

Shariat Bill in 1990—which the parliament had failed to pass during the Zia period—formed the Bayt al-Mal (Islamic Treasury or Fund) in 1992 to streamline collection and distribution of *zakat* funds, talked of creating an Islamic welfare state, and continued support for seminaries, Islamic courts, and Islamic laws.[133] His most ambitious undertaking in this regard was a new Shariat Bill that was passed in 1998 as the Fifteenth Amendment to Pakistan's constitution.

Second, the intense rivalry between the PPP and Muslim League turned attention away from ideological issues to political squabbles. In addition, economic hardship, the collapse of law and order, and ethnic tensions were deemed to be more pressing problems, and it was not readily apparent how they would tie in with Islamization. As a result, the ruling governments—and Nawaz Sharif in particular—found diminishing returns to pushing for Islamization and were not able to anchor politics in Islamization as had been the case in the 1980s. As a result, even when there was support for Islamization it failed to dominate politics as a national goal.

Third, in the 1990s the government found it increasingly difficult to sustain its financial support of Islamization. Economic crises forced the government to cutback on its expenditures. This made religious taxes, although meager, more important. For instance *zakat* revenues had increased from Rs. 2.19 billion ($168 million) to Rs. 4.65 billion ($357 million).[134] These funds were important in supporting the government's welfare expenditures (0.4% of GDP in 1994).[135] However, from the outset Islamization had been a source of patronage more than one of revenue. As a result, at a time of economic downturn Islamization came under pressure, and the political relations that it had spawned began to weaken. Flow of funds to seminaries declined—leading many to turn to foreign patrons or criminal activities—as did provision of jobs to seminary graduates. All this contributed to the growth of militancy in seminaries and reduced the state's control of them.[136] Insofar as control of seminaries in the 1980s had been an important extension of state authority into the religious spheres, in the 1990s that trend was reversed. Similarly, patronage of various other Islamic institutions and organizations was reduced.

The decade of democracy therefore witnessed gradual erosion of state power and authority, and decline in centrality of Islamization to politics and the working of the state. Still, there were attempts during this period to reverse this trend, most notably by Nawaz Sharif. Throughout the democratic period Nawaz Sharif followed the example of Zia to weave the demand for Islamization with his own project of power to create a stable ruling regime that would be able to augment state power and formulate and implement policies. His efforts in this regard were hampered by the absence of an effective parliamentary majority until 1997 and tensions with the presidency and the military, which controlled the levers of power and removed his government in 1993. However, these limitations were also instrumental in convincing him of the imperative of Islamization for consolidation of power under the Muslim League and the parliament and through them the state.

During Nawaz Sharif's initial stint as prime minister first signs of fissure in the anti-PPP forces surfaced. Tensions between Nawaz Sharif and the president at the time, Ghulam Ishaq Khan, who enjoyed the support of the military, led to Nawaz Sharif's dismissal, fresh elections, and Benazir Bhutto's return to power.[137] It was evident that Nawaz Sharif and the Muslim League would be able to exercise power only if that power was concentrated in the office of the prime minister, and if that office was able to lord over the presidency and the military. The fall of the Muslim League government in 1990 thus led that party to move away from the military and to look for ways of exercising power independent of the military. In this regard, Nawaz Sharif sought to appropriate the legacy of the Zia period and to fashion the Muslim League in lieu of the military as the vehicle for Islamization in Pakistan.

Although Islamization was in abeyance in the 1990s, Islam continued to be important to Pakistan's politics. Islamist forces enjoyed limited support, but Islamic values were important to a broader spectrum of voters. From 1993 onward the Muslim League sought to construct a stable right-of-center Islamic bloc that would appeal to that broad spectrum of voters, and would place the Muslim League in the position to capitalize on the Islamic vote to project power in the political arena. The upshot of this would be that the Muslim League would replace the military as the champion of Islamization. In this the Muslim League enjoyed some advantage over the military. Like UMNO, the Muslim League was a party and could more successfully represent an ideological and political platform. In fact, throughout the 1990s Nawaz Sharif looked to Malaysia as a model, not only in ensuring the Muslim League's domination over Islamist politics, but in using Islamization in the service of development. In this Nawaz Sharif went beyond the initial goals of the Zia regime, whose primary objective was restoration of state authority.

The results of the 1993 elections encouraged Nawaz Sharif and the Muslim League in this regard. In those elections the Muslim League and its brand of soft Islamism did well. It did not win the elections because the Jama'at and two other Islamist electoral coalitions took away votes from the Muslim League to PPP advantage. In at least ten constituencies the votes cast for Islamic parties and the Muslim League exceed those for PPP candidates, but the seats went to the PPP. Those ten seats may well have denied Benazir Bhutto her victory.

Islamist parties, however, did poorly. The Jama'at, which contested the elections on its own and challenged the Muslim League in several seats, won only three seats to the National Assembly, and its leader, Qazi Husain Ahmad, failed to win a seat. All Islamic parties put together won nine seats, trailing behind the religious minorities.[138] It was evident from the election results that whereas there was a repository of support for Islamic causes and values, there was little support for ardent Islamism and Islamist parties. The Muslim League stood to gain by posing as a moderate Islamic party that stood for the values and causes that the electorate favored, but not the kind of politics and policies that Islamist parties advocated. The Muslim League's approach to Islam and politics from this point forward would greatly resemble that of UMNO after 1980. Throughout the 1990s all attention was focused on the PPP and Benazir Bhutto whereas the real story in Pakistan was the rise of the Muslim League as claimant to power in that country.

The Muslim League's project of power faced resistance from two important political groups. The first were Islamist parties in general, and the most prominent among them, the Jama'at, in particular. The Muslim League and the Jama'at had both been a part of the Zia regime and had initially been allied in IDA against the PPP.[139] In this their relationship was very different from that of UMNO and PAS. By 1993, however, their competition for control of Islamist politics very much resembled the standoff between UMNO and PAS, with the difference that the Muslim League did not enjoy the same balance of power vis-à-vis the Jama'at that characterized UMNO's relations with PAS.

Islamist parties had been a pillar of the Zia regime and the strongest defender of its Islamization initiative. They were also among the most ardent opponents of the PPP. As a result, they quickly joined hands with the Muslim League in IDA to protect the values and policies of the Zia regime. When Benazir Bhutto fell from power in 1990 and was replaced by Nawaz Sharif, Islamist parties no longer saw any urgency in cooperating with the Muslim League. Islamist parties, and the Jama'at in particular, had all along viewed themselves as the rightful heirs to the Zia regime. They had hoped that once Benazir Bhutto and the PPP had been vanquished, the Jama'at who would assume the reigns of power in Pakistan. Islamist parties, therefore, viewed the Muslim League as a rival.

Islamist parties were conscious of the power and potential of Islam in the political arena and believed that as the rightful spokesmen for Islamism they had proprietary rights to Islamist politics: it should be they who would reap the political benefits of Islamization. Nawaz Sharif's attempts to relate his own project of power to a renewed Islamization initiative, therefore, set him on a collision course with Islamist parties. His Shariat Bill of 1990 elicited strong criticism from the Jama'at and its leader, Qazi Husain Ahmad, who described the bill as inadequate and a ruse designed to facilitate a power grab by the Muslim League.[140]

The rivalry between Islamists and the Muslim League led to the breakup of IDA in 1993, pursuant to which the Jama'at decided to contest the national elections on its own, and other Islamist parties congregated in two separate electoral alliances. The Jama'at, in particular, took the prospects for exceeding the Muslim League in importance and an Islamist victory at the polls most seriously. The party's leader, Qazi Husain Ahmad, posed as a national leader, on par with Benazir Bhutto and Nawaz Sharif. As mentioned earlier, the Jama'at's expectations came to naught, but that did not end Islamist rivalry with the Muslim League, which to some extent accounts for Nawaz Sharif's inability to successfully consolidate power under his party.[141]

The other source of resistance to Nawaz Sharif's project of power was the military. After Zia's death the military did not produce a national leader capable of carrying the mantle of "chief Islamizer." The military as an institution showed signs that it favored a return to professionalism in lieu of open advocacy of Islamization. It was the military's turn away from openly championing Islamization that opened the door for Nawaz Sharif to assume that position. The military was not, however, reconciled to the political implications of Nawaz Sharif and the Muslim League's assumption of the mantle of the Zia regime. For Nawaz Sharif's ultimate aim was to wrest power from those state institutions that had monopolized power under Zia and vest them in the parliament and the prime minister, and ultimately the Muslim League and himself. The relations between the military and the Muslim League therefore deteriorated throughout the 1990s. The military was behind efforts to limit Nawaz Sharif's power on several occasions and made tactical alliances with Islamist parties to do so. It was, however, only after Nawaz Sharif's project of power was not restoring power in the state—and hence, not reversing the political decay that democratization had augured—and also had begun to infringe on the prerogatives of the military that the generals intervened directly in the political process.[142] The military therefore remained the main obstacle to the prime minister—and Nawaz Sharif and the Muslim League—emerging as the true heirs to General Zia and replicating his use of Islamization to consolidate power.

The scope of Nawaz Sharif's use of Islamization to augment power became evident in the 1997–99 period. The general elections of 1997 followed the dismissal of the PPP government for corruption and mismanagement. At the time of the elections Benazir Bhutto and the PPP were at the nadir of their popularity, Pakistan faced a serious financial crisis, and the threat of political decay and loss of power at the center appeared more foreboding than ever. The elections greatly favored the Muslim League. The PPP was too unpopular to be a challenge, and other right-of-center and Islamist parties were unprepared to mount an effective campaign.[143] In fact, the Jama'at and JUP boycotted the elections fearing a repetition of the 1993 humiliation. Only JUI contested the elections.

The elections of 1997 were the first since 1988 to give a party a clear mandate to rule. The Muslim League won 136 of the 217 seats to the National Assembly, a 63% majority. The PPP managed only nineteen and JUI only two.[144] The election results produced the smallest contingent of Islamist representation in the parliament on record. This permitted Nawaz Sharif to more openly fashion the Muslim League on the model of UMNO. The Muslim League was to form a stable right-of-center government that would not be beholden to Islamist parties and would be able to govern Pakistan with a strong claim to representing popular national and religious aspirations. As a senior Muslim League leader, Mushahid Hussain, put it to me, "Nawaz Sharif will be both the Erbakan [leader of Turkey's Islamist Refah Party at the time] and Mahathir of Pakistan." The Muslim League's claim was bolstered by the fact that it had taken over seats that were once held by Islamist parties and had defeated those Islamist candidates that had participated in the elections. It argued that it could better serve the interests of the Islamic vote bank, given

that only it could keep the PPP out of office and put in place Islamic legislation. However, the Muslim League's power in 1997 was not based on the kind
of grassroots support that UMNO relies on, nor were Islamists as easily marginalized in Pakistan as were PAS and *dakwahs* in Malaysia.

Still, Nawaz Sharif was quick to set in place new directives for Islamization in the political process. Islamic symbols, laws, and policies would more
directly serve the aim of economic growth. Nawaz Sharif, who himself hails
from the private sector, emphasized the goal of rapid development—of turning Pakistan into another "Asian tiger." He believed that the example of Malaysia was germane, not only because UMNO served as an appropriate model
for the Muslim League, but also because Malaysian leaders Mahathir and
Anwar Ibrahim were respected by Islamists in Pakistan, and Malaysia's model
of development had been lauded by them. Malaysia therefore would serve as
an appropriate way of committing Pakistan to development through an example with which Pakistanis could identify, and which Islamists could support.

The first indication that Nawaz Sharif intended to appropriate the right to
interpret Islamism and the place of Islamic values in public life, and to do so
in the service of the state and its goal of development, was his move to
change the public holiday from Friday to Sunday. This was a demand of the
private sector that believed that such a change was necessary for greater international economic interactions. The move also symbolized the shift from
emphasis on Islam to emphasis on the economy. The change was not received
well in all quarters. Islamist parties had demanded that Friday (the Muslim
sabbath) be the public holiday in lieu of Sunday throughout the 1960s and the
1970s. In fact, it was to mollify his Islamist opposition that Z. A. Bhutto
changed the holiday to Friday. The change back was depicted as a reversal of
Islamization, marked an open breach between the Muslim league and Islamist parties, and underscored the difficulties that faced Nawaz Sharif in
successfully riding the tiger of Islamism.[145]

More important, however, were the implications of the electoral victory
and the Muslim League's assumption of the position of spokesman for Islam
in politics for restoration of state power and relations between the prime minister and other institutions of the state, the military in particular. For the first
time in Pakistan's history one party was in the position to control 75% (that
is, with its close allies) of the National Assembly, which allowed it to change
the constitution. There was then an opportunity to scrap the Eighth Amendment to the constitution that had been set in place by Zia to limit the powers
of the parliament and the prime minister in favor of those of the president—
a power that had been exercised three times since 1988 and had prevented all
three elected governments up to that time from completing their terms. The
Muslim League eventually removed the Eighth Amendment, thus once again
making the parliament and the office of the prime minister the preeminent instruments of power in the state.

This trend continued in 1997 and 1999 as Nawaz Sharif followed the example of Mahathir (versus the sultans and the judiciary) to concentrate power
under the prime minister's control. Nawaz Sharif forced the resignation of the

president, choosing his own candidate for the job, curtailed the powers of the judiciary after a public showdown with the Supreme Court, dismissed the chief of staff of the Army, and was about to do the same again when he was ousted in the coup of 1999. Nawaz Sharif also used his greater powers to crack down on his opposition, ordering arrest of protesters, closure of newspapers, and harassment of opponents. For instance, in May 1999 120 PPP activists were arrested in Lahore to prevent them from demonstrating against the government, and a number of prominent journalists were arrested after they criticized corruption in the government.[146] In Karachi, terrorism courts were used to silence Muhajir opposition to the government and intimidate opponents. All this occurred during a time of escalating economic crisis, which compelled the government to sign on to difficult IMF austerity packages.

When the Muslim League government assumed office, Pakistan's domestic and foreign debt had reached $50 billion (90% of GDP) and Pakistan had become reliant on IMF loans. Economic progress slowed after Pakistan faced trade sanctions that were imposed on the country for its testing of a nuclear weapon in 1998. In addition, the expansion of the prime minister's powers did not produce palpable improvements in administrative management and corruption. As a result, Nawaz Sharif's project of power—which unfolded more rapidly than that of Mahathir—was received with greater cynicism and faced greater resistance. That resistance culminated in the October 1999 coup, which promised to deliver on the promises of the Muslim League administration, but to do so without use of Islamization.

The 1999 coup marks the end of the Islamization era in Pakistan. General Parvez Musharraf quickly separated questions of power, administration, and growth from Islamization. The general's position suggests that the military no longer views Islamization as a useful tool for restoration of power to the state. In fact, the coup was staged to arrest erosion of state power and authority that occurred over the course of the last decade. Still, at its inception Islamization was designed to strengthen state control of society, and expand its powers and reach. It was a component of state leaders' project of power. That it did not fully accomplish that task owes to the interplay of a set of factors, ranging from Pakistan's social structure to the vicissitudes of democratization.

Conclusion

The Islamization Period in the Balance

The Islamization period in Malaysia and Pakistan lasted some two decades, beginning in 1979–81 and stretching through 1997. During that time it became entwined with state leaders' project of power and deeply influenced the working of the state. It affected the scope of state powers, policy making, and reach into society. Islamization redefined state-society relations, and changed the balance of power between the two. Islamization had its roots in the Islamist challenge to state authority in the 1970s. In time, however, it became the ideology of choice for state leaders in these weak postcolonial states that otherwise lacked strong ideological tools and enjoyed only precarious hegemony over society. Islamization thus became a phase in the life span of the postcolonial state in Malaysia and Pakistan. In the end, Islamization was not so much a reinvention of the state, but a tool to allow the postcolonial state to rise above the limitations before it. The cultural directives of Islamization were real, but its impact on state institutions, law, and policy making did not amount to creating the state de novo. To the contrary, the state during the Islamization period was very much the same as before, only now it was masquerading behind an Islamic veneer. The postcolonial state in Malaysia and Pakistan emerged from Islamization with its institutional design, trappings of power, and view of the role of the state and its relation with society very much intact. The Malaysian state under Mahathir at the time of the general elections of 1999 (which will be discussed later) was little different in its fundamental characteristics than before the Islamization period, save for the fact

158

that it was stronger in 1999. In Pakistan General Parvez Musharraf's military rule resembles Ayub Khan's regime more than that of Zia ul-Haq. After two decades of Islamization very little in the fundamental characteristics of the state has changed.

In the final analysis, Islamization was not so much about Islam as it was about the state. Despite its ideological and religious trappings, Islamization was a strategy of state formation. Its ultimate success or failure was determined in the political arena, and then as a measure of the extent to which it served the interests of the state. There is little doubt that Islamization did fulfill this function, and to that extent it was a useful tool in the hand of state leaders in both dealing with crises before the state at a critical juncture, and strengthening the state and expanding its reach. In both Malaysia and Pakistan Islamization in the first place allowed secular postcolonial states to survive the tidal wave of Islamist activism. In Malaysia, Islamization then served the state's goal of economic growth and development, whereas in Pakistan it was used first and foremost to restore state authority.

What the cases of Malaysia and Pakistan show is that states are governed by the imperative of hegemony and legitimacy, as well as the need to generate wealth and economic growth and extract revenue from society. Religion and, more broadly, culture are directly relevant to state reach and power, and hence, to the aforementioned imperatives. Far from static actors in politics, or antithetical to the goals and needs of the modern state, religion and culture are powerful and dynamic forces that serve the interests of that state. The role of religion and culture in politics, and their contribution to the project of state power, must be reexamined and understood more broadly than has been the case in the social sciences.

The turn to Islamization in Malaysia and Pakistan had to do with the particular characteristics of the state that go back to the colonial era. Malaysia and Pakistan were weak states that were conceived at the moment of independence, and lacked strong nationalist ideology and social cohesion. Their politics had been open to Islamist activism all along, and at the critical juncture of the late 1970s–early 1980s a new leadership rose to power that was more open to the presence of Islam in the political process.

In both Pakistan and Malaysia Islamization benefited and co-opted not the poor; but the middle and lower middle classes. It co-opted through its ideological appeal and patronage and corporatist practices the upwardly mobile and economically vibrant classes that were gaining political awareness but could not be accommodated in the elite and oligarchy-dominated power structures of the postcolonial states at the time. The co-optation of those classes precluded a middle class–lower class alliance against the ruling order that led to the revolution in Iran and continues to fuel Islamist challenges to the state in the Arab world.

Islamization also co-opted Islamist thinkers, activists, and movements, which weakened opposition to the state, but made state institutions the arena for struggles of power. As the state adopted Islamization, Islam ceased to be an important axis of conflict between state and society, but precipitated new conflicts between state actors and leaders. Therefore, under Islamization the state became larger and more domineering over society, but itself became open to conflict. In Malaysia these conflicts were evident in UMNO and manifested themselves with the dismissal of Anwar Ibrahim, and in Pakistan they defined the relations between the various institutions of power as well as with the state's Islamist clients.

In particular, the Islamizing state was able to remove ideology as a main axis of conflict in the political arena, but this did not mean the end of Islamist opposition to the state. With ideology out of the way Islamist parties more openly displayed their political and organizational interests, which were not served by the Islamization regimes. Islamization fulfilled the ideological demands of Islamism, but not the political and organizational interests of Islamists who were upstaged by the state and kept away from power. In Pakistan this produced tensions in Zia's relations with Islamist parties, most notably the Jama'at, and culminated in the breach between that party and the Muslim League in the 1990s.[1]

Islamist parties came to the conclusion that they would fare better in opposition to secular states and are likely to be marginalized by state-led Islamization. The Jama'at had reached the height of its power and popularity in opposition to Z. A. Bhutto and the PPP in the 1970s, and had witnessed a decline since then. The Jama'at therefore welcomed the removal of Nawaz Sharif, and quickly mobilized in opposition to General Musharraf's apparent turn to secularism after the coup of 1999 in the hope of gaining by polarization of politics between a secular state and its Islamist opposition.[2] Similarly, in Malaysia PAS has gained since the dismissal of Anwar Ibrahim (discussed later), and which reduced the state's hold on Islamist politics.

The outcomes of the Islamization initiative in Malaysia and Pakistan were quite different. In Malaysia, the state was able to successfully divide Islamist forces, and to co-opt some of them through UMNO and marginalize the rest. Islamization in Malaysia unfolded smoothly and produced both a stronger ruling party and state institutions—whose interaction and cooperation ensure state power. In Pakistan Islamization faced greater resistance, and as a result unfolded more unevenly in spurts and through negotiation. The state was able neither to successfully divide Islamist force nor to co-opt or marginalize them. There were a number of factors that were important in determining the varied outcome. The Malaysian state entered the Islamization era from a position of greater strength whereas state institutions in Pakistan faced a crisis at the end of the Bhutto era. Malaysian society is divided along ethnic lines, but there is little real division within Malay society. In Pakistan there are deep-seated ethnic and sectarian divisions among Muslims. As a result, in Malaysia Islamization was more readily acceptable to all Muslims than it was in Pakistan. In Malaysia Islamization to some extent became the ideology of the Malay community in face of competition with the Chinese and Indians. In Pakistan Islamization at all times remained an ideology of the state, over whose content there was disagreement. Finally, in Malaysia UMNO was at the forefront in the state's attempt to manage the society and govern the economy, whereas in Pakistan this task was performed by the military. As a party UMNO was better able to co-opt Islamist forces and formulate Islamization as a political platform. Even when the Muslim League replaced the military as the focus of Islamization, it lacked the infrastructural power and autonomy of UMNO.

Malaysian Islamism, too, was different from Pakistani Islamism. In Malaysia Islamism was divided between the more moderate ABIM and PAS, with the former dominating the Islamist scene in the 1970s. In Pakistan there was no moderate Islamist element, and Islamism as a whole wielded greater power on the eve of Islamization than did ABIM or PAS in Malaysia.

By the end of the 1990s the Malaysian state was moving away from Islamization, whereas Pakistan continued to be deeply involved in Islamization—promulgating a sweeping Shariat Bill in 1988 and again in 1998. In Malaysia the state had attained greater stability and social control, and its pursuit of economic growth continued unbridled. In Pakistan, by contrast, political decay and economic crisis eroded state authority and power, so much so that by the time of the coup of 1999 Pakistan was facing the same problematic that it did in 1977. During the Islamization era state power and authority had experienced a bell-curve rise and decline. The dissipation of Islamization in Malaysia in light of expansion of its state power and pace of its economic growth was proof that Islamization had attained its intended objectives— hence, why a strong Malaysian state, having experienced economic growth, could sublimate Islamization. Conversely, in Pakistan the continued salience of Islamization in the face of erosion of state power suggested the opposite, that Islamization had failed.

The end of Islamization also had to do with financial crises and IMF prescriptions. Both Malaysia and Pakistan faced economic downturns from 1997 onward, which changed the political equation that underpinned the Islamization regimes. The political fallout from the economic crises compelled the states to withdraw financial support from Islamization schemes, but, more important, to end political ties that had been spawned by Islamization.

The Asian Financial Crisis and the Fall of Anwar Ibrahim

In 1997 Southeast Asian economies were plunged into a financial crisis. The crisis was most severe in Thailand and Indonesia, but it affected Malaysia's economy as well. The Asian financial crisis opened a breach between Mahathir and his deputy prime minister, minister of finance, and heir apparent, Anwar Ibrahim. Anwar favored implementation of IMF prescriptions even on a voluntary basis. That would have meant reform and restructuring of the economy, withdrawal of government support for failing businesses and banks, and an end to lucrative government patronage of industrial projects. All of this would have adversely affected the Malay industrial elites and capitalists that had been carefully nurtured by Mahathir over the course of the previous two decades. Mahathir did not favor sacrificing gains made by

Malay capitalists to live by IMF prescriptions. There was also a great deal of pressure brought to bear on Mahathir from within UMNO where the Malay business elite wielded a great deal of power.[3] In the end Mahathir chose capital controls to prevent collapse of the Ringgit, and blamed international financiers and Western economic practices for Malaysian financial woes, thus using nationalism in place of economic reform.[4] The Malay industrial and business elite now viewed Anwar as a threat and began to look for ways of curtailing his power. It was clear that Anwar was not committed to the Malay millionaires that Mahathir had nurtured and was more interested in enriching the Malays as a whole, possibly through altogether different policies and institutions. This realization caused an open breach, first between Anwar and the Malay business interest, and then between Anwar and Mahathir. Mahathir indicated the direction that he was leaning by giving the control of the economy to Daim Zainuddin, who had been closely tied with the Malay business elite and the policy of supporting them in the 1980s.

The disagreement between Mahathir and Anwar over economic policy, however, quickly escalated into a struggle for power. It was an open secret in Malaysia that, encouraged by the fall of Suharto in Indonesia, Anwar was poised to challenge Mahathir for the leadership of UMNO.[5] Mahathir and the growing opposition to Anwar from among the Malay business elite within and outside UMNO therefore openly resisted a change in party leadership, and, following the lead of Daim Zainuddin, began an anti-Anwar campaign. The loss of support among the business elite all but ended Anwar's chances of assuming the party's leadership. The business elite were, however, wary of Anwar, and at any rate did not want him in control of the ministry of finance.[6]

Anwar responded to the concerted attack on his position by the business elite by turning to populism to shore up his authority. He began to criticize financial corruption involving UMNO leaders and business elite. Chandra Muzaffar writes that Anwar went so far as refusing to guarantee the immunity of Mahathir's family—some of whom have been engaged in questionable business practices.[7] Anwar took heart from the collapse of the Suharto regime in Indonesia, and quickly adopted the rhetoric of the prodemocracy movement there, and called for reform (*reformasi*) to depict Mahathir as an authoritarian ruler and his regime as corrupt and nepotistic.[8]

Mahathir, however, was not Suharto.[9] He was popular among Malays and had the backing of a powerful party. He was able to react to Anwar's challenge quickly, and did so ruthlessly.[10] He dismissed Anwar from his official positions, charging him with financial mismanagement, corruption, abuse of power, and sexual misconduct.[11] With this move Mahathir not only removed an immediate challenge to his own leadership and the financial interests of the Malay business elite, but also sought to end Anwar's political career altogether. Anwar's arrest and subsequent trial precipitated the most serious Malay anti-government protest movement since the May 1969 riots. Under the banner of *reformasi* Anwar's supporters demanded political and financial accountability from the powers-that-be. The movement gained momentum after it became apparent that Anwar had been beaten in jail, and the case against him had all the trappings of a staged political lynching.[12]

The arrest and trial of Anwar had broad implications for the relation of state to Islam, especially as charges of sexual misconduct caused as much consternation in Islamist circles abroad—leading to widespread condemnation of Mahathir—as they did domestically. It would also underscore the degree to which the state had gained in strength since 1980. Anwar Ibrahim had continued to be associated with ABIM, many of whose members were now working in various state institutions and in businesses, and who constituted the urban middle classes. The showdown between Mahathir and Anwar therefore put to question the loyalty of the ABIM constituency—to the extent to which it still existed—to UMNO and the state, and whether the two would be able to weather the consequences of the attack on Anwar. For the dismissal and trial of Anwar was popularly viewed as a divorce between UMNO and ABIM, and, hence, the end of the Islamization era. It had been the alliance between Mahathir and Anwar that had kept Islamism under state control and anchored in a moderate middle. The end of that alliance could have meant that the state would lose control of Islamism and that Islamism could gravitate toward greater radicalism. Mahathir had gambled his own future and that of UMNO on the fact that the party and the state were now sufficiently strong, and enjoyed enough social control, to purge Anwar and his ABIM constituency.

The Asian financial crisis thus parlayed into a struggle for power in Malaysia that drove a wedge between two of UMNO and the state's principal constituencies, the business elite and the pro-Islamist middle classes. Until 1997 UMNO and the state's political and economic platforms had successfully included both as Islamization had gone hand in hand with economic growth. In fact, Anwar had very much symbolized the convergence of interests of the two constituencies. After Anwar's dismissal a chasm opened between the business elite and the pro-Islamist forces in UMNO. Mahathir and UMNO elite chose the business elite. As a consequence, the pro-Islamist middle-class constituency was alienated from UMNO and became a stronger source of support for Anwar.

As UMNO's grip over that element of Islamism that it had co-opted in the 1980s weakened, others began to make a bid for it.[13] It had been the UMNO-ABIM compact that had marginalized PAS in the 1980s. With the end of that compact, PAS saw new opportunities before it.[14] For the first time since the late 1970s UMNO had no viable Islamic credentials, and Malaysian politics was becoming polarized between secularism and Islam, with the latter relegated to the opposition.[15] PAS saw this development as a threat to UMNO and escalated its attacks against the government, accusing it of corruption, authoritarianism, and un-Islamic practices. To underscore UMNO's Islamic legitimacy deficit in the wake of Anwar's trial, PAS upped the ante with Islamization by demanding the death penalty for apostasy. PAS leaders argued that Anwar had made a mistake to join UMNO in the first place, and that the interests of Islam would never be served in a secular party. PAS, however, was able to threaten UMNO only in the northern states and its rural areas and small towns. As significant as that threat would be, it would not be sufficient for undoing UMNO at the center. PAS had tempered its stance greatly since the 1970s in response to changes in urban Malay society and changes in Islamism in the Middle East—Khomeini's revolutionary rhetoric was replaced with overtures to democracy of Khatami of Iran and Ghannouchi of Tunisia.[16] Still, the party was hard-pressed to attract the urban Malays. In 1980 PAS was viewed by many in ABIM and its supporters in urban centers as too militant. The same ABIM members and supporters, after years of integration into the economy and mainstream society, were now even farther from PAS.

The other contender for the ABIM vote was the new party, Parti Keadilan Nasional (National Justice Party), that was formed by Anwar's wife, Wan Az-izah Isma`il. The National Justice Party's setup and program reflect the changes that have taken place in the ABIM constituency over the course of the past two decades. The party is not openly Islamic, but rather demands social justice, democracy, and economic reform. It also capitalizes on popular anger over the treatment of Anwar. The National Justice Party seeks to regroup the old ABIM and its supporters, but without an open call to Islam. The upwardly mobile ABIM constituency is no longer likely to respond to such a call, but would look favorably on a reconstitution of ABIM, albeit informally.

Thus with the end of the Mahathir-Anwar alliance Islam once again became an antiestablishment political force.[17] The extent to which it could threaten UMNO and make a bid for power would be decided in elections. As Malaysia's economy improved throughout 1999 UMNO felt more confident, leading Mahathir to call for general elections in November. The National Justice Party, PAS, and the Chinese Democratic Action Party formed an electoral alliance. The National Justice Party–PAS alliance was in essence the anti-UMNO ABIM-PAS alliance that had been on the table in the early 1980s.

The election results, however, attested not only to the power of UMNO and social control of the state but also to the continued salience of Islamism.[18] UMNO was able to use its considerable resources to ensure Barisan Nasional's victory at the polls—retaining its two-thirds majority in the parliament (winning 148 of the 193 seats to the parliament, down from 162 in 1995)[19]—proving that UMNO and the state were now strong enough to rule without Islamiza-tion.[20] That Mahathir and UMNO chose the business elite over Anwar and his constituency underscored where the aims and interests of the ruling party and the state lay. That Mahathir and UMNO could win the 1999 election in the face of a resurgent PAS and National Justice Party attests to the success of Islamization—producing a powerful state that can rule without Islamization, and even in spite of it—at least for now.

However, the election results were a setback for UMNO in other regards. Barisan Nasional's victory came from its constituent parties' strong showing in Borneo and southern Malaysia, and among the Chinese. The ruling alliance did not do as well among Malays, which could be interpreted as a defeat for UMNO. UMNO did poorly in the northern Malay-dominated states, and its total number of seats declined from eighty-eight in 1995 to seventy-two.[21] PAS retained control of Kelantan, won state elections in Terengganu (a critical state owing to its oil and natural resources), and improved its showing in provincial elections in Perlis and Kedah (Mahathir's home state). In Kelantan PAS won forty-one of forty-three seats to the state parliament, and in Terengganu, twenty-eight of thirty-two, virtually obliterating UMNO in those states. PAS also increased its presence in the national parliament from eight to twenty-seven.[22] The National Justice Party, however, did poorly. It won only five seats to the parliament, but none in Kuala Lumpur where its intended constituency is concentrated and where the opposition relied on the party to deliver the vote.

The election results prove that the collapse of the Mahathir-Anwar alliance has indeed opened up the political process to PAS and brought Islam to the center of national politics. The results also show that the ABIM constituency is either no longer there—given the fact that the National Justice Party did poorly—or that is has been divided up between UMNO and PAS. The elections therefore suggest that UMNO to some extent continues to be a player in Islamist politics, but its dominance has been lessened by PAS's resurgence. The power of UMNO and the state after two decades of Islamization is considerable, but its control of Islamism is not total. The state may not altogether be able to keep Islamism in the moderate middle as easily as it did in the 1980s and the 1990s. UMNO and state leaders will once again have to contend with Islamism as an oppositional force over which they cannot exercise absolute control. They will have to compete with PAS for that control.[23] Without Anwar UMNO will be at a disadvantage in that competition.

The IMF, the Bomb, and Collapse of Pro-Islamization Alliance

The failure of Nawaz Sharif and the Muslim League to effectively rule Pakistan also owed to financial crises facing the state. Here, too, the political cost of economic reform adversely affected the state's ability to continue to manage Islamism in the political process. This combined with the mounting political crisis facing the Muslim League in 1997–99 to precipitate a critical crisis of governability that ended with the military coup of 1999.

Pakistan was already facing a severe financial crisis when Nawaz Sharif assumed office in 1997. The financial crisis along with continued bickering with IMF over the implementation of its austerity package had been one of the principal reasons for the fall of the PPP government in 1996. The interim administration that governed Pakistan between the PPP and Muslim League governments addressed some of the immediate problems. The Muslim League, however, had to tackle the thornier issue of implementing an IMF austerity package that was unpopular in Pakistan and faced stiff political and social resistance.[24] The most contentious issues were IMF's recommendations regarding greater taxation of the agricultural sector, increase in the price of fuel and electricity, and an end to government subsidies.

The problem facing the government became more pronounced when in 1998 Pakistan followed India in testing a nuclear device. This led to economic sanctions that pushed Pakistan's already ailing economy to the brink of collapse. Nawaz Sharif's efforts to manage the resultant financial crisis and to put in place the IMF package began to divide the pro-Islamization alliance that had supported the government. The breakup of the political constituency that Nawaz Sharif had inherited from Zia and was to serve as the basis of the Muslim League's domination of the state, and, in turn, the state's domination of society and politics, made Nawaz Sharif and his party vulnerable to the resistance that his attempts to concentrate power was facing in other quarters.

Islamist parties had been moving away from the Muslim League since 1990, and more openly since 1993. However, before the financial crisis of 1997–99 these parties had not been able to draw away any social and political groups from the Muslim League. The government's response to the financial crisis, however, presented them with that opportunity.

Islamist parties, and the Jama'at in particular, have been active in opposition to IMF policy prescriptions since the early 1990s. When in 1993 the provisional government of Moeen Qureshi introduced an austerity package recommended by the IMF, the Jama'at quickly took the lead in protesting the rise in prices and cutbacks in social supports and services. While the party's aim was to establish a base of support among those the reforms would squeeze, it also used the IMF's Western image to link its own anti-imperialist rhetoric to a new populist stance.

This strategy found more coherent shape in the summer of 1996, when the PPP government introduced its new budget. The IMF had warned Pakistan that unless it introduced new taxes to cover the growing government deficit, the fund would withhold $600 million in new loans. The IMF favored new agricultural taxes that would extract resources from the landed elite, but the government was not eager to precipitate a showdown with that class, and instead sought to cover its deficit through new sales taxes and closing exemptions, all of which affected the industrialists, salaried middle classes, merchants, and lower middle classes, who were the Muslim League and Islamization's base of support. The new measures proved to be highly unpopular and led to demonstrations in several cities. The Jama'at was at the forefront of a number of these protests, characterizing the government's actions as protection of the wealthy and punishment of the poor. One showdown in Rawalpindi led to the death of four demonstrators at the hands of the police. Also important in opposing IMF prescriptions were merchants who precipitated a political crisis through a series of well-organized strikes.

Since 1996 the Jama'at has systematically rejected the IMF's prescriptions as unnecessary, excessive, and tantamount to enslavement. In recent years the anti-IMF position has gained strength in light of Mahathir's tirades against Western economic institutions during the Asian financial crisis. In 1998 as IMF prescriptions began to take effect, the Jama'at renewed its attacks on that institution, posing as the defender of national rights. Claiming to speak for the masses, the party warned the government against heeding the advice of the IMF. The Islamist opposition to the IMF thus distinguished the Islamist parties from the Muslim League, and laid the groundwork for it to benefit from the political fallout of the Muslim League's attempt to implement IMF's prescriptions in 1999 following Pakistan's nuclear test and the sanctions that followed it.

Both the private sector and the merchant classes—bazaar merchants, traders, and shopkeepers—had supported Pakistan's nuclear test. After sanctions were imposed on Pakistan, however, the private sector lobbied for signing of the Comprehensive Test Ban Treaty and an end to sanctions. The small-scale merchants, on the other hand, continued to support the nationalist and Islamist position that rejected any compromise on the nuclear issue. The private sector, moreover, openly supported implementation of the IMF plan in hope of reforming the economy and generating growth. The merchants followed the lead of the Islamists in rejecting IMF recommendations as imperialist dictates.[25] The private sector supported Nawaz Sharif whereas the merchants gravitated to Islamist parties. The breakup of the alliance between private sector and small merchants that had been forged since the resistance of both social groups to Bhutto in the 1970s greatly weakened the Muslim League. The merchants had been instrumental in the Muslim League's challenge to the PPP. For instance, between 1993 and 1996 the merchants orchestrated a number of strikes across Pakistan that undermined Benazir Bhutto's authority. That power had now passed out of the hands of the Muslim League and into that of its opposition. Moreover, since the private sector and the small merchants had been two of the principal sociopolitical pillars of Islamization their parting of the ways weakened that process as well. The military coup of 1999 and its secular orientation were a consequence of the weakening of both the Muslim League and the Islamization regime.

The defining issue in this process was the government's decision to implement a 12% general sales tax that was demanded by IMF as a way of generating revenue for the government. The small merchants were strongly opposed to this tax, for it would force them to reveal what they sold and at what prices. This would them make them liable to more efficient taxation by the government down the road. The merchants made their displeasure known through three days of strikes in Karachi, along with protests in other cities.[26] The opposition to the sales tax drove a wedge between the Muslim League and the merchants, who now openly joined the ranks of the opposition.

The sales tax issue was followed with renewed clashes between India and Pakistan in Kashmir, and the Pakistan military's decision to send guerilla forces into the Kargil region of Kashmir to bog down Indian troops there. This led to an international diplomatic crisis and brought India and Pakistan to the brink of war. The crisis was resolved owing to American pressure and pursuant to Nawaz Sharif's meeting with Bill Clinton in Washington. The withdrawal of the guerillas from Kargil was unpopular with the military, Islamists, and the small merchants—who unlike the private sector saw no benefits in either foreign trade or better relations with India. The Kargil episode thus created a common ground between these erstwhile supporters of Islamization who all stood opposed to Nawaz Sharif and the Muslim League. By the end of 1999 the Muslim League and its Islamization was narrowly based in the private sector and traditional Muslim League supporters. That made it vulnerable to a challenge by the military to resume its preeminent position in the state.

In the end Islamization failed to either ensure the long-run viability of the state or to produce a stable social base to support the state's domination of society. Islamization helped restore authority to the state in the 1980s, but failed to stop the erosion of that authority in the 1990s. Islamization produced a social base for military rule over Pakistan, but that was never integrated into a seamless source of support for state power. In fact, it came undone during the democratic period and as a consequence of financial crises.

In both Malaysia and Pakistan Islamization ultimately proved untenable. In Pakistan it lost its ability to bolster state authority and its social base became undone. In Malaysia the fundamental incompatibility of the underlying secularism of the postcolonial state and Islamist ideology surfaced to separate the state from Islam. Here, too, a financial crisis served as the catalyst. Still, the Asian financial crisis merely brought to a head the festering unease of UMNO elite and their business allies regarding Anwar's rise to the helm.

Was Islamization a failure? Was it a futile exercise? The answer is decidedly no. Islamization bore many costs for Malaysia and Pakistan, the most obvious of which are bad laws, discrimination against women and minorities, and ideologization of the public arena political discourse. It also encouraged Islamist activism and militant attitude.[27] However, judging Islamization as a tool that was used by state leaders to serve state interests, it was in good measure a successful strategy. Islamization served the interests of weak postcolonial states at a critical juncture. It allowed those states to survive serious challenges to their authority, and provided them with ideological tools that allowed them to expand their power and reach and to create greater harmony in state-society relations at a time when the society was turning to Islam. Malaysia used the ensuing stability more successfully to pursue economic growth. On the downside, Islamization allowed states to avoid fundamental reforms in their economies, political structures, and policy making as it facilitated expansion of state power through successful manipulation of ideology rather than rationalization of the structure and working of state institutions. Islamization also allowed the state to regulate more and to spread its tentacles into civil society and the private lives of its citizens. Whatever the merits and costs of Islamization, it was nevertheless an important phase in state formation in Malaysia and Pakistan, the understanding of which is necessary for taking stock of the powers and working of the state in these countries.

Notes

Introduction

1. For general discussions of Islamism, see John L. Esposito, *Islam and Politics*, 3rd ed. (Syracuse: Syracuse University Press, 1991); Nazih Ayubi, *Political Islam: Religion and Politics in the Arab World* (New York: Routledge, 1991); Dale F. Eickelman and James Piscatori, *Muslim Politics* (Princeton: Princeton University Press, 1996); Hamid Enayat, *Modern Islamic Political Thought* (Austin, TX: University of Texas Press, 1982); Henry Munson, Jr., *Islam and Revolution in the Middle East* (New Haven: Yale University Press, 1988); Ali Rahnema, ed., *The Pioneers of Islamic Revival* (London: Zed Books, 1994); Emmaneul Sivan, *Radical Islam: Medieval Theology and Modern Politics* (New Haven: Yale University Press, 1985); Nikki Keddie, "The Revolt of Islam, 1700 to 1993: Comparative Considerations and Relation to Imperialism," *Comparative Studies in Society and History,* 36, 3 (July 1994), pp. 463–87; Michael M. J. Fischer, "Islam and the Revolt of the Petit Bourgeoisie," *Dædalus,* 111 (Winter 1982), pp. 101–25; John O. Voll, "Fundamentalism in the Sunni Arab World: Egypt and the Sudan," in Martin Marty and R. Scott Appelby, eds., *Fundamentalisms Observed* (Chicago: University of Chicago Press, 1991), pp. 366–95.

2. See Peter B. Evans, Dietrich Rueschemeyer, and Theda Skocpol, eds., *Bringing the State Back In* (New York: Cambridge University Press, 1985).

3. For discussion of weak states, see Joel S. Migdal, *Strong Societies and Weak States: State-Society Relations and State Capabilities in the Third World* (Princeton: Princeton University Press, 1988).

4. On the importance of the colonial era to explaining later development patterns, see *ibid.;* Lisa Anderson, *The State and Social Transformation in Tunisia and Libya: 1830–1980* (Princeton: Princeton University Press, 1986); Crawford Young, *The African Colonial State in Comparative Perspective* (New Haven: Yale University Press, 1994); Atul Kohli, "Where Do High-Growth Political Economies Come From? The Japanese Lineage of Korea's 'Developmental State,'" in Meredith Woo-Cumings, ed.,

The Developmental State (Ithaca: Cornell University Press, 1999), pp. 93–136; and Catherine Boone, "States and Ruling Classes in Postcolonial Africa: The Enduring Contradictions of Power," in Joel S. Migdal, Atul Kohli, and Vivienne Shue, eds., *State Power and Social Forces* (New York: Cambridge University Press, 1994), pp. 108–40.

5. S. V. R. Nasr, "European Colonialism and the Emergence of Modern Muslim States," in John L. Esposito, ed., *The Oxford History of Islam* (New York: Oxford University Press, 1999), pp. 549–99.

6. Kathleen Thelen and Sven Steimo, "Historical Institutionalism in Comparative Perspective," in Sven Steimo, Kathleen Thelen, and Frank Longstreth, eds., *Structuring Politics: Historical Institutionalism in Comparative Analysis* (New York: Cambridge University Press, 1992), pp. 1–32; D. B. Robertson, "The Return to History and the New Institutionalism in American Political Science," *Social Science History,* 17, 1 (Spring 1993), pp. 1–36; Peter Hall and Rosemary Taylor, "Political Science and the Three New Institutionalisms," *Political Studies,* 44 (1996), pp. 936–57; and Ellen M. Immergut, "The Theoretical Core of the New Institutionalism," *Politics and Society,* 26, 1 (1998), pp. 5–34.

7. Hall and Taylor, "Political Science," p. 938.

8. Douglass C. North, "Economic Performance Through Time," in Lee Alston, Thrainn Eggertsson, and Douglass C. North, eds., *Empirical Studies in Institutional Change* (New York: Cambridge University Press, 1996), p. 344.

9. Jack Knight, "Models, Interpretations, and Theories: Constructing Explanations of Institutional Emergence and Change," in Jack Knight and Itai Sened, eds., *Explaining Social Institutions* (Ann Arbor: University of Michigan Press, 1995), pp. 95–120; K. Dowding, "The Compatibility of Behavioralism, Rational Choice, and New Institutionalism," *Journal of Theoretical Politics,* 6, 1 (January 1994), pp. 105–17; R. M. Smith, "Ideas, Institutions, and Strategic Choice," *Polity,* 28, 1 (Fall 1995), pp. 135–40; D. D. Searing, "Roles, Rules, and Rationality in the New Institutionalism," *American Political Science Review,* 85, 4 (December 1991), pp. 1239–60.

10. Theda Scokpol, "Analyzing Causal Configurations in History: A Rejoinder to Nichols," *Comparative Social Research,* 9 (1986), pp. 187–94.

11. On the importance of the state to change, see Ellen Trimberger, *Revolution from Above: Military Bureaucrats and Development in Japan, Turkey, Egypt, and Peru* (New Brunswick, NJ: Transaction Books, 1978).

12. Margaret Levi, *Of Rule and Revenue* (Berkeley: University of California Press, 1988), pp. 1–10.

13. Douglass C. North, *Structure and Change in Economic History* (New York: W. W. Norton, 1981), p. 24. The impact of provision of services on the shape of the state is also evident in an exaggerated fashion in rentier states, whose structure reflects their emphasis on allocation of resources; see Kiren Aziz Chaudhry, *The Price of Wealth: Economies and Institutions in the Middle East* (Ithaca: Cornell University Press, 1997), and Terry L. Karl, *The Paradox of Plenty: Oil Booms and Petro-States* (Berkeley: University of California Press, 1997).

14. Eric Nordlinger, "Taking the State Seriously," in Samuel P. Huntington and Myron Weiner, eds., *Understanding Political Development* (New York: HarperCollins, 1987), pp. 353–90.

15. Barbara Geddes, *Politician's Dilemma: Building State Capacity in Latin America* (Berkeley: University of California Press, 1994), pp. 1–2. Marxists and neo-Marxists emphasize the function of the state to serve class interests by extracting sur-

plus and transferring it to the elite classes and state institutions; Ralph Miliband, *The State in Capitalist Society* (London: Weidenfeld & Nicolson, 1969); Nicos Poulantzas, *Political Power and Social Classes* (London, NLB; Sheed and Ward, 1973); Martin Carnoy, *The State and Political Theory* (Princeton: Princeton University Press, 1984).

16. Martin Van Creveld, *The Rise and Decline of the State* (New York: Cambridge University Press, 1999), pp. 336–414.

17. Atul Kohli, *The State and Poverty in India: the Politics of Reform* (New York: Cambridge University Press, 1987), pp. 15–50; Joel S. Migdal, "Strong States, Weak States: Power and Accommodation," in Weiner and Huntington, *Understanding Political Development*, pp. 391–434.

18. Karl, *Paradox of Plenty*, p. 45; also see Otto Hintze, *The Historical Essays of Otto Hintze*, Felix Gilbert and Robert M. Berdahl, eds. (New York : Oxford University Press, 1975); Charles Tilly, ed., *The Formation of National States in Western Europe* (Princeton: Princeton University Press, 1975); Theda Skocpol, *States and Social Revolutions: A Comparative Analysis of France, Russia, and China* (New York: Cambridge University Press, 1979).

19. Nordlinger, "Taking the State Seriously," p. 373.

20. Ziya Önis, "The Logic of the Developmental State," *Comparative Politics*, 24, 1 (October 1991), pp. 109–26; Chalmers Johnson, *MITI and the Japenese Miracle* (Stanford: Stanford University Press, 1982); *idem*, "The Developmental State: Odyssey of a Concept," in Woo-Cumings, *The Developmental State*, pp. 32–60; Stephan Haggard, *Pathways from the Periphery: The Politics of Growth in the Newly Industrializing Countries* (Ithaca: Cornell University Press, 1990); and Peter Evans, *Embedded Autonomy: States and Industrial Transformation* (Princeton: Princeton University Press, 1995).

21. Michael Mann, "The Autonomous Power of the State: Its Origins, Mechanisms, and Results," *Archives Européene de Sociologie*, 25 (1984), p. 185.

22. Joel S. Migdal, "The State in Society: An Approach to Struggles of Domination," in Migdal, Kohli, and Shue, *State Power*, pp. 7–34.

23. *Ibid*, p. 8.

24. Alfred Stepan, *The State and Society: Peru in Comparative Perspective* (Princeton: Princeton University Press, 1978), pp. 40–45.

25. Timothy Mitchell, "The Limits of the State: Beyond Statist Approaches and Their Critics," *American Political Science Review*, 85, 1 (March 1991), pp. 77–96.

26. Young, *The African Colonial State*, pp. 35–40.

27. Charles Tilly, "War Making and State Making as Organized Crime," in Evans, Rueschemeyer, and Skocpol, *Bringing the State Back In*, pp. 169–91; *idem, Coercion, Capital, and European States, A. D. 990–1990* (Cambridge, MA: Blackwell, 1990); and Thomas Ertman, *Birth of Leviathan: Building States and Regimes in Medieval and Early Modern Europe* (New York: Cambridge University Press, 1997).

28. Young, *The African Colonial State*, pp. 258–59.

29. Michael Barnett, *Confronting the Costs of War: Military Power, State, and Society in Egypt and Israel* (Princeton: Princeton University Press, 1992).

30. Levi, *Of Rule and Revenue*, p. 10.

31. North, *Structure and Change*, p. 24.

32. See, for instance, David Camroux, "State Responses to Islamic Resurgence in Malaysia: Accommodation, Co-Option, and Confrontation," *Asian Survey*, 36, 9 (September 1996), pp. 852–68; Manning Nash, "Islamic Resurgence in Malaysia and Indonesia," in Martin Marty and R. Scott Appelby, eds., *Fundamentalisms Observed*

(Chicago: University of Chicago Press, 1991), pp. 691–739; Simon Barraclough, "Managing the Challenges of Islamic Revival in Malaysia: A Regime Perspective," *Asian Survey,* 23, 8 (August 1983), pp. 958–75; Jomo Kwame Sundaram and Ahmad Shabery Cheek, "The Politics of Malaysia's Islamic Resurgence," *Third World Quarterly,* 10, 2 (April 1988), pp. 843–68; Mumtaz Ahmad, "The Crescent and the Sword: Islam, the Military, and Political Legitimacy in Pakistan: 1977–1985," *The Middle East Journal,* 50, 3 (Summer 1996), pp. 372–86.

33. Conroy, *The State and Political Theory,* p. 134.

34. Adam Pzerworski and Michael Wallerstein, "Structural Dependence of the State on Capital," *American Political Science Review,* 82 (March 1988), pp. 11–29.

35. For a review of the field, see Marc Howard Ross, "Culture and Identity in Comparative Political Analysis," in Mark I. Lichbach and Alan S. Zuckerman, eds., *Comparative Politics: Rationality, Cutlture, and Structure* (New York: Cambridge University Press, 1997), pp. 42–80; and Samuel H. Barnes, "Politics and Culture," *Research on Democracy and Society,* 2 (1994), pp. 45–64.

36. See, for instance, Gabriel Almond and Sidney Verba, *The Civic Culture* (Princeton: Princeton University Press, 1963), and Lucian Pye, *Asian Power and Politics: The Cultural Dimensions of Authority* (Cambridge: Harvard University Press, 1985).

37. Clifford Geertz, *The Interpretation of Cultures* (New York: Basic Books, 1973), p. 310.

38. Haggay Ram, *Myth and Mobilization in Revolutionary Iran: The Use of the Friday Congregational Sermon* (Washington, DC: American University Press, 1994); Gilbert M. Joseph and Daniel Nugent, "Popular Culture and State Formation in Revolutionary Mexico," in Gilbert M. Joseph and Daniel Nugent, eds., *Everyday Forms of State Formation: Revolution and Negotiation of Rule in Modern Mexico* (Durham: Duke University Press, 1994), pp. 3–23; Hamza Alavi, "Ethnicity, Muslim Society, and the Pakistan Ideology," in Anita Weiss, eds., *Islamic Reassertion in Pakistan: The Application of Islamic Laws in a Modern State* (Syracuse: Syracuse University Press, 1986), pp. 21–47; Vali Nasr, "Pakistan: State, Agrarian Reform, and Islamization," *International Journal of Politics, Culture, and Society,* 10, 2 (Winter 1996), pp. 249–72; Mustapha Kamal Pasha, "Islamization, Civil Society, and the Politics of Transition in Pakistan," in Douglas Allen, ed., *Religion and Political Conflict in South Asia: India, Pakistan, and Sri Lanka* (Westport, CT: Greenwood Press, 1992), p. 116; Charles Tripp, "Islam and the Secular Logic of the State in the Middle East," in Abdel Salam Sidahmad and Anoushiravan Ehteshami, eds., *Islamic Fundamentalism* (Boulder, CO: Westview, 1996), pp. 57–60; and Heken Siu, "Recycling Rituals: Politics and Popular Culture in Contemporary Rural China," in Perry Link, Richard Madsen, and Paul Pickowicz, eds., *Unofficial China: Popular Culture and Thought in Peoples Republic* (Boulder, CO: Westview Press, 1989).

39. David Laitin, *Hegemony and Culture: Politics and Religious Change Among the Yoruba* (Chicago: University of Chicago Press, 1986), p. 11.

40. Paul Brass, *Ethnicity and Nationalism: Theory and Comparison* (London: Sage Publications, 1991), p. 8; and Vali Nasr, "International Politics, Domestic Imperatives, and the Rise of Politics of Identity: Sectarianism in Pakistan, 1979–1997," *Comparative Politics,* 32, 2 (January 2000), pp. 171–90; *idem,* "Communalism and Fundamentalism: A Re-examination of the Origins of Islamic Fundamentalism," *Contention,* 4, 2 (Winter 1995), pp. 121–39; and Nikki R. Keddie, "The New Religious Politics: Where, When, and Why Do 'Fundamentalisms' Appear?" *Comparative Studies in Society and History,* 40, 4 (October 1998), pp. 696–723.

41. Charles Tilly, "Contentious Repertoires in Great Britain, 1758–1834," in M. Traugott, ed., *Repertoires and Cycles of Collective Action* (Durham: Duke University Press, 1995), p. 26.

42. Joseph and Nugent, "Popular Culture and State Formation," pp. 3–23.

43. Clifford Geertz, *Negara: The Theatre State in Nineteenth-Century Bali* (Princeton: Princeton University Press, 1980), pp. 121–22.

44. Antonio Gramsci, *Selections from the Prison Notebooks,* ed. and trans. Quinten Hoare and Geoffrey Nowell Smith (London: Lawrence & Wishart, 1971).

45. James C. Scott, *Weapons of the Weak: Everyday Forms of Peasant Resistance* (New Haven: Yale University Press, 1985).

46. Pierre Bourdieu, *Outline of a Theory of Practice* (Cambridge: Cambridge University Press, 1977); p. 191; Timothy Mitchell, "Everyday Metaphors of Power," *Theory and Society,* 19 (1990), pp. 545–77.

47. North, *Structure and Change,* p. 49.

48. Joel S. Migdal, "Studying the State," in Mark I. Lichbach and Alan S. Zuckerman, eds., *Comparative Politics: Rationality, Culture, and Structure* (New York: Cambridge University Press, 1997), p. 212.

49. James C. Scott's contribution to "The Role of Theory in Comparative Politics: A Symposium," *World Politics,* 48, 1 (October 1995), pp. 28–37.

50. Migdal, "Studying the State," p. 229.

51. Geertz, *Interpretations of Culture,* pp. 222–24.

52. *Ibid.*

53. For an interesting discussion of the role of pomp and theater in the Syrian state, see Lisa Wadeen, *Ambiguities of Domination: Politics, Rhetoric, and Symbols in Contemporary Syria* (Chicago: University of Chicago Press, 1999).

54. Geertz, *Negara,* p. 13.

55. Migdal, "Studying the State," p. 230.

56. Ayesha Jalal, "Conjuring Pakistan: History as Official Imagining," *International Journal of Middle East Studies,* 27, 1 (February 1995), pp. 73–89.

57. Lauren Berlant, *The Anatomy of National Fantasy: Hawthorne, Utopia, and Everyday Life* (Chicago: University of Chicago Press, 1991), p. 20. Also see Ranjit Guha, *Dominance Without Hegemony: History and Power in Colonial India* (Cambridge: Harvard University Press, 1997).

58. Migdal, "Studying the State," p. 230.

59. David Laitin, "Political Culture and Political Preferences," *American Political Science Review,* 82 (1988), pp. 589–93.

60. *Idem, Hegemony and Culture,* p. 175.

61. *Idem, Politics, Language, and Thought: The Somali Experience* (Chicago: University of Chicago Press, 1977), p. 19.

62. Sandria Freitag writes of India that the masses better understood the modern message of nationalism once it was conveyed to them through the familiar language of religion; see *Collective Action and Community: Public Arenas and the Emergence of Communalism in North India* (Berkeley: University of California Press, 1989).

63. Migdal, *Strong Societies and Weak States;* and *idem,* "Strong States, Weak States," pp. 395–96. Also see Lisa Anderson, "The State in the Middle East and North Africa," *Comparative Politics,* 20, 1 (October 1987), pp. 1–18.

64. Young, *The African Colonial State,* p. 16.

65. Cyrus Ghani, *Iran and the Rise of Reza Shah: From Qajar Collapse to Pahlavi Power* (London: I. B. Tauris, 1998); and Hakkan Yavuz, "Search for a New Social

Contract in Turkey: Fethullah Gülen, the Virtue Party, and the Kurds," *SAIS Review* 19, 1 (1999), pp. 115–16.

66. James C. Scott, *Political Ideology in Malaysia: Reality and the Beliefs of an Elite* (Kuala Lumpur: University of Malaya Press, 1968), pp. 218–20.

67. Lisa Anderson, "The Traditions of Imperialism: The Colonial Antecedents of the Authoritarian Welfare State in the Arab World," paper presented at the American Political Science Association meeting in Chicago, 1995.

68. Scott, *Political Ideology*, p. 218.

69. H. E. Chehabi and Juan J. Linz, eds., *Sultanistic Regimes* (Baltimore: Johns Hopkins University Press, 1998). For a discussion of this issue in the Middle East, see Sami Zubaida, *Islam, the People, and the State: Political Ideals and Movements in the Middle East* (London: I. B. Tauris, 1993), pp. 121–82.

70. Scott, *Ideology and Politics*, p. 218.

71. Migdal, "The State in Society," p. 26; Hamza Alavi, "The State in Postcolonial Societies: Pakistan and Bangladesh," in Kathleen Gough and Hari P. Sharma, eds., *Imperialism and Revolution in South Asia* (New York: Monthly Review Press, 1973), p. 145; Hassan N. Gardezi, "Neocolonial Alliances and the Crisis of Pakistan," in Kathleen Gough and Hari P. Sharma, eds., *Imperialism and Revolution in South Asia* (New York: Monthly Review Press, 1973), pp. 130–44; James Puthucheary, *Ownership and Control in Malayan Economy* (Singapore: Eastern University Press, 1960); and Jomo Kwame Sundaram, *A Question of Class: Capital, the State, and Uneven Development in Malaya* (New York: Oxford University Press, 1986), p. 245.

72. Alavi, "Ethnicity," p. 24.

73. Anthony Milner, *The Invention of Politics in Colonial Malaya: Contesting Nationalism and Expansion of the Public Sphere* (New York: Cambridge University Press, 1994), p. 2

74. Benedict Anderson, *Imagined Communities: Reflections on the Origins and Spread of Nationalism*, 2nd ed. (New York: Verso, 1991), pp. 113–40.

75. Partha Chaterjee, *Nationalist Thought and the Colonial World: A Derivative Discourse?* (London: Zed Press, 1986).

76. Ibrahim Abu Rabi`, "Islamic Resurgence and the Problematic of Tradition in the Modern Arab World: The Contemporary Academic Debate," *Islamic Studies,* 34, 1 (Spring 1995), p. 51.

77. Thomas Blom Hansen, *The Saffron Wave: Democracy and Hindu Nationalism in Modern India* (Princeton: Princeton University Press, 1999), p. 50.

78. See, for instance, Clement Henry Moore, *Politics in North Africa: Algeria, Morocco, and Tunisia* (Boston: Little, Brown, 1970); and Ali Gheissari, *Iranian Intellectuals in the Twentieth Century* (Austin: University of Texas Press, 1998).

79. Adeed Dawisha and I. William Zartman, *Beyond Coercion: Durability of the Arab State* (London: Croom Helm, 1988).

80. John P. Entelis, "The Crisis of Authoritarianism in North Africa: The Case of Algeria," *Problems of Communism,* 41 (May–June 1992), pp. 71–81.

81. Ayubi, *Political Islam, p.* 5.

82. Thomas R. Metcalf, *Ideologies of the Raj* (New York: Cambridge University Press, 1994); and Young, *The African Colonial State,* pp. 43–76 and 222–43.

83. Anderson, *The State and Social Transformation*, p. 273.

84. Timothy Mitchell, *Colonising Egypt* (Berkeley: University of California Press, 1991).

85. Migdal, "The State in Society," p. 26. Also see Chandra Muzaffar, *Challenges and Choices in Malaysian Politics and Society* (Penang: ALIRAN, 1989), p. 492.

86. Rupert Emerson, *From Empire to Nation: The Rise of Self-Assertion of Asian and African Peoples* (Cambridge, MA: Harvard, 1960); and Gyanendra Pandey, *The Construction of Communalism in Colonial North India* (Delhi: Oxford University Press, 1990).

87. Hansen, *The Saffron Wave,* p. 47.

88. Young, *The African Colonial State,* pp. 287–88.

89. Alan Richards and John Waterbury, *A Political Economy of the Middle East* (Boulder, CO: Westview Press, 1990); and Robert Malley, *The Call from Algeria: Third Worldism, Revolution, and the Turn to Islam* (Berkeley: University of California Press, 1996).

90. Mumtaz Ahmad, "Islamization and the Structural Crises of the State in Pakistan," *Issues in Islamic Thought,* 12 (1993), pp. 304–10.

91. François Burgat, *L'Islamisme en Face* (Paris : Découverte/Poche, 1996).

92. On the evolution of Islamist ideology and its principle directives, see Hamid Dabashi, *Theology of Discontent* (New York: New York University Press, 1993); Said A. Arjomand, "Ideological Revolution in Shi`ism," in Said A. Arjomand, ed., *Authority and Political Culture in Shi`ism* (Albany, NY: SUNY Press, 1988), pp. 178–209; Seyyed Vali Reza Nasr, *Mawdudi and the Making of Islamic Revivalism* (New York: Oxford University Press, 1996); and Voll, "Fundamentalism in the Sunni Arab World."

93. Keddie, "The Revolt of Islam." Also see, for instance, Hamid Algar, ed. and trans., *Islam and Revolution: Writings and Declarations of Imam Khomeini* (Berkeley: Mizan Press, 1981), pp. 27–28, 33–39, and 195–99.

94. Cited in Gilles Kepel, *Allah in the West: Islamic Movements in America and Europe* (Stanford: Stanford University Press, 1997), p. 160.

95. On the social base of Islamism, see Leonard Binder, *Islamic Liberalism: A Critique of Development Ideologies* (Chicago: University of Chicago Press, 1988), pp. 328–41; Abdallah Laroui, *L'ideologie arabe contemporaine* (Berkeley: University of California Press, 1967); Said Amir Arjomand, *The Turban for the Crown: The Islamic Revolution in Iran* (New York: Oxford University Press, 1988); Henry Munson, Jr., *Islam and Revolution in the Middle East* (New Haven: Yale University Press, 1988), pp. 98–104; Seyyed Vali Reza Nasr, *The Vanguard of the Islamic Revolution: The Jama`at-i Islami of Pakistan* (Berkeley: University of California Press, 1994); Judith Nagata, *The Reflowering of Malaysian Islam: Modern Religious Radicals and Their Roots* (Vancouver: University of British Columbia Press, 1984); Ayubi, *Political Islam,* pp. 158–77; Giles Kepel, *Muslim Extremism in Egypt: The Prophet and Pharoah* (Berkeley: University of California Press, 1985), p. 206; Saad Eddin Ibrahim, "Anatomy of Egypt's Militant Islamic Groups: Methodological Note and Preliminary Findings," in *International Journal of Middle East Studies,* 12 (1980), pp. 423–53; and Fischer, "Islam and the Revolt of the Petit Bourgeoisie."

96. Denis J. Sullivan and Sana Abed-Kotob, *Islam in Contemporary Egypt: Civil Society vs. the State* (Boulder, CO: Lynne Rienner, 1999).

97. José Casanova, *Public Religions in the Modern World* (Chicago: University of Chicago Press, 1994), pp. 5–39.

98. On the challenge of religion to secular states, see Mark Jurgensmeyer, "The New Religious State," *Comparative Politics,* 27, 4 (July 1995), pp. 379–91.

99. Although it has often been characterized as such by some observers; see, for instance, Sivan, *Radical Islam: Medieval Theology and Modern Politics,* Bruce Lawrence, *Defenders of God: The Fundamentalist Revolt Against the Modern Age* (San Francisco: Harper and Row, 1989); and Hrair R. Dekmejian, *Islam and Revolution* (Syracuse: Syracuse University Press, 1985).

100. Daniel Pipes, "The Western Mind of Radical Islam," *First Things*, 58 (December 1995), pp. 18–23.

101. Nasr, *Mawdudi and the Making of Islamic Revivalism*, pp. 49–106.

102. Brian H. Smith, "Religion and Politics: A New Look Through an Old Prism," in H. E. Chehabi and Alfred Stepan, eds., *Politics, Society, and Democracy: Comparative Studies* (Boulder, CO: Westview, 1995), pp. 73–88.

103. Geertz, *Interpretations of Culture*, p. 259–78.

104. See *Toward Islamization of Disciplines* (Herndon, VA: IIIT, 1988); *Islamization of Knowledge: General Principles and Work Plan* (Herndon, VA: IIIT, 1989); Farid Alatas, "Reflections on the Idea of Islamic Social Science," *Comparative Civilizations Review*, 17 (1987), pp. 60–86; Fazlur Rahman, "Islamization of Knowledge: A Response," *The American Journal of Islamic Social Sciences*, 5, 1 (1988), pp. 3–11; Seyyed Vali Reza Nasr, "Islamization of Knowledge; A Critical Overview," *Islamic Studies*, 30, 3 (Autumn 1991), pp. 387–400; *idem*, "Islamic Economics: Novel Perspectives on Change in the Middle East," *Middle Eastern Studies*, 25, 4 (October 1989), pp. 516–530; Timur Kuran, "The Economic Impact of Islamic Fundamentalism," in Martin Marty and R. Scott Appelby, eds., *Fundamentalisms and the State* (Chicago: University of Chicago Press, 1993), pp. 302–41; *idem*, "Islamic Economics and the Islamic Subeconomy," *Journal of Economic Perspectives*, 9, 4 (Fall 1995), pp. 155–73; Ishtiaq Ahmed, *The Concept of an Islamic State:An Analysis of the Ideological Controversy in Pakistan* (New York: St. Martin's Press, 1987).

105. Seyyed Vali Reza Nasr, "Ideology and Institutions in Islamist Approaches to Public Policy," in Sohrab Behdad and Farhad Nomani, eds., *International Review of Comparative Public Policy* 9 (1997), pp. 41–67.

106. This trend is particularly evident in the manner in which International Islamic Universities in Islamabad, Pakistan, and Kuala Lumpur, Malaysia, along with many other state-sponsored institutions, absorbed Islamist thinkers and co-opted them into the state; see the entries on the two universities in John L. Esposito, ed., *The Oxford Encyclopedia of the Modern Islamic World* (New York: Oxford University Press, 1995). Similar institutions have also emerged in Saudi Arabia, Indonesia, and the emirates of the Persian Gulf to serve the same function.

107. For instance, by taking over Islamic financial activities and taxation, Malaysia and Pakistan have compromised Islamism's financial autonomy; on the use of Islamic banks and taxation for Islamist activism, see Timur Kuran, "The Economic Impact of Islamic Fundamentalism," p. 307.

108. Olivier Roy, "The Crisis of Religious Legitimacy in Iran," *Middle East Journal*, 53, 2 (Spring 1999), pp. 210–11.

109. On the relation between clarity of state-society boundaries and state power, see Mitchell, "The Limits of the State: Beyond Statist Approaches."

110. Jamal Malik, "Islamization in Pakistan in 1977–1985: The Ulama and Their Places of Learning," *Islamic Studies*, 28, 1 (Spring 1989), p. 23.

111. Nasr, "Pakistan: State, Agrarian Reform, and Islamization."

112. Basit Koshul, for instance, argues that the Islamization of the constitution in Pakistan has supported greater authoritarian tendencies of the state, and has adversely affected individual liberties and their guarantees in the constitution. See Basit Koshul, "The Islamization of Pakistan's Constitution: A Critical Analysis," *Middle East Affairs Journal*, 4, 1–2 (Winter/Spring 1998), pp. 129–44.

113. Casanova, *Public Religions*, pp. 11–39.

114. Bryan S. Turner, "Religion and State-Formation: A Commentary on Recent Debates," *Journal of Historical Sociology*, 1, 3 (September 1988), pp. 322–33.

115. Michael Mann, "State and Society, 1130–1815: An Analysis of English State Finances," in M. Zeitlin, ed., *Political Power and Social Theory* (Greenwich, CT: JAI Press, 1980), vol.1, pp. 165–208.

116. Thomas Ertman, *Birth of the Leviathan: Building States and Regimes in Medieval and Early Modern Europe* (New York: Cambridge University Press, 1997), pp. 35–89.

117. *Ibid*, p. 44.

118. Robert Wuthnow, *Communities of Discourse: Ideology and Social Structure in the Reformation, the Enlightenment, and European Socialism* (Cambridge: Harvard University Press, 1989), pp. 67–71.

119. *Ibid*, p. 70.

120. *Ibid*, pp. 71–82.

121. *Ibid*, p. 76.

122. Wolfrem Fischer and Peter Lundgreen, "The Recruitment and Training of Administrative and Technical Personnel," in Tilly, *The Formation of National States in Western Europe*, pp. 456–561.

123. Turner, "Religion and State-Formation," p. 326.

124. Wuthnow, *Communities of Discourse*, p. 80.

125. *Ibid*, pp. 67–82.

126. Philip S. Gorski, "The Protestant Ethic Revisited: Disciplinary Revolution and State Formation in Holland and Prussia," *American Journal of Sociology*, 99, 2 (September 1993), pp. 265–316.

127. *Ibid*, p. 269.

128. Richards and Waterbury, *A Political Economy of the Middle East*, pp. 187–218.

129. H. E. Chehabi, "Staging the Emperor's New Clothes: Dress Codes and Nation-Building Under Reza Shah," *Iranian Studies*, 26, 3–4 (Summer/Fall 1993), pp. 209–29.

130. See, for instance, Shahrough Akhavi, *Religion and Politics in Contemporary Iran: Clergy-State Relations in the Pahlavi Period* (Albany, NY: SUNY Press, 1980).

131. M. Hakan Yavuz, "Political Islam and the Welfare (*Refah*) Party in Turkey," *Comparative Politics*, 30, 1 (October 1997), pp. 64–65, and Daniel Crescilius, "Non-ideological Responses of Egyptian Ulama to Modernization," in Nikki R. Keddie, ed., *Scholars, Saints, and Sufis: Muslim Religious Institutions Since 1500* (Berkeley: University of California Press, 1972), pp. 167–210.

132. Malika Zeghal, "Religion and Politics in Egypt: the Ulema of al-Azhar, Radical Islam, and the State (1952–94)," *International Journal of Middle East Studies*, 31, 3 (August 1999), pp. 373–75.

133. Arjomand, *Turban for the Crown*, and *idem*, "Traditionalism in Twentieth Century Iran," in Said A. Arjomand, ed., *From Nationalism to Revolutionary Islam* (Albany, NY: SUNY Press, 1984), pp. 195–232.

134. Jean-Claude Vatin, "Popular Puritanism Versus State Reformism: Islam in Algeria," in James Piscatori, ed., *Islam in the Political Process* (New York: Cambridge University Press, 1983), p. 99.

135. Tripp, "Islam and the Secular Logic of the State," p. 57.

136. Michael Willis, *The Islamist Challenge in Algeria: A Political History* (New York: New York University Press, 1997); Dirk Vandewalle, "Islam in Algeria: Religion, Culture, and Opposition in a Rentier State," in John L. Esposito, ed., *Political Islam: Revolution, Radicalism, or Reform?* (Boulder, CO: Lynne Rienner, 1997), pp. 33–52; Yavuz, "Search for a New Social Contract in Turkey," pp. 114–43.

137. Ali Hillal Dessouki, "Official Islam and Political Legitimation in the Arab Countries," in Barbara F. Stowasser, ed., *The Islamic Impulse* (London: Croom Helm, 1987), pp. 135–41.

138. Quintan Wiktorowicz, "Regulating Religious Contention: Islamic Collective Action and Patterns of Mobilization in Jordan," Ph.D. dissertation submitted to School of Public Affairs of the American University, 1998.

139. Simon Barraclough reports that the Egyptian government has proposed to hand over control of some 50,000 private (*ahli*) mosques to the al-Azhar Islamic institution by 2002. This will increase the government's reach and social control and deny Islamists space and recruiting and social control grounds; see Simon Barraclough, "Al-Azhar: Between the Government and the Islamists," *Middle East Journal,* 52, 2 (Spring 1998), p. 239. Also see Linda S. Adams, "Political Liberalization in Jordan: An Analysis of the State's Relationship with the Muslim Brotherhood," *Journal of Church and State,* 38, 3 (Summer 1996), pp. 507–28; and Abdullah Akailah, "The Experience of the Jordanian Islamic Movement," in Azzam Tamimi, ed., *Power-Sharing Islam?* (London: Liberty for the Muslim World Publications, 1993), pp. 93–101.

140. Nash, "Islamic Resurgence in Malaysia and Indonesia," pp. 691–739.

141. Anne Sophie Roald, *Tarbiya: Education and Politics in Islamic Movements in Jordan and Malaysia* (Lund: Lund University, 1994).

142. Raymond W. Baker, *Sadat and After: Struggles for Egypt's Political Soul* (Cambridge, MA: Harvard University Press, 1990); Sana Abed Kotob, "The Accommodationists Speak: Goals and Strategies of the Muslim Brotherhood," *International Journal of Middle East Studies,* 27, 3 (August 1995), pp. 321–39; and Hamied Ansari, "The Islamic Militants in Egyptian Politics," *International Journal of Middle East Studies,* 16, 1 (March 1984), p. 129.

143. John L. Esposito, *The Islamic Threat: Myth or Reality?* (New York: Oxford University Press, 1992), pp. 138–39.

144. Sakallioglu, "Parameters and Strategies," pp. 231–51. The tendency to use Islam as a counterweight to leftist activism dated back to the 1950s; Sencer Ayata, "Patronage, Party, and the State: The Politicization of Islam in Turkey," *Middle East Journal,* 50, 1 (Winter 1996), pp. 43–44.

145. Ziya Önis, "The Political Economy of Islamic Resurgence in Turkey: The Rise of the Welfare Party in Perspective," *Third World Quarterly,* 18, 4 (September 1997), pp. 743–66.

146. *The Economist,* February 26, 2000, p. 62.

147. Vali Nasr, "Secular States and Religious Oppositions," *SAIS Review,* 18, 2 (Summer/Fall 1998), pp. 32–37.

148. Olivier Roy, "Changing Patterns Among Radical Islamic Movements," *Brown Journal of International Affairs,* 6, 1 (Winter/Spring 1999), pp. 112–13.

149. Yavuz, "Search for a New Social Contract in Turkey," pp. 114–43; *idem,* "Turkey's Fault Lines and the Crisis of Kemalism," *Current History,* 99, 633 (January 2000), pp. 33–38.

150. Jakob Skovgaard-Petersen, *Defining Islam for the Egyptian State: Muftis and Fatwas of Dar al-Ifta* (Leiden: E. J. Brill, 1997); and Barraclough, "Al-Azhar," pp. 236–49.

151. Syed Mujawar Hussain Shah, *Religion and Politics in Pakistan (1972–88)* (Islamabad: Quaid-i-Azam University, 1996); and Ahmad, "Islam and the State," pp. 230–40.

152. Seyyed Vali Reza Nasr, "Pakistan: Islamic State, Ethnic Polity," *Fletcher Forum of World Affairs,* 16, 2 (Summer 1992), pp. 81–90.

153. Hussin Mutalib, *Islam and Ethnicity in Malay Politics* (Singapore: Oxford University Press, 1990); Fred von der Mehden, "Islamic Resurgence in Malaysia," in John L. Esposito, ed., *Islam and Development: Religion and Sociopolitical Change* (Syracuse: Syracuse University Press, 1980), pp. 163–80; Mohamad Abu Bakar, "Islamic Revivalism and the Political Process in Malaysia," *Asian Survey,* 21, 10 (October 1981), pp. 1040–59; and Judith Nagata, "Religious Ideology and Social Change: The Islamic Revival in Malaysia," *Pacific Affairs,* 53, 3 (Fall 1980), pp. 405–39.

154. Musa Hitam, "Malaysia's Strategic Vision: Into the Twenty-first Century," in *Malaysia: Past, Present, and Future* (Kuala Lumpur: ISIS, 1987), p. 6.

155. Seyyed Vali Reza Nasr, "Islamic Opposition to the Islamic State: The Jama'at-i Islami, 1977–1988," *International Journal of Middle East Studies,* 25, 2 (May 1993), pp. 261–83.

1. The Colonial Legacy

1. K. C. Tregonning, *The British in Malaya: The First Forty Years* (Tucson: University of Arizona Press, 1965), p. 165.

2. Anthony Milner, *The Invention of Politics in Colonial Malaya: Contesting Nationalism and Expansion of the Public Sphere* (New York: Cambridge University Press, 1994), p. 3; William R. Roff, *The Origins of Malay Nationalism,* 2nd ed. (New York: Oxford University Press, 1994), pp. 11–12.

3. Donald M. Nonini, *British Colonial Rule and the Resistance of the Malay Peasantry, 1900–1957* (New Haven: Yale University Southeast Asia Studies, 1992), p. 18.

4. *Ibid,* pp. 20–21.

5. Yeo Kim Wah, *The Politics of Decentralization: Colonial Controversy in Malaya, 1920–1929* (Kuala Lumpur: Oxford University Press, 1982), p. 8.

6. Rupert Emerson, *Malaysia: A Study in Direct and Indirect Rule* (Kuala Lumpur: University of Malaya Press, 1964), pp. 119–23.

7. *Ibid,* pp. 112–34.

8. *Ibid,* pp. 135–268.

9. Nonini, *British Colonial Rule,* p. 45.

10. John G. Butcher, *The British in Malaya: 1880–1941: The Social History of a European Community in Colonial South-East Asia* (Kuala Lumpur: Oxford University Press, 1979), p. 4.

11. Alasdair Bowie, *Crossing the Industrial Divide: State, Society, and the Politics of Economic Transformation in Malaysia* (New York: Columbia University, 1991), pp. 34–35.

12. Butcher, *The British in Malaya,* p. 14.

13. *Ibid,* p. 16. Commercial competition with the Dutch and rivalry with the French were also instrumental in nudging the British in the direction of tightening their hold over the Malayan Peninsula; Hon-Chan Chai, *The Development of British Malaya, 1896–1909* (Kuala Lumpur: Oxford University Press, 1964), pp. 1–2.

14. Butcher, *The British in Malaya,* pp. 7–8.

15. N. J. Funston, *Malay Politics in Malaysia: A Study of United Malays National Organisation and Party Islam* (Kuala Lumpur: Heinemann, 1980), pp. 24–25.

16. Roff, *The Origins of Malay Nationalism,* p. 93.

17. Hussin Mutalib, *Islam and Ethnicity in Malay Politics* (Singapore: Oxford University Press, 1990), pp. 15–16.

18. Chandra Muzaffar, *Challenges and Choices in Malaysian Politics and Society* (Penang: ALIRAN, 1989), p. 490.

19. Syed Husin Ali, *The Malays: Their Problems and Future* (Kuala Lumpur: Heinemann, 1981), p. 27.

20. Butcher, *The British in Malaya*, p. 8.

21. Mutalib, *Islam and Ethnicity*, pp. 15–17.

22. On the *Kaum Muda*, see William R. Roff, "Patterns of Islamization in Malaysia, 1890s–1990s: Exemplars, Institutions, and Vectors," *Journal of Islamic Studies*, 9, 2 (July 1998), pp. 216–17.

23. Harry Benda, "Southeast Asian Islam in the Twentieth Century," in P. M. Holt et al., eds., *The Cambridge History of Islam* (Cambridge: Cambridge University Press, 1970), vol.2, pp. 182–209.

24. S. U. Balogun, "The Status of *Shari`ah* in Malaysia," *Hamdard Islamicus*, 20, 2 (April–June 1997), p. 55.

25. Mutalib, *Islam and Ethnicity*, pp. 15–17.

26. John L. Esposito and John O. Voll, *Islam and Democracy* (New York: Oxford University Press, 1996), p. 125.

27. Bowie, *Crossing the Industrial Divide*, p. 36.

28. Chai, *The Development of British Malaya*, pp. 10–15.

29. Roff, *The Origins of Malay Nationalism*, pp. 94–98.

30. Nonini, *British Colonial Rule*, p. 77.

31. Roff, *The Origins of Malay Nationalism*, pp. 43–44.

32. *Ibid*, p. 22.

33. Nonini, *British Colonial Rule*, p. 77.

34. Chai, *The Development of British Malaya*, p. 56.

35. Paul Lubeck, "Malaysian Industrialization, Ethnic Divisions, and the NIC Model: The Limits to Replication," in Richard P. Appelbaum and Jeffrey Henderson, eds., *State and Development in the Asian Pacific Rim* (Newbury Park: Sage Press, 1992), pp. 188–89.

36. Jomo Kwame Sundaram [Jomo K. S.], *A Question of Class: Capital, the State, and Uneven Development in Malaya* (New York: Oxford University Press, 1986), p. 245.

37. Funston, *Malay Politics in Malaysia*, pp. 14–15.

38. Milner, *The Invention of Politics*, pp. 283 and 294–95.

39. James C. Scott, *Political Ideology in Malaysia: Reality and the Beliefs of an Elite* (Kuala Lumpur: University of Malaya Press, 1968), pp. 215–18.

40. Funston, *Malay Politics in Malaysia*, pp. 39–68.

41. Roff, *The Origins of Malay Nationalism*, pp. 113–25.

42. On expansion of the colonial economy, see Jomo K. S., *A Question of Class*, pp. 135–202.

43. Edmund T. Gomez and Jomo K. S., *Malaysia's Political Economy: Politics, Patronage, and Profits* (New York: Cambridge University Press, 1997), p. 10.

44. Butcher, *The British in Malaya*, p. 12.

45. Cited in Bowie, *Crossing the Industrial Divide*, p. 42.

46. Emerson, *Malaysia*, pp. 129–57.

47. Bowie, *Crossing the Industrial Divide*, p. 42.

48. Gomez and Jomo K. S., *Malaysia's Political Economy*, p. 10.

49. Paul H. Kratoska, "Rice Cultivation and Ethnic Division of Labor in British Malaya," *Comparative Studies in Society and History*, 24 (1982), pp. 280–314.

50. Nonini, *British Colonial Rule*, p. 24; and Syed Hussein Alatas, *The Myth of the Lazy Native: A Study of the Image of the Malays, Filipinos, and Javanese from the*

Sixteenth to the Twentieth Century and Its Function in the Ideology of Colonial Capitalism (London: F. Cass, 1977).

51. Ozay Mehmet, *Islamic Identity and Development: Studies of the Islamic Periphery* (New York: Routledge, 1990), p. 102.

52. Jomo K. S., *A Question of Class*, pp. 35–133 and 244–45; Paul H. Kratoska, "Ends That We Cannot Foresee: Malay Reservations in British Malaya," *Journal of Southeast Asian Studies*, 14 (1983), p. 149.

53. Bowie, *Crossing the Industrial Divide*, pp. 36–38.

54. Mehmet, *Islamic Identity*, p. 102.

55. Roff, *The Origins of Malay Nationalism*, pp. 56–90; idem, "Patterns of Islamization," pp. 210–13.

56. Roff, *The Origins of Malay Nationalism*, p. 26; Mohamad Abu Bakar, "Islam and Nationalism in Contemporary Malay Society," in Taufik Abdullah and Sharon Siddique, eds., *Islam and Society in Southeast Asia* (Singapore: Institute of Southeast Asian Studies, 1986), p. 156.

57. Funston, *Malay Politics in Malaysia*, pp. 29–35.

58. On the rise of the PAS, see *ibid*, pp. 75–96.

59. Wah, *The Politics of Decentralization*, p. 14.

60. *Ibid*, p. 65.

61. In addition, the centralized administrative system in Kuala Lumpur had begun to suffer from over-bureaucratization. It consumed as much if not more revenue than it generated; Emerson, *Malaysia*, pp. 156–57. Decentralization, therefore, was also a measure of fiscal and administrative reform at a time when the British Empire and its constituent parts faced shortage of funds.

62. Butcher, *The British in Malaya*, pp. 19–21

63. Wah, *The Politics of Decentralization*, p. 69.

64. On the British order in post–World War I Middle East, see Elizabeth Monroe, *Britain's Moment in the Middle East, 1914–1956* (Baltimore: Johns Hopkins Press, 1963).

65. Wah, *The Politics of Decentralization*, p. 326.

66. Boon Kheng Cheah, "Sino-Malay Conflicts in Malaya, 1945–46: Communist Vendetta and Islamic Resistance," *Journal of Southeast Asian Studies*, 12 (1981), pp. 108–17.

67. A. J. Stockwell, *British Policy and Malay Politics During the Malayan Union Experiment, 1942–1948*, monograph number 8 (Kuala Lumpur: Malaysian Branch of the Royal Asiatic Society, 1979).

68. Scott, *Political Ideology*, p. 9.

69. Edmund Terence Gomez, *Political Business: Corporate Involvement in Malaysian Political Parties* (Townsville, Australia: Center for South-East Asian Studies, James Cook University, 1994), p. 49.

70. Ozay Mehmet, *Islamic Identity and Development: Studies of the Islamic Periphery* (New York: Routledge, 1990), pp. 21–22.

71. Gomez and Jomo K. S., *Malaysia's Political Economy*, p. 11.

72. *Ibid*.

73. Philip Woodruff, *The Men Who Ruled India*, 2 vols. (London: Jonathan Cape, 1953 and 1954).

74. C. A. Bayly, *Rulers, Townsmen, and Bazaars: North Indian Society in the Age of British Expansion, 1770–1870* (Cambridge: Cambridge University Press, 1983); and idem, *Indian Society and the Making of the British Empire* (New York: Cambridge University Press, 1988).

75. B. R. Tomlinson, *The Political Economy of the Raj, 1914–1947: The Economics of Decolonization in India* (London: Macmillan, 1979), p. 28.

76. *Ibid*, pp. 1–29.

77. *Ibid*, pp. 153–54.

78. Bernard S. Cohen, "Representing Authority in Victorian India," in Eric Hobsbawm and Terence Ranger, eds., *The Invention of Tradition* (Cambridge: Cambridge University Press, 1983), p. 180.

79. Lawrence James, *Raj: The Making and Unmaking of British India* (New York: St. Martin's Press, 1998), pp. 190–91

80. Thomas R. Metcalf, *Land, Landlords, and the British Raj: Northern India in the Nineteenth Century* (Berkeley: University of California Press, 1979).

81. *Idem, Ideologies of the Raj* (New York: Cambridge University Press, 1994).

82. David Gilmartin, *Empire and Islam: Punjab and the Making of Pakistan* (Berkeley: University of California Press, 1988), p. 11.

83. Metcalf, *Ideologies of the Raj*, pp. 139–44.

84. *Ibid*, pp. 140–48.

85. Markus Daechsel, "Military Islamisation in Pakistan and the Spectre of Colonial Perceptions," *Contemporary South Asia*, 6, 2 (July 1997), pp. 141–60.

86. Bernard S. Cohn, *Colonialism and Its Forms of Knowledge: The British in India* (Princeton: Princeton University Press, 1996), pp. 57–75.

87. Thomas Blom Hansen, *The Saffron Wave: Democracy and Hindu Nationalism in Modern India*, (Princeton: Princeton University Press, 1999), pp. 34–35.

88. David Washbrook, "Law, State, and Agrarian Society in Colonial India," *Modern Asian Studies*, 15, 3 (1981), pp. 653–54.

89. Hansen, *The Saffron Wave*, pp. 34–35.

90. Michael R. Anderson, "Islamic Law and the Colonial Encounter in British India," in Chibli Mallat and Jane Connors, eds., *Islamic Family Law* (London: Graham & Trotman, 1990), pp. 205–6.

91. David Gilmartin, "Customary Law and *Sharî`at* in British Punjab," in Katherine P. Ewing, ed., *Sharî`at and Ambiguities in South Asian Islam* (Berkeley: University of California Press, 1988), pp. 43–62.

92. *Idem, Empire and Islam*, pp. 12–13.

93. *Ibid*, p. 13.

94. *Ibid*, pp. 18–26.

95. *Ibid*, pp. 24–39.

96. David Page, *Prelude to Partition: The Indian Muslims and the Imperial System of Control, 1920–1932* (Delhi: Oxford University Press, 1982), p. 13.

97. On the socioreligious role of these offices, see Katherine P. Ewing, *Arguing Sainthood: Modernity, Psychoanalysis, and Islam* (Durham: Duke University Press, 1997).

98. Gilmartin, *Empire and Islam*, pp. 53–55.

99. On these movements, see J. M. S. Baljon, *Religion and Thought of Shah Wali Allah Dihlawi, 1703–1762* (Leiden: E. J. Brill, 1986); Barbara Metcalf, *Islamic Revival in British India: The Deoband, 1860–1900* (Princeton: Princeton University Press, 1982); S. V. R. Nasr, *Mawdudi and the Making of Islamic Revivalism* (New York: Oxford University Press, 1996), pp. 9–46.

100. Farzana Shaikh, *Community and Consensus in Islam: Muslim Representation in Colonial India, 1860–1947* (New York: Cambridge University Press, 1989); and I. H. Qureshi, *Ulema in Politics: A Study Relating to the Political Activities of the Ulema in the South-Asian Subcontinent from 1556 to 1947* (Karachi: Ma'aref, 1972).

101. Jamal Malik, *Colonization of Islam: Dissolution of Traditional Institutions in Pakistan* (Delhi: Manohar, 1996), pp. 55–56.

102. Gilmartin, "Customary Law," pp. 51–53.

103. Page, *Prelude to Partition,* pp. 14–15.

104. Gilmartin, "Customary Law," p. 60.

105. Riazul Hasan Gilani, "A Note on Islamic Family Law and Islamization in Pakistan," in Chibli Mallat and Jane Connors, eds., *Islamic Family Law* (London: Graham & Trotman, 1990), pp. 339–46.

106. Ian Talbot, *Provincial Politics and the Pakistan Movement: The Growth of the Muslim League in North-West and North-East India, 1937–1947* (Karachi: Oxford University Press, 1988).

107. Hamza Alavi, "Ethnicity, Muslim Society, and the Pakistan Ideology," in Anita Weiss, ed., *Islamic Reassertion in Pakistan* (Syracuse: Syracuse University Press, 1986), pp. 21–48.

108. Gilmartin, *Empire and Islam,* pp. 71–72.

109. On Jinnah, the Muslim League, and the Pakistan movement, see Stanley Wolpert, *Jinnah of Pakistan* (New York: Oxford University Press, 1984); Ayesha Jalal, *The Sole Spokesman: Jinnah, the Muslim League, and the Demand for Pakistan* (New York: Cambridge University Press, 1985); Shaikh, *Community and Consensus;* and Akbar S. Ahmed, *Jinnah, Pakistan, and Islamic Identity: The Search for Saladin* (New York: Routledge, 1997).

2. From Independence to 1969

1. N. J. Funston, *Malay Politics in Malaysia: A Study of United Malays National Organisation and Party Islam* (Kuala Lumpur: Heinemann, 1980), p. 12.

2. Syed Farid Alatas, *Democracy and Authoritarianism in Indonesia and Malaysia: The Rise of the Post-Colonial State* (New York: St. Martin's Press, 1997).

3. Charles H. Kennedy, *Bureaucracy in Pakistan* (Karachi: Oxford University Press, 1987).

4. Boon Kheng Cheah, "Sino-Malay Conflicts in Malaya, 1945–46: Communist Vendetta and Islamic Resistance," *Journal of Southeast Asian Studies,* 12 (1981), pp. 108–17.

5. Hussin Mutalib, *Islam and Ethnicity in Malay Politics* (Singapore: Oxford University Press, 1990), p. 33.

6. S. V. R. Nasr, "Pakistan: Islamic State, Ethnic Polity," *Fletcher Forum of World Affairs,* 16, 2 (Summer 1992), pp. 81–90.

7. Rounaq Jahan, *Pakistan: Failure in National Integration* (New York: Columbia University Press, 1972), p. 12; and Philip Oldenburg, "'A Place Insufficiently Imagined': Language, Belief, and the Pakistan Crisis of 1971," *Journal of Asian Studies,* 44, 4 (August 1985), pp. 715–23.

8. William R. Roff, "Patterns of Islamization in Malaysia, 1890s-1990s: Exemplars, Institutions, and Vectors," *Journal of Islamic Studies,* 9, 2 (July 1998), pp. 216–17.

9. S. U. Balogun, "The Status of *Shari`ah* in Malaysia," *Hamdard Islamicus,* 20, 2 (April–June 1997), p. 55.

10. John L. Esposito and John O. Voll, *Islam and Democracy* (New York: Oxford University Press, 1996), p. 126; and Ozay Mehmet, *Islamic Identity and Development: Studies of the Islamic Periphery* (New York: Routledge, 1990), p. 109.

11. Alasdair Bowie, *Crossing the Industrial Divide: State, Society, and the Politics of Economic Transformation in Malaysia* (New York: Columbia University, 1991), p. 73.

12. Harold Crouch, *Government and Society in Malaysia* (Ithaca: Cornell University Press, 1996), p. 91.

13. *Ibid*, pp. 69–72.

14. James Puthucheary, *Ownership and Control in Malayan Economy* (Singapore: Eastern University Press, 1960).

15. Bowie, *Crossing the Industrial Divide*, pp. 69–72.

16. Edmund T. Gomez and Jomo K. S., *Malaysia's Political Economy: Politics, Patronage, and Profits* (New York: Cambridge University Press, 1997), p. 14.

17. Funston, *Malay Politics*, p. 5.

18. Bowie, *Crossing the Industrial Divide*, pp. 69–74.

19. *Ibid*, p. 73.

20. James C. Scott, *Political Ideology in Malaysia: Reality and the Beliefs of an Elite* (Kuala Lumpur: University of Malaya Press, 1968), pp. 76–77.

21. Jomo K. S., *A Question of Class: Capital, the State, and Uneven Development in Malaya* (New York: Oxford University Press, 1986), p. 271.

22. Edmund Terence Gomez, *Political Business: Corporate Involvement in Malaysian Political Parties* (Townsville, Australia: Center for South-East Asian Studies, James Cook University, 1994), pp. 49–53.

23. Jomo K. S., *A Question of Class*, pp. 245 and 271.

24. Gomez, *Political Business*, p. 34.

25. Judith Nagata, "Ethnonationalism Versus Religious Transnationalism: Nation-Building and Islam in Malaysia," *The Muslim World*, 87, 2 (April 1997), p. 134.

26. Mutalib, *Islam and Ethnicity*, p. 23.

27. Balogun, "The Status of *Shari`ah* in Malaysia," p. 54.

28. Mutalib, *Islam and Ethnicity*, pp. 21–22; and Funston, *Malay Politics*, p. 146..

29. Scott, *Political Ideology*, pp. 72–74.

30. Mutalib, *Islam and Ethnicity*, pp. 31–32; and Mohamad Abu Bakar, "Islam and Nationalism in Contemporary Malay Society," in Taufik Abdullah and Sharon Siddique, eds., *Islam and Society in Southeast Asia* (Singapore: Institute of Southeast Asian Studies, 1986), p. 159.

31. Mutalib, *Islam and Ethnicity*, p. 34.

32. On origins of PAS, see Funston, *Malay Politics;* and Clive Kessler, *Islam and Politics in a Malay State: Kelantan, 1838–1969* (Ithaca: Cornell University Press, 1978).

33. A. B. Shamsul, *From British to Bumiputera Rule: Local Politics and Rural Development in Peninsular Malaysia* (Singapore: Institute of Southeast Asian Studies, 1986).

34. Fred von der Mehden, "Islamic Resurgence in Malaysia," in John L. Esposito, ed., *Islam and Development: Religion and Sociopolitical Change* (Syracuse: Syracuse University Press, 1980), p. 167.

35. Mutalib, *Islam and Ethnicity*, pp. 89–90.

36. *Ibid*, p. 35.

37. *Ibid*, p. 36.

38. *Ibid*, pp. 42–43.

39. Harold Crouch, *Government and Society in Malaysia* (Ithaca: Cornell University Press, 1996), p. 189.

40. Charles Hirschman, "Development and Inequality in Malaysia," *Pacific Affairs*, 62, 1 (Spring 1989), p. 76.

41. Mutalib, *Islam and Ethnicity*, p. 58.

42. *Ibid.*

43. On ethnic tensions in Malaysia and the May riots, see Milton J. Esman, *Ethnic Politics* (Ithaca: Cornell University Press, 1994), pp. 49–74; Donald Horowitz, *Ethnic Groups in Conflict* (Berkeley: University of California Press, 1985); Karl von Vorys, Democracy Without Consensus: Communalism and Political Stability in Malaysia (Princeton: Princeton University Press, 1975); Felix Gagliano, *Violence in Malaysia, 1969: The Political Aftermath* (Athens: Ohio University Center for International Studies, 1970).

44. Judith Nagata, "Religious Ideology and Social Change: The Islamic Revival in Malaysia," *Pacific Affairs*, 53, 3 (Fall 1980), p. 407.

45. Alasdair Bowie, "The Dynamics of Business-Government Relations in Industrialising Malaysia," in Andrew MacIntyre, ed., *Business and Government in Industrialising Asia* (Ithaca: Cornell University Press, 1994), pp. 170–71.

46. H. F. Goodnow, *The Civil Service of Pakistan* (New Haven: Yale University Press, 1964).

47. Brian Cloughy, *A History of the Pakistan Army* (Karachi: Oxford University Press, 1999).

48. Hamza Alavi, "Ethnicity, Muslim Society, and the Pakistan Ideology," in Anita Weiss, eds., *Islamic Reassertion in Pakistan: The Application of Islamic Laws in a Modern State* (Syracuse: Syracuse University Press, 1986), pp. 21–47; and Ayesha Jalal, *The State of Martial Rule: The Origins of Pakistan's Political Economy of Defence* (Cambridge: Cambridge University Press, 1990).

49. Allen McGrath, *The Destruction of Pakistan's Democracy* (Karachi: Oxford University Press, 1996).

50. Ian Talbot, *Provincial Politics and the Pakistan Movement: The Growth of the Muslim League in North-West and North-East India, 1937–1947* (Karachi: Oxford University Press, 1988).

51. Jalal, *The State of Martial Rule.*

52. For an examination of the relation of feudalism to state power, see Michael Mann, "The Autonomous Power of the State: Its Origins, Mechanisms, and Results," *Archives Européennes de Sociologie*, 25, 2 (1984), pp. 189–90.

53. For a more detailed discussion of this issue, see S. V. R. Nasr, "Pakistan: State, Agrarian Reform, and Islamization," *International Journal of Politics, Culture, and Society*, 10, 2 (Winter 1996), pp. 249–72.

54. Catherine Boone has written about similar relations between the state and rural strongmen in Senegal; see "States and Ruling Classes in Postcolonial Africa: The Enduring Contradictions of Power," in Joel S. Migdal, Atul Kohli, and Vivienne Shue, eds., *State Power and Social Forces* (New York: Cambridge University Press, 1994), pp. 108–40.

55. On the patterns of extraction or transfer of surplus from agriculture to industry, see Ashutosh Varshney, "Urban Bias in Perspective," *Journal of Development Studies*, 29, 4 (July 1993), pp. 3–22.

56. Tahir Amin, *Ethno-National Movements in Pakistan: Domestic and International Factors* (Islamabad: Institute of Policy Studies, 1988), p. 72. This trend, in fact, predated partition. Muslim minority areas of India, from where the Muslim League drew its support, favored a strong center in Delhi with a strong Muslim party to rep-

resent their ideas. The Muslim majority areas, which became Pakistan, however, had no need for protection by a strong party in a strong center, and, in fact, favored a weak center; see Astma Barlas, *Democracy, Nationalism, and Communalism: The Colonial Legacy in South Asia* (Boulder, CO: Westview Press, 1995), p. 157.

57. M. Afzal, *Political Parties in Pakistan, 1947–1958* (Islamabad: National Commission on Historical and Cultural Research, 1976); and K. K. Aziz, *Party Politics in Pakistan, 1947–1958* (Islamabad: National Commission on Historical and Cultural Research, 1976).

58. Jahan, *Pakistan,* pp. 25–27.

59. Although East Pakistanis outnumbered West Pakistanis, East Pakistanis accounted for only 11% of the civil service and 1.5% of military officers; *ibid.,* pp. 25–27.

60. In fact, the prospect for a constitution that would give significant powers to East Pakistan led the governor-general, Ghulam Muhammad, to dismiss the Constituent Assembly in 1954; see McGrath, *The Destruction of Pakistan's Democracy.*

61. On debates over the role of Islam, see Binder, *Religion and Politics in Pakistan* (Berkeley: University of California Press, 1961). On the issue of the role of East Pakistan in the state, see Anwar H. Syed, *Pakistan: Islam, Politics, and National Solidarity* (New York: Praeger, 1982).

62. Lawrence Ziring, *Pakistan in the Twentieth Century: A Political History* (Karachi: Oxford University Press, 1997), pp. 146–99.

63. Muhammad Munir, *From Jinnah to Zia* (Lahore: Vanguard, 1980).

64. Binder, *Religion and Politics;* Freeland Abbott, *Islam and Pakistan* (Ithaca: Cornell University Press, 1968); and S. V. R. Nasr, *The Vanguard of the Islamic Revolution: The Jama`at-i Islami of Pakistan* (Berkeley: University of California Press, 1994).

65. Said A. Arjomand, "Religion and Constitutionalism in Western History and in Modern Iran and Pakistan," in Said A. Arjomand, ed., *The Political Dimensions of Religion* (Albany: SUNY Press, 1993), pp. 69–99.

67. Afzal Iqbal, *Islamisation in Pakistan* (Lahore: Vanguard, 1986), pp. 42–57.

68. For more on the constitutional debates in 1950, see Binder, *Religion and Politics;* and Iqbal, *Islamisation,* pp. 65–74.

69. On the Ayub Khan era, see Lawrence Ziring, *The Ayub Khan Era: Politics of Pakistan, 1958–69* (Syracuse: Syracuse University Press, 1971); *idem, Pakistan in the Twentieth Century: A Political History,* pp. 251–316; and Altaf Gauhar, *Ayub Khan, Pakistan's First Military Ruler* (Lahore: Sang-e-Meel Publications, 1993).

70. H. Feldman, *Revolution in Pakistan: A Study of the Martial Law Administration* (Karachi: Oxford University Press, 1967).

71. Nasr, *The Vanguard,* pp. 147–48.

72. On the growing power of the military after 1958, see Mumtaz Ahmad, "Islamization and the Structural Crises of the State in Pakistan," *Issues in Islamic Thought,* 12 (1993), p. 305.

73. Fazlur Rahman, "Some Islamic Issues in the Ayub Khan Era," in Donald P. Little, ed., *Essays on Islamic Civilization Presented to Niyazi Berkes* (Leiden: E. J. Brill, 1976), p. 285.

74. Syed Mujawar Hussain Shah, *Religion and Politics in Pakistan, 1972–88* (Islamabad: Quaid-i-Azam University, 1996), pp. 60–64.

75. For more on Ayub Khan's policies, see Mumtaz Ahmad, "Islam and the State: The Case of Pakistan," in Matthew Moen and Lowell Gustafson, eds., *The Religious Challenge to the State* (Philadelphia: Temple University Press, 1992), pp. 239–67; and Nasr, *Vanguard,* pp. 147–69.

76. Rahman, "Some Islamic Issues," p. 284.

77. Nasr, *Vanguard,* pp. 148–50.

78. Ahmad, "Islam and the State," p. 239.

79. Katherine Ewing, "The Politics of Sufism: Redefining the Saints of Pakistan," *Journal of Asian Studies,* 42, 2 (February 1983), pp. 251–68; and Arthur Beuller, "Currents of Sufism in Nineteenth and Twentieth Century Indo-Pakistan," *Muslim World,* 87, 3–4 (July–October 1997), pp. 299–314.

80. Ahmad, "Islam and the State," p. 244.

81. Nasr, "Pakistan: State, Agrarian Reform, and Islamization."

82. Ahmad, "Islam and the State," p. 245; and Ewing, "The Politics of Sufism."

83. Ahmad, "Islam and the State," p. 244.

84. *Ibid,* p. 245.

85. The text of the speech is enclosed with United Kingdom High Commission, Karachi, dispatch #INT.48/47/1, 5/25/1959, DO35/8962, Public Records Office, England.

86. Omar Noman, *Political Economy of Pakistan, 1947–85* (London: KPI, 1988), pp. 33–35.

87. Jamal Malik, *Colonization of Islam: Dissolution of Traditional Institutions in Pakistan* (Delhi: Manohar, 1996), pp. 35–36.

88. Fazlur Rahman, "The Controversy Over the Muslim Family Laws," in Donald E. Smith, ed., *South Asian Religion and Politics* (Princeton: Princeton University Press, 1966), pp. 414–27.

890. Iqbal, *Islamisation,* pp. 75–83.

90. Nasr, *Vanguard,* pp. 147–69.

91. *Idem,* "Islamic Opposition in the Political Process: Lessons from Pakistan," in John L. Esposito, ed., *Political Islam: Revolution, Radicalism, or Reform?* (Boulder, CO: Lynne Rienner, 1997), pp. 142–45.

92. Mumtaz Ahmad, "Islamization and Sectarian Violence in Pakistan," *Intellectual Discourse,* 6, 1 (1998), p. 17.

93. Shahid Javed Burki, "Pakistan's Economy in Year 2000: Two Possible Scenarios," in J. Henry Korson, ed., *Contemporary Problems of Pakistan* (Boulder, CO: Westview Press, 1993), p. 6.

94. Rashid Amjad, *Pakistan's Growth Experience: Objectives, Achievement, and Impact on Poverty, 1947–1977* (Lahore: Progressive Publishers, 1978).

95. Khalid B. Sayeed, *Politics in Pakistan: The Nature and Direction of Change* (New York: Praeger, 1980), pp. 54–83.

96. S. M. Naseem, "Mass Poverty in Pakistan: Some Preliminary Findings," *Pakistan Development Review,* 12, 4 (Winter 1973), pp. 322–25.

97. For a discussion of the impact of economic changes during Ayub Khan's rule on the distribution of wealth between the provinces, see Jahan, *Pakistan,* pp. 51–107.

98. Mahbub ul-Haq, *The Poverty Curtain: Choices for the Third World* (New York: Columbia University Press, 1976), pp. 7–8.

3. Secular States in Crisis

1. Chandra Muzaffar, *Challenges and Choices in Malaysian Politics and Society* (Penang: ALIRAN, 1989), p. 19.

2. Harold Crouch, *Government and Society in Malaysia* (Ithaca: Cornell University Press, 1996); Haji Ahmad Zakaria, "Malaysia: Quasi-Democracy in a Divided Society," in Larry Diamond, Juan Linz, and Seymour Martin Lipset, eds., *Democracy in*

Developing Counties, vol. 3 (Boulder, CO: Lynne Rienner, 1989), pp. 347–82; W. Case, "Malaysia: The Semi-Democratic Paradigm," *Asian Survey,* 36, 9 (September 1996), pp. 852–68; Clark Neher, "Asian Style Democracy," *Asian Survey,* 34, 11 (November 1994), pp. 949–61; and p. R. Moody, Jr., "Asian Values," *Journal of International Affairs* (Summer 1996), pp. 166–92.

3. Jomo K. S., *A Question of Class: Capital, the State, and Uneven Development in Malaya* (New York: Oxford University Press, 1986), p. 271.

4. Ozay Mehmet, *Islamic Identity and Development: Studies of the Islamic Periphery* (New York: Routledge, 1990), p. 155.

5. Alasdair Bowie, "The Dynamics of Business-Government Relations in Industrialising Malaysia," in Andrew MacIntyre, ed., *Business and Government in Industrialising Asia* (Ithaca: Cornell University Press, 1994), p. 167.

6. Edmund T. Gomez, *Political Business: Corporate Involvement in Malaysian Political Parties* (Townsville, Australia: Center for South-East Asian Studies, James Cook University, 1994), pp. 10–11.

7. James Jesundason, *Ethnicity and the Economy: The State, Chinese Business, and Multinationals in Malaysia* (Singapore: Oxford University Press, 1989), p. 102.

8. Bowie, "The Dynamics of Business-Government Relations," p. 171.

9. For discussions of NEP, see Edmund T. Gomez and Jomo K. S., *Malaysia's Political Economy: Politics, Patronage, and Profits* (New York: Cambridge University Press, 1997), pp. 24–74; Jomo K. S., *A Question of Class,* pp. 256–68; and Paul Lubeck, "Malaysian Industrialization, Ethnic Divisions, and the NIC Model: The Limits to Replication," in Richard p. Appelbaum and Jeffrey Henderson, eds., *State and Development in the Asian Pacific Rim* (Newbury Park: Sage Press, 1992), pp. 176–98.

10. Hussin Mutalib, *Islam and Ethnicity in Malay Politics* (Singapore: Oxford University Press, 1990), p. 57.

11. Mehmet, *Islamic Identity,* p. 150; and *idem, Development in Malaysia: Poverty, Wealth, and Trusteeship* (London: Croom Helm, 1986).

12. Mehmet, *Islamic Identity,* pp. 132–52.

13. Edmund T. Gomez, *Politics in Business: UMNO's Corporate Investments* (Kuala Lumpur: Forum, 1990), p. vii.

14. Mutalib, *Islam and Ethnicity,* p. 58.

15. Muzaffar, *Challenges and Choices,* pp. 32–33.

16. Gordon R. Means, *Malaysian Politics: The Second Generation* (Singapore: Oxford University Press, 1991), pp. 27–32.

17. Bowie, "The Dynamics of Business-Government Relations," pp. 172–73.

18. *Ibid,* p. 175.

19. Mahathir had been earlier expelled from UMNO for his criticisms of Tunku Abdul Rahman. Along with Musa Hitam and other "Ultras," Mahathir continued to argue for more aggressively pro-Malay government policies; Means, *Malaysian Politics,* p. 83.

20. Gomez, *Politics in Business.*

21. *Ibid,* p. vii, and Mehmet, *Islamic Identity and Development,* p. 155.

22. Gomez and Jomo K. S. write that in 1981 still 41% of delegates to UMNO's General Assembly were teachers. That number fell to 32% in 1984 and 19% in 1987. By 1995 20% of UMNO's division chairmen were millionaire businessmen; Gomez and Jomo K. S., *Malaysia's Political Economy,* p. 26.

23. Mehmet, *Islamic Identity,* pp. 195–96.

24. *Ibid,* pp. 49–50; and Gomez, *Political Business,* p. 34.

25. Mehmet, *Islamic Identity and Development,* p. 155.

26. *Ibid,* pp. 109–10.

27. Anthony Milner, *The Invention of Politics in Colonial Malaya: Contesting Nationalism and Expansion of the Public Sphere* (New York: Cambridge University Press, 1994).

28. Judith Nagata, "Religious Ideology and Social Change: The Islamic Revival in Malaysia," *Pacific Affairs,* 53, 3 (Fall 1980), p. 412.

29. Chandra Muzaffar, *Islamic Resurgence in Malaysia* (Petaling Jaya: Penerbit Fajar Bakti, 1987), pp. 18–20.

30. Mehmet, *Islamic Identity and Development,* pp. 48–49.

31. Zainah Anwar, *Islamic Revivalism in Malaysia: Dakwah Among the Students* (Petaling Jaya: Peladunk, 1987), pp. 10–11.

32. Mutalib, *Islam and Ethnicity,* p. 58.

33. Nagata, "Religious Ideology," p. 411.

34. Means, *Malaysian Politics,* p. 66; and Jomo K. S. and Ahmad Shabery Cheek, "The Politics of Malaysia's Islamic Resurgence," *Third World Quarterly,* 10, 2 (April 1988), pp. 844–45.

35. Muzaffar, *Islamic Resurgence,* pp. 20–21.

36. Nagata, "Religious Ideology," pp. 407–8.

37. Alfred Stepan, *The State and Society: Peru in Comparative Perspective* (Princeton: Princeton University Press, 1978), pp. 44–45.

38. S. V. R. Nasr, The Vanguard of the Islamic Revolution: The Jama'at-i Islami of Pakistan (Berkeley: University of California Press, 1994), pp. 161–65; Markus Daechsel, "Military Islamisation in Pakistan and the Specter of Colonial Perceptions," *Contemporary South Asia* 6, 2 (July 1997), pp. 153–54.

39. For the specifics of these demands, known as the "six-point" plan, and their implications, see Richard Sisson and Leo E. Rose, *War and Secession: Pakistan, India, and the Creation of Bangladesh* (Berkeley: University of California Press, 1990), pp. 19–21.

40. Vali Nasr, "The Negotiable State: Borders and Power-Struggles in Pakistan," forthcoming, in Ian Lustick, Thomas Callaghy, and Brendan O'Leary, eds., *Rightsizing the State: The Politics of Moving Borders.*

41. On the Bhutto era see Shahid Javed Burki, *Pakistan Under Bhutto, 1971–1977* (London: Macmillan, 1980); Stanley Wolpert, *Zulfi Bhutto of Pakistan: His Life and Times* (New York: Oxford University Press, 1993); Rafi Raza, *Zulfikar Ali Bhutto and Pakistan, 1967–1977* (Karachi: Oxford University Press, 1997); Salmaan Taseer, *Bhutto: A Political Biography* (London: Ithaca Press, 1979); and Anwar H. Syed, *The Discourse and Politics of Zulfikar Ali Bhutto* (New York: St. Martin's Press, 1992).

42. Syed Mujawar Hussain Shah, *Religion and Politics in Pakistan, 1972–88* (Islamabad: Quaid-I-Azam University, 1996), pp. 98–101.

43. For an excellent analysis of this theme, with special reference to the case of Afghanistan, see Barnett R. Rubin, "Redistribution and the State in Afghanistan: The Red Revolution Turns Green," in Myron Weiner and Ali Banuazizi, eds., *The Politics of Social Transformation in Afghanistan, Iran, and Pakistan* (Syracuse: Syracuse University Press, 1994), pp. 187–227.

44. Omar Noman, *The Political Economy of Pakistan, 1947–85* (London: KPI, 1988), pp. 74–95.

45. John Adams, "Pakistan's Economic Performance in the 1980s: Implications for Political Balance," in Craig Baxter, ed., *Zia's Pakistan: Politics and Stability in a Frontline State* (Boulder, CO: Westview Press, 1985), p. 52.

46. Nasr, *Vanguard,* p. 171; Mir Zohair Hussain, "Islam in Pakistan under Bhutto and Zia-ul-Haq," in Hussin Mutalib and Taj ul-Islam Hashmi, eds., *Islam, Muslims, and the Modern State* (New York: St. Martin's Press, 1994), p. 52; and Hussain Shah, *Religion and Politics,* pp. 133–39.

47. Nasr, *Vanguard,* p. 171.

48. Stephen Cohen, *The Pakistan Military* (Berkeley: University of California Press, 1984).

49. Mumtaz Ahmad, "Islamization and the Structural Crises of the State in Pakistan," *Issues in Islamic Thought,* 12 (1993), p. 306.

50. Afzal Iqbal, *Islamisation of Pakistan* (Lahore: Vanguard, 1986), pp. 84–95.

51. Hussain Shah, *Religion and Politics,* pp. 151–56.

52. Mumtaz Ahmad, "Islam and the State: The Case of Pakistan," in Matthew Moen and L. Gustafson, eds., *Religious Challenge to the State* (Philadelphia: Temple University Press, 1992), p. 254; and General Khalid Mahmud Arif, *Working with Zia: Pakistan's Power Politics, 1977–88* (Karachi: Oxford University Press, 1995).

53. On diversity of Islamic expression in Pakistan's politics, see Nasim Ahmad Jawed, *Islam's Political Culture: Religion and Politics in Predivided Pakistan* (Austin: University of Texas Press, 1999).

54. Hussain, "Islam in Pakistan," pp. 51–53; and Fazlur Rahman, "Islam in Pakistan," *Journal of South Asian and Middle Eastern Studies,* 8 (Summer 1985), pp. 50–51.

55. Akbar S. Ahmed, *Discovering Islam: Making Sense of Muslim History and Society* (New York: Routledge & Kegan Paul, 1988), pp. 81–83.

56. Hussain Shah, *Religion and Politics,* pp. 106–7.

57. Iqbal, *Islamisation,* pp. 100–101.

58. Ahmad, "Islam and the State," pp. 255–56; and Hussain Shah, *Religion and Politics,* pp. 161–64.

59. On PNA and Nizam-i Mustafa, see Abdu'l-Ghafur Ahmad, *Pher Martial Law A-Giya* (Then Came Martial Law) (Lahore: Jang Publications, 1988); Kausar Niazi, *Zulfiqar Ali Bhutto of Pakistan: The Last Days* (New Delhi: Vikas Publishing House, 1992); and General Faiz Ali Chishti, *Betrayals of Another Kind: Islam, Democracy, and the Army in Pakistan* (Cincinnati: Asia Publishing House, 1990).

60. General Khalid Mahmud Arif, *Working with Zia: Pakistan's Power Politics, 1977–88* (Karachi: Oxford University Press, 1995), p. 69.

61. Ahmad, "Islam and the State," pp. 255–56.

4. The Islamist Challenge in Malaysia and Pakistan

1. Chandra Muzaffar, *Islamic Resurgence in Malaysia* (Petaling Jaya: Penerbit Fajar Bakti, 1987), pp. 4–5.

2. Anthony Milner, *The Invention of Politics in Colonial Malaya: Contesting Nationalism and Expansion of the Public Sphere* (New York: Cambridge University Press, 1994), p. 3.

3. Mohamad Abu Bakar, "Islam and Nationalism in Contemporary Malay Society," in Taufik Abdullah and Sharon Siddique, eds., *Islam and Society in Southeast Asia* (Singapore: Institute of Southeast Asian Studies, 1986), pp. 162–63; and Judith Nagata, "Ethnonationalism Versus Religious Transnationalism: Nation-Building and Islam in Malaysia," *Muslim World,* 87, 2 (April 1997), pp. 129–50.

4. Zainah Anwar, *Islamic Revivalism in Malaysia: Dakwah Among the Students* (Petaling Jaya: Peladunk, 1987), p. 21; and Raymond Lee, "The State, Religious Na-

tionalism, and Ethnic Rationalization in Malaysia," *Ethnic and Racial Studies,* 13, 4 (October 1990), pp. 482–502.

5. Manning Nash, "Islamic Resurgence in Malaysia and Indonesia," in Martin Marty and R. Scott Appelby, eds., *Fundamentalisms Observed* (Chicago: University of Chicago Press, 1991), p. 700.

6. A. B. Shamsul, "The Economic Dimension of Malay Nationalism: Identity Formation in Malaysia Since 1988; the Social-Historical Roots of the New Economic Policy and Its Contemporary Implications," *Developing Economies,* 35, 2 (September 1997), pp. 240–61.

7. Ozay Mehmet, *Islamic Identity and Development: Studies of the Islamic Periphery* (New York: Routledge, 1990), pp. 48–49; Jomo K. S. and Ahmad Shabery Cheek, "The Politics of Malaysia's Islamic Resurgence," *Third World Quarterly,* 10, 2 (April 1988), pp. 844–45; Clive S. Kessler, "Malaysia: Islamic Revivalism and Political Disaffection in a Divided Society," *Southeast Asia Chronicle,* 75 (October 1980), pp. 3–11; and Muzaffar, *Islamic Resurgence,* pp. 15–21.

8. Judith Nagata, "Religious Ideology and Social Change: The Islamic Revival in Malaysia," *Pacific Affairs,* 53, 3 (Fall 1980), p. 412.

9. Muzaffar, *Islamic Resurgence,* pp. 55–64.

10. Nash, "Islamic Resurgence," p. 703.

11. Jomo K. S. and Cheek, "The Politics of Malaysia's Islamic Resurgence," p. 847; M. R. J. Vatikiotis, *Political Change in Southeast Asia: Trimming the Banyan Tree* (London: Routledge, 1996), p. 162.

12. Gordon P. Means, *Malaysian Politics: The Second Generation* (Singapore: Oxford University Press, 1991), pp. 28 and 88–89; and Syed Ahmad Hussein, "Muslim Politics and Discourse of Democracy in Malaysia," in Loh Kok Wah and Khoo Boo Teik, eds., *Democracy in Malaysia: Discourses and Practices* (London: Curzon, 2000).

13. Anwar, *Islamic Revivalism;* and Judith Nagata, *The Reflowering of Malaysian Islam: Modern Religious Radicals and Their Roots* (Vancouver: University of British Columbia Press, 1984).

14. Mohamad Abu Bakar, "Islamic Revivalism and the Political Process in Malaysia," *Asian Survey,* 21, 10 (October 1981), pp. 1040–41.

15. Hussin Mutalib, *Islam and Ethnicity in Malay Politics* (Singapore: Oxford University Press, 1990), p. 90.

16. On al-Arqam, see Nagata, *Reflowering of Malaysian Islam,* pp. 104–16; Mutalib, *Islam and Ethnicity,* pp. 73–101; and Muhammad Syukri Sallaeh, *An Islamic Approach to Rural Development: The Arqam Way* (London: ASOIB International, 1992).

17. Anwar, *Islamic Revivalism,* pp. 10–11.

18. Mutalib, *Islam and Ethnicity,* p. 58.

19. *Ibid,* p. 59.

20. Nagata, *Reflowering of Malaysian Islam,* p. 56.

21. Anwar, *Islamic Revivalism,* p. 22.

22. Mehmet, *Islamic Identity,* p. 49.

23. On Anwar Ibrahim's political career, see John L. Esposito and John O. Voll, *The Makers of Contemporary Islam* (New York: Oxford University Press, 2001), pp. 177–98.

24. K. J. Ratham and R. S. Milne, "The 1969 Parliamentary Elections in West Malaysia," *Pacific Affairs,* 43, 2 (Summer 1970), pp. 203–26.

25. Fred von der Mehden, "Malaysia: Islam and Multiethnic Politics," in John L. Esposito, ed., *Islam in Asia: Religion, Politics, and Society* (New York: Oxford University Press, 1987), pp. 177–201.

26. Nagata, "Ethnonationalism Versus Religious Transnationalism," pp. 129–50.

27. John L. Esposito and John O. Voll, *Islam and Democracy* (New York: Oxford University Press, 1996), pp. 137–38; Shanti Nair, *Islam in Malaysian Foreign Policy* (New York: Routledge, 1997), pp. 29–30.

28. Mehmet, *Islamic Identity,* pp. 104–6.

29. Mohamad Abu Bakar, "External Influences on Contemporary Islamic Resurgence in Malaysia," *Contemporary Southeast Asia,* 13, 2 (September 1991), pp. 220–28.

30. Rose Ismail, ed., *Hudud in Malaysia: The Issues at Stake* (Kuala Lumpur: SISI Forum, 1995).

31. Fred von der Mehden, "Islamic Resurgence in Malaysia," in John L. Esposito, ed., *Islam and Development: Religion and Sociopolitical Change* (Syracuse: Syracuse University Press, 1980), p. 168.

32. *Idem, Two Worlds of Islam: Interactions Between Southeast Asia and the Middle East* (Gainesville: University Press of Florida, 1993), pp. 23–33.

33. *Ibid,* p. 18.

34. Mehmet, *Islamic Identity,* pp. 104–6; Mutalib, *Islam and Ethnicity,* p. 73.

35. Muzaffar, *Islamic Resurgence,* pp. 31–32.

36. Alias Mohamed, *PAS' Platform: Development and Change, 1951–1986* (Petaling Jaya: Gateway Publishing, 1994), pp. 138–64.

37. Nagata, "Religious Ideology," p. 429.

38. Mutalib, *Islam and Ethnicity,* pp. 83–84

39. Mohamamd Abu Bakar, "Islam in Malaysia's Foreign Policy," *Hamdard Islamicus,* 13, 1 (Spring 1981), pp. 6–7.

40. Anwar, *Islamic Revivalism,* pp. 25–31.

41. Mutalib, *Islam and Ethnicity,* p. 60; Abu Bakar, "Islamic Revivalism," pp. 1042–43.

42. Anwar, *Islamic Revivalism,* pp. 27–28; and Nair, *Islam in Malaysian Foreign Policy,* p. 30.

43. Anwar, *Islamic Revivalism,* pp. 27–28.

44. Abu Bakar, "Islamic Revivalism," p. 1042.

45. Anwar, *Islamic Revivalism,* pp. 30–31.

46. On the roots of Anwar Ibrahim and ABIM's views, see Esposito and Voll, *Makers of Contemporary Islam,* pp. 177–98.

47. On ABIM, see Mutalib, *Islam and Ethnicity,* pp. 73–101; *idem,* "ABIM," in John L. Esposito, ed., *The Oxford Encyclopedia of the Modern Islamic World* (New York: Oxford University Press, 1995); Nagata, *Reflowering of Malaysian Islam,* pp. 87–104; Muzaffar, *Islamic Resurgence,* pp. 48–52; Esposito and Voll, *Islam and Democracy,* pp. 130–33.

48. Anwar, *Islamic Revivalism,* p. 12.

49. *Ibid.*

50. Abu Bakar, "Islamic Revivalism," p. 1046–47; and Nagata, "Religious Ideology," p. 428.

51. Esposito and Voll, *Makers of Contemporary Islam,* pp. 177–98.

52. Interviews with Anwar Ibrahim, Siddiq Fazil, and Muhammad Nur Manuty, June–August 1997, Kuala Lumpur.

53. Nagata, *Reflowering of Malaysian Islam,* p. 95.

54. Nash, "Islamic Resurgence," p. 707.

55. Nair, *Islam in Malaysian Foreign Policy,* p. 29; and Mutalib, *Islam and Ethnicity,* p. 77.

56. Abu Bakar, "Islamic Revivalism," p. 1048.

57. Esposito and Voll, *Islam and Democracy,* p. 131.

58. Cited in Muzaffar, *Islamic Resurgence,* pp. 12–13.

59. Simon Barraclough, "Managing the Challenges of Islamic Revival in Malaysia: A Regime Perspective," *Asian Survey,* 23, 8 (August 1983), pp. 958–75.

60. Nagata, "Religious Ideology," pp. 415–16.

61. Mutalib, *Islam and Ethnicity,* p. 66.

62. Abu Bakar, "Islamic Revivalism," p. 1051.

63. Mutalib, *Islam and Ethnicity,* p. 65.

64. Anwar, *Islamic Revivalism,* p. 23; Means, *Malaysian Politics,* p. 37.

65. Nair, *Islam in Malaysian Foreign Policy,* p. 31.

66. Nash, "Islamic Resurgence," p. 714.

67. *Ibid,* p. 96.

68. Nagata, "Religious Ideology," p. 412.

69. Barraclough, "Managing the Challenges," p. 961.

70. For a general discussion of government Islam strategy, see David Camroux, "State Responses to Islamic Resurgence in Malaysia: Accommodation, Co-Option, and Confrontation," *Asian Survey,* 36, 9 (September 1996), pp. 856–57.

71. *Ibid,* p. 960.

72. Hussein, "Muslim Politics."

73. Esposito and Voll, *Islam and Democracy,* p. 134.

74. Delair Noer, "Contemporary Political Dimensions of Islam," in M. B. Hooker, *Islam in South-East Asia* (Leiden: E. J. Brill, 1983), p. 200.

75. On the UMNO-PAS conflict, see Muzaffar, *Islamic Resurgence,* pp. 84–87.

76. On Awang, see Mohamed, *PAS' Platform,* pp. 165–200.

77. Mutalib, *Islam and Ethnicity,* pp. 114–23.

78. Interviews with Anwar Ibrahim, Fazil Siddiq, Muhammad Nur Manuty, and Khalid Ja`far, June–August 1997, Kuala Lumpur.

79. Interview with Anwar Ibrahim in Joyce M. Davis, *Between Jihad and Salaam: Profiles in Islam* (New York: St. Martin's Press, 1997), p. 299.

80. *Ibid,* pp. 300–301.

81. On these parties, see Charles H. Kennedy, "Jam`iyatul `Ulama-i Islam" and S. V. R. Nasr, "Jam`iyatul `Ulama-i Pakistan," in John L. Esposito, ed., *The Oxford Encyclopedia of the Modern Islamic World* (New York: Oxford University Press, 1995).

82. For more on the Jama`at, see Mumtaz Ahmad, "Islamic Fundamentalism in South Asia: The Jamaat-i-Islami and the Tablighi Jamaat," in Martin E. Marty and R. Scott Appleby, eds., *Fundamentalisms Observed* (Chicago: University of Chicago Press, 1991), pp. 457–530; Rafiuddin Ahmed, "Redefining Muslim Identity in South Asia: The Transformation of the Jama`at-i Islami," in Martin E. Marty and R. Scott Appleby, eds., *Accounting for Fundamentalisms: The Dynamic Character of Movements* (Chicago: University of Chicago Press, 1994), pp. 699–705; Kalim Bahadur, *The Jama`at-i Islami of Pakistan* (New Delhi: Chetana Publications, 1977); and Seyyed Vali Reza Nasr, *The Vanguard of the Islamic Revolution: The Jama`at-i Islami of Pakistan* (Berkeley: University of California Press, 1994).

83. For a biography of Mawdudi, see Seyyed Vali Reza Nasr, *Mawdudi and the Making of Islamic Revivalism* (New York: Oxford University Press, 1996); and Charles J. Adams, "The Ideology of Mawlana Mawdudi," in Donald E. Smith, ed., *South Asian Politics and Religion* (Princeton: Princeton University Press, 1966), pp. 371–97.

84. Said A. Arjomand, "Religion and Constitutionalism in Western History and in Modern Iran and Pakistan," in Said Amir Arjomand, ed., *The Political Dimensions of Religion* (Albany: SUNY Press, 1993), pp. 69–99.

85. Nasr, *Vanguard,* pp. 132–41; Ayesha Jalal, *The State of Martial Rule: The Origins of Pakistan's Political Economy of Defence* (Cambridge: Cambridge University Press, 1990), p. 153.

86. On IJT, see Seyyed Vali Reza Nasr, "Students, Islam, and Politics: Islami Jami'at-i Tulaba in Pakistan." *The Middle East Journal,* 46, 1 (Winter 1992), pp. 59–76.

87. Quoted in Khalid B. Sayeed, *Politics in Pakistan: The Nature and Direction of Change* (New York: Praeger, 1980), p. 162.

88. Shahid Javed Burki, *Pakistan Under Bhutto, 1971–1977* (London: Macmillan, 1980), p. 53.

89. Muhammad Salahu'ddin, *Peoples Party: Maqasid Awr Hikmat-i `Amali* (Karachi, 1982).

90. On the importance of this issue in the eventual fall of the Bhutto government, see `Abdu'l-Ghafur Ahmad, *Pher Martial Law A-Giya* (Lahore: Jang, 1988), p. 101.

91. Sharif al-Mujahid, "The 1977 Pakistani Elections: An Analysis," in Manzooruddin Ahmad, ed., *Contemporary Pakistan: Politics, Economy, and Society* (Karachi: Royal Books Company, 1980), pp. 63–91.

92. Cited in Niazi, *Zulfiqar Ali Bhutto,* p. 91.

93. *Ibid,* pp. 239–41; and Lt. General Faiz Ali Chishti, *Betrayals of Another Kind: Islam, Democracy, and the Army in Pakistan* (Cincinnati: Asia, 1990), p. 66.

94. S. V. R., Nasr, "Ideology and Institutions in Islamist Approaches to Public Policy," in Sohrab Behdad and Farhad Nomani, eds., *International Review of Comparative Public Policy,* 9 (1997), pp. 41–67.

5. Malaysia, 1981–1997

1. *Asiaweek,* April 25, 1997, p. 71.

2. Chandra Muzaffar, "Two Approaches to Islam: Revisiting Islamic Resurgence in Malaysia," unpublished manuscript, p. 16.

3. Alasdair Bowie, *Crossing the Industrial Divide: State, Society, and the Politics of Economic Transformation in Malaysia* (New York: Columbia University, 1991), pp. 111–52.

4. Chandra Muzaffar, *Challenges and Choices in Malaysian Politics and Society* (Penang: ALIRAN, 1989), p. 498.

5. Jomo K. S. and Ahmad Shabery Cheek, "The Politics of Malaysia's Islamic Resurgence," *Third World Quarterly,* 10, 2 (April 1988), p. 855.

6. Gordon P. Means, *Malaysian Politics: The Second Generation* (Singapore: Oxford University Press, 1991), p. 180.

7. Farish Noor, "Caught Between the Ulama: How the Conflict Between the Government and the Islamist Opposition Is Bringing Malaysia to an Islamic State," forthcoming in *The German Journal of International Politics and Society.*

8. Jomo K. S. and Cheek, "The Politics of Malaysia's Islamic Resurgence," p. 867.

9. Mohamad Abu Bakar, "Islamic Revivalism and the Political Process in Malaysia," *Asian Survey,* 21, 10 (October 1981), pp. 1051.

10. On these issues, see Means, *Malaysian Politics,* pp. 91–98.

11. Jomo K. S. and Cheek, "The Politics of Malaysia's Islamic Resurgence," p. 855; and John L. Esposito and John O. Voll, *Islam and Democracy* (New York: Oxford University Press, 1996), pp. 140–45.

12. Esposito and Voll, *Islam and Democracy*, pp. 139–46.

13. Alasdair Bowie, "The Dynamics of Business-Government Relations in Industrialising Malaysia," in Andrew MacIntyre, ed., *Business and Government in Industrialising Asia* (Ithaca: Cornell University Press, 1994), p. 175.

14. Edmund Terence Gomez, *Political Business: Corporate Involvement in Malaysian Political Parties* (Townsville, Australia: Center for South-East Asian Studies, James Cook University, 1994), p. 7.

15. W. Goh and Jomo K. S., "Efficiency and Consumer Welfare," in Jomo K. S., ed., *Privatizing Malaysia: Rents, Rhetoric, and Realities* (Boulder, CO: Westview, 1995), pp. 154–71.

16. Bowie, "The Dynamics of Business-Government Relations," pp. 178–79.

17. Gomez, *Political Business*, p. 34.

18. Harold Crouch, *Government and Society in Malaysia* (Ithaca: Cornell University Press, 1996), p. 183.

19. Paul Lubeck, "Malaysian Industrialization, Ethnic Divisions, and the NIC Model: The Limits to Replication," in Richard p. Appelbaum and Jeffrey Henderson, eds., *State and Development in the Asian Pacific Rim* (Newbury Park: Sage Press, 1992), p. 179.

20. Bowie, "The Dynamics of Business-Government Relations," pp. 186–87.

21. Cited in Gomez, *Political Business, p. 7*.

22. *Ibid*, pp. 7–8.

23. *Ibid*, pp. 9–10 and 14–21; also see Patricia Sloane, *Islam, Modernity, and Entrepreneurship Among Malays* (London: Macmillan, 1999), pp. 171–86.

24. Khoo Boo Teik, *Paradoxes of Mahathirism: An Intellectual Biography of Mahathir Mohamad* (Kuala Lumpur: Oxford University Press, 1995), pp. 110–12.

25. Diane K. Mauzy and R. S. Milne, "The Mahathir Administration in Malaysia: Discipline Through Islam," *Pacific Affairs*, 56, 4 (Winter 1983), p. 630.

26. Jomo K. S., *Growth and Structural Change in Malaysian Economy* (London: Macmillan, 1990).

27. *Ibid*, p. 624.

28. Teik, *Paradoxes*, p. 73.

29. Mauzy and Milne, "The Mahathir Administration," p. 628.

30. Crouch, *Government and Society*, p. 171.

31. Teik, *Paradoxes*, p. 180.

32. Muzaffar, "Two Approaches," p. 7.

33. Mauzy and Milne, "The Mahathir Administration," p. 636; Judith Nagata, "Religious Ideology and Social Change: The Islamic Revival in Malaysia," *Pacific Affairs*, 53, 3 (Fall 1980), p. 430.

34. Mohamad Abu Bakar, "Islam and Nationalism in Contemporary Malay Society," in Taufik Abdullah and Sharon Siddique, eds., *Islam and Society in Southeast Asia* (Singapore: Institute of Southeast Asian Studies, 1986), pp. 167–68.

35. Gomez, *Political Business*.

36. Jomo K. S. and Ishak Shari, *Development Policies and Income Inequality in Peninsular Malaysia* (Kuala Lumpur: Institute of Advanced Studies, University of Malaya, 1986); Teik, *Paradoxes*, pp. 209–24.

37. Ozay Mehmet, *Islamic Identity and Development: Studies of the Islamic Periphery* (New York: Routledge, 1990), p. 9.

38. Diane Mauzy, "Malaysia: Malay Political Hegemony and Chinese Consociationalism," in John McGarry and Brendan O'Leary, eds., *The Politics of Ethnic Conflict Regulation* (London: Routledge, 1993), pp. 106–27.

39. Alias Mohamed, *PAS' Platform: Development and Change, 1951–1986* (Darul Ihsan: Gateway Publishing, 1994).

40. Edmund T. Gomez and Jomo K. S., *Malaysia's Political Economy: Politics, Patronage, and Profits* (New York: Cambridge University Press, 1997), pp. 10–12.

41. Simon Barraclough, "Managing the Challenges of Islamic Revival in Malaysia: A Regime Perspective," *Asian Survey*, 23, 8 (August 1983), pp. 958–75.

42. For a discussion of the relation of Islam to entrepreneurship and capitalist development under Mahathir, see Sloane, *Islam, Modernity, and Entrepreneurship*, pp. 57–88.

43. *Ibid*, p. 968.

44. Judith Nagata, "Ethnonationalism Versus Religious Transnationalism: Nation-Building and Islam in Malaysia," *Muslim World*, 87, 2 (April 1997), pp. 129–50.

45. Lubeck, "Malaysian Industrialization," p. 179.

46. Fred R. von der Mehden, *Two Worlds of Islam: Interactions between Southeast Asia and the Middle East* (Gainesville: University Press of Florida, 1993), pp. 64–79.

47. Shanti Nair, *Islam in Malaysian Foreign Policy* (New York: Routledge, 1997).

48. Mohamad Abu Bakar, "Islam in Malaysia's Foreign Policy," *Hamdard Islamicus*, 13, 1 (Spring 1981), pp. 10–11.

49. Fred von der Mehden, "Islamic Resurgence in Malaysia," in John L. Esposito, ed., *Islam and Development: Religion and Sociopolitical Change* (Syracuse: Syracuse University Press, 1980), p. 168; Rose Islamil, ed., *Hudud in Malaysia: The Issues at Stake* (Kuala Lumpur: SISI Forum, 1995).

50. Cited in Nagata, "Ethnonationalism," p. 142.

51. *New Straits Times,* July 17, 1982.

52. Mauzy and Milne, "The Mahathir Administration," p. 635.

53. Hussin Mutalib, *Islam and Ethnicity in Malay Politics* (Singapore: Oxford University Press, 1990), p. 123.

54. Barraclough, "Managing the Challenges," p. 967; and David Camroux, "State Responses to Islamic Resurgence in Malaysia: Accommodation, Co-Option, and Confrontation," *Asian Survey*, 36, 9 (September 1996), pp. 852–68.

55. *New Straits Times,* September 9, 1981.

56. Chandra Muzaffar, *Islamic Resurgence in Malaysia* (Petaling Jaya: Penerbit Fajar Bakti, 1987), p. 78.

57. *New Straits Times,* April 5, 1982.

58. Cited in Mauzy and Milne, "The Mahathir Administration," p. 644.

59. Judith Nagata, *The Reflowering of Malaysian Islam: Modern Religious Radicals and Their Roots* (Vancouver: University of British Columbia Press, 1984), p. 162.

60. Mohamad Abu Bakar, "Islamic Revivalism and the Political Process in Malaysia," *Asian Survey*, 21, 10 (October 1981), pp. 1055–56.

61. Interviews with Anwar Ibrahim, Khalid Ja`far, and Fazil Siddique.

62. Teik, *Paradoxes,* p. 37.

63. Abu Bakr, "Islamic Revivalism," p. 1056.

64. Mohamed, *PAS' Platform*, pp. 165–200.

65. Simon Barraclough, "Managing the Challenges of Islamic Revival in Malaysia: A Regime Perspective," *Asian Survey*, 23, 8 (August 1983), p. 971.

66. Farish Noor, "PAS's Victory Is a Political One," *Commentary*, 31 (December 1999).

67. Muhammad Kamal Hassan, "The Response of Muslim Youth Organizations to Political Change: HMI in Indonesia and ABIM in Malaysia," in William R. Roff, ed., *Islam and the Political Economy of Meaning: Comparative Studies of Muslim Discourse* (Berkeley: University of California Press, 1987), p. 193.

68. John L. Esposito and John O. Voll, *The Makers of Contemporary Islam* (New York: Oxford University Press, 2001), pp. 177–98.

69. Anwar, *Islamization in Malaysia*, p. 3.

70. Esposito and Voll, *Makers of Contemporary Islam*, pp. 177–98.

71. These ideas are elaborated upon in the pro-Mahathir writer Aidit Ghazali's books, *Development: An Islamic Perspective* (Selangor: Peladunk, 1990) and *Industrialization from an Islamic Perspective* (Kuala Lumpur: IKIM, 1993).

72. Rodney Wilson, "Islam and Malaysia's Economic Development," *Journal of Islamic Studies*, 9, 2 (July 1998), pp. 264–66.

73. *Ibid*, p. 267.

74. Muzaffar, "Two Approaches to Islam," p. 20.

75. On Wahid, see Esposito and Voll, *Makers of Contemporary Islam*, pp. 199–216.

76. Norani Othman, "The Sociopolitical Dimensions of Islamisation in Malaysia: A Cultural Accommodation or Social Change," in Norani Othman, ed., *Shari'a Law and the Modern Nation-State: A Malaysian Symposium* (Kuala Lumpur: SIS Forum, 1994), p. 134; and Mohamed, *PAS' Platform*, pp. 201–7.

77. Abu Bakar, "Islamic Revivalism," pp. 1052–53.

78. Mutalib, *Islam and Ethnicity*, p. 148.

79. Means, *Malaysian Politics*, p. 71; and Hussin Mutalib, "Islamization in Malaysia: Between Ideals and Realities," in Hussin Mutalib and Taj ul-Islam Hashmi, eds., *Islam, Muslims, and the Modern State: Case Studies of Muslims in Thirteen Countries* (New York: St. Martin's Press, 1994), pp. 164–65; Hussein, "Muslim Politics."

80. *Far Eastern Economic Review*, May 26, 1994, pp. 35–36; Camroux, "State Responses," pp. 863–65.

81. Mutalib, *Islam and Ethnicity*, p. 150.

82. Nair, *Islam in Malaysia's Foreign Policy*.

83. Means, *Malaysian Politics*, pp. 113.

84. *Ibid*, pp. 113–20; Khoo Boo Teik, *Paradoxes of Mahathirism: An Intellectual Biography of Mahathir Mohamad* (Kuala Lumpur: Oxford University Press, 1995), pp. 202–9; and Harold Crouch, *Government and Society in Malaysia* (Ithaca: Cornell University Press, 1996), pp. 142–48.

85. Muzaffar, *Challenges*, p. 8.

86. Nair, *Islam in Malaysia's Foreign Policy*, pp. 133–34.

87. Means, *Malaysian Politics*, pp. 90 and 125.

88. Nagata, "Ethnonationalism," p. 146.

89. Muzaffar, "Two Approaches," pp. 1–2; and S. U. Balogun, "The Status of Shari'ah in Malaysia," *Hamdard Islamicus*, 20, 2 (April–June 1997), pp. 51–58.

90. Teik, *Paradoxes*, pp. 286–94.

91. Nagata, *Reflowering*, p. 159.

92. Esposito and Voll, *Islam and Democracy*, p. 130.

93. Nair, *Islam in Malaysia's Foreign Policy*, p. 109.

94. Muzaffar, *Islamic Resurgence*, p. 77.

95. Nair, *Islam in Malaysia's Foreign Policy*, p. 112.

96. Sharifah Zaleha, "Surau and Mosques in Malaysia," *ISIM Newsletter*, 3 (1999), p. 9.

97. Mutalib, *Islam and Ethnicity,* p. 149.

98. On Islamic economics, see Farhad Nomani and Ali Rahnema, *Islamic Economic Systems* (London: Zed Press, 1994); Seyyed Vali Reza Nasr, "Towards a Philosophy of Islamic Economics," *Muslim World,* 77, 3–4 (July–October 1987), pp. 175–96; *idem,* "Islamic Economics: Novel Perspectives on Change in the Middle East," *Middle Eastern Studies,* 25, 4 (October 1989), pp. 516–530; Timur Kuran, "The Economic Impact of Islamic Fundamentalism," in Martin Marty and R. Scott Appleby, eds., *Fundamentalisms and the State* (Chicago: University of Chicago Press, 1993), pp. 175–96; *idem,* Timur Kuran, "Behavioral Norms in the Islamic Doctrine of Economics: A Critique," *Journal of Economic Behavior and Organization,* 4 (1983), pp. 353–79; and *idem,* "The Economic System in Contemporary Islamic Thought," *International Journal of Middle East Studies,* 18, 2 (May 1986), pp. 135–64.

99. Anwar, *Islamization,* p. 5.

100. Muzaffar, "Two Approaches," p. 14.

101. Jomo K. S. and Cheek, "The Politics of Malaysia's Islamic Resurgence," p. 865; and Muzaffar, *Two Approaches,* p. 11.

102. *Ibid.*

103. Fred von der Mehden, *Religion and Modernization in Southeast Asia* (Syracuse: Syracuse University Press, 1986), p. 58.

104. *Ibid.*

105. *Ibid,* p. 60.

106. Kuran, "The Economic Impact of Islamic Fundamentalism," p. 320.

107. Von der Mehden, *Religion and Modernization,* p. 62.

108. Nair, *Islam in Malaysia's Foreign Policy,* p. 144.

109. Von der Mehden, *Religion and Modernization,* p. 64.

110. Rodney Wilson, "Islam and Malaysia's Economic Development," *Journal of Islamic Studies,* 9, 2 (July 1998), p. 269.

111. William R. Roff, "Patterns of Islamization in Malaysia, 1890s–1990s: Exemplars, Institutions, and Vectors," *Journal of Islamic Studies,* 9, 2 (July 1998), pp. 222–23.

112. Radia Abdul Kader and Mohamed Ariff, "The Political Economy of Islamic Finance: The Malaysian Experience," in Masudul Alam Choudhry, Abdad M. Z., and Muhammad Syukri Salleh, eds., *Islamic Political Economy in Capitalist Globalization: An Agenda for Change* (Kuala Lumpur: IPIPE, 1997), pp. 262–63.

113. Anwar, *Islamization,* p. 5.

114. Wilson, "Islam and Malaysia's Economic Development," p. 269.

115. Mehmet, *Islamic Identity,* pp. 159–60.

116. Wilson, "Islam and Malaysia's Economic Development," p. 267.

117. Judith Nagata, "Religious Correctness and the Place of Islam in Malaysia's Economic Policies," in Timothy Brook and Hy V. Luong, eds., *Culture and Economy: The Shaping of Capitalism in Eastern Asia* (Ann Arbor: University of Michigan Press, 1997), p. 92.

118. Anne Sophie Roald, *Tarbiya: Education and Politics in Islamic Movements in Jordan and Malaysia* (Lund: Lund University, 1994), pp. 233–34; Anwar, *Islamization,* p. 2; Means, *Malaysian Politics,* pp. 133–34.

119. Roald, *Tarbiya,* pp. 241–45.

120. Esposito and Voll, *Makers of Contemporary Islam,* pp. 177–98.

121. On Faruqi, see John L. Esposito, "Ismail R. al-Faruqi: Muslim Scholar-Activist," in Yvonne Haddad, ed., *Muslims of America* (New York: Oxford University Press, 1991), pp. 65–79.

122. Fazlur Rahman, "Islamization of Knowledge: A Response," *American Journal of Islamic Social Sciences,* 5, 1 (1988), pp. 3–11; Seyyed Vali Reza Nasr, "Islamization of Knowledge: A Critical Overview," *Islamic Studies,* 30, 3 (Autumn 1991), pp. 387–400.

123. Wilson, "Islam and Malaysia's Economic Development," p. 261.

124. Nair, *Islam in Malaysia's Foreign Policy,* p. 34.

125. Anwar, *Islamization,* p. 6.

126. Mutalib, *Islam and Ethnicity,* p. 134; *idem,* "Islamization in Malaysia," p. 152.

127. Mutalib, *Islam and Ethnicity,* p. 129.

128. Anwar, *Islamization,* p. 6.

129. *Ibid,* pp. 7–8; and Mutalib, "Islamization in Malaysia," pp. 155–56.

130. Anwar, *Islamization,* p. 9.

131. Esposito and Voll, *Islam and Democracy,* p. 149.

132. Cited in Mutalib, *Islam and Ethnicity,* p. 145.

133. Nagata, "Religious Correctness," pp. 87–90.

134. Muzaffar, "Two Approaches," p. 7.

135. Statement is propagated by IKIM in its literature.

136. Muzaffar, "Two Approaches," and Nagata, "Ethnonationalism," p. 141.

137. Bruce B. Lawrence, *Shattering the Myth: Islam Beyond Violence* (Princeton: Princeton University Press, 1998), pp. 157–86.

138. Ghazali, *Development;* other titles from IKIM in this regard include Nik Mustapha Nik Hassan, *Values-Based Management: The Way Forward for the Next Millennium;* Syed Othman Alhabshi and Aidit Ghazali, *Islamic Values and Management;* Syed Othman Alhabshi and Nik Mustapha Nik Hassan, *Islam, Knowledge, and Ethics: A Pertinent Culture for Managing Organisations.*

139. Lawrence, *Shattering the Myth,* p. 161.

140. Camroux, "State Responses," p. 855; IKIM's titles in this regard include Abu Bakar Abdul Majeed, Shaikh Saifuddeen Shaikh, and Mohd Salleh, eds., *Islam and Development in Asia; Kongres Menjelang Abad 21: Islam dan Wawasan 2020* (Congress on the Twenty-first Century: Islam and Vision 2020) (IKIM, 1993); Nik Mustapha Nik Hassan, Shaikh Saifuddeen, Shaikh Mohd Salleh, and Hamiza Ibrahim, *Globalisasi: Peranan Ekonomi dan Kewangan Islam Penyunting* (Globalization: The Role of Islamic Economics and Finance) (IKIM, nd).

141. Lawrence, *Shattering the Myth,* p. 167.

142. Ghazali, *Industrialization from an Islamic Perspective.*

143. Nagata, "Religious Correctness," p. 89.

144. W. Case, "The 1996 UMNO Party Elections: Two for the Show," *Pacific Affairs,* 70, 3 (Fall 1997), pp. 393–411.

6. Pakistan, 1977–1997

1. See Abd al-Ghafur Ahmad, *Phir martial law a-giya* (Then Came Martial Law) (Lahore: Jang Publications, 1988); and Kausar Niazi, *Zulfiqar Ali Bhutto of Pakistan: The Last Days* (New Delhi: Vikas Publishing House, 1992).

2. Lt.-General Faiz Ali Chishti, *Betrayals of Another Kind: Democracy and the Army in Pakistan* (Cincinnati: Asia Publishing House, 1990), p. 67.

3. Hasan-Askari Rizvi, *The Military and Politics in Pakistan, 1947–86* (Delhi: Konark, 1988), p. 226.

4. General Khalid Mahmud Arif, *Working with Zia: Pakistan's Power Politics, 1977–88* (Karachi: Oxford University Press, 1995), p. 72–81.

5. *Ibid,* p. 1; Chishti, *Betrayals,* pp. 66–69.

6. Mohammad Waseem, *Pakistan Under Martial Law, 1977–1985* (Lahore: Vanguard, 1987), pp. 1–4.

7. Rizvi, *The Military and Politics in Pakistan,* pp. 229–30.

8. Saeed Shafqat, *Civil-Military Relations in Pakistan: From Zulfiqar Ali Bhutto to Benazir Bhutto* (Boulder, CO: Westview Press, 1997).

9. Mohammad Asghar Khan, *Generals in Politics: Pakistan 1958–1982* (Delhi: Vikas, 1983), pp. 154–55; and Syed Mujawar Hussain Shah, *Religion and Politics in Pakistan (1972–88)* (Islamabad: Quaid-i-Azam University, 1996), pp. 271–72.

10. S. V. R. Nasr, "Islamic Opposition to the Islamic State: The Jama'at-i Islami 1977–1988," *International Journal of Middle East Studies,* 25, 2 (May 1993), pp. 268.

11. *Idem,* "Democracy and Islamic Revivalism," *Political Science Quarterly,* 110, 2 (Summer 1995), pp. 275–78.

12. Mumtaz Ahmad, "The Crescent and the Sword: Islam, the Military, and Political Legitimacy in Pakistan: 1977–1985," *Middle East Journal,* 50, 3 (Summer 1996), pp. 372–86.

13. S. V. R. Nasr, *The Vanguard of the Islamic Revolution: The Jama'at-i Islami of Pakistan* (Berkeley: University of California Press, 1994), p. 190.

14. Charles Kennedy, *Islamization of Laws and Economy: Case Studies on Pakistan* (Islamabad: Institute of Policy Studies, 1996), p. 44.

15. Omar Noman, *Pakistan: A Political and Economic History Since 1947* (London: KPI, 1990), pp. 144–56.

16. Dietrich Reetz, "National Consolidation or Fragmentation of Pakistan: The Dilemma of General Zia-ul-Haq (1977–88)," in Diethelm Weidemann, ed., *Nationalism, Ethnicity, and Political Development: South Asian Perspectives* (Delhi: Manohar, 1991), p. 131.

17. Mushahid Hussain, *Pakistan's Politics: The Zia Years* (Lahore: Progressive Publishers, 1990).

18. G. W. Choudhury, *Pakistan: Transition from Military to Civilian Rule* (Burkenhurst Hill, Essex: Scorpion, 1988), pp. 35–36.

19. Shahid Javed Burki, "Pakistan Under Zia, 1977–1988," *Asian Survey,* 28, 10 (October 1988), p. 1093.

20. Cited in Ayesha Jalal, *Democracy and Authoritarianism in South Asia* (New York: Cambridge University Press, 1995), p. 154.

21. *Government of Pakistan: Economic Survey, 1987–1988* (Islamabad: Finance Division, 1988), p. 115.

22. Reetz, "National Consolidation," p. 131.

23. *Government of Pakistan: Economic Survey, 1987–1988* (Islamabad: Finance Division, 1988), p. 115.

24. *Ibid.*

25. Marvin Weinbaum, *Pakistan and Afghanistan: Resistance and Reconstruction* (Boulder, CO: Westview Press, 1994), p. 18.

26. Barnett R. Rubin, *The Fragmentation of Afghanistan: State Formation and Collapse in the International System* (New Haven: Yale University Press, 1995), pp. 196–97.

27. Burki, "Pakistan Under Zia," pp. 1090–91.

28. John Adams, "Pakistan's Economic Performance in the 1980s: Implications for Political Balance," in Craig Baxter, ed., *Zia's Pakistan: Politics and Stability in a Frontline State* (Boulder, CO: Westview Press, 1985), pp. 47–48.

29. Burki, "Pakistan Under Zia," p. 1093.

30. For a discussion of the economy during this period, see Omar Noman, *Economic and Social Progress in Asia: Why Pakistan Did Not Become a Tiger* (Karachi: Oxford University Press, 1997), pp. 195–277.

31. Reetz, "National Consolidation," p. 131.

32. Adams, "Pakistan's Economic Performance," p. 57.

33. For a general study of this class in Pakistan, see Anita Weiss, *Culture, Class, and Development in Pakistan: The Emergence of an Industrial Bourgeoisie in Punjab* (Boulder, CO: Westview Press, 1991).

34. Rizvi, *Military and Politics*, pp. 245–53.

35. Paula R. Newberg, *Judging the State: Courts and Constitutional Politics in Pakistan* (New York: Cambridge University Press, 1995), pp. 180–81.

36. Nasr, "Islamist Opposition," p. 265.

37. Arif, *Working with Zia*, pp. 241–46.

38. *Ibid*, Chishti, *Betrayals*, pp. 63–64.

39. Chishti, *Betrayals*, pp. 97–101. Muhammad Afzal, who served as advisor to Zia in the 1980s, as well as in his cabinets, argues that Zia was alone among the top rank of the military in his belief in the political utility of Islamization, and had to do much to convince them; interview with Afzal, Islamabad, 1997.

40. Arif, *Working with Zia*, p. 120.

41. Mir Zohair Hussain, "Islam in Pakistan under Bhutto and Zia-ul-Haq," in Hussin Mutalib and Taj ul-Islam Hashmi, eds., *Islam, Muslims, and the Modern State* (New York: St. Martin's Press, 1994), p. 59.

42. Stanley Wolpert, *Zulfi Bhutto of Pakistan: His Life and Times* (New York: Oxford University Press, 1993), pp. 280–81.

43. Cited in Khalid B. Sayeed, *Politics in Pakistan: The Nature and Direction of Change* (New York: Praeger, 1980), p. 162.

44. Markus Daechsel, "Military Islamisation in Pakistan and the Spectre of Colonial Perceptions," *Contemporary South Asia*, 6, 2 (July 1997), p. 155.

45. Cited in *ibid*.

46. Ahmad, "Crescent and the Sword," p. 374.

47. Arif, *Working with Zia*, p. 79.

48. S. V. R. Nasr, *Mawdudi and the Making of Islamic Revivalism* (New York: Oxford University Press, 1996), pp. 80–106.

49. *Idem, Vanguard*, p. 191.

50. Alfred Stepan, *The State and Society: Peru in Comparative Perspective* (Princeton: Princeton University Press, 1978).

51. Ahmad, "Crescent and the Sword," pp. 381–82.

52. Mustapha Kamal Pasha, "Islamization, Civil Society, and the Politics of Transition in Pakistan," in Douglas Allen, ed., *Religion and Political Conflict in South Asia* (Westport, CT: Greenwood Press, 1992), pp. 128.

53. Mumtaz Ahmad, "Islamization and the Structural Crises of the State in Pakistan," *Issues in Islamic Thought*, 12 (1993), p. 306.

54. Charles Kennedy, "Islamization of Real Estate: Pre-emption and Land Reforms in Pakistan, 1978–1992," *Journal of Islamic Studies*, 4, 1 (January 1993), pp. 71–83.

55. Jamal Malik, *Colonization of Islam: Dissolution of Traditional Institutions in Pakistan* (Delhi: Manohar, 1996), pp. 63–64.

56. Hussain Shah, *Religion and Politics*, p. 247.

57. *Ibid*, pp. 247–48.

58. Hussain, "Islam in Pakistan," p. 60; and Malik, *Colonization,* pp. 55–74.

59. Mumtaz Ahmad, "Islamization and Sectarian Violence in Pakistan," *Intellectual Discourse,* 6, 1 (1998), p. 18.

60. *Ibid,* pp. 38–47.

61. Arif, *Working with Zia,* pp. 135–50.

62. Ahmad, "Islamization," pp. 17–18.

63. Arif, *Working with Zia,* p. 250.

64. Ahmad, "Islamization," pp. 19–20.

65. Charles Kennedy, "Islamization in Pakistan: Implementation of Hudood Ordinances," *Asian Survey,* 28, 3 (March 1988), pp. 307–16.

66. Mumtaz Ahmad, "Islam and the State: The Case of Pakistan," in Matthew Moen and L. Gustafson, eds., *Religious Challenge to the State* (Philadelphia: Temple University Press, 1992), p. 263.

67. Kemal A. Faruki, "Pakistan: Islamic Government and Society," in John L. Esposito, ed., *Islam in Asia: Religion, Politics, and Society* (New York: Oxford University Press, 1987), p. 63.

68. Afzal Iqbal, *Islamisation of Pakistan* (Lahore: Vanguard, 1986), p. 112.

69. Hussain, *Religion and Politics,* p. 250.

70. Charles Kennedy, "Repugnancy to Islam—Who Decides? Islam and Legal Reform in Pakistan," *International and Comparative Law Quarterly,* 41, 4 (October 1992), pp. 772.

71. Arif, *Working with Zia,* p. 255.

72. *Ibid,* p. 132.

73. Hussain, *Religion and Politics,* pp. 253–55.

74. *Ibid,* p. 252.

75. Malik, *Colonization,* p. 65.

76. Newberg, *Judging the State,* p. 184.

77. Hussain, *Religion and Politics,* pp. 259–60.

78. Faruki, "Pakistan," p. 59.

79. Malik, *Colonization,* p. 38.

80. Rizvi, *Military and Politics,* pp. 233–34.

81. Hussain, *Religion and Politics,* pp. 267–73.

82. S. V. R. Nasr, "The Rise of Sunni Militancy in Pakistan: The Changing Role of Islamism and the Ulama in Society and Politics," *Modern Asian Studies,* 34; 1 (January 2000), pp. 155–65.

83. Malik, *Colonization,* pp. 85–119.

84. *Idem,* "Islamization in Pakistan, 1977–1985: The Ulama and Their Places of Learning," *Islamic Studies,* 28, 1 (Spring 1989), p. 13.

85. Malik, "Islamization," pp. 9–10.

86. Muhammad Qasim Zaman, "Religious Education and the Rhetoric of Reform: The Madrasah in British India and Pakistan," *Comparative Studies in Society and History,* 41, 2 (April 1999), 294–323.

87. Malik, "Islamization," pp. 11–12.

88. *Ibid,* p. 16.

89. *Ibid,* p. 12.

90. *Idem, Colonization,* pp. 133–36.

91. *Idem,* "Dynamics Among Traditional Religious Scholars and Their Institutions in Contemporary South Asia," *Muslim World,* 87, 3–4 (July–October 1997), pp. 216–17.

92. Nasr, "Islamic Opposition to the Islamic State," pp. 261–83.

93. Iqbal, *Islamisation*, pp. 109–12.

94. Shahid Javed Burki, "Economic Management Within an Islamic Context," in Anita Weiss, eds., *Islamic Reassertion in Pakistan: The Application of Islamic Laws in a Modern State* (Syracuse: Syracuse University Press, 1986), pp. 51–52.

95. *Ibid*, p. 56.

96. In 1986–87 Khurshid Ahmad of the Jama'at claimed that despite Islamization 95–97% of all banking remained "un-Islamic"; cited in Timur Kuran, "The Economic Impact of Islamic Fundamentalism," in Martin Marty and R. Scott Appleby, eds., *Fundamentalisms and the State* (Chicago: University of Chicago Press, 1993), p. 315.

97. Hussain, *Religion and Politics*, pp. 260–67.

98. Ann Elizabeth Mayer, "Islamization and Taxation in Pakistan," in Anita Weiss, ed., *Islamic Reassertion in Pakistan* (Syracuse: Syracuse University Press, 1986), p. 60.

99. Grace Clark, "Pakistan's Zakat and 'Ushr as a Welfare System," in Weiss, *Islamic Reassertion in Pakistan*, p. 79.

100. Ahmad, "Islamization and Structural Crises," p. 307.

101. Mayer, "Islamization," p. 60.

102. For a discussion of this issue, see Rafiq Ahmad, "Taxation and Agricultural Incomes in Pakistan," in Richard Stanford, ed., *Rural Development in Pakistan* (Durham: Carolina Academic Press, 1980), pp. 40–47.

103. Clark, "Pakistan's Zakat and 'Ushr," p. 86.

104. Ahmad, "Islamization," p. 17.

105. Mohammad Waqar-ul-Haq and Jameel Ahmed Saleemi, *Manual of Zakat and Ushr Laws* (Lahore: Nadeem Law Book House, 1990), pp. 77–115.

106. Ann Elizabeth Mayer, "Islamization and Taxation in Pakistan," in Weiss, *Islamic Reassertion*, p. 67.

107. *Zakat and Ushr System in Pakistan* (Islamabad: Central Zakat Administration, Ministry of Finance, 1991), p. 2. Ghulam Ishaq Khan, the minister of finance under Zia gives a higher figure: Rs. 32.2 billion ($239 million) for 1980–83 alone; cited in Faruki, "Pakistan," p. 63.

108. Kuran, "Economic Impact," pp. 321–22.

109. *Zakat and Ushr System*, p. 2.

110. *The Economist*, August 6, 1994, p. 9; on the problem of welfare in Pakistan, see Noman, *Economic and Social Progress*, pp. 278–94.

111. On the relevance of redistribution resources to state power, see Atul Kohli, *The State and Poverty in India: The Politics of Reform* (New York: Cambridge University Press, 1987); and Barnett R. Rubin, "Redistribution and the State in Afghanistan: The Red Revolution Turns Green," in Myron Weiner and Ali Banuazizi, eds., *The Politics of Social Transformation in Afghanistan, Iran, and Pakistan* (Syracuse: Syracuse University Press, 1994), pp. 187–227.

112. S. V. R. Nasr, "Pakistan: State, Agrarian Reform, and Islamization," *International Journal of Politics, Culture, and Society*, 10, 2 (Winter 1996), pp. 249–72.

113. On these conflicts, see Tahir Amin, *Ethno-National Movements in Pakistan: Domestic and International Factors* (Islamabad: Institute of Policy Studies, 1988); Leonard Binder, "Islam, Ethnicity, and the State in Pakistan," in Banuazizi and Weiner, *The State, Religion, and Ethnic Politics*, pp. 259–66; Hamza Alavi, "Nationhood and Communal Violence in Pakistan," *Journal of Contemporary Asia*, 21, 2 (1991), pp. 152–77; Charles H. Kennedy, "Policies of Ethnic Preference in Pakistan," *Asian Survey*, 24, 6 (June 1984), pp. 938–55.

114. Akmal Hussain, "The Karachi Riots of 1986: Crisis of State and Civil Society in Pakistan," in Veena Das, ed., *Mirrors of Violence: Communities, Riots, and Sur-*

vivors in South Asia (Delhi: Oxford University Press, 1990), pp. 185–93; and Farida Shaheed, "The Pathan-Muhajir Conflict, 1985–6: A National Perspective," in *ibid*, pp. 194–214.

115. S. V. R. Nasr, "Pakistan: Islamic State, Ethnic Polity," *The Fletcher Forum of World Affairs*, 16, 2 (Summer 1992), pp. 81–90.

116. *Idem*, "International Politics, Domestic Imperatives, and the Rise of Politics of Identity: Sectarianism in Pakistan, 1979–1997," forthcoming in *Comparative Politics*.

117. Muhammad Qasim Zaman, "Sectarianism in Pakistan: The Radicalization of Shi'i and Sunni Identities," *Modern Asian Studies* 32 (July 1998), pp. 687–716; and Malik, "Islamization," pp. 5–28.

118. Nasr, "The Rise of Sunni Militancy in Pakistan, pp. 139–80.

119. On politics during time period, see Lawrence Ziring, *Pakistan in the Twentieth Century: A Political History* (Karachi: Oxford University Press, 1997), pp. 423–502.

120. Hussain Shah, *Religion and Politics*, pp. 274–78.

121. Malik, *Colonization*, p. 43.

122. Omar Asghar Khan, "Political and Economic Aspects of Islamisation," in Asghar Khan, ed., *Islam, Politics, and the State: The Pakistan Experience* (London: Zed Books, 1985), pp. 127–63.

123. Waseem, *Pakistan Under Martial Law*, pp. 4–6; Arif, *Working with Zia*, pp. 218–20.

124. Ahmad, "Crescent and the Sword," p. 375.

125. Vali Nasr, "The Negotiable State: Borders and Power-Struggles in Pakistan," forthcoming in Ian Lustick, Thomas Callaghy, and Brendan O'Leary, eds., *Rightsizing the State: The Politics of Moving Borders;* Noman, *Pakistan*, pp. 130–33; Arif, *Working with Zia*, pp. 233–41.

126. Muhammad Waseem, "Pakistan's Lingering Crisis of Dyarchy," *Asian Survey*, 32, 7 (July 1992), pp. 617–34.

127. Hussain Shah, *Religion and Politics*, pp. 286–90.

128. Kennedy, "Repugnancy to Islam," pp. 774–77.

129. Qazi Husain Ahmad, *Shariat Bill: Uski Zarurat Awr Us Par I`tirazat Ja'izah* (Shariat Bill: Its Necessity and An Examination of the Objections to It) (Lahore: Mutahhidah Shariat Mahaz, 1986).

130. S. V. R. Nasr, "Democracy and the Crisis of Governability in Pakistan," *Asian Survey*, 32, 6 (June 1992), pp. 521–37.

131. On Pakistan's politics during the democratic period, see Ayesha Jalal, *Democracy and Authoritarianism in South Asia* (New York: Cambridge University Press, 1995), pp. 140–55; Ziring, *Pakistan*, pp. 503–47.

132. See comments by army chief Jahangir Karamat on the imperative of institution building in *Dawn* (Karachi), October 6, 1998, p. 1.

133. On the Shariat Bill of 1990 and Nawaz Sharif's Islamization policies, see Ann Elizabeth Mayer, "The Fundamentalist Impact on Law, Politics, and Constitutions in Iran, Pakistan, and the Sudan," in Martin E. Marty and R. Scott Appleby, eds., *Fundamentalisms and the State: Remaking Polities, Economies, and Militance* (Chicago: University of Chicago Press, 1993), pp. 131–32.

134. Figures provided by Central Zakat Commission and the State Bank of Pakistan.

135. *Ibid*.

136. Mumtaz Ahmad, "Revivalism, Islamization, Sectarianism, and Violence in Pakistan," in Craig Baxter and Charles H. Kennedy, eds., *Pakistan 1997* (Boulder, CO: Westview Press, 1998), pp. 101–21.

Bibliography

Abbot, Freeland, *Islam and Pakistan* (Ithaca: Cornell University Press, 1968).

Abu Bakar, Mohamad, "External Influences on Contemporary Islamic Resurgence in Malaysia," *Contemporary Southeast Asia,* 13, 2 (September 1991): 220–28.

———, "Islam and Nationalism in Contemporary Malay Society," in Taufik Abdullah and Sharon Siddique, eds., *Islam and Society in Southeast Asia* (Singapore: Institute of Southeast Asian Studies, 1986): 155–75.

———, "Islamic Revivalism and the Political Process in Malaysia," *Asian Survey,* 21, 10 (October 1981): 1040–59.

———, "Islam in Malaysia's Foreign Policy," *Hamdard Islamicus,* 13, 1 (Spring 1981): 3–13.

Abu Rabi`, Ibrahim, "Islamic Resurgence and the Problematic of Tradition in the Modern Arab World: The Contemporary Academic Debate," *Islamic Studies,* 34, 1 (Spring 1995): 43–65.

Adams, Charles J., "The Ideology of Mawlana Mawdudi," in Donald E. Smith, ed., *South Asian Politics and Religion* (Princeton: Princeton University Press, 1966): 371–97.

Adams, John, "Pakistan's Economic Performance in the 1980s: Implications for Political Balance," in Craig Baxter, ed., *Zia's Pakistan: Politics and Stability in a Frontline State* (Boulder, CO: Westview, 1985): 47–62.

Adams, Linda S., "Political Liberalization in Jordan: An Analysis of the State's Relationship with the Muslim Brotherhood," *The Journal of Church and State,* 38, 3 (Summer 1996): 507–28.

Afzal, M., *Political Parties in Pakistan, 1947–1958* (Islamabad: National Commission on Historical and Cultural Research, 1976).

Ahmad, Abdu'l-Ghafur, *Pher Martial Law A-Giya* (Then Came Martial Law) (Lahore: Jang Publications, 1988).

Ahmad, Mumtaz, "The Crescent and the Sword: Islam, the Military, and Political Legitimacy in Pakistan: 1977–1985," *The Middle East Journal,* 50, 3 (Summer 1996): 372–86.

————, "Democracy on Trial in Malaysia," *Studies in Contemporary Islam,* 1, 1 (Spring 1999): 72–81.

————, "From Nawaz to General Musharraf," *The Frontier Post* (Peshawar), October 28, 1999.

————, "Islam and the State: The Case of Pakistan," in Matthew Moen and Lowell L. Gustafson, eds., *The Religious Challenge to the State* (Philadelphia: Temple University Press, 1992): 239–67.

————, "Islamic Fundamentalism in South Asia: The Jamaat-i-Islami and the Tablighi Jamaat," in Martin E. Marty and R. Scott Appleby, eds., *Fundamentalisms Observed* (Chicago: University of Chicago Press, 1991): 457–530.

————, "Islamization and Sectarian Violence in Pakistan," *Intellectual Discourse,* 6, 1 (1998): 17, 18.

————, "Islamization and the Structural Crises of the State in Pakistan," *Issues in Islamic Thought,* 12 (1993): 304–10.

————, "Revivalism, Islamization, Sectarianism, and Violence in Pakistan," in Craig Baxter and Charles H. Kennedy, eds., *Pakistan 1997* (Boulder, CO: Westview Press, 1998): 101–21.

Ahmad, Qazi Husain, *Shariat Bill: Uski Zarurat Awr Us Par I`tirazat Ja'izah* (Shariat Bill: Its Necessity and an Examination of the Objections to It) (Lahore: Mutahhidah Shariat Mahaz, 1986).

Ahmad, Rafiq, "Taxation and Agricultural Incomes in Pakistan," in Richard Stanford, ed., *Rural Development in Pakistan* (Durham: Carolina Academic Press, 1980): 40–47.

Ahmed, Akbar S., *Discovering Islam: Making Sense of Muslim History and Society* (New York: Routledge & Kegan Paul, 1988).

————, *Jinnah, Pakistan, and Islamic Identity: The Search for Saladin* (New York: Routledge, 1997).

Ahmed, Ishtiaq, *The Concept of an Islamic State: An Analysis of the Ideological Controversy in Pakistan* (New York: St. Martin's Press, 1987).

Ahmed, Rafiuddin, "Redefining Muslim Identity in South Asia: The Transformation of the Jama'at-i Islami," in Martin E. Marty and R. Scott Appleby, eds., *Accounting for Fundamentalisms: The Dynamic Character of Movements* (Chicago: University of Chicago Press, 1994): 699–705.

Akailan, Abdullah, "The Experience of the Jordanian Islamic Movement," in Azzam Tamimi, ed., *Power-Sharing Islam?* (London: Liberty for the Muslim World Publications, 1993): 93–101.

Akhavi, Shahrough, *Religion and Politics in Contemporary Iran: Clergy-State Relations in the Pahlavi Period* (Albany: SUNY Press, 1980).

Alatas, Syed Farid, *Democracy and Authoritarianism in Indonesia and Malaysia : The Rise of the Post-Colonial State* (New York: St. Martin's Press, 1997).

————, "Reflections on the Idea of Islamic Social Science," *Comparative Civilizations Review,* 17 (1987): 60–86.

Alatas, Syed Hussein, *The Myth of the Lazy Native: A Study of the Image of the Malays, Filipinos, and Javanese from the 16th to the 20th Century and Its Function in the Ideology of Colonial Capitalism* (London: F. Cass, 1977).

Alavi, Hamza, "Ethnicity, Muslim Society, and the Pakistan Ideology," in Anita Weiss, ed., *Islamic Reassertion in Pakistan: The Application of Islamic Laws in a Modern State* (Syracuse: Syracuse University Press, 1986): 21–47.

————, "Nationhood and Communal Violence in Pakistan," *Journal of Contemporary Asia,* 21, 2 (1991): 152–77.

————, "The State in Postcolonial Societies: Pakistan and Bangladesh," in Kathleen Gough and Hari P. Sharma, eds., *Imperialism and Revolution in South Asia* (New York: Monthly Review Press, 1973): 145.

Algar, Hamid, ed. and trans., *Islam and Revolution: Writings and Declarations of Imam Khomeini* (Berkeley: Mizan Press, 1981).

Ali, Syed Husin, *The Malays: Their Problems and Future* (Kuala Lumpur: Heinemann, 1981).

Almond, Gabriel, and Sidney Verba, *The Civic Culture* (Princeton: Princeton University Press, 1963).

al-Mujahid, Sharif, "The 1977 Pakistani Elections: An Analysis," in Manzooruddin Ahmad, ed., *Contemporary Pakistan: Politics, Economy, and Society* (Karachi: Royal Books Company, 1980): 63–91.

Amin, Tahir, *Ethno-National Movements in Pakistan: Domestic and International Factors* (Islamabad: Institute of Policy Studies, 1988).

————, "Pakistan in 1993," *Asian Survey,* 34, 2 (February 1994): 191–99.

Amjad, Rashid, *Pakistan's Growth Experience: Objectives, Achievement, and Impact on Poverty, 1947–1977* (Lahore: Progressive Publishers, 1978).

Anderson, Benedict, *Imagined Communities: Reflections on the Origins and Spread of Nationalism,* 2nd ed., (New York: Verso, 1991).

Anderson, Lisa, *The State and Social Transformation in Tunisia and Libya: 1830–1980* (Princeton: Princeton University Press, 1986).

————, "The State in the Middle East and North Africa," *Comparative Politics,* 20, 1 (October 1987): 1–18.

————, "The Traditions of Imperialism: The Colonial Antecedents of the Authoritarian Welfare State in the Arab World," paper presented at the American Political Science Association meeting in Chicago, August 1995.

Anderson, Michael R., "Islamic Law and the Colonial Encounter in British India," in Chibli Mallat and Jane Connors, eds., *Islamic Family Law* (London: Graham & Trotman, 1990): 205–6.

Ansari, Hamied, "The Islamic Militants in Egyptian Politics," *International Journal of Middle East Studies,* 16, 1 (March 1984): 123–44.

Anwar, Zainah, *Islamic Revivalism in Malaysia: Dakwah Among the Students* (Petaling Jaya: Peladunk, 1987).

Arif, General Khalid Mahmud, *Working with Zia: Pakistan's Power Politics, 1977–88* (Karachi: Oxford University Press, 1995).

Arjomand, Said A., "Ideological Revolution in Shi`ism," in Said A. Arjomand, ed., *Authority and Political Culture in Shi`ism* (Albany: SUNY Press, 1988): 178–209.

————, "Religion and Constitutionalism in Western History and in Modern Iran and Pakistan," in Said A. Arjomand, ed., *The Political Dimensions of Religion* (Albany: SUNY Press, 1993): 69–99.

————, "Traditionalism in Twentieth Century Iran," in Said A. Arjomand, ed., *From Nationalism to Revolutionary Islam* (Albany: SUNY Press, 1984): 195–232.

————, *The Turban for the Crown: The Islamic Revolution in Iran* (New York: Oxford University Press, 1988).

Ayata, Sencer, "Patronage, Party, and the State: The Politicization of Islam in Turkey," *The Middle East Journal,* 50, 1 (Winter 1996): 40–56.

Ayubi, Nazih, *Political Islam: Religion and Politics in the Arab World* (New York: Routledge, 1991).

Aziz, K. K., *Party Politics in Pakistan, 1947–1958* (Islamabad: National Commission on Historical and Cultural Research, 1976).

Bahadur, Kalim, *The Jama`at-i Islami of Pakistan* (New Delhi: Chetana Publications, 1977).

Baker, Raymond W., *Sadat and After: Struggles for Egypt's Political Soul* (Cambridge, MA: Harvard University Press, 1990).

Baljon, J. M. S., *Religion and Thought of Shah Wali Allah Dihlawi, 1703–1762* (Leiden: E. J. Brill, 1986).

Balogun, S. U., "The Status of *Shari`ah* in Malaysia," *Hamdard Islamicus,* 20, 2 (April–June 1997): 51–58.

Barlas, Astma, *Democracy, Nationalism, and Communalism: The Colonial Legacy in South Asia* (Boulder, CO: Westview Press, 1995).

Barnes, Samuel H., "Politics and Culture," *Research on Democracy and Society,* 2 (1994): 45–64.

Barnett, Michael, *Confronting the Costs of War: Military Power, State, and Society in Egypt and Israel* (Princeton: Princeton University Press, 1992).

Barraclough, Simon, "Al-Azhar: Between the Government and the Islamists," *Middle East Journal,* 52, 2 (Spring 1998): 236–49.

———, "Managing the Challenges of Islamic Revival in Malaysia: A Regime Perspective," *Asian Survey,* 23, 8 (August 1983): 958–75.

Bayly, C. A., *Indian Society and the Making of the British Empire* (New York: Cambridge University Press, 1988).

———, *Rulers, Townsmen, and Bazaars: North Indian Society in the Age of British Expansion, 1770–1870* (Cambridge: Cambridge University Press, 1983).

Benda, Harry, "Southeast Asian Islam in the Twentieth Century," in P. M. Holt et al., eds., *The Cambridge History of Islam* (Cambridge: Cambridge University Press, 1970), vol. 2:182–209.

Berlant, Lauren, *The Anatomy of National Fantasy: Hawthorne, Utopia, and Everyday Life* (Chicago: University of Chicago Press, 1991).

Beuller, Arthur, "Currents of Sufism in Nineteenth and Twentieth Century Indo-Pakistan," *The Muslim World,* 87, 3–4 (July–October 1997): 299–314.

Binder, Leonard, "Islam, Ethnicity, and the State in Pakistan," in Ali Banuazizi and Myron Weiner, *The State, Religion, and Ethnic Politics: Afghanistan, Iran, and Pakistan* (Syracuse: Syracuse University Press, 1986): 259–66.

———, *Islamic Liberalism: A Critique of Development Ideologies* (Chicago: University of Chicago Press, 1988).

———, *Religion and Politics in Pakistan* (Berkeley: University of California Press, 1961).

Boone, Catherine, "States and Ruling Classes in Postcolonial Africa: The Enduring Contradictions of Power," in Joel S. Migdal, Atul Kohli, and Vivienne Shue, eds., *State Power and Social Forces* (New York: Cambridge University Press, 1994): 108–40.

Bourdieu, Pierre, *Outline of a Theory of Practice* (Cambridge: Cambridge University Press, 1977).

Bowie, Alasdair, *Crossing the Industrial Divide: State, Society, and the Politics of Economic Transformation in Malaysia* (New York: Columbia University, 1991).

———, "The Dynamics of Business-Government Relations in Industrialising Malaysia," in Andrew MacIntyre, ed., *Business and Government in Industrialising Asia* (Ithaca: Cornell University Press, 1994): 167–94.

Brass, Paul, *Ethnicity and Nationalism: Theory and Comparison* (London: Sage Publications, 1991).

Burgat, François, *L'Islamisme en Face* (Paris : Découverte/Poche, 1996).

Burki, Shahid Javed, "Economic Management Within an Islamic Context," in Anita Weiss, ed., *Islamic Reassertion in Pakistan: The Application of Islamic Laws in a Modern State* (Syracuse: Syracuse University Press, 1986): 49–58.

———, "Pakistan's Economy in Year 2000: Two Possible Scenarios," in J. Henry Korson, ed., *Contemporary Problems of Pakistan* (Boulder, CO: Westview Press, 1993): 1–15.

———, *Pakistan Under Bhutto, 1971–1977* (London: Macmillan, 1980).

———, "Pakistan Under Zia, 1977–1988," *Asian Survey*, 28, 10 (October 1988): 1082–89.

Butcher, John G., *The British in Malaya, 1880–1941: The Social History of a European Community in Colonial South-East Asia* (Kuala Lumpur: Oxford University Press, 1979).

Camroux, David, "State Responses to Islamic Resurgence in Malaysia: Accommodation, Co-Option, and Confrontation," *Asian Survey*, 36, 9 (September 1996): 852–68.

Carnoy, Martin, *The State and Political Theory* (Princeton: Princeton University Press, 1984).

Casanova, José, *Public Religions in the Modern World* (Chicago: University of Chicago Press, 1994).

Case, W., "Malaysia: the Semi-Democratic Paradigm," *Asian Survey*, 36, 9 (September 1996): 852–68.

———, "The 1996 UMNO Party Elections: Two for the Show," *Pacific Affairs*, 70, 3 (Fall 1997): 393–411.

Chai, Hon-Chan, *The Development of British Malaya, 1896–1909* (Kuala Lumpur: Oxford University Press, 1964).

Chaterjee, Partha, *Nationalist Thought and the Colonial World: A Derivative Discourse?* (London : Zed Press, 1986).

Chaudhry, Kiren Aziz, *The Price of Wealth: Economies and Institutions in the Middle East* (Ithaca: Cornell University Press, 1997).

Cheah, Kheng Cheah, "Sino-Malay Conflicts in Malaya, 1945–46: Communist Vendetta and Islamic Resistance," *Journal of Southeast Asian Studies*, 12 (1981): 108–17.

Chehabi, H. E., "Staging the Emperor's New Clothes: Dress Codes and Nation-Building Under Reza Shah," *Iranian Studies*, 26, 3–4 (Summer/Fall 1993): 209–29.

Chehabi, H. E., and Juan J. Linz, eds., *Sultanistic Regimes* (Baltimore: Johns Hopkins University Press, 1998).

Chishti, Lt. General Faiz Ali, *Betrayals of Another Kind: Islam, Democracy, and the Army in Pakistan* (Cincinnati: Asia, 1990).

Choudhury, G. W., *Pakistan: Transition from Military to Civilian Rule* (Burkenhurst Hill, Essex: Scorpion, 1988).

Clark, Grace, "Pakistan's Zakat and 'Ushr as a Welfare System," in Anita Weiss, ed., *Islamic Reassertion in Pakistan* (Syracuse: Syracuse University Press, 1986): 79–95.

Cloughy, Brian, *A History of the Pakistan Army* (Karachi: Oxford University Press, 1999).

Cohen, Bernard S., *Colonialism and Its Forms of Knowledge: The British in India* (Princeton: Princeton University Press, 1996).

———, "Representing Authority in Victorian India," in Eric Hobsbawm and Terence Ranger, eds., *The Invention of Tradition* (Cambridge: Cambridge University Press, 1983): 165–210.

Cohen, Stephen, *The Pakistan Military* (Berkeley: University of California Press, 1984).

Crescilius, Daniel, "Nonideological Responses of Egyptian Ulama to Modernization," in Nikki R. Keddie, ed., *Scholars, Saints, and Sufis: Muslim Religious Institutions Since 1500* (Berkeley: University of California Press, 1972): 167–210.

Crouch, Harold, *Government and Society in Malaysia* (Ithaca: Cornell University
Press, 1996).

Dabashi, Hamid, *Theology of Discontent* (New York: New York University Press,
1993).

Daechsel, Markus, "Military Islamisation in Pakistan and the Specter of Colonial Perceptions," *Contemporary South Asia*, 6, 2 (July 1997): 141–60.

Davis, Joyce M. *Between Jihad and Salaam: Profiles in Islam* (New York: St. Martin's
Press, 1997).

Dawisha, Adeed, and Zartman, I. William, *Beyond Coercion: Durability of the Arab
State* (London: Croom Helm, 1988).

Dekmejian, Hrair R., *Islam and Revolution* (Syracuse: Syracuse University Press,
1985).

Dessouki, Ali Hillal, "Official Islam and Political Legitimation in the Arab Countries," in Barbara F. Stowasser, ed., *The Islamic Impulse* (London: Croom Helm,
1987): 135–41.

Dowding, K., "The Compatibility of Behavioralism, Rational Choice, and New Institutionalism," *Journal of Theoretical Politics* 6, 1 (January 1994): 105–17.

Eickelman, Dale F., and Piscatori, James, *Muslim Politics* (Princeton: Princeton University Press, 1996).

Emerson, Rupert, *From Empire to Nation: The Rise of Self-Assertion of Asian and African Peoples* (Cambridge, MA: Harvard, 1960).

———, *Malaysia: A Study in Direct and Indirect Rule* (Kuala Lumpur: University of
Malaya Press, 1964).

Enayat, Hamid, *Modern Islamic Political Thought* (Austin: University of Texas Press,
1982).

Entelis, John P., "The Crisis of Authoritarianism in North Africa: The Case of Algeria," *Problems of Communism*, 41 (May–June 1992): 71–81.

Ertman, Thomas, *Birth of the Leviathan: Building States and Regimes in Medieval
and Early Modern Europe* (New York: Cambridge University Press, 1997).

Esman, Milton J., *Ethnic Politics* (Ithaca: Cornell University Press, 1994): 49–74.

Esposito, John L., *Islam and Politics*, 3rd ed. (Syracuse: Syracuse University Press,
1991).

———, *The Islamic Threat: Myth or Reality?* (New York: Oxford University Press,
1992).

———, "Ismail R. al-Faruqi: Muslim Scholar-Activist," in Yvonne Haddad, ed.,
Muslims of America (New York: Oxford University Press, 1991): 65–79.

———, ed., *The Oxford Encyclopedia of the Modern Islamic World* (New York: Oxford University Press, 1995).

Esposito, John L., and John O. Voll, *Islam and Democracy* (New York: Oxford University Press, 1996).

———, *The Makers of Contemporary Islam* (New York: Oxford University Press,
2001).

Evans, Peter, *Embedded Autonomy: States and Industrial Transformation* (Princeton:
Princeton University Press, 1995).

Evans, Peter B., Dietrich Rueschemeyer, and Theda Skocpol, eds., *Bringing the State
Back In* (New York: Cambridge University Press, 1985).

Ewing, Katherine P., *Arguing Sainthood: Modernity, Psychoanalysis, and Islam* (Durham: Duke University Press, 1997).

———, "The Politics of Sufism: Redefining the Saints of Pakistan," *Journal of Asian Studies,* 42, 2 (February 1983): 251–68.

Faruki, Kemal A., "Pakistan: Islamic Government and Society," in John L. Esposito, ed., *Islam in Asia: Religion, Politics, and Society* (New York: Oxford University Press, 1987): 53–78.

Feldman, H., *Revolution in Pakistan: A Study of the Martial Law Administration* (Karachi: Oxford University Press, 1967).

Fischer, Michael M. J., "Islam and the Revolt of the Petit Bourgeoisie," *Dædalus,* 111 (Winter 1982): 101–25.

Fischer, Wolfrem and Peter Lundgreen, "The Recruitment and Training of Administrative and Technical Personnel," in Charles Tilly, *The Formation of National States in Western Europe* (Princeton: Princeton University Press, 1975): 456–561.

Freitag, Sandria, *Collective Action and Community: Public Arenas and the Emergence of Communalism in North India* (Berkeley: University of California Press, 1989).

Funston, N. J., *Malay Politics in Malaysia: A Study of United Malays National Organisation and Party Islam* (Kuala Lumpur: Heinemann, 1980).

Gagliano, Felix, *Violence in Malaysia 1969: The Political Aftermath* (Athens: Ohio University Center for International Studies, 1970).

Gardezi, Hassan N., "Neocolonial Alliances and the Crisis of Pakistan," in Kathleen Gough and Hari P. Sharma, eds., *Imperialism and Revolution in South Asia* (New York: Monthly Review Press, 1973): 130–44.

Gauhar, Altaf, *Ayub Khan, Pakistan's First Military Ruler* (Lahore: Sang-e-Meel Publications, 1993).

Geddes, Barbara, *Politician's Dilemma: Building State Capacity in Latin America* (Berkeley: University of California Press, 1994).

Geertz, Clifford, *The Interpretation of Cultures* (New York: Basic Books, 1973).

———, *Negara: The Theatre State in Nineteenth-Century Bali* (Princeton: Princeton University Press, 1980).

Ghani, Cyrus, *Iran and the Rise of Reza Shah: From Qajar Collapse to Pahlavi Power* (London: I. B. Tauris, 1998).

Ghazali, Aidit, *Development: An Islamic Perspective* (Selangor: Peladunk, 1990).

———, *Industrialization from an Islamic Perspective* (Kuala Lumpur: IKIM, 1993).

Gheissari, Ali, *Iranian Intellectuals in the Twentieth Century* (Austin: University of Texas Press, 1998).

Gilani, Riazul Hasan, "A Note on Islamic Family Law and Islamization in Pakistan," in Chibli Mallat and Jane Connors, eds., *Islamic Family Law* (London: Graham & Trotman, 1990): 339–46.

Gilmartin, David, "Customary Law and *Sharî`at* in British Punjab," in Katherine P. Ewing, ed., *Sharî`at and Ambiguities in South Asian Islam* (Berkeley: University of California Press, 1988): 43–62.

———, *Empire and Islam: Punjab and the Making of Pakistan* (Berkeley: University of California Press, 1988).

Goh, W., and Jomo K. S., "Efficiency and Consumer Welfare," in Jomo K. S., ed., *Privatizing Malaysia: Rents, Rhetoric, and Realities* (Boulder, CO: Westview Press, 1995): 154–71.

Gomez, Edmund T., and Jomo K. S.,*Malaysia's Political Economy: Politics, Patronage, and Profits* (New York: Cambridge University Press, 1997).

Gomez, Edmund T., *Political Business: Corporate Involvement in Malaysian Political Parties* (Townsville, Australia: Center for South-East Asian Studies, James Cook University, 1994).

————, *Politics in Business: UMNO's Corporate Investments* (Kuala Lumpur: Forum, 1990).

Goodnow, H. F., *The Civil Service of Pakistan* (New Haven: Yale University Press, 1964).

Gorski, Philip S., "The Protestant Ethic Revisited: Disciplinary Revolution and State Formation in Holland and Prussia," *American Journal of Sociology,* 99, 2 (September 1993): 265–316.

Government of Pakistan: Economic Survey, 1987–1988 (Islamabad: Finance Division, 1988).

Gramsci, Antonio, *Selections from the Prison Notebooks,* ed. and trans. Quinten Hoare and Geoffrey Nowell Smith (London: Lawrence & Wishart, 1971).

Guha, Ranjit, *Dominance Without Hegemony: History and Power in Colonial India* (Cambridge: Harvard University Press, 1997).

Haggard, Stephan, *Pathways from the Periphery: The Politics of Growth in the Newly Industrializing Countries* (Ithaca: Cornell University Press, 1990).

Hall, Peter, and Rosemary Taylor, "Political Science and the Three New Institutionalisms," *Political Studies* 44 (1996): 936–57.

Hansen, Thomas Blom, *The Saffron Wave: Democracy and Hindu Nationalism in Modern India* (Princeton: Princeton University Press, 1999).

Hassan, Muhammad Kamal, "The Response of Muslim Youth Organizations to Political Change: HMI in Indonesia and ABIM in Malaysia," in William R. Roff, ed., *Islam and the Political Economy of Meaning: Comparative Studies of Muslim Discourse* (Berkeley: University of California Press, 1987): 180–96.

Hintze, Otto, *The Historical Essays of Otto Hintze,* Felix Gilbert and Robert M. Berdahl, eds., (New York: Oxford University Press, 1975).

Hirschman, Charles, "Development and Inequality in Malaysia," *Pacific Affairs,* 62, 1 (Spring 1989): 72–81.

Hitam, Musa, "Malaysia's Strategic Vision: Into the Twenty-first Century," in *Malaysia: Past, Present, and Future* (Kuala Lumpur: ISIS, 1987).

Horowitz, Donald, *Ethnic Groups in Conflict* (Berkeley: University of California Press, 1985).

Hussain, Akmal, "The Karachi Riots of 1986: Crisis of State and Civil Society in Pakistan," in Veena Das, ed., *Mirrors of Violence: Communities, Riots, and Survivors in South Asia* (Delhi: Oxford University Press, 1990): 185–93.

Hussain, Mir Zohair, "Islam in Pakistan under Bhutto and Zia-ul-Haq," in Hussin Mutalib and Taj ul-Islam Hashmi, eds., *Islam, Muslims, and the Modern State* (New York: St. Martin's Press, 1994): 47–79.

Hussain, Mushahid, *Pakistan's Politics: The Zia Years* (Lahore: Progressive Publishers, 1990).

Hussein, Syed Ahmad, "Muslim Politics and Discourse of Democracy in Malaysia," forthcoming in Loh Kok Wah and Khoo Boo Teik, eds., *Democracy in Malaysia: Discourses and Practices* (London: Curzon, 2000).

Ibrahim, Saad Eddin, "Anatomy of Egypt's Militant Islamic Groups: Methodological Note and Preliminary Findings," in *International Journal of Middle East Studies,* 12, 4 (December 1980): 423–53.

Immergut, Ellen M., "The Theoretical Core of the New Institutionalism," *Politics and Society,* 26, 1 (1998): 5–34.

Iqbal, Afzal, *Islamisation in Pakistan* (Lahore: Vanguard, 1986).

Islamil, Rose, ed., *Hudud in Malaysia: The Issues at Stake* (Kuala Lumpur: SISI Forum, 1995).

Islamization of Knowledge: General Principles and Work Plan (Herndon, VA: IIIT, 1989).

Jahan, Rounaq, *Pakistan: Failure in National Integration* (New York: Columbia University Press, 1972).

Jalal, Ayesha, "Conjuring Pakistan: History as Official Imagining," *International Journal of Middle East Studies*, 27, 1 (February 1995): 73–89.

———, *Democracy and Authoritarianism in South Asia* (New York: Cambridge University Press, 1995): 140–55.

———, *The Sole Spokesman: Jinnah, the Muslim League, and the Demand for Pakistan* (New York: Cambridge University Press, 1985).

———, *The State of Martial Rule: The Origins of Pakistan's Political Economy of Defence* (Cambridge: Cambridge University Press, 1990).

James, Lawrence, *Raj: The Making and Unmaking of British India* (New York: St. Martin's Press, 1998).

Jawed, Nasim Ahmad, *Islam's Political Culture: Religion and Politics in Predivided Pakistan* (Austin: University of Texas Press, 1999).

Jesundason, James, *Ethnicity and the Economy: The State, Chinese Business, and Multinationals in Malaysia* (Singapore: Oxford University Press, 1989).

Johnson, Chalmers, "The Developmental State: Odyssey of a Concept," in Meredith Woo-Cumings, *The Developmental State* (Ithaca: Cornell University Press, 1999): 32–60.

———, *MITI and the Japanese Miracle* (Stanford: Stanford University Press, 1982).

Joseph, Gilbert M., and Daniel Nugent,"Popular Culture and State Formation in Revolutionary Mexico," in Gilbert M. Joseph and Daniel Nugent, eds., *Everyday Forms of State Formation: Revolution and Negotiation of Rule in Modern Mexico* (Durham: Duke University Press, 1994): 3–23.

Jurgensmeyer, Mark, "The New Religious State," *Comparative Politics*, 27, 4 (July 1995): 379–91.

Kader, Radia Abdul, and Ariff, Mohamed, "The Political Economy of Islamic Finance: The Malaysian Experience," in Masudul Alam Choudhry, Abdad M. Z., and Muhammad Syukri Salleh, eds., *Islamic Political Economy in Capitalist Globalization: An Agenda for Change* (Kuala Lumpur: IPIPE, 1997): 262–63.

Karl, Terry L., *The Paradox of Plenty: Oil Booms and Petro-States* (Berkeley: University of California Press, 1997).

Keddie, Nikki R., "The New Religious Politics: Where, When, and Why Do "Fundamentalisms" Appear?" *Comparative Studies in Society and History*, 40, 4 (October 1998): 696–723.

———, "The Revolt of Islam, 1700 to 1993: Comparative Considerations and Relation to Imperialism," *Comparative Studies in Society and History*, 36, 3 (July 1994): 463–87.

Kennedy, Charles H., *Bureaucracy in Pakistan* (Karachi: Oxford University Press, 1987).

———, "Islamization in Pakistan: Implementation of Hudood Ordinances," *Asian Survey*, 28, 3 (March 1988): 307–16.

———, *Islamization of Laws and Economy: Case Studies on Pakistan* (Islamabad: Institute of Policy Studies, 1996).

———, "Islamization of Real Estate: Pre-emption and Land Reforms in Pakistan, 1978–1992," *Journal of Islamic Studies*, 4, 1 (January 1993): 71–83.

————, "Jam'iyatul 'Ulama-i Islam," in John L. Esposito, ed., *The Oxford Encyclopedia of the Modern Islamic World* (New York: Oxford University Press, 1995).

————, "Policies of Ethnic Preference in Pakistan," *Asian Survey,* 24, 6 (June 1984): 938–55.

————, "Repugnancy to Islam—Who Decides? Islam and Legal Reform in Pakistan," *International and Comparative Law Quarterly,* 41, 4 (October 1992): 769–87.

Kepel, Gilles, *Allah in the West: Islamic Movements in America and Europe* (Stanford: Stanford University Press, 1997).

————, *Muslim Extremism in Egypt: The Prophet and Pharoah* (Berkeley: University of California Press, 1985).

Kessler, Clive S., *Islam and Politics in a Malay State: Kelantan, 1838–1969* (Ithaca: Cornell University Press, 1978).

————, "Malaysia: Islamic Revivalism and Political Disaffection in a Divided Society," *Southeast Asia Chronicle,* 75 (October 1980): 3–11.

Khan, Mohammad Asghar, *Generals in Politics: Pakistan 1958–1982* (Delhi: Vikas, 1983).

Khan, Omar Asghar, "Political and Economic Aspects of Islamisation," in Asghar Khan, ed., *Islam, Politics, and the State: The Pakistan Experience* (London: Zed Books, 1985): 127–63.

Knight, Jack, "Models, Interpretations, and Theories: Constructing Explanations of Institutional Emergence and Change," in Jack Knight and Itai Sened, eds., *Explaining Social Institutions* (Ann Arbor: University of Michigan Press, 1995): 95–120.

Kohli, Atul, "Where Do High-Growth Political Economies Come From? The Japanese Lineage of Korea's "Developmental State," in Meredith Woo-Cumings, ed., *The Developmental State* (Cornell: Cornell University Press, 1999): 93–136.

————, *The State and Poverty in India: The Politics of Reform* (New York: Cambridge University Press, 1987).

Koshul, Basit, "The Islamization of Pakistan's Constitution: A Critical Analysis," *Middle East Affairs Journal,* 4, 1–2 (Winter/Spring 1998): 129–44.

Kotob, Sana Abed, "The Accommodationists Speak: Goals and Strategies of the Muslim Brotherhood," *International Journal of Middle East Studies,* 27, 3 (August 1995): 321–39.

Kratoska, Paul H., "Ends That We Cannot Foresee: Malay Reservations in British Malaya," *Journal of Southeast Asian Studies,* 14 (1983): 149–68.

————, "Rice Cultivation and Ethnic Division of Labor in British Malaya," *Comparative Studies in Society and History,* 24 (1982): 280–314.

Kuran, Timur, "Behavioral Norms in the Islamic Doctrine of Economics: A Critique," *Journal of Economic Behavior and Organization,* 4 (1983): 353–79.

————, "The Economic System in Contemporary Islamic Thought," *International Journal of Middle East Studies,* 18, 2 (May 1986): 135–64.

————, "The Economic Impact of Islamic Fundamentalism," in Martin Marty and R. Scott Appleby, eds., *Fundamentalisms and the State* (Chicago: University of Chicago Press, 1993): 175–96, 302–41.

————, "Islamic Economics and the Islamic Subeconomy," *Journal of Economic Perspectives,* 9, 4 (Fall 1995): 155–73.

Laitin, David, *Hegemony and Culture: Politics and Religious Change Among the Yoruba* (Chicago: University of Chicago Press, 1986).

————, "Political Culture and Political Preferences," *American Political Science Review,* 82 (1988): 589–93.

———, *Politics, Language, and Thought: The Somali Experience* (Chicago: University of Chicago Press, 1977).

Laroui, Abdallah, *L'ideologie arabe contemporaine* (Berkeley: University of California Press, 1967).

Lawrence, Bruce B., *Defenders of God: The Fundamentalist Revolt Against the Modern Age* (San Francisco: Harper and Row, 1989).

———, *Shattering the Myth: Islam Beyond Violence* (Princeton: Princeton University Press, 1998).

Lee, Raymond, "The State, Religious Nationalism, and Ethnic Rationalization in Malaysia," *Ethnic and Racial Studies,* 13, 4 (October 1990): 482–502.

Levi, Margaret, *Of Rule and Revenue* (Berkeley: University of California Press, 1988).

Lubeck, Paul, "Malaysian Industrialization, Ethnic Divisions, and the NIC Model: The Limits to Replication," in Richard P. Appelbaum and Jeffrey Henderson, eds., *State and Development in the Asian Pacific Rim* (Newbury Park: Sage Press, 1992): 176–98.

Majeed, Abu Bakar Abdul, Shaikh Saifuddeen Shaikh and Mohd Salleh, eds., *Islam and Development in Asia: Kongres Menjelang Abad 21: Islam dan Wawasan 2020* (Congress on the Twenty-first Century: Islam and Vision 2020) (IKIM, 1993).

Malik, Jamal, *Colonization of Islam: Dissolution of Traditional Institutions in Pakistan* (Delhi: Manohar, 1996).

———, "Dynamics Among Traditional Religious Scholars and Their Institutions in Contemporary South Asia," *The Muslim World,* 87, 3–4 (July–October 1997): 216–17.

———, "Islamization in Pakistan 1977–1985: The Ulama and Their Places of Learning," *Islamic Studies,* 28, 1 (Spring 1989): 5–28.

Malley, Robert, *The Call from Algeria: Third Worldism, Revolution, and the Turn to Islam* (Berkeley: University of California Press, 1996).

Mann, Michael, "The Autonomous Power of the State: Its Origins, Mechanisms, and Results," *Archives Européennes de Sociologie,* 25, 2 (1984): 185–213.

———, "State and Society, 1130–1815: An Analysis of English State Finances," in M. Zeitlin, ed., *Political Power and Social Theory* (Greenwich, CT: JAI Press, 1980), vol. 1: 165–208.

Mauzy, Diane, "Malaysia: Malay Political Hegemony and Chinese Consociationalism," in John McGarry and Brendan O'Leary, eds., *The Politics of Ethnic Conflict Regulation* (London: Routledge, 1993): 106–27.

Mauzy, Diane K., and R. S. Milne, "The Mahathir Administration in Malaysia: Discipline Through Islam," *Pacific Affairs,* 56, 4 (Winter 1983).

Mayer, Ann Elizabeth, "The Fundamentalist Impact on Law, Politics, and Constitutions in Iran, Pakistan, and the Sudan," in Martin E. Marty and R. Scott Appleby, eds., *Fundamentalisms and the State: Remaking Polities, Economies, and Militance* (Chicago: University of Chicago Press, 1993): 110–51.

———, "Islamization and Taxation in Pakistan," in Anita Weiss, ed., *Islamic Reassertion in Pakistan* (Syracuse: Syracuse University Press, 1986): 59–77.

McGrath, Allen, *The Destruction of Pakistan's Democrcay* (Karachi: Oxford University Press, 1996).

Means, Gordon P., *Malaysian Politics: The Second Generation* (Singapore: Oxford University Press, 1991): 83, 88–89, 180.

Mehmet, Ozay, *Development in Malaysia: Poverty, Wealth, and Trusteeship* (London: Croom Helm, 1986).

————, *Islamic Identity and Development: Studies of the Islamic Periphery* (New York: Routledge, 1990).

Metcalf, Barbara, *Islamic Revival in British India: The Deoband, 1860–1900* (Princeton: Princeton University Press, 1982).

Metcalf, Thomas R., *Ideologies of the Raj* (New York: Cambridge University Press, 1994).

————, *Land, Landlords, and the British Raj: Northern India in the Nineteenth Century* (Berkeley: University of California Press, 1979).

Migdal, Joel S., "The State in Society: An Approach to Struggles of Domination," in Joel S. Migdal, Atul Kohli, and Vivienne Shue, *State Power and Social Forces: Domination and Transformation in the Third World* (New York: Cambridge University Press, 1994): 7–34.

————, *Strong Societies and Weak States: State-Society Relations and State Capabilities in the Third World* (Princeton: Princeton University Press, 1988).

————, "Strong States, Weak States: Power and Accommodation," in Myron Weiner and Samuel P. Huntington, *Understanding Political Development* (New York: HarperCollins, 1987): 391–434.

————, "Studying the State," in Mark I. Lichbach and Alan S. Zuckerman, eds., *Comparative Politics: Rationality, Culture, and Structure* (New York: Cambridge University Press, 1997): 208–35.

Miliband, Ralph, *The State in Capitalist Society* (London: Weidenfeld & Nicolson, 1969).

Milner, Anthony, *The Invention of Politics in Colonial Malaya: Contesting Nationalism and Expansion of the Public Sphere* (New York: Cambridge University Press, 1994): 2, 3.

Mitchell, Timothy, *Colonising Egypt* (Berkeley: University of California Press, 1991).

————, "Everyday Metaphors of Power," *Theory and Society,* 19 (1990): 545–77.

————, "The Limits of the State: Beyond Statist Approaches and Their Critics," *American Political Science Review,* 85, 1 (March 1991): 77–96.

Mohamed, Alias, *PAS' Platform: Development and Change, 1951–1986* (Petaling Jaya: Gateway Publishing, 1994).

Monroe, Elizabeth, *Britain's Moment in the Middle East, 1914–1956* (Baltimore: Johns Hopkins Press, 1963).

Moody, P. R., Jr., "Asian Values," *Journal of International Affairs* (Summer 1996): 166–92.

Moore, Clement Henry, *Politics in North Africa: Algeria, Morocco, and Tunisia* (Boston: Little, Brown, 1970).

Munir, Muhammad, *From Jinnah to Zia* (Lahore: Vanguard, 1980).

Munson, Henry, Jr., *Islam and Revolution in the Middle East* (New Haven: Yale University Press, 1988).

Mutalib, Hussin, "ABIM," in John L. Esposito, ed., *The Oxford Encyclopedia of the Modern Islamic World* (New York: Oxford University Press, 1995).

————, *Islam and Ethnicity in Malay Politics* (Singapore: Oxford University Press, 1990).

————, "Islamization in Malaysia: Between Ideals and Realities," in Hussin Mutalib and Taj ul-Islam Hashmi, eds., *Islam, Muslims, and the Modern State: Case Studies of Muslims in Thirteen Countries* (New York: St. Martin's Press, 1994): 152–73.

Muzaffar, Chandra, "The Administration of Justice," *Commentary,* 19 (December 1999).

———, "Anwar Ibrahim and the Crisis in Malaysia," *Commentary,* 18 (November 1998).

———, *Challenges and Choices in Malaysian Politics and Society* (Penang: ALIRAN, 1989).

———, "From Lenders to Loansharks: International Banks Take Advantage of Asia's Weakness to Hijack the Agenda for Growth," *Commentary* (Kuala Lumpur), 25 (June 1999).

———, *Islamic Resurgence in Malaysia* (Petaling Jaya: Penerbit Fajar Bakti, 1987).

———, "The People's Verdict," *Commentary,* 24 (May 1999).

———, "A Travesty of Justice," *Commentary* (Kuala Lumpur), 21 (February 1999).

———, "Two Approaches to Islam: Revisiting Islamic Resurgence in Malaysia," unpublished manuscript.

Nagata, Judith, "Ethnonationalism Versus Religious Transnationalism: Nation-Building and Islam in Malaysia," *The Muslim World,* 87, 2 (April 1997): 129–50.

———, *The Reflowering of Malaysian Islam: Modern Religious Radicals and Their Roots* (Vancouver: University of British Columbia Press, 1984).

———, "Religious Correctness and the Place of Islam in Malaysia's Economic Policies," in Timothy Brook and Hy V. Luong, eds., *Culture and Economy: The Shaping of Capitalism in Eastern Asia* (Ann Arbor: University of Michigan Press, 1997): 79–101.

———, "Religious Ideology and Social Change: The Islamic Revival in Malaysia," *Pacific Affairs,* 53, 3 (Fall 1980): 405–39.

Nair, Shanti, *Islam in Malaysian Foreign Policy* (New York: Routledge, 1997).

Naseem, S. M., "Mass Poverty in Pakistan: Some Preliminary Findings," *Pakistan Development Review,* 12, 4 (Winter 1973): 322–25.

Nash, Manning, "Islamic Resurgence in Malaysia and Indonesia," in Martin Marty and R. Scott Appleby, eds., *Fundamentalisms Observed* (Chicago: University of Chicago Press, 1991): 691–739.

Nasr, Seyyed Vali Reza, "Communalism and Fundamentalism: A Re-examination of the Origins of Islamic Fundamentalism," *Contention,* 4, 2 (Winter 1995): 121–39.

———, "Democracy and Islamic Revivalism," *Political Science Quarterly,* 110, 2 (Summer 1995): 275–78.

———, "Democracy and the Crisis of Governability in Pakistan," *Asian Survey,* 32, 6 (June 1992): 521–37.

———, "European Colonialism and the Emergence of Modern Muslim States," in John L. Esposito, ed., *The Oxford History of Islam* (New York: Oxford University Press, 1999): 549–99.

———, "Ideology and Institutions in Islamist Approaches to Public Policy," in Sohrab Behdad and Farhad Nomani, eds., *International Review of Comparative Public Policy,* 9 (1997): 41–67.

———, "International Politics, Domestic Imperatives, and the Rise of Politics of Identity: Sectarianism in Pakistan, 1979–1997," *Comparative Politics,* 32, 2 (January 2000): 171–90.

———, "Islamic Economics: Novel Perspectives on Change in the Middle East," *Middle Eastern Studies,* 25, 4 (October 1989): 516–30.

———, "Islamic Opposition in the Political Process: Lessons from Pakistan," in John L. Esposito (ed.), *Political Islam: Revolution, Radicalism, or Reform?* (Boulder, CO: Lynne Rienner, 1997): 142–45.

———, "Islamic Opposition to the Islamic State: The Jama'at-i Islami, 1977–1988," *International Journal of Middle East Studies* 25, 2 (May 1993): 261–83.

————, "Islamization of Knowledge: A Critical Overview," *Islamic Studies,* 30, 3 (Autumn 1991): 387–400.

————, "Jam`iyatul `Ulama-i Pakistan," in John L. Esposito, ed., *The Oxford Encyclopedia of the Modern Islamic World* (New York: Oxford University Press, 1995).

————, *Mawdudi and the Making of Islamic Revivalism* (New York: Oxford University Press, 1996): 9–46.

————, "The Negotiable State: Borders and Power-Struggles in Pakistan," forthcoming in Ian Lustick, Thomas Callaghy, and Brendan O'Leary, eds., *Rightsizing the State: The Politics of Moving Borders.*

————, "Pakistan at Crossroads: The February Elections and Beyond," *Muslim Politics* (Council on Foreign Relations), 12 (March/April, 1997): 1–4.

————, "Pakistan: Islamic State, Ethnic Polity," *The Fletcher Forum of World Affairs,* 16, 2 (Summer 1992): 81–90.

————, "Pakistan: State, Agrarian Reform, and Islamization," *International Journal of Politics, Culture, and Society,* 10, 2 (Winter 1996): 249–72.

————, "The Rise of Sunni Militancy in Pakistan: The Changing Role of Islamism and the Ulama in Society and Politics," *Modern Asian Studies,* 34, 1 (January 2000): 155–65.

————, "Secular States and Religious Oppositions," *SAIS Review,* 18, 2 (Summer/Fall 1998): 32–37.

————, "Students, Islam, and Politics: Islami Jami`at-i Tulaba in Pakistan," *The Middle East Journal,* 46, 1 (Winter 1992): 59–76.

————, "Towards a Philosophy of Islamic Economics," *The Muslim World,* 77, 3–4 (July–October 1987): 175–196.

————, *The Vanguard of the Islamic Revolution: The Jama`at-i Islami of Pakistan* (Berkeley: University of California Press, 1994): 161–65, 190.

Neher, Clark D., "Asian Style Democracy," *Asian Survey,* 34, 11 (November 1994): 949–61.

————, *Southeast Asia in the New International Era* (Boulder, CO: Westview Press, 1999).

Newberg, Paula R., *Judging the State: Courts and Constitutional Politics in Pakistan* (New York: Cambridge University Press, 1995).

Niazi, Kausar, *Zulfiqar Ali Bhutto of Pakistan: The Last Days* (New Delhi: Vikas Publishing House, 1992).

Noer, Delair, "Contemporary Political Dimensions of Islam," in M. B. Hooker, *Islam in South-East Asia* (Leiden: E. J. Brill, 1983): 200.

Noman, Omar, *Economic and Social Progress in Asia: Why Pakistan Did Not Become a Tiger* (Karachi: Oxford University Press, 1997).

————, *Pakistan: A Political and Economic History Since 1947* (London: KPI, 1990).

————, *The Political Economy of Pakistan, 1947–85* (London: KPI, 1988).

Nomani, Farhad, and Ali Rahnema, *Islamic Economic Systems* (London: Zed Press, 1994).

Nonini, Donald M., *British Colonial Rule and the Resistance of the Malay Peasantry, 1900–1957* (New Haven: Yale University Southeast Asia Studies, 1992).

Noor, Farish, "Caught Between the Ulama: How the Conflict Between the Government and the Islamist Opposition Is Bringing Malaysia to an Islamic State," forthcoming in *The German Journal of International Politics and Society.*

————, "Malaysia," paper presented at Georgetown and Thammasat Universities' conference, "Asian Islam in the Twenty-first Century," Bangkok, February 2000.

————, "PAS's Victory Is a Political One," *Commentary,* 31 (December 1999).

————, "A Race for Islamization," *Asiaweek,* March 31, 2000, the internet edition: http://www.cnn.com/ASIANOW/asiaweek/magazine/2000/0331/nat.viewpoint. html.

Nordlinger, Eric, "Taking the State Seriously," in Samuel P. Huntington and Myron Weiner, eds., *Understanding Political Development* (New York: HarperCollins, 1987): 353–90.

North, Douglass C., "Economic Performance Through Time," in Lee Alston, Thrainn Eggertsson, and Douglass C. North, eds., *Empirical Studies in Institutional Change* (New York: Cambridge University Press, 1996): 342–55.

————, *Structure and Change in Economic History* (New York: W. W. Norton, 1981).

Oldenburg, Philip, " 'A Place Insufficiently Imagined': Language, Belief, and the Pakistan Crisis of 1971," *Journal of Asian Studies,* 44, 4 (August 1985): 715–23.

Önis, Ziya, "The Logic of the Developmental State," *Comparative Politics,* 24, 1 (October 1991): 109–26.

————, "The Political Economy of Islamic Resurgence in Turkey: The Rise of the Welfare Party in Perspective," *Third World Quarterly,* 18, 4 (September 1997): 743–66.

Othman, Norani, "The Sociopolitical Dimensions of Islamisation in Malaysia: A Cultural Accommodation or Social Change?" in Norani Othman, ed., *Shari'a Law and the Modern Nation-State: A Malaysian Symposium* (Kuala Lumpur: SIS Forum, 1994): 123–43.

Page, David, *Prelude to Partition: The Indian Muslims and the Imperial System of Control, 1920–1932* (Delhi: Oxford University Press, 1982).

Pandey, Gyanendra, *The Construction of Communalism in Colonial North India* (Delhi: Oxford University Press, 1990).

Pasha, Mustapha Kamal, "Islamization, Civil Society, and the Politics of Transition in Pakistan," in Douglas Allen, ed., *Religion and Political Conflict in South Asia: India, Pakistan, and Sri Lanka* (Westport, CT: Greenwood Press, 1992): 113–32.

Pipes, Daniel, "The Western Mind of Radical Islam," *First Things,* 58 (December 1995): 18–23.

Poulantzas, Nicos, *Political Power and Social Classes* (London, NLB; Sheed and Ward, 1973).

Puthucheary, James, *Ownership and Control in Malayan Economy* (Singapore: Eastern University Press, 1960).

Pye, Lucian, *Asian Power and Politics: The Cultural Dimensions of Authority* (Cambridge, MA: Harvard University Press, 1985).

Pzerworski, Adam, and Michael Wallerstein, "Structural Dependence of the State on Capital," *American Political Science Review,* 82 (March 1988): 11–29.

Qureshi, I. H., *Ulema in Politics: A Study Relating to the Political Activities of the Ulema in the South-Asian Subcontinent from 1556 to 1947* (Karachi: Ma'aref, 1972).

Rahman, Fazlur, "The Controversy Over the Muslim Family Laws," in Donald E. Smith, ed., *South Asian Religion and Politics* (Princeton: Princeton University Press, 1966): 414–27.

————, "Islam in Pakistan," *Journal of South Asian and Middle Eastern Studies,* 8 (Summer 1985): 34–61.

————, "Islamization of Knowledge: A Response," *The American Journal of Islamic Social Sciences,* 5, 1 (1988): 3–11.

————, "Some Islamic Issues in the Ayub Khan Era," in Donald P. Little, ed., *Essays on Islamic Civilization Presented to Niyazi Berkes* (Leiden: E. J. Brill, 1976): 284–302.

Rahnema, Ali, ed., *The Pioneers of Islamic Revival* (London: Zed Books, 1994).

Ram, Haggay, *Myth and Mobilization in Revolutionary Iran: The Use of the Friday Congregational Sermon* (Washington DC: American University Press, 1994).

Ratham, K. J., and R. S. Milne, "The 1969 Parliamentary Elections in West Malaysia," *Pacific Affairs,* 43, 2 (Summer 1970): 203–26.

Raza, Rafi, *Zulfikar Ali Bhutto and Pakistan, 1967–1977* (Karachi: Oxford University Press, 1997).

Reetz, Dietrich, "National Consolidation or Fragmentation of Pakistan: The Dilemma of General Zia-ul-Haq (1977–88)," in Diethelm Weidemann, ed., *Nationalism, Ethnicity, and Political Development: South Asian Perspectives* (Delhi: Manohar, 1991): 123–43.

Richard, Alan, and John Waterbury, *A Political Economy of the Middle East* (Boulder, CO: Westview Press, 1990).

Rizvi, Hasan-Askari, *The Military and Politics in Pakistan, 1947–86* (Delhi: Konark, 1988).

Roald, Anne Sophie, *Tarbiya: Education and Politics in Islamic Movements in Jordan and Malaysia* (Lund: Lund University, 1994).

Robertson, D. B., "The Return to History and the New Institutionalism in American Political Science," *Social Science History* 17, 1 (Spring 1993): 1–36.

Roff, William R., *The Origins of Malay Nationalism,* 2nd ed., (New York: Oxford University Press, 1994).

———, "Patterns of Islamization in Malaysia, 1890s–1990s: Exemplars, Institutions, and Vectors," *Journal of Islamic Studies,* 9, 2 (July 1998): 210–28.

Ross, Marc Howard, "Culture and Identity in Comparative Political Analysis," in Mark I. Lichbach and Alan S. Zuckerman, eds., *Comparative Politics: Rationality, Culture, and Structure* (New York: Cambridge University Press, 1997): 42–80.

Roy, Olivier, "Changing Patterns Among Radical Islamic Movements," *The Brown Journal of International Affairs,* 6, 1 (Winter/Spring 1999): 109–20.

———, "The Crisis of Religious Legitimacy in Iran," *The Middle East Journal,* 53, 2 (Spring 1999): 201–16.

Rubin, Barnett R., *The Fragmentation of Afghanistan: State Formation and Collapse in the International System* (New Haven: Yale University Press, 1995).

———, "Redistribution and the State in Afghanistan: The Red Revolution Turns Green," in Myron Weiner and Ali Banuazizi, eds., *The Politics of Social Transformation in Afghanistan, Iran, and Pakistan* (Syracuse: Syracuse University Press, 1994): 187–227.

Umit Cizre Sakallioglu, "Parameters and Strategies of Islam-State Interaction in Republican Turkey," *International Journal of Middle East Studies,* 28, 2 (May 1996): 231–51.

Salahu'ddin, Muhammad, *People's Party: Maqasid Awr Hikmat-i `Amali* (People's Party: Goals and Policies) (Karachi, 1982).

Sallaeh, Muhammad Syukri, *An Islamic Approach to Rural Development: The Arqam Way* (London: ASOIB International, 1992).

Sayeed, Khalid B., *Politics in Pakistan: The Nature and Direction of Change* (New York: Praeger, 1980).

Scott, James C., *Political Ideology in Malaysia: Reality and the Beliefs of an Elite* (Kuala Lumpur: University of Malaya Press, 1968).

———, "The Role of Theory in Comparative Politics: A Symposium," *World Politics,* 48, 1 (October 1995): 28–37.

———, *Weapons of the Weak: Everyday Forms of Peasant Resistance* (New Haven: Yale University Press, 1985).

Searing, D. D., "Roles, Rules, and Rationality in the New Institutionalism," *American Political Science Review,* 85, 4 (December 1991): 1239–60.

Shafqat, Saeed, *Civil-Military Relations in Pakistan from Zulfiqar Ali Bhutto to Benazir Bhutto* (Boulder, CO: Westview Press, 1997).

Shah, Syed Mujawar Hussain, *Religion and Politics in Pakistan (1972–88)* (Islamabad: Quaid-i-Azam University, 1996).

Shaheed, Farida, "The Pathan-Muhajir Conflict, 1985–6: A National Perspective," in Veena Das, ed., *Mirrors of Violence: Communities, Riots, and Survivors in South Asia* (Delhi: Oxford University Press, 1990), 194–214.

Shaikh, Farzana, *Community and Consensus in Islam: Muslim Representation in Colonial India, 1860–1947* (New York: Cambridge University Press, 1989).

Shamsul, A. B., "The Economic Dimension of Malay Nationalism: Identity Formation in Malaysia Since 1988: The Social-Historical Roots of the New Economic Policy and Its Contemporary Implications," *The Developing Economies,* 35, 2 (September 1997): 240–61.

———, *From British to Bumiputera Rule: Local Politics and Rural Development in Peninsular Malaysia* (Singapore: Institute of Southeast Asian Studies, 1986).

Sisson, Richard, and Leo E. Rose, *War and Secession: Pakistan, India, and the Creation of Bangladesh* (Berkeley: University of California Press, 1990).

Siu, Heken, "Recycling Rituals: Politics and Popular Culture in Contemporary Rural China," in Perry Link, Richard Madsen, and Paul Pickowicz, eds., *Unofficial China: Popular Culture and Thought in Peoples Republic* (Boulder, CO: Westview Press, 1989): 121–37.

Sivan, Emmanuel, *Radical Islam: Medieval Theology and Modern Politics* (New Haven: Yale University Press, 1985).

Skockpol, Theda, "Analyzing Causal Configurations in History: A Rejoinder to Nichols," *Comparative Social Research,* 9 (1986): 187–94.

———, *States and Social Revolutions: A Comparative Analysis of France, Russia, and China* (New York: Cambridge University Press, 1979).

Skovgaard-Petersen, Jakob, *Defining Islam for the Egyptian State: Muftis and Fatwas of Dar al-Ifta* (Leiden: E. J. Brill, 1997).

Sloane, Patricia, *Islam, Modernity, and Entrepreneurship Among Malays* (London: Macmillan, 1999): 171–86.

Smith, Brian H., "Religion and Politics: A New Look Through an Old Prism," in H. E. Chehabi and Alfred Stepan, eds., *Politics, Society, and Democracy: Comparative Studies* (Boulder, CO: Westview Press, 1995): 73–88.

Smith, R. M., "Ideas, Institutions, and Strategic Choice," *Polity* 28, 1 (Fall 1995): 135–40.

Stepan, Alfred, *The State and Society: Peru in Comparative Perspective* (Princeton: Princeton University Press, 1978).

Stockwell, A. J., *British Policy and Malay Politics During the Malayan Union Experiment, 1942–1948,* monograph number 8 (Kuala Lumpur: Malaysian Branch of the Royal Asiatic Society, 1979).

Sullivan, Denis J., and Sana Abed-Kotob, *Islam in Contemporary Egypt: Civil Society vs. the State* (Boulder, CO: Lynne Rienner, 1999).

Sundaram, Jomo Kwame [Jomo K. S.], *Growth and Structural Change in Malaysian Economy* (London: Macmillan, 1990).

———, *A Question of Class: Capital, the State, and Uneven Development in Malaya* (New York: Oxford University Press, 1986): 245, 271.

Sundaram, Jomo Kwame [Jomo K. S.], and Ahmad Shabery Cheek, "The Politics of Malaysia's Islamic Resurgence," *Third World Quarterly,* 10, 2 (April 1988): 843–68.

Sundaram, Jomo Kwame and Ishak Shari, *Development Policies and Income Inequality in Peninsular Malaysia* (Kuala Lumpur: Institute of Advanced Studies, University of Malaya, 1986).

Syed, Anwar H., *The Discourse and Politics of Zulfikar Ali Bhutto* (New York: St. Martin's Press, 1992).

———, *Pakistan: Islam, Politics, and National Solidarity* (New York: Praeger, 1982).

Talbot, Ian, *Provincial Politics and the Pakistan Movement: The Growth of the Muslim League in North-West and North-East India, 1937–1947* (Karachi: Oxford University Press, 1988).

Taseer, Salmaan, *Bhutto: A Political Biography* (London: Ithaca Press, 1979).

Tate, D. J. Muzaffar, "The Malaysian Dilemma," *Commentary,* 24 (May 1999).

Teik, Khoo Boo, *Paradoxes of Mahathirism: An Intellectual Biography of Mahathir Mohamad* (Kuala Lumpur: Oxford University Press, 1995).

Thelen, Kathleen, and Sven Steimo, "Historical Institutionalism in Comparative Perspective," in Sven Steimo, Kathleen Thelen, and Frank Longstreth, eds., *Structuring Politics: Historical Institutionalism in Comparative Analysis* (New York: Cambridge University Press, 1992): 1–32.

Tilly, Charles, *Coercion, Capital, and European States, A. D. 990–1990* (Cambridge, MA: Blackwell, 1990).

———, "Contentious Repertoires in Great Britain, 1758–1834," in M. Traugott, ed., *Repertoires and Cycles of Collective Action* (Durham: Duke University Press, 1995): 26.

———, ed., *The Formation of National States in Western Europe* (Princeton: Princeton University Press, 1975).

———, "War Making and State Making as Organized Crime," in Peter B. Evans, Dietrich Rueschemeyer, and Theda Skocpol, eds., *Bringing the State Back In* (New York: Cambridge University Press, 1985): 169–91.

Tomlinson, B. R., *The Political Economy of the Raj, 1914–1947: The Economics of Decolonization in India* (London: Macmillan, 1979).

Toward Islamization of Disciplines (Herndon, VA: IIIT 1988).

Tregonning, K. C., *The British in Malaya: The First Forty Years* (Tucson: University of Arizona Press, 1965).

Trimberger, Ellen, *Revolution from Above: Military Bureaucrats and Development in Japan, Turkey, Egypt, and Peru* (New Brunswick, NJ: Transaction Books, 1978).

Tripp, Charles, "Islam and the Secular Logic of the State in the Middle East," in Abdel Salam Sidahmad and Anoushiravan Ehteshami, eds., *Islamic Fundamentalism* (Boulder, CO: Westview Press, 1996): 57–60.

Turner, Bryan S., "Religion and State-Formation: A Commentary on Recent Debates," *Journal of Historical Sociology,* 1, 3 (September 1988): 322–33.

ul-Haq, Mahbub, *The Poverty Curtain: Choices for the Third World* (New York: Columbia University Press, 1976).

Van Creveld, Martin, *The Rise and Decline of the State* (New York: Cambridge University Press, 1999).

Vandewalle, Dirk, "Islam in Algeria: Religion, Culture, and Opposition in a Rentier State," in John L. Esposito, ed., *Political Islam: Revolution, Radicalism, or Reform?* (Boulder, CO: Lynne Rienner, 1997): 33–52.

Varshney, Ashutosh, "Urban Bias in Perspective," *The Journal of Development Studies,* 29, 4 (July 1993): 3–22.

Vatikiotis, M. R. J., *Political Change in Southeast Asia: Trimming the Banyan Tree* (London: Routledge, 1996).

Vatin, Jean-Claude, "Popular Puritanism Versus State Reformism: Islam in Algeria," in James Piscatori, ed., *Islam in the Political Process* (New York: Cambridge University Press, 1983): 98–121.

Voll, John O., "Fundamentalism in the Sunni Arab World: Egypt and the Sudan," in Martin Marty and R. Scott Appleby, eds., *Fundamentalisms Observed* (Chicago: University of Chicago Press, 1991): 366–95.

Von der Mehden, Fred R., "Islamic Resurgence in Malaysia," in John L. Esposito, ed., *Islam and Development: Religion and Sociopolitical Change* (Syracuse: Syracuse University Press, 1980): 163–80.

———, "Malaysia: Islam and Multiethnic Politics," in John L. Esposito, ed., *Islam in Asia: Religion, Politics, and Society* (New York: Oxford University Press, 1987): 177–201.

———, *Religion and Modernization in Southeast Asia* (Syracuse: Syracuse University Press, 1986).

———, *Two Worlds of Islam: Interactions Between Southeast Asia and the Middle East* (Gainesville: University Press of Florida, 1993).

Von Vorys, Karl, *Democracy Without Consensus: Communalism and Political Stability in Malaysia* (Princeton: Princeton University Press, 1975).

Wadeen, Lisa, *Ambiguities of Domination: Politics, Rhetoric, and Symbols in Contemporary Syria* (Chicago: University of Chicago Press, 1999).

Wah, Yeo Kim, *The Politics of Decentralization: Colonial Controversy in Malaya, 1920–1929* (Kuala Lumpur: Oxford University Press, 1982).

Waqar-ul-Haq, Mohammad, and Jameel Ahmed Saleemi, *Manual of Zakat and Ushr Laws* (Lahore: Nadeem Law Book House, 1990).

Waseem, Mohammad, "Pakistan's Lingering Crisis of Dyarchy," *Asian Survey,* 32, 7 (July 1992): 617–34.

———, *Pakistan Under Martial Law, 1977–1985* (Lahore: Vanguard, 1987).

Washbrook, David, "Law, State, and Agrarian Society in Colonial India," *Modern Asian Studies,* 15, 3 (1981): 653–54.

Weinbaum, Marvin, *Pakistan and Afghanistan: Resistance and Reconstruction* (Boulder, CO: Westview Press, 1994).

Weiss, Anita, *Culture, Class, and Development in Pakistan: The Emergence of an Industrial Bourgeoisie in Punjab* (Boulder, CO: Westview Press, 1991).

Wiktorowicz, Quintan, "Regulating Religious Contention: Islamic Collective Action and Patterns of Mobilization in Jordan," Ph.D. dissertation submitted to the School of Public Affairs of the American University, 1998.

Willis, Michael, *The Islamist Challenge in Algeria: A Political History* (New York: New York University Press, 1997).

Wilson, Rodney, "Islam and Malaysia's Economic Development," *Journal of Islamic Studies,* 9, 2 (July 1998): 259–76.

Wolpert, Stanley, *Jinnah of Pakistan* (New York: Oxford University Press, 1984).

———, *Zulfi Bhutto of Pakistan: His Life and Times* (New York: Oxford University Press, 1993).

Woodruff, Philip, *The Men Who Ruled India,* 2 vols., (London: Jonathan Cape, 1953 and 1954).

Wuthnow, Robert, *Communities of Discourse: Ideology and Social Structure in the Reformation, the Enlightenment, and European Socialism* (Cambridge: Harvard University Press, 1989).

Yavuz, M. Hakan, "Political Islam and the Welfare (*Refah*) Party in Turkey," *Comparative Politics,* 30, 1 (October 1997): 64–65.

————, "Search for a New Social Contract in Turkey: Fethullah Gülen, the Virtue Party, and the Kurds," *SAIS Review,* 19, 1 (1999): 115–16.

————, "Turkey's Fault Lines and the Crisis of Kemalism," *Current History,* 99, 633 (January 2000): 33–38.

Young, Crawford, *The African Colonial State in Comparative Perspective* (New Haven: Yale University Press, 1994).

Zakaria, Haji Ahmad, "Malaysia: Quasi-Democracy in a Divided Society," in Larry Diamond, Juan Linz, and Seymour Martin Lipset, eds., *Democracy in Developing Countries,* vol. 3 (Boulder: Lynne Rienner, 1989): 347–82.

Zakat and Ushr System in Pakistan (Islamabad: Central Zakat Administration, Ministry of Finance, 1991).

Zaleha, Sharifah, "Surau and Mosques in Malaysia," *ISIM Newsletter,* 3 (1999): 9.

Zaman, Muhammad Qasim, "Religious Education and the Rhetoric of Reform: The Madrasah in British India and Pakistan," *Comparative Studies in Society and History,* 41, 2 (April 1999): 294–323.

————, "Sectarianism in Pakistan: The Radicalization of Shi'i and Sunni Identities," *Modern Asian Studies,* 32 (July 1998): 687–716.

Zeghal, Malika, "Religion and Politics in Egypt: The Ulema of al-Azhar, Radical Islam, and the State (1952–94)," *International Journal of Middle East Studies,* 31, 3 (August 1999): 373–75.

Ziring, Lawrence, *The Ayub Khan Era: Politics of Pakistan, 1958–69* (Syracuse: Syracuse University Press, 1971).

————, "Dilemma and Challenge in Nawaz Sharif's Pakistan," in Charles H. Kennedy, ed., *Pakistan 1992* (Boulder, CO: Westview Press, 1993): 1–18.

————, *Pakistan in the Twentieth Century: A Political History* (Karachi: Oxford University Press, 1997).

————, "The Second Stage in Pakistan Politics," *Asian Survey,* 33, 12 (December 1993): 1175–85.

Zubaida, Sami, *Islam, the People, and the State: Political Ideals and Movements in the Middle East* (London: I. B. Tauris, 1993).

Index